STUDIES IN ANTISEMITISM

Alvin H. Rosenfeld, editor

INDIANA UNIVERSITY PRESS

Bloomington & Indianapolis

European Muslim ANTISEMITISM

European Muslim ANTISEMITISM

Why Young Urban Males Say They Don't Like Jews

Günther Jikeli

This book is a publication of

INDIANA UNIVERSITY PRESS
Office of Scholarly Publishing
Herman B Wells Library 350
1320 East 10th Street
Bloomington, Indiana 47405 USA

iupress.indiana.edu

Publication of this book was supported in part by grants from the following: the Friedrich-Ebert Foundation; The Hans-Böckler-Foundation, a non-profit German foundation committed to the advancement of democracy and the improvement of people's working lives on behalf of the German Confederation of Trade Unions (DGB); and the Robert A. and Sandra S. Borns Jewish Studies Program at Indiana University.

∞ The paper used in this publication meets the minimum requirements of the American National Standard for Information Sciences–Permanence of Paper for Printed Library Materials, ANSI Z39.48–1992.

Manufactured in the United States of America

Library of Congress Cataloging-in-Publication Data

Jikeli, Günther, author.
European Muslim antisemitism : why young urban males say they don't like Jews / Günther Jikeli.
pages cm. – (Studies in antisemitism)
Includes bibliographical references and index.
ISBN 978-0-253-01518-1 (cl : alk. paper) – ISBN 978-0-253-01525-9 (eb)
1. Antisemitism – Europe, Western – History – 21st century. 2. Jews – Europe – Public opinion. 3. Public opinion – Europe, Western. 4. Muslim youth – Europe, Western – Attitudes. 5. Muslim men – Europe, Western – Attitudes. 6. Urban youth – Europe, Western – Attitudes. 7. Europe, Western – Ethnic relations – History – 21st century. I. Title.
DS146.E85J56 2015
305.892'404 – dc23
2014029057

1 2 3 4 5 20 19 18 17 16 15

This book is dedicated to my parents, who taught me to speak out against bigotry.

Barbarism is not the inheritance of our prehistory.
It is the companion that dogs our every step.

ALAIN FINKIELKRAUT

Contents

Acknowledgments

I HAVE RECEIVED SUPPORT FROM A LARGE NUMBER OF INDIVIDUALS and institutions, and this book would not have been possible without their help. I am most grateful to all of them.

But it is only thanks to Alvin H. Rosenfeld that I was able to publish this book in its current form. His encouragement and support as well as comments and suggestions on earlier versions have been invaluable. My stay at IU's Institute for the Study of Contemporary Antisemitism as the Justin M. Druck Family Visiting Scholar in Spring 2014 semester led to substantial improvements of the manuscript, and a grant from the Justin M. Druck Family helped to support the publication of the book.

I also want to thank Janet Rabinowitch from Indiana University Press for her careful reading of the manuscript. M. Alison Hunt, David Szonyi, and Eric Schramm did a great job of reviewing the manuscript.

I am proud that three important organizations valued this study and supported the research project financially: the Fondation pour la Mémoire de la Shoah, the Task Force for International Cooperation on Holocaust Education, Remembrance, and Research (International Holocaust Remembrance Alliance from 2013), and the Hans-Böckler-Foundation.

Research for this book relied on the cooperation with a number of institutes and individuals. At the Center for Research on Antisemitism, Technical University Berlin, I would like to thank Wolfgang Benz, who encouraged, advised, and supported me throughout my years there, as well as Werner Bergmann and Juliane Wetzel, who not only gave me valuable advice from the very beginning, but who also helped me discuss the results of my research in conferences and academic publications.

I am also grateful to the following institutions and their staff members: the Kantor Center for the Study of Contemporary European Jewry, the United States Holocaust Memorial Museum, the Wiener Library, the Borns Jewish Studies Program at Indiana University, the Institute for the Study of Contemporary Antisemitism, the Groupe Sociétés, Religions, Laïcités/Centre National de la Recherche Scientifique, the Centre d'anthropologie sociale at Toulouse University, the Institute for Education and Research on Antisemitism, the Vidal Sassoon International Center for the Study of Antisemitism at Hebrew University, the research group "Jews Color Race" at the Van Leer Jerusalem Institute, and the Institute for the Study of Global Antisemitism and Policy. They gave me the opportunity to discuss results of my study in their seminars and informally with colleagues during the time I have spent there. I want to thank especially Joëlle Allouche-Benayoun, Ben Barkow, Chantal Bordes-Benayoun, Lars Breuer, Diane Druck, Hagai van der Horst, Metin Irencin, Josefine Jikeli, Stephanie Jikeli, Serdar Kaya, Doris Krüger, Doerte Letzmann, Götz Nordbruch, Yves Pallade, Dina Porat, Jessica Ring, Antonia Schmid, Efraim Sicher, Charles Small, Philip Spencer, Roni Stauber, Karin Stögner, Kim Robin Stoller, Richard Timmis, Esther Webman, and Robert S. Wistrich for their help, critiques, hints, and, last but not least, their moral support. I am also grateful to the participants in the study for their time and honest responses regarding their views and private lives. For any errors or inadequacies that may remain in this work, of course, the responsibility is entirely my own.

European Muslim ANTISEMITISM

Introduction

ANTISEMITISM IN EUROPE HAS INCREASED DRAMATICALLY SINCE the beginning of the twenty-first century. Antisemitic parties, although still a minority, are now members of the European Parliament and some national parliaments. Antisemitic stereotypes meet with high approval rates in surveys, and in some countries the majority of the population shares these views. Antisemitic acts have increased and become radicalized; violence has become more frequent and many Jews in Europe feel under threat. In recent years, the most violent antisemitic acts have been committed by individuals of Muslim background. However, little is known about their views of Jews and why many have negative views of Jews.

In 2004 and 2005, I was involved in educational projects in Berlin, Germany, that aimed to combat antisemitic attitudes. We worked with students from different backgrounds, including many Muslims. Young Muslims were not the only students who exhibited worrisome antisemitic attitudes, but my colleagues and I knew the least about both their views of Jews and their rationales and motives. I was professionally interested in the kinds of tropes young Muslims use so that we would be able to work on them with the students. I participated in meetings with other educators from across the country – and even from other European countries – to learn from their experiences. Many educators have come to deal with antisemitism among Muslim students. In these years I emerged as one of the few "experts" on antisemitism among young Muslims and was invited to inform German president Horst Köhler on that matter before his first official trip to Israel.

I read the literature on contemporary antisemitism and spoke to scholars in the field to find that almost no studies had dealt with antisemitism among Muslims living in Germany or in other European countries. One valuable early resource proved to be the report by Werner Bergmann and Juliane Wetzel from the Center for Research on Antisemitism entitled "Manifestations of Anti-Semitism in the European Union; First Semester 2002." They noted: "Physical attacks on Jews and the desecration and destruction of synagogues were acts mainly committed by young Muslim perpetrators mostly of Arab descent in the monitoring period."[1] Since this report, however, few scientific studies have investigated the sources of antisemitism among Muslims in any European country. Nevertheless, the issue has drawn public interest. Public debates have taken place with regard to cases of violent assaults on Jews perpetrated by youths of Muslim or Arab background. In summer 2014, during the war between Israel and Hamas in Gaza, many pro-Palestinian rallies turned antisemitic with slogans and, at times, violence. Many perpetrators had a Muslim background. "Allahu Akbar" became a battle cry, and during some of these rallies Jews and Jewish institutions were directly targeted. This led to a brief public outcry and strong condemnation of antisemitism by political leaders. One of the most infamous cases, however, is the 2006 torture and murder of Ilan Halimi in Paris by a large group of mostly Muslim youths;[2] but there have also been a number of relatively less violent incidents, such as the violent attack on a rabbi and his six-year-old daughter in Berlin in August 2012[3] and an attack on Jewish dancers at a local festival in Hanover, Germany, in 2010.[4] Public debates in Britain on antisemitism among Muslims have revolved around Islamist organizations[5] or the curricula of Islamic schools.[6] Muslim antisemitism is also a problem in an educational context, as reports and teachers' testimonies in Germany,[7] France,[8] and Britain[9] have shown. Problematic views are often voiced in the context of education about the Holocaust.[10]

Surprisingly, the antisemitic killing spree by Mohamed Merah at a Jewish school in Toulouse, which resulted in the death of three children and a teacher (and father) shot at close range on March 19, 2012,[11] did not lead to major debates about antisemitism, although the incident signifies a new dimension of antisemitic attacks in twenty-first-century Europe.

This has changed to some extent with the cold-blooded shooting at the Jewish Museum in Brussels on May 24, 2014, which left four dead. The case of the presumed murderer, French Jihadist Mehdi Nemmouche, made it clear that radicalized Muslims pose a serious and growing terrorist threat first to Jewish communities but also to the wider public. Nemmouche grew up in France and was radicalized in prison. He then participated in the Syrian civil war, most likely on the part of the Islamic State of Iraq and Syria (ISIS).

However, those radicalized extremists are (dangerous) exceptions and the large majority of European Muslims condemns attacks against Jews. In recent years, a number of representatives of Muslim communities have publicly condemned violence and hatred against Jews,[12] and a few Muslim individuals have also spoken out explicitly and self-critically against widespread antisemitism within Muslim communities.[13]

Discussing Muslim antisemitism is politically challenging. It can be feared that naming the problem contributes to further stigmatization of Muslim minorities.[14] I argue that scholarly discussions about antisemitism among Muslims in Europe are necessary for a detailed understanding of the phenomenon and its sources, which might inform the development of effective tools for fighting antisemitism in Europe. It is only if Muslims are essentialized, that is, if it is wrongly assumed that people of Muslim background necessarily or "naturally" adhere to certain attitudes, that they become further stigmatized. Neglecting specific forms of antisemitism and groups of antisemitic perpetrators, on the other hand, is detrimental to the struggle against antisemitism.

The lack of investigation into antisemitism among Muslims in Europe represents a research gap, and simultaneously points to the necessity of additional studies that can add insight with the goal of fostering a more nuanced public debate on Muslim minorities and Muslim antisemitism. Due to this large research gap, I have chosen an exploratory approach for my investigation. The principle questions of this book are the following: What stereotypes of Jews exist among young European Muslims? What kinds of arguments do they use to support hostility against Jews? What role does the perception of the Middle East conflict play? Does Islamist ideology influence young European Muslims? What are the possible sources for their antisemitic views? Are discrimination, specific perceptions of Islam, foreign television, and friends and parents relevant factors for the genesis of antisemitic resentments? And what are the motives among Muslims to actively oppose antisemitism?

These questions are interesting to look at from a comparative perspective among people living in European countries – particularly Germany, France, and Great Britain, which together are home to approximately 70 percent of European Muslims. The differences between these countries regarding policies of migration and integration and the ethnic background of most Muslims are substantial. Muslims in Germany are mostly of Turkish origin; the majority of Muslims in France have a Maghrebian background; and most Muslims in Britain stem from South Asian countries of Pakistan, India, and Bangladesh.

Islamic organizations in Europe, many of them with Islamist tendencies, are not representative of European Muslims, and the mass media geared specifically toward Muslim communities in Europe tend to be marginal. Thus, the best option for an investigation of views and attitudes was face-to-face interviews. A few interviewers, including myself, asked young Muslims in Berlin, Paris, and London open-ended questions about their experiences of discrimination, views on international conflicts, and opinions of Jews. For practical reasons, we had to restrict the participants to male interviewees. After interviewing more than one hundred young male Muslims, it became clear that the arguments and responses were (largely) repetitive; the sample was saturated. The interviewees in each city roughly represent their ethnic minority groups in their respective countries; that is, in Berlin the majority of interviewees were of Turkish heritage, in Paris of North African origin, and in London of South Asian background. What we found were patterns of argumentations for negative views of Jews, as well as interesting results regarding perceptions of discrimination, exclusion, and self-identification with the national identity of the country of residence.

I provide an overview of relevant aspects of the Muslim communities in Germany, France, and Britain in chapter 1. Muslim communities in the three countries are diverse, and individuals' attitudes even more so. I focus on the different histories of immigration, the social situations, migration policies, Islamic organizations, and the discrimination that Muslims face. I relate this to interviewees' perceptions of discrimination, exclusion, and self-identification with their country of residence.

The comparative approach reveals significant differences between the three countries.

In chapter 2, I discuss the literature, reports, and surveys on antisemitism among European Muslims and show that some forms of antisemitism are more pronounced among Muslims than in the general society. Above all, however, a review of the literature reveals relevant research questions that have been included in this study, such as the role of self-identification of Muslims and the question of what kinds of ideologies influence antisemitic patterns of thinking.

Detailed description of the methods in chapter 3 helps the reader to comprehend the research process and the way in which I arrived at my results and conclusions. I discuss my prior understanding, motivation, and expectations, and the definition of antisemitism I use, as well as how respondents were approached, what they were asked, and how the conversations went. The analytical strategy explains how patterns of argumentations for negative attitudes toward Jews evolved, how I came to my conclusions, and how the results enrich a better understanding of antisemitism among European Muslims beyond the sample of interviewees. This chapter also provides information on the interviewees. Who are they in terms of background and age? What is their economic, educational, and ethnic background? What does Islam mean to them? How do they view discrimination and exclusion and how do they identify themselves? And what is their everyday life like? The answers are very different for individual participants. A table of all interviewees can be found in Appendix B and will help the reader see the overall picture.

Chapters 4–8 provide a detailed description of patterns of argumentation for negative views of Jews. Four main categories of patterns emerged from the interviews:

(1) *"Classic" antisemitic attitudes.* This category comprises antisemitic conspiracy theories and well-known stereotypes of Jews, such as assumptions that they are rich or stingy.

(2) *Antisemitism related to Israel.* Here, antisemitic views are often based on a conflation of Jews and Israelis and a Manichean view of the Palestinian-Israeli conflict. Certain tropes, such as "Jews kill children," are used to justify hatred against Jews, including local Jews. Negative views of Israel are used to justify antisemitism.

(3) *Negative views of Jews with direct reference to Islam, Muslim identity, or the person's ethnic identity.* This is often voiced in such assumptions as "Muslims hate Jews." Negative associations of Jews made in accordance with the collective identity or with perceptions of "Islam" make it difficult for young Muslims to distance themselves from such assumptions.

(4) *Expressions of hostility against Jews in which the person does not bother to give any arguments for such enmity.* This reveals a normalization of negative views of Jews and/or the true character and irrationality of antisemitism; Jews are hated simply because they are Jews.

However, these categories overlap in some argumentations, and respondents use differing, and often contradictory, arguments. An important insight I gained from this study is that attitudes toward Jews are usually fragmented and full of contradictions.[15] It is only a small minority that expresses (relatively) coherent antisemitic views.[16] However, the study shows that those who have only a fragmented and contradictory antisemitic view can still pose a threat to Jews. Antisemitic attitudes do not have to be coherent to translate into passive or active support of harassment and violence against Jews.

In chapter 9, views of the Holocaust are discussed. European Muslims are influenced by discourses about the Holocaust in their countries of residence, their countries of origin, or their respective social circles. Almost all interviewees share a certain core knowledge of the Holocaust, although one that is at times very limited. Views of Jews and of the Holocaust are interrelated, and distorted views of the Holocaust and inappropriate comparisons are rooted in negative views of Jews rather than in lack of knowledge.

Chapter 10, a discussion of possible sources of antisemitic attitudes, is based on what respondents mentioned as sources of their negative views of Jews. Friends and family play an important role in the respondents' attitudes, particularly if a norm of negative views of Jews exists. Domestic and foreign media are often referred to as sources of certain negative views of Jews, particularly with regard to the Middle East conflict, but also in the case of conspiracy theories. Frequently, however, the source of antisemitic assumptions cannot be identified. Interviewees often referred vaguely to "what people say," to rumors rather than concrete facts or sources. I add my observations on some possible reasons for the adoption of antisemitic attitudes, including the influence of education, and, particularly, on perceptions of the ethnic and religious collective identity and discrimination. I also explore possible projections of interviewees' suppressed feelings onto Jews.[17]

In chapter 11, I present portraits of young Muslims who reject antisemitic attitudes, each for different reasons. Their views demonstrate that not only is the genesis of antisemitism multi-determined, but so is its rejection. These young men's outspoken rejection of antisemitic attitudes was found to be related to many factors: their belief in human rights, strong individualism, life experiences, critical views of irrational assumptions, or close contacts with Jews.

Finally, in the conclusion, I offer a summary on differences among the three cities and ethnic groups and an analysis of the functions of the different patterns of argumentation.

This study is rich in empirical data. The aim is to provide the reader as much as possible with direct insights about how antisemitism is actually voiced by young Muslims. I present much of the original material through direct quotation of the interviewees that reflect the uncorrected spoken language used by the young people. Translations from French and German are mine.[18] I have chosen a descriptive approach and aim to be as transparent as possible in my analysis, allowing contradictions and various interpretations to be debated.

I hope that this book will prove useful in several ways: to advance an understanding of antisemitism among European Muslims today, to encourage scholars to investigate their own questions on the issue, and to verify, debate, quantify, or specify particular findings and theses; to assist policymakers and educators in working with Muslim students to eventually overcome any existing biased attitudes toward Jews; and to contribute in a positive way to public debates on Muslim antisemitism by providing comprehensive and nuanced insights into the various ways young Muslim men think of Jews, and by acknowledging that Muslims are an integral part of European societies today who themselves still face discrimination on racial, ethnic, social, cultural, and also religious grounds.

ONE

European Muslims: Between Integration and Discrimination

MUSLIMS ARE THE LARGEST RELIGIOUS MINORITY IN EUROPE, while Islam is the fastest growing religion: there are an estimated 15–20 million Muslims in the European Union,[1] contributing to a total population of over 500 million Europeans. Approximately 70 percent of European Muslims live in Germany, France, or Great Britain. Europe's Muslim population is also diverse religiously, culturally, ethnically, and economically. Far from a homogeneous religion, Islam is interpreted differently by various sub-groups, ideological streams, and individuals.

Most Muslims in Europe are immigrants or descendants of immigrants from a variety of African, South Asian, and Middle Eastern countries, as well as from Turkey and the former Yugoslavia. The history and context of migration and the origins of European Muslims vary from country to country, often due to the country's colonial history, special ties with particular Muslim countries, and distinctive immigration policies.

MUSLIMS AND MUSLIM ORGANIZATIONS IN GERMANY

The estimated number of Muslims in Germany is between 3.0 and 4.3 million, up to 45 percent of whom are German citizens.[2] Muslims, therefore, form approximately 5 percent of the population in Germany, with higher percentages residing in urban areas. The large majority are Turkish immigrants or their descendants, roughly one quarter of whom are ethnic Kurds.[3] The second-largest group comes from the former Yugoslavia, followed by the Middle East, North Africa, and South Asia.[4]

A significant migration of Muslims to Germany started in the early 1960s when West Germany officially began to recruit low-skilled workers from Turkey for Germany's growing industry in the postwar era. Recruitment contracts were later signed with other countries; those signed with Muslim populations included Morocco, Tunisia, and Yugoslavia.

In 1973, the economic recession brought an end to the recruitment of the "Gastarbeiter" ("guest" or foreign-born workers). Foreign workers, Muslims and non-Muslims alike, were expected to go back to their countries of origin, but only half of the four million migrants at the time actually left Germany.[5] Clearly, the end of the recruitment program did not have the intended effect of diminishing the number of foreigners. On the contrary, fearing even stricter controls on immigration, many "guest workers" brought their families *to* Germany. Family reunion and marriage migration subsequently became the dominant form of migration after 1973.

Due to this change in the character of migration, the migrants moved out of workers' accommodations, often to run-down, inner-city areas. Even today most Muslims live in current or former industrial areas, often concentrated in certain districts, while only a few live on the territory of the former German Democratic Republic.[6] Another wave of Muslim immigrants arrived in the early 1980s and onward as refugees or asylum seekers. Many political refugees came from Turkey as a result of the coup d'état in 1980 and the civil war in southeast Turkey. Others came from the Middle East, North Africa, and the former Yugoslavia. The introduction of restrictive laws in 1991 and 1993 drastically reduced the number of refugees coming to Germany.

Most Muslims in Germany are Sunni, but about 13 percent are Alevis, a particular liberal current of Islam. Shiites form approximately 7 percent of Muslims in Germany, while others, such as Ahmadiyas and Sufis, comprise about 6 percent of the Muslim population.[7]

Muslim organizations are often formed along ethnic lines, but relatively few organizations are formed as an explicitly Turkish or another ethnic (as opposed to Islamic) group primarily, such as the Türkischer Bund Deutschland. The diversity of the Muslim population is reflected in the diversity of Muslim organizations. In 2003, there were about 2,400 local associations, along with a number of associations on the regional and federal level.[8] However, official membership in these organizations is low (about 10 percent).[9] In 2006, the German government established the German Islam Conference, where Muslim representatives, including those from the major organizations, meet representatives of the government on a regular basis.[10]

The Türkisch-Islamische Union der Anstalt für Religion (Turkish-Islamic Union for Religious Affairs, DİTİB) is the largest Muslim organization in Germany. It has strong ties to the Turkish government and therefore has a secular orientation, abiding to the strong secular traditions and laws of the Turkish state. However, the ruling party in Turkey today, the Justice and Development Party, is considered to be Islamist[11] and influences DİTİB.

The Islamische Gemeinschaft Milli Görüş (IGMG) is the second-largest organization, heading 323 mosques and cultural associations in Germany. The IGMG is closely related to the Islamist Milli Görüş movement in Turkey, which held Necmettin Erbakan as its leader until his death in February 2011. The movement aims to establish a global Islamic society founded upon Shari'a law. Representatives regularly denounce capitalism, imperialism, Zionism, and racism.[12] The Islamrat, acting as a representative body on a national level, is almost identical to the IGMG.

The Verband Islamischer Kulturzentren (VIKZ) boasts the third-largest membership. Its anti-Western indoctrination of students in their facilities has often been criticized.[13]

The Zentralrat der Muslime in Deutschland (ZMD) encompasses three main subgroups among its nineteen member organizations: the Union der Türkisch-Islamischen Kulturvereine in Europa (ATIP), a religious spinoff of the extremist-nationalist Turkish group Grey Wolves, with approximately 8,000 members; networks associated with the Muslim Brotherhood, such as the Islamische Gemeinschaft in Deutschland (IGD); and Iran-oriented Shiites of various origins.[14] The Islamische Gemeinschaft der Bosniaken is an associated member of the ZMD and is linked to the Islamic Association in Bosnia-Herzegovina.

The secular Alevitische Gemeinde Deutschland represents some ninety local Alevite organizations with Turkish and Kurdish members.[15]

Due to the strong Turkish community and the ties of many Muslim organizations to Turkey, Islam in Germany is still very much influenced by Turkish interpretations of Islam. However, Muslim organizations are not representative and many Muslims are not even aware of them. The best known is DITIB (44 percent knew of the organization in 2008), but only 39 percent of those who were familiar with the organization felt represented by it. In 2008, 50 percent of Muslims in Germany did not feel represented by any Muslim organization on religious issues.[16]

MUSLIMS AND MUSLIM ORGANIZATIONS IN FRANCE

The estimated number of Muslims in France is 4–5 million, representing 6–7.5 percent of the population, with a significantly higher percentage in some regions, particularly Ile-de-France, Provence-Alpes-Côte d'Azur, Rhône-Alpes, and Nord-Pas-de-Calais.[17] Some 80 percent of Muslims in France are immigrants or descendants of immigrants from former colonies in the Maghreb – most are Arabs, but many are also Berbers, coming from Algeria, Morocco, and Tunisia. Other ethnicities include people from Turkey, Sub-Saharan Africa, and the Middle East.

Before World War II, only a small number of Muslim workers migrated to France, and those who did were mainly Berbers from North Africa. Additionally, some of the 86,000 men from North Africa who served in the French army in World War I settled in France. After World War II the growing economy of the 1950s required manpower, which was a major factor contributing to immigration from colonies, and also led to bilateral agreements with such countries as Morocco and Turkey to recruit workers. Muslim immigration from Algeria also brought about the arrival of pro-French refugees before Algeria's independence in 1962.[18]

With the economic crisis of the early 1970s, the recruitment programs were stopped and legislation made immigration to France from non-EU countries difficult. Migration then consisted largely of people arriving to reunite with their families.[19] Another wave of Muslim immigrants arrived with the rise of refugees, who hailed largely from Turkey in the 1980s and Bosnia in the 1990s.[20]

In 1994, there were 1,685 Muslim prayer rooms in France, only some of which were mosques.[21] The estimated number today is more than 2,000. Most Islamic organizations in France are influenced by foreign countries. This influence of foreign countries has been a cause for concern for the French authorities since the 1980s, due to the fact that some organizations promote Islamist ideologies and the interests of foreign states.[22] Despite France's strong secular tradition, the French government enhanced the establishment of the Muslim umbrella organization Conseil français du culte musulman (CFCM) in 2003 with the aim of creating a representative body for Muslim organizations. Its representativeness for Muslims in France is disputed, however, because only 25 percent of French Muslims regularly visit a mosque. Critics charge the CFCM with supporting extremists and, indeed, some leading organizations within the group promote Islamist ideologies.[23]

There are six main Muslim associations in France, all represented within the CFCM:

(1) The Institut Musulman de la Mosquée de Paris, which was formed in 1916 and historically linked to Algeria, and is attached to the Paris Mosque.
(2) The Union des Organisations Islamiques de France (UOIF), which is an affiliate of the Federation of Islamic Organizations in Europe and close to the Muslim Brotherhood, was formed in 1983 and is the largest Muslim organization in France today.[24]
(3) The Fédération Nationale des Musulmans de France (FNMF) was established in 1985 and is supported by Morocco.[25]
(4) The Fédération Invitation et Mission pour la Foi et la Pratique is the French chapter of the orthodox group Tablighi Jamaat, one of the largest transnational Muslim movements.
(5) The Fédération française des associations islamiques d'Afrique, des Comores et des Antilles is an umbrella organization for Muslims who adhere to a traditional form of Islam rooted in African and French West Indian culture.
(6) The Comité de Coordination des Musulmans Turcs de France (CCMTF) is linked to the DİTİB (Turkish-Islamic Union for Religious Affairs) in Turkey.[26]

The more moderate umbrella organization Rassemblement des Musulmans de France (RMF) was founded in 2006 to complement the CFCM and is supported by Morocco.[27] It participated in the 2011 elections of the Conseil français du culte musulman and won the majority of seats, while the UOIF boycotted the elections in 2011 and 2013.

MUSLIMS AND MUSLIM ORGANIZATIONS IN GREAT BRITAIN

In the 2011 UK census, 2.7 million people identified as Muslim, a sharp increase from 1.6 million in 2001. The majority hold British citizenship.[28] Muslims make up the country's second-largest religious community, comprising 4.8 percent of the population, with a higher percentage in urban areas.[29] Approximately one million Muslims live in London. The London Borough of Tower Hamlets hosted the highest proportion of Muslims at 34.5 percent.[30]

Most Muslims are immigrants or their descendants from former British colonies in South Asia, today's Pakistan, Bangladesh, and India. In 2001, 74 percent of the Muslim population had a South Asian background, while 4 percent were white British Muslims, 7 percent were other white Muslims, 4 percent identified as partly Muslim and partly adherents of another religion, and 6 percent were black African.

Whereas a Muslim presence in Britain can be traced back 300 years to sailors who were employed with the British East India Company, Muslim migration on a larger scale started only after World War II, in a context similar to that in Germany and France. The first phase spanned from 1945 to the early 1970s, and included mainly young male migrants from Commonwealth countries who had come to work as unskilled laborers in Britain's growing economy.[31] Until the Commonwealth Immigrants Act in 1962, entry to the UK was unrestricted for Commonwealth citizens. The expulsion of South Asians from East Africa during the time of "Africanization" in the late 1960s and early 1970s brought another group of Muslim immigrants to Britain.[32] Many of those who arrived initially as pioneers were joined by members of their villages or kin networks in a process often described as "chain migration."[33] Particularly in the years and months before the restrictive Immigration Act 1970, many brought over their families, wives, and children.

The second phase, which lasted until around 1990, was characterized by the formation of new families and the creation of a Britain-born generation. The third phase covers those who arrived from the 1990s as refugees rather than economic migrants.[34] Political persecutions and civil wars were major factors that drove asylum seekers from Turkey, the former Yugoslavia, North Africa, Somalia, and the Middle East to Britain. Today, the largest group of newly arriving immigrants to the UK are students,[35] many of whom are Muslim.

Although there are no official figures for the number of mosques in the UK, one oft-quoted estimate is a figure of around 1,600.[36] In 2004, there were five Muslim State schools in England and 120 private Muslim schools in Britain.[37]

Britain hosts a large number of Muslim organizations, many of which have links to radical Islamist groups. For many years Britain had a noteworthy policy that tolerated Islamist radicals and their organizations that were banned in their own countries. Consequently, a number of international Islamist organizations have established themselves in the UK; some of them have their headquarters in the UK, such as the Federation of Islamic Organisations in Europe and the associated European Council for Fatwa and Research, both of which serve to advance the Muslim Brotherhood ideology.[38] Some prominent organizations like Hizb-ut Tahir and now-banned radical groups such as Al Muhajiroun and Sharia4Britain openly strive for an Islamic state and frequently express hatred against Jews and the West.

Muslim organizations with links to Islamism exert influence on Muslims via mosques, *madrasas,* Muslim religious schools, the internet, and newspapers and magazines targeting a British Muslim audience.[39]

The Muslim Council of Britain (MCB) was established in 1997 as an umbrella organization and represents more than 350 mosques around the country. The MCB is linked to two international Islamist organizations, the Muslim Brotherhood and Jamaat-I-Islami.[40] However, the majority group of Sufi Muslims established their own council in 2006, the Sufi Muslim Council.

The strength of Islamist groups in Britain has been bolstered by both Iranian support and a flow of money from Saudi Arabia and Pakistan to be used for new religious facilities, buildings, publications, and education resources.[41] Wahabism, the dominant form of Islam in Saudi Arabia, and Deobandism, centered primarily in Pakistan and India, are fundamentalist movements active in Britain that are largely funded from abroad. The latter is influential in more than a third of British mosques and produces the majority of domestically trained clerics.[42] Tablighi Jamaat is the largest Muslim group in the UK and promotes the ideas of Deobandism. The group claims to be purely apolitical and preaches strict religious practice, but it has also been criticized for Islamist tendencies.[43] In recent years, some, though still marginal, secular groups such as Progressive British Muslims and Muslims for Secular Democracy have also raised their voices.

However, as in Germany and France, the majority of British Muslims (51 percent) do not feel represented by any existing Islamic organization.[44] Thus, despite the existence of a number of Islamist organizations and the influence of Islamism in major Muslim organizations in Europe,[45] the observation of Muslim organizations should not be the only approach to evaluating attitudes among the diverse Muslim communities.

SOCIAL DISADVANTAGE AND DISCRIMINATION AGAINST MUSLIMS: A COMPLEX REALITY

Although the majority of European Muslims are by now a long-standing and integral part of the fabric of the cities, regions, and countries in which they reside, many experience social and economic discrimination. The large majority still has a working class background and shares social disadvantages, even compared to other groups with a similar history of immigration. Unemployment rates are particularly high among Muslims, the average level of formal qualifications is relatively low, and housing conditions are also poorer for this group.[46] Even so, unemployment can vary considerably between Muslims of different ethnic origins. In 2001 the unemployment rate was measured at 11 percent for male Indian Muslims in the UK, while the rate for Black Muslims was a significantly higher 28 percent.[47] However, in recent years, economic, social, and political integration of European Muslims seems to be growing for some parts of Muslim communities, as a number of success stories illustrate.[48]

Two major contributing factors are discussed in the literature for the social disadvantage of Muslims: first, the decline of traditional industries in which many Muslims worked as unskilled laborers; and second, racist and religious discrimination in employment, promotion, housing, and education.[49] The history of migration and the social (class) background of many Muslims, as well as insecure residence status and legal restrictions of access to the labor market, particularly for asylum seekers,[50] are additional factors.

Muslims in Europe face stereotypes, negative views, discrimination, and hatred in multiple facets of their lives. Most Muslims are regarded as immigrants and non-white and are therefore targeted by xenophobia and racism. Additionally, sentiments against their Muslim identity and against Islam are rising. All three aspects can be found in (a) political discourse and attitude surveys of mainstream society; (b) studies on experiences of discrimination; and (c) reports on threats and even violent incidents against Muslims.

DISCOURSES AND ATTITUDE SURVEYS

Debates about discrimination against Muslims have been linked to debates on integration, social cohesion, and security. Within these debates, stereotypes and essentializing generalizations are often voiced. Young Muslims or young men of "Arab origin" in France are often associated with riots in French suburbs. Muslims are generally associated with violence and Islamic fundamentalism. Some public debates focus on issues such as polygamy that are a problem among only a very small number of Muslims.[51] In the UK, South Asian Muslims, particularly men, are often represented as fitting into a false binary, with Islamic fundamentalists on one side and drug-addled criminals on the other. Such portrayals are not only extreme misrepresentation, but also focus on religion at the expense of culture and gender-related issues. Furthermore, Muslim men's "unacceptable" behavior is often misread as an inevitable part of their religious and cultural background.[52]

An international survey from 2008 found that 50 percent of the population in Germany, 62 percent in Britain, and 40 percent in France agreed that there were too many immigrants in their country.[53] And about a third of the population in these countries agreed that "there is a natural hierarchy between black and white people,"[54] an indication of widespread racist attitudes. Comparing studies on xenophobia and racism in the three countries reveals a slightly different focus of hostile attitudes and discourse toward immigrants and their descendants, including Muslims. In Germany, negative attitudes regarding "foreigners" seem to be particularly common.[55] In France, negative stereotypes of Maghrebians and Arabs are widespread.[56] The perception of discrimination is particularly strong among young Muslims, who often complain about stigmatization and not being fully accepted in French society.[57] In the UK, the focus is rather on (South) "Asians" and blacks.[58] Anti-Muslim and anti-Islamic attitudes seem to be growing in all three countries.[59] Agreement with the statement that there were "too many Muslims in the country" was lower than respective attitudes toward immigrants but still significant: respective figures concerning Muslims were 46 (Germany), 45 (UK), and 36 (France) percent.[60] Another survey confirmed three years later that in Germany, Muslims were seen the least favorably (only 46 percent had a favorable view of Muslims) compared to France and Britain (both 64 percent).[61] A large majority in Germany and almost half of the population in France and Britain associated Muslims with fanaticism or violence in 2006.[62] This was not necessarily a manifestation of hatred, but at the very least can be interpreted as an over-generalization and stereotype.[63]

Since the mid-1990s, concerns about a rise of a particular enmity toward Muslims, or Islamophobia, have been voiced, particularly in Britain. These concerns were supported by the first comprehensive report to address discrimination and harassment against Muslims, which was published in 1997.[64] Other reports have followed,[65] but maintaining the distinction between racist and anti-Muslim incidents remains challenging, as does drawing the distinction between legitimate criticism of Islamic practice and doctrine and illegitimate anti-Muslim discourse and discrimination.[66]

STUDIES ON EXPERIENCES OF DISCRIMINATION

Muslims in the European Union perceive discrimination to be based on a number of factors, most significantly racism. In 2008, one in three Muslims in the EU stated that he/she had suffered discrimination in the previous twelve months.[67] However, this number varied according to country and ethnic background, and was even higher among other minority groups: 47 percent of Roma and 41 percent of people with Sub-Saharan African background had been discriminated against in the previous twelve months.[68] Thirty-two percent of the Muslim respondents believed that the discrimination they experienced was based on ethnic or immigrant origin; 10 percent thought it was based on religion or belief; and 43 percent assumed that it was a combination of all of the above.[69] These findings were confirmed in national studies. Descendants of immigrants in France perceived discrimination in 2008 as being based on their country of origin (65 percent), skin color (28 percent), neighborhood (13 percent), and religion (13 percent). Immigrants assign an even smaller role to religion than their descendants do.[70] According to an ongoing study, 40 percent of Muslims in France between ages eighteen and fifty feel subjected to racism, but only 5 percent believe that the discrimination against them is based on religion.[71] In Germany, the minority group that receives the highest level of discrimination is black people, indicating that racism still is the dominant factor of discrimination in Germany.[72]

A distinction should be made between personal discrimination and group-focused enmity. A major study in Germany, for example, found only very weak correlations among Muslims between experiences of personal discrimination and their perception of general bias against Muslims.[73]

However, there is a growing sense of victimhood based on Islamic belief. Muslim organizations point to mounting fears in the community about the rise of anti-Muslim sentiments in society.[74] Moreover, debates about Islamic fundamentalism, increased anti-terror measurements after September 11, 2001, the public's response to Islamist terrorist acts in Europe, and even the simple mention of the fact that such acts have been perpetrated by Muslims in the name of Islam are often perceived as biases against Muslims.

Interviewees' Perceptions of Discrimination

The different factors of discrimination are also well reflected in the views and experiences by the young Muslim interviewees of this study. They are described in more detail in chapter 3. The international comparison and qualitative analysis of their views on discrimination give some additional insights, particularly on differences between the three countries.[75] While the majority of interviewees reported experiences of discrimination or of being subjected to negative stereotypes and prejudices, they perceive their "otherness" in different ways. Generally, interviewees in Germany feel that discrimination exists against "foreigners" (who might have German nationality) based on skin and hair color. In France, the impression is that discrimination focuses foremost on "Arabs" and "blacks," based on skin color, Arab names, and places of residence. In Britain, many respondents think that they encounter discrimination based on skin color, too, but others believe that anti-Muslim prejudices prevail. Stop-and-search controls by police are often considered to be biased, particularly in France but also in Britain, and less so in Germany.[76]

In everyday life, interviewees from all three countries feel most directly affected by hostile looks, which usually occurs in areas where very few people of their own ethnic background reside. Additionally, some feel discriminated against in the job market, or have experienced verbal abuse or even physical threats and assaults. Interviewees also reported discrimination based on prejudice against their social background, their neighborhood,[77] or their status of residence.

The question of whether discrimination is rooted in racism or in anti-Muslim prejudice is probably less pressing for Muslim immigrants and their descendants than it seems to be for scholars. Interviewees rightly complained about the effects of discrimination and prejudice and are less concerned about the motives or ideological reasons behind this discrimination. A French interviewee, who believes that he is affected by racial rather than religious discrimination, said: "*No, I don't think it's because of religion. But, I dunno, honestly, I'm not in their heads, so I can't know why*" (Farouk, Paris).[78]

A prominent opinion, particularly among interviewees in Britain, is that there has been a rise in discrimination against Muslims since the terrorist attacks of September 11, 2001, in the United States and July 7, 2005, in London. In contrast to these perceptions, surveys have shown that negative attitudes toward Muslims are particularly high in Germany compared to Britain and France.[79] However, many interviewees, again particularly in Britain, feel that a prejudice exists against Islam and Muslims or that they are indirectly affected by the attack of Muslims in other countries, even if they do not feel personally targeted. Some of these perceptions are intrinsically problematic: those who see the wars in Afghanistan or Iraq as an attack and a form of bias by "the West" against "the Muslims" will always feel under attack by proxy. We will come back to such binary perceptions of the world in later chapters. As noted above, a distinction should be made between personal discrimination and perceptions of bias against one's religious group as a whole, and lines must certainly be drawn between personal discrimination and negative attitudes or attacks against adherents of the same religion in other countries. The wars in Iraq or Afghanistan do not target Muslims as Muslims and are certainly not an attack against "the Muslims" worldwide.

REPORTS ON THREATS AND VIOLENT INCIDENTS AGAINST MUSLIMS

Hostile attitudes, unfortunately, can not only spill over into discrimination, but also into outright hostile behavior and hate crimes. Some figures are available for Germany, France, and the UK, although, due to their different nature, these figures are not internationally comparable. The Crown Prosecution Service in Britain publishes annual reports on racially and religiously aggravated hate crimes. In 2011–12, the number of prosecuted racially aggravated hate crimes stood at 11,774 and the number of religiously aggravated hate crimes at 593, including anti-Muslim and antisemitic hate crimes.[80]

In the year 2012, the French authorities registered 724 racist and xenophobic acts (threats and acts of violence), 614 antisemitic acts, and 201 anti-Muslim acts. The majority of all violent acts (excluding threats) were antisemitic. Racist and xenophobic threats and violence increased from fewer than 200 in 1992 to 724 in 2012. Anti-Muslim incidents rose from 116 in 2010, the first year such acts were recorded, to 201 in 2012.[81]

The German authorities only publish data on "politically motivated crimes," distinguishing between perpetrators of the extreme right and extreme left, as well as foreigners. Perpetrators of the extreme right were responsible for 350 xenophobic and 22 antisemitic violent crimes in 2011.[82] It can be assumed that the total number of xenophobic, racist, antisemitic, and anti-Muslim incidents is in fact much higher than the registered violent crimes by perpetrators of the extreme right.

Figures for the United States are also available. In 2011, 2,917 racist incidents, 771 anti-Jewish incidents, and 157 anti-Islamic incidents were registered.[83] However, such a comparison may be misleading because it may reflect only a better (or different) recording system for such incidents, as well as a discrepancy in population figures.

MUSLIMS GENERALLY IDENTIFY STRONGLY BOTH WITH THE COUNTRY OF RESIDENCE AND ISLAM

The majority of European Muslims value their religion and religious identity. Some surveys point to country-specific differences: In 2009, 75 percent among the Muslim population in Britain said that they "extremely strongly" or "very strongly" identify with their religion versus 58 percent of Muslims in France and 59 percent in Germany.[84] The strong identification with Islam has been confirmed in other studies; it is significantly higher than religious identification among Christians, including those with migrant backgrounds.[85] This might explain why many European Muslims consider themselves Muslim first with regard to identification as national citizens.[86] But identification with the country of residence is strong, despite experiences of discrimination. In Germany and in Britain, in 2009, the percentage of those who identified strongly with their country of residence was even higher among Muslims than among non-Muslims, while the difference in France was marginal.[87]

Again, there are country-specific differences: most Muslims in Germany feel a strong sense of belonging and loyalty to Germany, similar to people with migrant backgrounds of other religions. Only a minority identify as German, however.[88] The identification of Muslims in France as French is strong. In 2008, 60 percent considered themselves equally French and Muslim, 14 percent predominantly French, and only 22 percent predominantly Muslim.[89] The majority of British Muslims identify strongly with both Britain and their religion, and identification with the country of residence is considerably stronger than in Germany and

France.[90] Thus, a strong identification with Islam does not seem to be related to a lack of identification with the country of residence.

EXPLAINING COUNTRY-SPECIFIC DIFFERENCES OF NATIONAL IDENTIFICATION CONFIRMED IN INTERVIEWS

Self-identifications as German, French, or British differ significantly. In Germany, the young Muslim interviewees feel that they are not seen as Germans despite their German nationality. They accept and internalize their non-acceptance as Germans, and demand to be accepted as "foreigners" or as "Turks" or "Arabs" in Germany. German national identity is seen as existing in opposition to the strong identification with ethnic backgrounds. Representative studies confirm that most Muslims in Germany do not identify as German.[91] In France, by contrast, most interviewees consider themselves to be French, although many harbor the feeling that they are not perceived that way. This gap between their personal identification and society's wrongful interpretation of said identification leads to a feeling of injustice and an insistence on being accepted as French. However, in some situations they consider themselves as Arab, Algerian, Moroccan, Tunisian, black, or belonging to some other ethnic or racial group rather than, and sometimes in opposition to, "French."

In Britain, the non-acceptance of Muslims as British seems to be less of an issue than in France or Germany, even though some interviewees voiced concerns about non-acceptance and discrimination as members of ethnic or religious minorities.[92] Most respondents identify Britishness as one important dimension of their identity, often in combination with their ethnic background and in self-descriptions such as "British Asian."

The disparate concepts of national identity and immigration policies in the three countries influence the self-identification of young European Muslims. The claim for acceptance of one's own ethnic community or of "foreigners" in general, rather than acceptance as a German, can be regarded as an internalization of an ethnic concept of nationality in Germany. The French civic model of a "territorial community" allows immigrants to identify as French, which most respondents do to some extent. However, their experiences and perceptions of exclusion and discrimination lead to a feeling of injustice. Furthermore, the French model of assimilative integration, as opposed to the British multicultural approach, might be an additional factor for self-descriptions such as "French" and "French of [country] origin," as opposed to explicitly dual self-descriptions, such as "British Asian." The multicultural concept in Britain seems to facilitate such dual self-identification, although some respondents in France and Germany use it too. The different integration models and nationality concepts of each of the three countries can explain differences in European Muslims' national self-identification. However, other factors such as the disparate backgrounds of Muslims might also be relevant.

Muslim identity and identification as German, French, or British are usually not perceived as contradictory, although Manichean perceptions of a struggle between Islam/Muslims and non-Muslims can be problematic. A strong belief in a global Muslim identity can lead to alienation of the British, German, or French identity if the global Muslim identity is defined in direct opposition to the national or "Western" identity.

TENSIONS, CONFLICTING IDENTITIES, AND DEBATES ON INTEGRATION

Despite strong identification with the country of residence, a hefty minority among Muslims believe that there is a "natural conflict between being a devout Muslim and living in a modern society"; according to a survey from 2006, 36 percent of Muslims in Germany agreed to this statement, as did 28 percent in France and 47 percent in Great Britain.[93]

However, the diversity of Muslim communities and individuals in Europe, as well as the fact that the large majority is law-abiding and strongly committed to the democratic society of the country of residence, should be kept in mind when discussing controversial opinions among Muslims.

A minority of Muslims have attitudes that contradict those of the majority societies in which they live. Different issues in public discourse in recent years can be regarded as signs of tension between Muslim minorities in Europe and the majority societies. These frictions vary from country to country and include public approval of some of the Shari'a, violent clashes in reaction to cartoons mocking the prophet Muhammad, public discussions about Muslim women wearing a veil, forced marriages, "honor killings," plots of terrorism by young European Muslims, and suicide bombings or approval of Islamist terrorism. Debates about these issues often wrongly stereotype Muslims as culturally alien and dangerous in general, disregarding the fact that these issues only concern a minority of Muslims.

However, two-thirds of Muslims in six European countries (Germany, France, the Netherlands, Belgium, Austria, Sweden) believe that religious rules are more important than secular laws, and the majority believe that "the West is out to destroy Islam"[94] – a belief that nurtures various conspiracy theories, as we see in later chapters. The EURISLAM survey in six European countries, on the other hand, found a generally strong commitment to democracy among Muslims but discovered significantly less progressive attitudes compared to the national majority concerning abortion, homosexuality, and premarital sex.[95] Polls in Germany showed that Muslims had greater misogynistic or conservative attitudes on gender issues than the general population[96] and that some Muslims do not embrace democratic values.[97]

Many British Muslims hold negative opinions of Westerners, often to a much greater degree than their coreligionists in Germany or France. For instance, while 57 percent of British Muslims associated immorality with Westerners, only 32 percent of German and 30 percent of French Muslims held such views in 2006.[98]

A large majority of French Muslims supports the separation of state and religion. However, 54 percent stated in a survey in 2008 that the Shari'a should be applied fully or partly in every country.[99] Such percentages might be skewed depending on the way the questions were asked. In Germany, Muslims were asked in a representative survey if they supported introduction of beating as a punishment by law with reference to Shari'a law in Germany; 9.4 percent agreed. The large majority supported basic democratic rights such as freedom of speech and minority rights.[100] Support for violence as a means to reach political ends or to "defend Islam" is relatively weak.[101] In fact, Muslims in Europe are generally concerned about the rise of Islamic extremism.[102]

EXCURSUS: DIFFERENCES BETWEEN DISCRIMINATION AGAINST MUSLIMS AND ANTISEMITISM (CO-AUTHORED BY DOERTE LETZMANN)

Some scholars see similarities between discrimination against Muslims or what is sometimes called Islamophobia and antisemitism.[103] Others fiercely oppose such comparisons.[104] However, despite some polemics, no serious scholar claims that Muslims in Europe or the United States are facing persecution today that remotely resembles the persecution and genocidal murder of Jews during the Holocaust, or that Muslims in the European Union are threatened by genocide. Activists might be tempted to implicitly or explicitly build an analogy between Muslim sufferings or Islamophobia and the Holocaust or the threat of a "Holocaust" against Muslims in order to highlight Muslim victimization. This is only possible, however, if "the Holocaust" is used simply as a metaphor for evil, devoid of its specific content.[105]

While analogies between Muslim suffering today and the Holocaust are dishonest, there might be some merit in comparing discrimination and hatred against Muslims with antisemitism before or after the Holocaust. It is therefore important to look at what exactly is being compared and what analogies are implied in order to see if such comparisons advance a better understanding of the phenomena.

Comparisons always consist of at least three elements: the phenomena that are compared with each other and a *tertium comparationis,* an overlapping aspect that forms the basis of the comparison.[106] Thus, equation of at least one aspect or dimension is the basis of any comparison. In the case of comparing so-called Islamophobia and antisemitism, it is usually unclear what exactly is being compared: is it stereotypes, negative attitudes, images, discrimination, physical attacks, hatreds, or worldviews?

The term Islamophobia remains ill defined and controversial due to the conflation of criticism of Islam and Islamic practice with hatred against and stereotyping of Muslims.[107] Additionally, the term blurs the fact that a good part of the discrimination that Muslims have to face is rooted in racism and xenophobia. I therefore use the term "discrimination against Muslims," which is, as shown above, a sad reality in Europe today, including bias specifically against Muslim identity.

Comparisons between discrimination against Muslims and antisemitism are made either within the same time period or between different periods. Historic comparisons of different phenomena in different historic periods are generally challenging. They become ahistorical and thus highly questionable if they do not account adequately for the different sociohistoric settings. David Cesarani analyzed an attempt to draw parallels between the situation and views of Jews in the 1890s in Britain and Muslims in Britain today, showing that the different backgrounds of Jews then and Muslims today are incomparable. "Despite superficial similarities between the Jewish experience and the position of Muslims now," he concluded, "it is only possible to create a parallel by distorting history."[108] This statement is supported in a number of other examples.

In his 1978 book *Orientalism,* Edward Said wrote: "The transference of a popular anti-Semitic animus from a Jewish to an Arab target was made smoothly, since the figure was essentially the same."[109] Said referred to Arabs, not Muslims, but a number of historical comparisons between hatred against Jews and against Muslims refer to his concept of orientalism.[110] Said made this comment with reference to caricatures about Arabs in the context of the oil crisis in the 1970s in which he found "'Semitic' features: sharply hooked noses, the evil mustachioed leer on their faces." He interpreted this as evidence that "Semites" are seen to be "at the bottom of all 'our' troubles, which in this case was principally a gasoline shortage."[111] Notwithstanding the fact that there are no "Semite" people but, rather, Semitic languages, including Arabic and Hebrew, Said inferred from some resemblances in stereotypes that the imaginary Jew and the imaginary Arab are similar. A closer analysis of the images and of the historical context would have shown that Arab oil oligarchs were portrayed in a biased way through the use of some racist physical features that are derived from antisemitic caricatures. However, the accusation that Arabs controlled the oil market had some roots in reality and therefore cannot be compared to delusional conspiracy theories of Jews allegedly controlling the world. Others compare the situation and images of Jews in late nineteenth-century Germany and France to the situation and images of Muslims in these countries today. Back then, it is argued, Jewish men were portrayed as lecherous; today, Muslim men are often seen as "sexually overactive."[112]

With regard to Germany, Sabine Schiffer and Constantin Wagner claim that Muslims today are the 'Others' to German society just as Jews were at the end of the nineteenth century. They see value in a comparison between antisemitism and Islamophobia in its potential to avoid a worst-case scenario: a new crime against humanity.[113] According to their book, there are common characteristics of antisemitism at the end of the nineteenth century and Islamophobia today. Both, they write, have a long history, in the form of Christian anti-Judaism and Orientalism and colonialism, respectively.[114] Schiffer and Wagner also give examples of how random citations from the Torah in nineteenth-century Germany and the Qur'an in Germany today were and are used in similar ways to show that Jews then and Muslims now are a danger to Western society. Both forms of racism, as they categorize it, rely on irrational conspiracy theories, and both Jews in the past and Muslims today are faced with the demand to fully assimilate into German society, while at the same time accused of faking their allegiance to the German nation.[115] Although Schiffer and Wagner point out that there are also important differences between antisemitism and Islamophobia, their approach is flawed in a number of ways.

First, Schiffer and Wagner fail to account for the different historical situation of the newly founded Germany state in the nineteenth century and the reunited state of the early twenty-first century: in the legal system, relevant political groups, political violence, and relations to the international community, to name but a few. Concerning racism there is also a fundamental difference: whereas race theories were accepted in the nineteenth century, both socially and, in part, scientifically, such theories have no public or scientific legitimacy today.

Second, the situation and background of German Jews then and Muslims today are entirely different. German Jews had gone through the so-called emancipation period: most of them had been living in Germany for many generations and were indeed assimilated. Antisemites wanted to reverse this process. Muslims in Germany today, on the other hand, are almost exclusively immigrants or descendants of immigrants who came to Germany, often with the initial intention to go back to their country of origin. A common reproach against them is an alleged lack of willingness for integration or assimilation.

Third, and most important, the hostilities against Jews in nineteenth-century Germany and Muslims today are of an entirely different quality and scope. Many organizations, including political parties, passed antisemitic constitutions that explicitly excluded Jews from their organizations. There were international and national self-proclaimed antisemites' congresses of political parties.[116] Sea resorts propagated and officially advertised themselves to be "judenrein." Antisemitic preachers such as court chaplain Adolf Stoecker agitated against Jews with the authority of the state and the church. The government only intervened when antisemitic riots threatened public order, such as during the antisemitic riots in Pomerania in 1881.[117] All this is not the case today. The German government condemns hate crimes against Muslims (and Jews) and takes action against its perpetrators.

Fourth, even if we compare the images and stereotypes, as Schiffer and Wagner claim to be doing, we see two entirely different situations aside from a few isolated examples. In contrast to the anti-Jewish attitudes in German society in the late nineteenth century, which were marked by an obsession with Jews in the political field and by conspiracy theories, particularly with regard to assimilated Jews,[118] anti-Muslim stereotypes today exaggerate and generalize the behavior of only a small group of Muslim extremists. Furthermore, attacks target visible Muslims and Islamic symbols rather than assimilated Muslims. A common generalized accusation against Muslims is their alleged refusal to integrate into German society, not the accusation that they undermine society through assimilation.

A more sophisticated comparison between past antisemitism and contemporary Islamophobia was presented by sociologists Nasar Meer and Tehseen Noorani, who analyzed reactions to Jewish and Muslim minorities in British society at the end of the nineteenth century and today, respectively. Meer and Noorani argue that there are "important analogies in the racial content of anti-Semitism and anti-Muslim sentiment."[119] They categorize both antisemitism and Islamophobia as forms of cultural racism. In this prevalent form of contemporary racism, they argue, "cultural difference functions like nature." They believe that because there had been a focus on cultural difference alongside alleged biological difference in pre–Second World War antisemitism, early "cultural difference" can be understood as a prototype of cultural racism. Thus, there are "forms of pathologising" earlier Jewish minorities and today's Muslim minorities that are "constituted through a cultural racism." They see the main point of comparison in "the way in which British Jews were associated with anarchism and Bolshevism," for which an analogy operates for "fundamentalist Muslims/Islamic Terrorists."[120] It is important to note, however, that the anarchism/Bolshevism accusation is only one stereotype that was attributed to Jews at the time, and that Jews were nevertheless mostly seen as economic individualists harming British society. So although many Jews at the time were employed in the tailoring trade, there was the assumption that "in every Jewish tailor there was a Rothschild just bursting to get out."[121]

As Meer and Noorani show, there are some similarities between the situation of Jews and Muslims in Britain. Parts of the Jewish community and Muslims as immigrants were affected by exclusionary national identity formation, immigration legislation, and discrimination. But not only is it important to acknowledge the different historical contexts, it is also necessary to see the differences between the alleged characteristics that were attributed to Jews at the time and to the Muslims today. While Jews were largely seen as ruthless entrepreneurs striving to control the economy and at the same time responsible for communism and anarchy, Muslims are seen as backward and violent. Meer and Noorani explicitly use "cultural racism" as the *tertium comparationis* to compare antisemitism to Islamophobia. Their approach is thus more academic and credible. However, they only succeed in this by ignoring important aspects of antisemitism that go beyond cultural racism.

But aside from particular stereotypes, which often seem to have been picked selectively in order to support a preconceived notion, comparisons between antisemitism and Islamophobia have also been made on conceptual levels. According to Matti Bunzl, antisemitism was closely related to nationalism and resulted in the rejection of the Jews. Today's European identity, by contrast, allegedly questions the participation of Muslims and their ability to be "good Europeans." Antisemitism, he writes, is therefore in decline while Islamophobia is on the rise.[122] This simplistic view is tempting but plainly wrong: First, Europe is still organized in nations and European identifications are weaker than national identifications; second, antisemitism is not in decline; and third, antisemitism is not solely related to nationalism.

What is more, such comparisons do not take into account the existence of varied historical and social situations. German or French Jews in the nineteenth century had been living in those countries for centuries as second-class citizens; while often persecuted, they acquired equal rights with emancipation in emerging democracies. Today, these countries are solid democracies with equal rights for all citizens and protection of minorities, although discrimination and prejudices still are a problem.

Another category of questionable comparison has been made between the situation of Jews and Muslims in Spain's fifteenth century. Jewish and Muslim communities, even those who had converted, as well as those with Amerindian, Asian, or African ancestry, were excluded from Christian society, infamously documented in Toledo in 1449 with the "Limpieza de sangre" (cleanliness of blood). Jews faced expulsion in 1492 and Muslims ten years later in 1502. However, Jews (including converts to Christianity) were facing even fiercer persecution than Muslims (and Muslim converts)[123] despite the military conflict with Muslim kingdoms on the Iberian Peninsula since 711 and the Reconquista. An analogy of the persecution of Jews with the persecution of Muslims in fifteenth-century Spain risks omitting not only important aspects of Christian antisemitism, such as the accusation of deicide, but also specific anti-Muslim aspects of the Reconquista.

Negative and stereotypical images of Muslims were used in the context of multiple armed conflicts: during the time of the crusades, between the thirteenth and late seventeenth century throughout the conquests of the Ottoman Empire, and even beyond the seventeenth century until the collapse of the Ottoman Empire. An equation of such images ignores the fundamental difference between biases against external (real) enemies who pose a military threat and prejudice toward enemies from within, such as Jews, who have never posed a physical threat to European societies. Some stereotypes may bear resemblance to others, but the implications and consequences are fundamentally different.

The most fruitful comparisons are those that compare antisemitism to hatred and discrimination against today's Muslims on a qualitative basis.[124] A better understanding of these fundamental differences can be achieved through studies that analyze the forms and tropes of images of Jews and Muslims. A study from Spain by Alejandro Baer and Paula López published in 2012 is revealing. They found images portraying Jews as "'ultra-modern': intelligent, rational, business oriented," while images of Muslims implied that they were "'still in the Middle Ages': religious, backwards, sexist." The imaginary Jew is perceived as being "the incarnation of the values of the modern mercantile world" and is thought to govern the world behind the scenes, whereas "an 'imaginary Arab' [is perceived as] a noble savage uncontaminated by the spirit of modern economics."[125]

Even those qualitative studies that assume parallels between anti-Jewish and anti-Muslim conspiracy theories note the differences: whereas Jews are accused of governing the world and world finances, Muslims are accused of "flooding the country" and acquiring power through demographic developments[126] – "classic xenophobic accusations.

Other fruitful comparisons analyze images of Muslims and Jews in the Middle Ages. Suzanne Conklin Akbari scrutinized late medieval English literature and found that biblical Jews formed the model for Christian depictions of Muslims in the Middle Ages.[127]

To conclude, comparisons between the hatred against Muslims and that against Jews only advance a better understanding of these phenomena if the specific images are taken into consideration and contrasted and if the historical contexts are taken into account.

What is more, hatred against Jews cannot be discussed in abstraction of the Holocaust because antisemitism and the Holocaust are intertwined in the world's collective memory today, and because antisemitism today still aims, eventually, for the annihilation of the Jews. This is why comparisons between hatred of Jews and Muslims so easily slip into dishonest polemics: such comparisons often result in direct or indirect allegations that Muslims face similar threats as Holocaust-era Jews did.

TWO

Debates and Surveys on European Muslim Antisemitism

MOST SCHOLARS ACKNOWLEDGE THAT ANTISEMITISM AMONG Muslims is a relevant factor in European antisemitism today, and yet there remains a void in research on the particularities of the Muslim case. This gap fuels both denial of antisemitism among European Muslims and demagogic accusations against "the Muslims."[1] Although Muslim perpetrators of antisemitic incidents are mostly young individuals rather than organized groups, some Muslim organizations are responsible for disseminating antisemitic ideology.

Scholars disagree on the magnitude of Muslim antisemitism compared to that of other groups, despite the mounting evidence summarized below. However, antisemitism is still widespread in the general, largely non-Muslim society, as surveys and reports on antisemitic incidents show.[2] Twenty-four percent of the population in Western Europe agreed to at least six out of eleven antisemitic stereotypes in the 2014 Anti-Defamation League survey.[3] Results vary by country and stereotype. However, a comparative look at Anti-Defamation League surveys from 2002 to 2014 shows that while agreement with antisemitic stereotypes wax and wane, they remain at a relatively high level in many countries. In Spain, between 45 (2005) and 63 (2002) percent of the population believed that it is probably true that "Jews have too much power in the business world." Fifty-three percent agreed in 2014. In Germany, between 20 (2005) and 33 (2014) percent agreed; in France between 25 and 51 percent; and in the United Kingdom between 14 (2005) and 22 (2007) percent. A comparative study from 2009 of eight European countries revealed that, with substantial differences between the countries, 24.5 percent agreed that Jews have too much influence in their country, and 41.2 percent maintain that "Jews try to take advantage of having been victims during the Nazi era."[4] A group of German scholars and experts, commissioned by the German parliament, for example, reported that up to 20 percent of Germans are estimated to be antisemitic.[5] Major disagreement exists on the sources of antisemitism among European Muslims. Are these attitudes solely related to the Israeli-Palestinian conflict? Are hostile attitudes toward Jews a result of the influence of Islamist ideology, or of discrimination and exclusion? The research deficit on this issue was assessed at an international conference in 2006 on antisemitism among people of Muslim or Arab background in Europe,[6] but only a few studies have touched on it since.

ANTISEMITIC ATTACKS

Werner Bergmann and Juliane Wetzel of the Center for Research on Antisemitism in Berlin were the first to point out the specific phenomenon of antisemitism among young European Muslims. They based their findings on comprehensive empirical data that was gathered by agencies from all European countries in 2002 on behalf of the European Monitoring Centre on Racism and Xenophobia (EUMC, now FRA). In their report they note: "Physical attacks on Jews and the desecration and destruction of synagogues were acts mainly committed by young Muslim perpetrators, mostly of Arab descent."[7] The available data today are more detailed for some countries, such as France and the United Kingdom, and reveal that while people of Muslim background are far from the only perpetrators of antisemitic violence, they nonetheless are disproportionally represented among perpetrators of such acts.

Graphs 2.1 and 2.2 illustrate the overall figures of antisemitic acts in France from 1994 to 2012 and in Britain from 1996 to 2012. The figures are based on the annual reports by the French Commission nationale consultative des droits de l'homme (CNCDH) and the Service de Protection de la Communauté Juive (SPCJ) in France and the annual reports by the Community Security Trust (CST) in the UK.

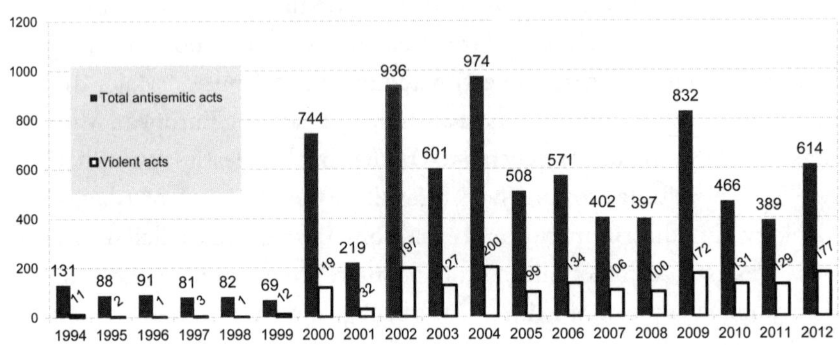

Graph 2.1

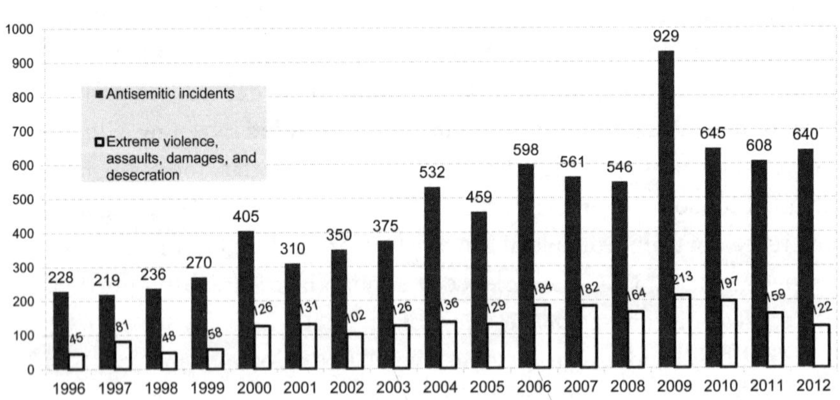

Graph 2.2

Percentage of Identified Arab-Muslim Perpetrators of All Antisemitic Acts (Threats and Violence) in France 1994 - 2007

Source: CNCDH, author's illustration

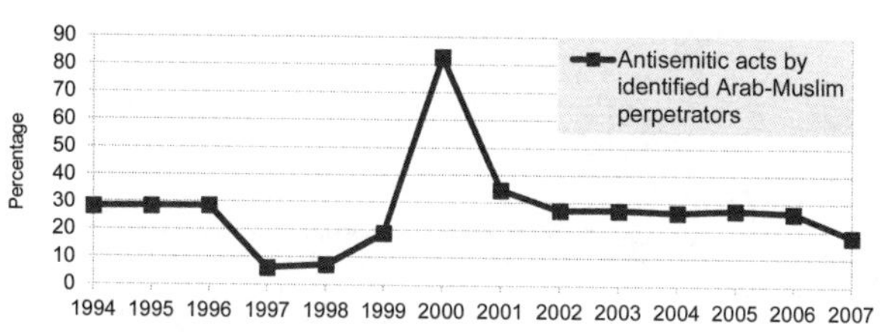

The actual percentage of Arab-Muslim perpetrators is signicifantly higher; it can be assumed that many among the non-identified perpetrators are also Arabs/Muslims.

The CNCDH reports since 2008 do not provide any information on perpetrators of antisemitic threats with Arab-Muslim background. However, for the years between 2008 and 2011, the CNCDH reports indicate the number of violent acts by identified Arab-Muslim perpetrators.

Graph 2.3

Many of the peaks in antisemitic incidents are related to eruptions of violence in the Israeli-Palestinian conflict. The outbreak of the Second Intifada in 2000, the war between Israel and Hamas in December 2008/January 2009, but also the Iraq war and even the murders at a Jewish school in Toulouse (France) were all followed by a rise of antisemitic acts, both in France and in Britain. This connection becomes even more obvious in a month-by-month analysis.[8] However, the number of incidents have increased considerably since the 1990s even without these peaks.

What percentage of attacks come from Muslim perpetrators? The exact figures are difficult to establish. They are based mainly on victims' or police reports, usually centered on the perpetrators' ethnic backgrounds. Some reports make reference to Islam during the antisemitic incident. The percentage of incidents in which perpetrators have been identified at all varies from year to year. In France, the number of identified perpetrators of violent antisemitic acts has been above 26 percent from 1997 to 2011, although their total number is relatively small. In Britain, the percentage of ethnically identified perpetrators of all incidents has varied between 26 percent (2012) and 44 percent (2007).

The annual reports of the CNCDH provide figures for the percentage of Arab-Muslim perpetrators of all antisemitic acts in France for the years 1994–2007, as illustrated in Graph 2.3. The percentage was roughly

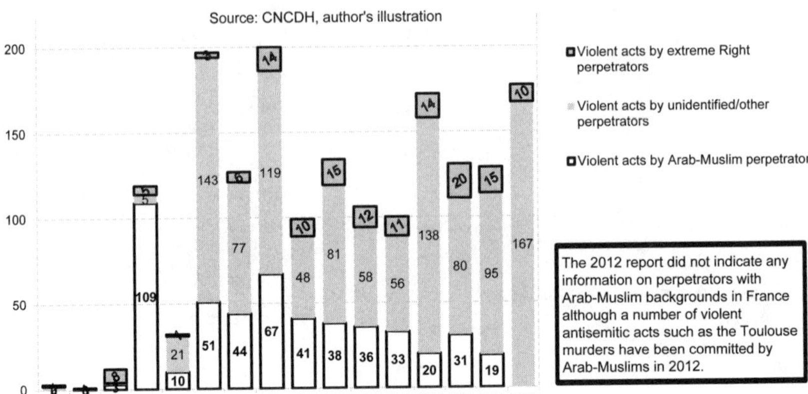

Graph 2.4

30 percent in that period, with a drop to less than 10 percent in 1997 and 1998 and a notable peak of 83 percent in 2000. However, the overall figures indicate that the rise of antisemitism since 2000 cannot be blamed solely on Muslim or Arab perpetrators. The percentage of Arab-Muslim perpetrators was just under 30 percent from 1994 to 1997, similar to the period from 2002 to 2006.

Graph 2.4 provides the number of identified perpetrators of violent antisemitic acts in France from 1997 to 2012. Since 2000, the number of identified Arab Muslim perpetrators has exceeded the number of identified perpetrators of the extreme right. The majority of identified perpetrators of violent antisemitic acts in France are Arab Muslim. The figures also show again the sharp rise of antisemitic violence since 2000 in France.

In 2011, 129 acts of antisemitic violence were registered. Nineteen were committed by people of Arab origin and/or Muslim background and 15 with reference to those of neo-Nazi ideology. The ethnic origin or religious background of a large proportion of the perpetrators, however, was not identified.[9] The 2012 report did not divulge any information on perpetrators with Arab-Muslim background in France, although Arab-

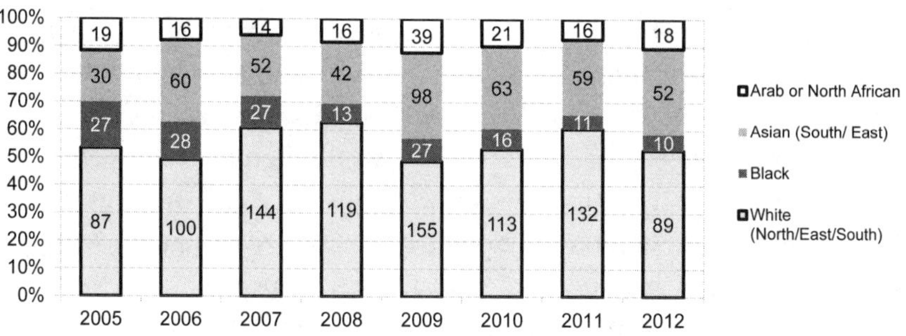

Graph 2.5

Muslims have been identified as perpetrators in a number of incidents. Among the most violent antisemitic incidents in France in 2012 was the murder of three small children and a father and teacher at the Jewish school Ozar Hatorah in Toulouse by French Jihadist Mohamed Merah, as well as the hand grenade attack on a kosher supermarket in Sarcelles, also involving a Muslim perpetrator.[10] An analysis of antisemitic incidents in France from 2000 to 2012 by Marc Knobel confirmed the significant role played by Muslims in antisemitic acts.[11]

In the United Kingdom, the CST provides numbers regarding the ethnicity of identified perpetrators, as shown in Graph 2.5. The CST reports show that since 2005, 27 to 43 percent of perpetrators of antisemitic incidents in which the ethnicity has been identified were classified as being of (South) Asian or Arab appearance, while the majority are white perpetrators. The percentage of black perpetrators ranged between 5 and 14 percent.[12] Based on these figures and religious allocations of "whites," "blacks," "Arabs," and "Asians" in the UK census,[13] the percentage of Muslim perpetrators can be estimated at between 20 and 30 percent, while the percentage of Muslims in the general population stands at 5 percent. This disproportion can only partly be explained by geographic proximity of the two communities in cities such as London and Manchester, where most incidents were reported.

Data provided by the German Federal Office for the Protection of the Constitution (Verfassungsschutz), Germany's domestic intelligence agency, indicate that the percentage of right-wing perpetrators of antisemitic attacks is particularly high in Germany (accounting for about 80 percent of violent antisemitic acts)[14] and that the percentage of Muslim perpetrators is lower there than in the United Kingdom and France. However, the Verfassungsschutz registers only three groups of perpetrators of antisemitic acts: right-wing, left-wing, and "foreign" perpetrators. Obviously, foreign perpetrators cannot automatically be equated with Muslims, but it can be assumed that, given the large percentage of Muslims among foreigners in Germany, many individuals in this category are in fact Muslim. In 2009, 22 percent of antisemitic violent acts were committed by foreigners, and the figure stood at 17 percent in 2010.[15] A report on Berlin shows that 12 of 33 acts of antisemitic and anti-Israeli violence between 2003 and 2005 were committed by "foreigners" and 15 by right-wing extremists.[16]

To resume, despite the poor data available for Germany, it can be assumed that the percentage of Muslim perpetrators of violent antisemitic acts is lower in Germany than in France and Britain, but it is still disproportionately high compared to the percentage of Muslims in Germany (4–5 percent).

These statistics are supported by newspaper reports of antisemitic incidents in which Muslims (or people of Arab origin) are often identified as perpetrators.[17] However, other crimes, such as the frequent desecration of Jewish cemeteries, are almost exclusively committed by the extreme right, at least in Germany.[18] While the share of Muslim perpetrators in all three countries is disproportionately high for violent antisemitic attacks, it might be lower for other forms of antisemitism.[19]

Another source of data points even more clearly to the important share of Muslim perpetrators. Jews who had become victims of antisemitic incidents were asked to provide details of their victimizers. The European Union Agency for Fundamental Rights (FRA) published a survey in 2013 on experiences of antisemitism in eight countries: Belgium, France, Germany, Hungary, Italy, Latvia, Sweden, and the United Kingdom.[20] The survey included 5,847 self-identified Jews. A third had

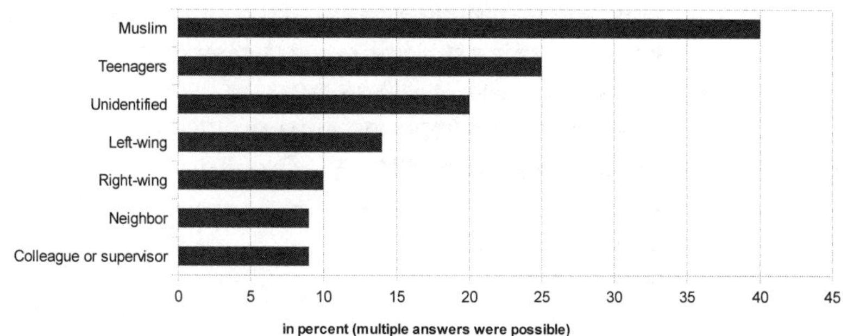

Graph 2.6

experienced antisemitic harassments in the past five years, and 7 percent reported antisemitic violence or threats against them. The most important group of perpetrators of harassment, violence, and threats were Muslim.

Forty percent of the victims of antisemitic violence or threats across the eight countries said that the perpetrators of the worst incident in the past five years had a Muslim background.[21] Given the fact that there are only a few thousand Muslims in Hungary and Latvia, it can be assumed that the percentage is higher for Belgium, France, Germany, Italy, Sweden, and the United Kingdom. (In contrast to other questions, the FRA report does not provide detailed figures on perpetrators for each country.) However, respondents could give multiple answers and about a third used this category in combination with "teenagers," the second-largest group of perpetrators of violent incidents and threats (25 percent). Perpetrators from the political left (14 percent) or right (10 percent) are relatively few.

The differences between these groups of perpetrators are somewhat smaller with regard to harassments. While Muslims remain the largest group of perpetrators (27 percent), they are closely followed by perpetra-

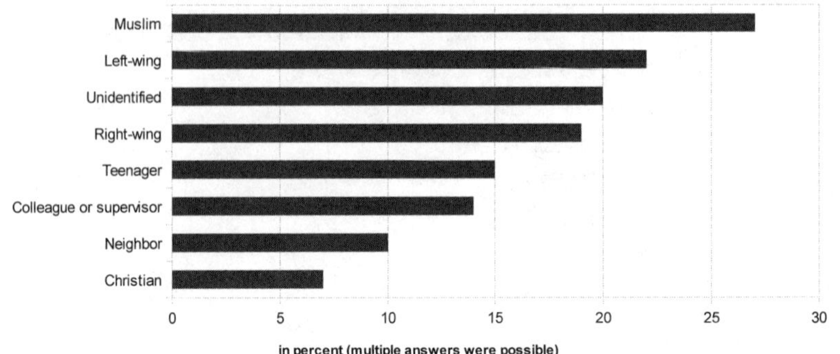

Graph 2.7

tors of the political left (22 percent) and the political right (19 percent). Interestingly, there are more perpetrators identified with the left than with the right, both for harassments and violence and threats.

The British All-Party Parliamentary Inquiry found that the majority of antisemitic incidents are "committed by individuals rather than organized groups" and are "either opportunistic or aggravated, indicating an undercurrent of anti-Jewish prejudice that is part of everyday life and that comes to the surface when there are tensions or trigger events."[22] A comprehensive study on antisemitic incidents in London from 2001 to 2004 shows that most suspects are male (83.4 percent) and that the largest proportion of suspects are between 16 and 20 years old.[23] Perpetrators in London were disproportionately and often described as "Arab Egyptians," "African Caribbean," and "Dark European." However, perpetrators described as white European still formed 56.9 percent of suspects of antisemitic incidents.[24]

Concerning the French context, Michel Wieviorka stressed that most perpetrators of North African origin are men with a low level of education who were largely unable to articulate a political rationale for their antisemitic actions. Additionally, many had been known previously by the police to be responsible for petty crime.[25]

Recognizable Jews – Jews who wear symbols of Judaism or who visit Jewish institutions such as synagogues and schools – are particularly at risk in Europe. Many Jews therefore disguise their Jewish identity. According to the FRA study, 60 percent of Jews in Sweden, 51 percent in France, 31 percent in Germany, and 21 percent in the UK frequently or always avoid wearing, carrying, or displaying items in public that might allow people to recognize them as Jews. And 30 percent of polled Jews in Sweden, 27 percent in France, 19 percent in Germany, and 16 percent in the UK at least sometimes avoid visiting Jewish events or sites because they do not feel safe as Jews there, or on the way there. On average, across all eight countries (Belgium, France, Germany, Hungary, Italy, Latvia, Sweden, and the United Kingdom), 46 percent worry about verbal insults or harassment and 21 percent have faced such incidents. Almost a third has considered emigrating in the past five years because they do not feel safe as Jews.[26] Antisemitic harassment and violence has become a daily concern for many Jews in Europe again, and Muslim antisemitism has a significant share in this.

ANTISEMITIC ATTITUDES

In Germany and France, antisemitic attitudes among young Muslims have been intensely discussed in the context of schools and education.[27] In Britain and some other European countries, anecdotes of antisemitism in schools have been published.[28] Antisemitism among European Muslims and Muslim organizations has also become visible in pro-Palestinian demonstrations in Germany,[29] France,[30] Britain,[31] and other European countries.[32] But these pro-Palestine Muslim protesters are hardly representative of European Muslims in general; their statements are made in a specific context. Even so, surveys consistently show that antisemitic attitudes are stronger and more common among European Muslims than non-Muslims.[33]

In 2006, the Pew Global Attitudes Project asked Muslims and non-Muslims in a number of countries if they have a "favorable or unfavorable opinion of Jews." In the UK 7 percent of the general population and 47 percent of Muslims stated that they do have an unfavorable opinion of Jews. In France the figures were 13 and 28 percent, respectively, while

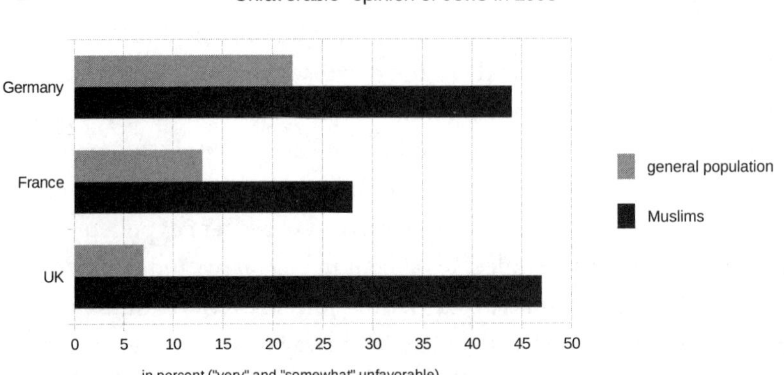

Graph 2.8

in Germany they were 22 and 44 percent. The differences are even stronger when attitudes of "very unfavorable opinion of Jews" are compared.[34] This can be explained by stronger and more widespread antisemitic attitudes among European Muslims compared to non-Muslims, by less reluctance among these Muslims to show openly negative opinions of Jews, or both. Unfortunately, no other items on antisemitic attitudes were included in the Pew survey.

Another international survey by the prestigious WZB Berlin Social Science Center reveals similar tendencies. This major study, led by Ruud Koopmans and published in 2013, focuses on religious fundamentalism and out-group hostility among Muslims and Christians in Western Europe. In Germany, 28 percent of Muslims and 10.5 percent of Christians agreed with the statement that "Jews cannot be trusted"; in France, 43.4 percent of Muslims and 7.1 percent of Christians agreed. The survey shows similar results for the Netherlands, Belgium, Austria, and Sweden. The authors explicitly exclude socioeconomic marginalization, exclusion, alienation and a lack of religious rights for Muslims as explanatory factors for religious fundamentalism and out-group hostility.[35]

Other surveys from European countries confirm that anti-Jewish attitudes are stronger among European Muslims than among the general population, even though more surveys are needed to establish the differences on a representative national level in various European countries. In Germany, Katrin Brettfeld and Peter Wetzels included one item on antisemitism in their questionnaire completed by 2,683 students, including 500 Muslims, in Cologne, Hamburg, and Augsburg; they found that 15.7 percent of Muslims of migrant background, 7.4 percent of non-Muslims of such background, and 5.4 percent of non-Muslims without any background of migration strongly believe that "people of Jewish faith are arrogant and greedy."[36] Another study, also commissioned by the German Ministry of the Interior, focused on radicalization of young Muslims (14–32 years old) and surveyed 200 German Muslims, 517 non-German Muslims, and a representative sample of 200 young non-Muslim Germans in 2009 and 2010. The questionnaire included two items on antisemitic attitudes, both related to Israel: (1) "Israel is exclusively to be blamed for the origin and continuation of the Middle East conflicts," and (2) "It would be better if the Jews would leave the Middle East." About 25 percent of both German and non-German Muslim participants and less than 5 percent of non-Muslim Germans agreed to both items. Antisemitic attitudes varied between different ethnic and religious groups.[37] A survey published already in 1997 asked youths of Turkish background if they think that Zionism threatens Islam; 33.2 percent agreed that it does.[38] Jürgen Mansel and Viktoria Spaiser conducted the most detailed survey on the issue.[39] In 2010, they surveyed 2,404 students with different backgrounds in Bielefeld, Cologne, Berlin, and Frankfurt. Antisemitic attitudes related to Israel, religious antisemitism, classic antisemitism, and equations between Israel and the Nazis were significantly higher among Muslim students, and Arab students in particular, than among other students.[40] Religious antisemitism was measured with two items: 15.2 percent of students with Turkish background, 18.2 percent of those with Arab background, and 20.8 of those with Kurdish background completely agreed with the statement, "In my religion they warn us against trusting Jews." Only 2.8 percent of those without any migrant background did so. Similarly, 15.9 percent of students with Turkish background, 25.7 percent of those with Arab background, and 16.7 of those with Kurdish background completely agreed with the statement, "In my religion, it is the Jews who drive the world to disaster."

However, Muslim students showed less anti-Jewish attitudes related to so-called "secondary" antisemitism ("I am fed up with hearing about the crimes against the Jews"). The authors noticed a correlation between antisemitic attitudes and religious fundamentalism among Muslims. Another study from 2012 conducted in Germany also found that Muslims endorse classic antisemitic statements more often than their non-Muslim counterparts; approval of "secondary" antisemitism, which is related to the Holocaust, was slightly weaker.[41]

A 2009 study from Denmark by the Institute for Political Science at Aarhus University conducted interviews with 1,503 immigrants with Turkish, Pakistani, Somali, Palestinian, and (former) Yugoslavian backgrounds, as well as 300 ethnic Danes. Analysis of the study revealed that a number of antisemitic stereotypes are significantly more common (up to 75 percent) among immigrants than among ethnic Danes (up to 20 percent). The study also showed that anti-Jewish attitudes are more widespread among Muslim than among Christian immigrants.[42]

In Brussels, 2,837 students in thirty-two Dutch-speaking high schools were polled. About half of the Muslim respondents agreed with the following statements:

(1) "Jews want to dominate everything" (total, 31.4 percent; Muslims, 56.8 percent; non-Muslims, 10.5 percent).
(2) "Most Jews think they're better than others" (total, 29.9 percent Muslims, 47.1 percent; Non-Muslims, 12.9 percent).
(3) "If you do business with Jews, you should be extra careful" (total, 28.6 percent; Muslims, 47.5 percent; non-Muslims, 12.9 percent).
(4) "Jews incite to war and blame others" (total, 28.4 percent; Muslims, 53.7 percent; non-Muslims, 7.7 percent).

The antisemitic attitudes were unrelated to low educational level or social disadvantage.[43] Mark Elchardus confirmed the findings two years later in 2013 with a study of 863 students from Ghent and Antwerp, including 346 Muslim students. While 45–50 percent of Muslim students revealed antisemitic attitudes, "only" about 10 percent of non-Muslims did so.[44]

In 2013, 937 teachers in the Netherlands participated in a survey about antisemitic attitudes and Holocaust diminishment among their students. Both are vastly more common in schools with a higher percentage of students of Turkish or Moroccan background (who are predominantly Muslim). In schools with under 5 percent of students with Turkish or Moroccan background, 28 percent of the teachers reported that their students made hurtful remarks about Jews or diminished the Holocaust once or a few times during the preceding year. In schools where the student population is over 25 percent Turkish or Moroccan, 43 percent of the teachers gave this answer. Interestingly, when we exclude insults made in the context of the Middle East or soccer, the percentage of insults against Jews is also significantly higher in schools with many students of Turkish or Moroccan background. According to teacher reports, perpetrators with Moroccan or Turkish backgrounds are overrepresented, forming 10 and 8 percent of the perpetrators, respectively, while the figure stands at 3 percent for both student groups in the Netherlands.[45]

In Britain in December 2005, the polling institute Populus interviewed 500 Muslims on their views of Jews but did not make inquiries into the views of the general population. In this survey, 53 percent agreed that Jews in Britain "have too much influence over the direction of UK foreign policy," 46 percent said that "they are in league with the Freemasons to control the media and politics," and 37 percent disclosed that Jews of the Jewish community in Britain "are legitimate targets as part of the ongoing struggle for justice in the Middle East."[46]

A comprehensive survey published in 2004 (2005 in English) in Sweden analyzed the results of more than 10,000 questionnaires filled out by pupils that included six items on antisemitic attitudes. Muslims showed the highest percentage of strong antisemitic attitudes with 8.3 percent versus 3.7 percent among Christians, but were followed closely by those considering themselves non-religious (7.6 percent). The survey also revealed significant differences among male and female respondents; 12.9 percent of Muslim boys were found to be "intolerant" toward Jews but only 4.8 percent of Muslim girls were reported as such.[47] The study by Wolfgang Frindte et al. on young Muslims in Germany found no gender differences.[48]

But not all negative attitudes toward Jews are necessarily antisemitic. A survey in Germany compared the attitudes of people of Turkish origin, who are mostly Muslim,[49] with those of ethnic Germans. Forty-eight percent of those of Turkish origin but "only" 20 percent of Germans stated that they would feel uncomfortable if a practicing Jew married a member of his or her family. However, 40 percent of the population of Turkish origin in Germany rejected practicing Christians in the same way and 69 percent rejected atheists, while 8 percent rejected practicing Muslims.[50] Therefore, the rejection of having practicing Jews in the family might more likely be motivated from valuing one's own religious affiliation rejecting non-Muslims in the family rather than in hostility against Jews in particular.

SCHOLARLY DISCUSSIONS AND SPECULATIONS ON POSSIBLE SOURCES OF ANTISEMITIC ATTITUDES

Scholars have discussed the possible sources of anti-Jewish attitudes among European Muslims, but due to a lack of empirical data, they have often based their reflections on anecdotal or historical observations, or on interpretations of a rise of European anti-Jewish incidents at times of heightened tensions in the Israeli-Palestinian conflict. Robert Wistrich describes Muslim antisemitism as one important factor today in antisemitism in Europe and suggests that Islamists have spread the "Palestinian war against the Jews" from the Middle East to the European Union. Wistrich states that the EU is "perceived as dar al-Kufr, the land of impiety. This is the soil on which fundamentalist paranoia can best flourish."[51] Klaus Holz acknowledges that a major group of perpetrators have a Muslim or migrant background, but rightly insists that "there is no necessary or monocausal relation between their background and their antisemitism."[52] He believes that their experiences of social, racist, and religious exclusion are major factors for antisemitism.[53] John Bunzl and Brian Klug see attacks against Jewish individuals and property by "alienated Moroccan and Algerian youths in the banlieues of Paris" as "an ethno-religious conflict between two communities with opposed identifications: roughly, French Muslims with Palestinian Arabs versus French Jews with Israeli Jews."[54]

For the French context, however, Michel Wieviorka's study disproves the thesis that antisemitism among young Muslims is largely based around an ethnic conflict between Jews and Muslims by comparing neighborhoods with and without a visible Jewish community. Wieviorka even dedicated a chapter to the issue with the telling title "Un antisémitisme (presque) sans Juifs" (Antisemitism [almost] without Jews).[55] Klug further interprets anti-Jewish attacks by "young Muslim immigrants" as "political outrage, not bigotry" and explicitly not antisemitic. He suggests that these attacks are motivated by anti-Zionism and believes that "it is closer to the truth to say that anti-Zionism today takes the form of anti-Semitism rather than the other way round."[56] Pierre-André Taguieff, on the other hand, insists that "the new Judeophobia which can be observed in the post-Nazi period appears to be centered on a mythical 'anti-Zionism' which treats 'Zionism' like the incarnation of absolute evil."[57]

Attacks against Jews and Jewish property in Europe have been interpreted as a result of anger over Israeli policies and, indeed, tensions and violence in the Israeli-Palestinian conflict often correlate with a rise in anti-Jewish incidents. But a closer look into these correlations shows that, first, antisemitic incidents are also correlated to other conflicts and, second, the Israeli-Palestinian conflict has been used for some time to stir up hatred against Jews.[58]

Paul A. Silverstein offers two other far-fetched theories. He sees attacks against Jews by North African immigrants and their children in France as part of a reaction to the violence they experience from the French state "directed back at the state and those (including Jews) who seem to represent it."[59] Why then are the attacks not directed against symbols of the state? If "the Jews," including Jewish neighbors and synagogues, are seen as representative of the French state, this is already an antisemitic perception in the first place. He also frames hostility against Jews as a result of immigrant identification with Palestinians over their perceived shared oppressive colonial experiences, together with the perception that Jews are privileged over Muslims in Europe and thus "iconic of all which is intolerable in their own lives."[60] Similarly, Matti Bunzl believes that Muslims attack Jews because they see Jews as part of a European hegemony that both marginalizes them and accounts for the suffering of Palestinians. He explains that "Muslim violence against Europe's Jews [is] the extension of an anti-colonial struggle."[61] Such assumptions take antisemitic interpretations of an "anti-colonial struggle" or antisemitic amalgamation of European Jews with Israel or with European governments as explanation for antisemitic attitudes and behavior, which is absurd. Additionally, such "explanations" tend to deny that attacks on European Jews are antisemitic in effect, if not in intent. Götz Nordbruch links antisemitic incidents by young Muslims to an increasing identification with the Muslim community and "Palestine" and as a reaction to discrimination and frustration about their standing in society. Taking the example of Germany, he argues that Muslims are often stigmatized by mainstream German society and thus rarely identify themselves with Germany, but rather with their religious identity.[62] Klaus Holz and Michael Kiefer see "Islamist antisemitism" as an import from Europe and make the general re-Islamization of the Muslim population responsible for the reimportation of this variation of modern antisemitism back to Europe. Some of these explanations seem to avoid placing any responsibility for antisemitic attitudes on European Muslims.

However, Holz and Kiefer provide evidence of antisemitic ideology on the part of major Muslim organizations in Germany[63] and point to popular antisemitic Turkish and Arab TV series and films. In their overview of the current state of research on "Islamist" or "Islamicized" antisemitism in Germany, they deplore the lack of research on said topic. They also voice a number of relevant questions, such as those that seek to examine the influence of Islamist ideology, and ask if antisemitism is seen as being connected to Islamic tradition. They point out that antisemitic attitudes about Jews should be analyzed in relation to images of self-identification, asking, "What is the role of self-identification as Muslim for the disposition of Jew-hatred?"[64] They also suggest investigating possible links between identification with "the Palestinians" and European Muslims' social exclusion and lack of "cultural acknowledgment" as an explanation for Jew hatred.

The most comprehensive research on antisemitism among European Muslims was undertaken by Michel Wieviorka in France, although he and his team based their analysis on "disenfranchised youths," many of Muslim background, as part of a larger analysis of contemporary antisemitism in France. They derived data from interviews and meetings with social workers, local politicians, and youths in the district Trois-Ponts in Roubaix, in the north of France, and Sarcelles, a town close to Paris.[65]

Trois-Ponts is a rather quiet neighborhood, characterized by social exclusion and inhabited mainly by Maghrebian immigrants; it has no visible Jewish community. In contrast, Sarcelles has strong and visible Jewish communities. The majority of the Muslim population, as well as most members of the Jewish communities, are immigrants from North Africa and their descendants. The researchers observed blunt antisemitic attitudes in both areas that were voiced openly, and sometimes in public. Antisemitic discourse is widespread and the use of the words "Juif" and "Feuj" (Jew) as insults indicate that negative views of Jews are taken for granted in some social circles. They observed that the use of antisemitic language among youths puts pressure on individuals to use this very language and to adopt an anti-Jewish discourse.[66] This phenomenon was also found in another study by Didier Lapeyronnie.[67] My own research on antisemitism in France and Germany confirms that these results are mirrored in the German context and show that anti-Jewish attitudes have materialized and are reinforced in the everyday language used by youths from different backgrounds, including Muslim youths.[68] Anecdotal evidence and a survey given among Dutch teachers both indicate that this phenomenon is more frequent among Muslim youths. While 16 percent of teachers in schools with under 5 percent Moroccan or Turkish students reported that students insult each other with the term "Jew," the number was 48 percent in schools with more than 25 percent of students with Moroccan or Turkish background.[69]

However, Wieviorka and his colleagues noted that, in contrast to Lapeyronnie, those who voiced antisemitic attitudes did not intend to act further on them. Interestingly, the researchers found the same antisemitic tropes, discourses, and resentments on the local level and in certain Middle Eastern media. Attitudes were often voiced in combination with hatred against Israel and also against the United States. The researchers observed that both the popular identification with the Palestinian cause and Islamism and the perception of a war of religions are all too often embedded in antisemitic views. Still, they concluded that the dynamics of antisemitic discourses in such areas stem from a combination of social exclusion and racist discrimination, which seems to contradict their own observations. Jonathan Laurence and Justin Vaisse come to similar conclusions on "the deeper cause of anti-Semitism," even if said conclusions also partially contradict their otherwise excellent literature review on antisemitism among Muslims in France.[70] A study based on interviews with 25 young Muslim men and women from Berlin found that the interviewees often interpret their own disadvantaged position in an antisemitic way, making the Jews responsible for inequality and exploitation and blaming "the Jews" for controlling the media, therefore effectively holding Jews responsible for an alleged negative image of Muslims and Islam in the media.[71] Thus, discrimination, (alleged) negative views of Muslims and Islam, and the economy can be interpreted in an antisemitic way, but this does not mean that they cause such views. The essence of antisemitic worldviews are antisemitic interpretations of the world around. It is true that many European Muslims suffer from exclusion and discrimination, but this also holds true for other minorities who manifest fewer antisemitic attitudes. The discrimination against Muslims alone cannot explain Muslim antisemitism.

Interestingly, Wieviorka's analysis of Muslim antisemitism in French prisons confirmed that there is not a single "type" of antisemitism among Muslims. Two different images of the Jews recur: in a more local context, Jews in France are seen as privileged and successful; they are often envied and contrasted to one's own underprivileged situation. In a global context, the Jews are seen as agents of Israeli and American hegemony who rely upon the oppression of "the Palestinians" in particular, and "the Arabs," or Muslims, in general. Anti-Jewish attitudes are part of a Manichean vision of the world: the all-powerful Jew incarnates evil, while the oppressed Muslim incarnates good. This vision, the researchers in Wieviorka's team stated, is used to justify violence by Muslims against Jews, allegedly as an answer to the "humiliation" in the banlieus – an image amplified by TV reports of Israeli tanks shooting young Palestinians armed with stones.[72]

Two studies, based on surveys in France and in Germany, demonstrate that antisemitic attitudes among Muslims are correlated to ethnic origin and religious orientation but not to economic disadvantages or discrimination.[73] A survey of Muslim and non-Muslim students in Brussels found that antisemitic attitudes among Muslims are unrelated to low educational level and social disadvantage.[74]

Sylvain Brouard and Vincent Tiberj analyzed data from a representative poll in 2005 on antisemitism among French citizens of African and Turkish descent in comparison to the general electorate. They pointed out that 33 percent of those of African or Turkish origin showed antisemitic attitudes in a number of items versus 18 percent of the general population. However, antisemitic attitudes recede with time spent in France, and the second generation born in France reaches figures below even the general population (17 percent). Interestingly, they demonstrate that antisemitism among this population is only weakly related to conservative attitudes, ethnocentrism, and authoritarianism but correlates strongly with the level of Islamic practice.[75] According to Tiberj, education, the social jealousy hypothesis that explains antisemitic attitudes stem from economic disadvantages, and even negative attitudes toward Israel cannot be explanatory factors, as respective correlations are relatively weak. In fact, the level of hostility toward Israel is similar among people of African and Turkish origin and the general French population.[76]

The study by Frindte et al. on young Muslims in Germany demonstrates that antisemitic attitudes are not related to gender, income, or perceptions of discrimination. However, the survey reveals differences related to ethnic origin and religious orientation. Among those surveyed, 42.1 percent of young Muslims born in the Middle East and the Arabian Peninsula (Israel, Lebanon, Palestine, Oman, etc.), 31.8 percent from Africa (Libya, Morocco, Tunisia, Sudan, Somalia, etc.), 29.4 percent born in Turkey, 28.1 percent of Muslims born in Germany, 14.8 percent born in Afghanistan, Iraq, Iran, Pakistan, and 11.8 percent born in the Balkans (Kosovo, etc.) agreed that "Israel is exclusively to be blamed for the origin and continuation of the Middle East conflicts," and that "it would be better if the Jews would leave the Middle East." Interestingly, differences with regard to the religious orientation were only found for the first statement. Regarding various religious strands among Muslims, 48.2 percent of Shiites, 42.4 percent of Sunnis, 31.6 percent of Ahmadis, and only 10 percent of Alevis agreed that "Israel is exclusively to be blamed for the origin and continuation of the Middle East conflicts." In addition, the authors found that authoritarian views have a significant effect on antisemitic attitudes of non-German Muslims but no effect on those of German Muslims.[77]

ANTISEMITISM IN ISLAMISM, ARAB NATIONALISM, AND ANTISEMITIC DISCOURSES IN THE COUNTRIES OF ORIGIN

The influence of Islamist movements and Arab nationalism on European Muslims is difficult to assess.[78] Both movements emerged in the first half of the twentieth century and adhere to antisemitic interpretations of the world.[79] Today, views of Jews in Arab and Muslim-majority countries are influenced by Islamist and Arab nationalist ideologies.[80] Surveys show that negative views of Jews are shared by the overwhelming majority of the population in countries with Muslim majorities. In 2011, 69 percent of the population in Turkey had a very unfavorable view of Jews and 14 percent had a somewhat unfavorable view of Jews. The figures were similar for Pakistan. Sixty-nine percent had a very unfavorable view, while 8 percent had a somewhat unfavorable view of Jews. In Egypt, 94 percent had a very unfavorable view of Jews. Compared to Egypt, the attitudes were slightly better in the Palestinian territories: 89 percent had a very unfavorable view of Jews.[81] The 2014 ADL survey confirms the widespread hatred of Jews in Muslim and Arab countries, many of them countries of origin of European Muslims. In Algeria, 87 percent of the population agreed to at least 6 out of 11 antisemitic stereotypes, 80 percent in Morocco, 87 percent in Tunisia, and 69 percent in Turkey.[82] These anti-Jewish attitudes are often embedded in negative views of the Western world in general.[83] Characteristics of contemporary antisemitism in Arab and Muslim-majority countries have been described as chimeric lies about Jews, such as making "the Jews" responsible for the attacks of September 11, 2001, the phenomenon of Holocaust denial, and a revival of the "Protocols of the Elders of Zion," including the blood libel.[84] These characteristics indicate that the sources of hostility against Jews are rooted in modern antisemitism rather than religious animosity. On the other hand, countless religious leaders have been recorded while disseminating hatred against Jews.[85] Many use negative statements about Jews in the Qur'an or the Hadith to justify hatred against Jews. Views of the Holocaust in Arab and Muslim countries are also often influenced by antisemitic and anti-Zionist attitudes.[86]

As mentioned earlier, many Muslim organizations in Europe are affiliated with or linked to global Islamist movements, such as the Muslim Brotherhood. In Germany, the second-largest Muslim organization, Milli Görüş, is thought to be a non-violent Islamist organization[87] with strong links to Turkey and ideologically close to the Brotherhood. In France, the majority of Muslim organizations of the Conseil français du culte musulman, created as a representative body for Muslims in France, have strong ties to Islamist organizations.[88] The Muslim Council of Britain (MCB) is linked to the international Islamist organizations Muslim Brotherhood and Jamaat-I-Islami.[89] On a European level, the most prominent Muslim organization is the European Council for Fatwa and Research, headed by Yusuf al-Quaradawi, a prominent Egyptian Islamic theologian and one of the main ideologues of the Muslim Brotherhood. These and other Islamist organizations have published antisemitic statements and some have close contacts to openly antisemitic organizations. Milli Görüş in Germany, for instance, has not severed its links to the antisemitic pro-Hamas organization IHH,[90] even after the latter was outlawed in Germany. Book fairs in mosques associated with Milli Görüş have displayed blunt antisemitic literature.[91] Similarly, the orthodox Sunni Union des Organisations Islamiques de France (UOIF) supports the pro-Hamas Committee for Charity and Assistance to Palestinians (CBSP).[92] The leading Deobandi figure in the UK, Abu Yusuf Riyadhul Haq, is known for the blunt antisemitic statements he has uttered in public.[93] The list goes on: the Muslim Association of Britain became prominent after its pro-Palestinian rally that equated Israel with Nazi Germany.[94] The British All-Party Parliamentary Inquiry into Antisemitism of 2006 offered examples of overtly antisemitic statements by Islamists and Islamist organizations, namely Hizb ut-Tahir, Al-Muhajiroun, and the Muslim Public Affairs Committee (MPACUK). The report also mentioned the availability of antisemitic propaganda, such as *Mein Kampf* and *The Protocols of the Elders of Zion* in Arabic bookshops in London and additional locations.[95]

An investigation in the UK of available literature in mosques, Islamic schools, and Islamic cultural centers found that some of Britain's mainstream Islamic institutions provide cause for concern. The literature available in a number of British mosques contains hatred against Jews and the West and antisemitic conspiracy theories, including positive reference to *The Protocols of the Elders of Zion*.[96] Islamic literature inciting hatred can also be found in a number of public libraries without any critical comment.[97]

Another study on Muslim schools published in 2009 revealed that some of the estimated 166 full-time Muslim schools in Britain teach the rejection of Western values and hatred of Jews. Many display some degree of affiliation with puritan and separatist movements, such as Wahhabis, Salafis, Deobandis, and the Muslim Brotherhood. The study gives evidence that individuals and organizations associated with some Muslim schools and even textbooks used in those schools harbor antisemitic stereotypes and worldviews.[98] However, as mentioned, Islamist organizations are hardly representative of the Muslim population in Europe, despite their prominence and influence in many European mosques.

JEW HATRED IN ISLAM

The influence of Islam on negative views of Jews has also been widely discussed. From a sociological perspective, Islam does not exist as a unitary category; there are as many different interpretations of Islam as there are Muslims. There is no "Islam" as such, so if anti-Jewish attitudes are justified with Islamic sources, then they are interpretations of the religion for which individuals are responsible, rather than "Islam." Therefore, linking Islam or Muslims with antisemitism in an essentializing way is wrong.[99] However, Islamic scripture, including parts of the Qur'an and the Hadith, do convey derogatory views of Jews or suggest an enmity between Muslims and Jews, and are used to justify anti-Jewish hostility. [100] More importantly, these passages are rarely contextualized, let alone criticized, by authoritative Islamic figures. The widespread understanding of the Qur'an as Allah's direct word and the idealization of Muhammad's life makes it difficult for many to criticize hostile messages in Islamic scripture against non-Muslims. Some translations from the Arabic are more hostile than others. However, often quoted examples include depictions of Jews as apes and swines, an alleged curse on Jews by Allah, accusations of treachery, and calls for the mistreatment and even murder of Jews. Furthermore, historically, Jews have often been discriminated against under Islamic rule.[101] A number of publications in the past decade have revealed links and cooperation between leading Muslims and National Socialism. Some Muslim leaders have adopted antisemitic ideology from the Nazis.[102] But again, these are acts of individuals and particular organizations. The overall impact of Islam on European Muslims and their attitudes toward Jews remains unclear. However, as we will see, certain perceptions of Islam among "ordinary" young European Muslims are directly related to antisemitic views.

EUROPEAN ANTISEMITIC DISCOURSES

Muslims in Europe are an integral part of European societies. It would be surprising if they were not influenced by antisemitic discourses in mainstream society, be it in private, in the culture, or in the media. Unfortunately, I cannot reflect here on the vast literature on contemporary antisemitism in different European countries today. But it is important to note that there are major differences with regard to antisemitism between European countries, both historically and today, both in quantitative and qualitative terms.[103] Research on Holocaust-related "secondary" antisemitism, for example, has demonstrated that some motives for negative views of Jews are country-specific, which result from a projective rejection of guilt for the Holocaust.[104] This study shows that some country-specific tropes are also repeated by Muslims living in these countries, pointing to a direct influence of views of Jews from mainstream European societies on European Muslims.

The role of antisemitism in general society, or rather the role of tolerance for antisemitism, as a factor among Muslims in the French context is discussed by Taguieff and Jean-Christophe Rufin. They argue that antisemitism among young French Arabs is tolerated by general society because anti-Israel and antiracist sympathies exist within the larger society.[105] Both antisemitic and anti-antisemitic attitudes, as well as tolerance of antisemitism within the general society, are relevant factors for an assessment of Jew hatred.[106]

I had no illusion that the artificiality of the interview situation would get them to offer a specific "presentation of self" that would reflect only one of their potentially numerous putative "authentic selves" – I was convinced, as I still am, that recognizing the artificiality of the conditions under which social science data are collected (even in naturalistic experiments) is an essential dimension of the production of sound research in the social sciences.

MICHÈLE LAMONT

THREE

Interviews with Young Muslim Men in Europe

METHODS AND EVALUATION OF RESEARCH PROCESS

I have chosen a qualitative approach in this study for two reasons. First, the lack of data on antisemitism among people of Muslim background demands an explorative approach and a qualitative description of relevant tropes before questions and items for a representative study are chosen. Second, the goal of understanding how young people of Muslim background argue in antisemitic ways, and how they convey their arguments, demands an in-depth description of these arguments. Such an approach also allows the researcher to consider the informants' subjective perspectives and everyday contexts.

The cross-national comparison enables one to take into account the identification of commonalities and transnational aspects, as well as national differences. The national contexts and discourses on integration and antisemitism and the history and origin of Muslim immigrants are very different in Germany, France, and Britain, which makes comparisons methodologically challenging. One must keep in mind the different national contexts, both in the presentation of research and in analytical strategies. From the start, the reader is reminded of these different contexts. In all steps of the analytical process, I compare responses in the three countries against their respective national contexts.[1]

Standardization of procedures is limited in qualitative studies. Reliability and validity are ensured not only by rigorous research but also by documentation and reflection on all steps of the research process.[2] Here I discuss my prior understanding, motivation, and expectations, my method of collecting data, decisions in the research process, and reflections on the interviewers and on myself as a subjective investigator, as well as my analytical strategy to enhance transparency and comprehensibility.

Prior Understanding, Motivation, and Expectations

This research project was developed in 2004 and 2005, when I worked as one of the co-founders of the Kreuzberger Initiative gegen Antisemitismus in Berlin on extracurricular education on antisemitism.[3] The majority of students were Muslims of Turkish and Arab background. At the time, available educational materials focused primarily on antisemitism and its sources and history among ethnic Germans, and was not designed for mixed classrooms of students with and without foreign origin. We therefore felt the need to develop our own material and included themes in our workshops that were related to the countries in which our students or their parents were born. We dealt with specific elements of antisemitism in Turkey, such as the figure of the "Dönme"[4] or reactions to the antisemitic terror attacks in Istanbul in 2003. We also developed a workshop on the roots of the Middle East conflict in order to counter dualistic and antisemitic assumptions surrounding it. One of our cognitive educational approaches was to expose popular antisemitic tropes and to deconstruct them. However, we could only make informed guesses about relevant expressions of contemporary antisemitism among students from our own experiences and anecdotal evidence.[5]

Thus, my research interest came directly from my work in education on antisemitism. I was interested in the rationales and patterns of antisemitic argumentation of the students with whom we were working. I wanted to know what arguments they use to justify hostility against Jews in order to be able to critically analyze, together with the students, these arguments and their underlying motivations.

In 2004 and 2005, I participated in a number of conferences and meetings of experts working on education on antisemitism in Germany, France, and Great Britain. These meetings showed that experts from elsewhere had similar questions, including the following: Are there specific patterns of argumentation or tropes among Muslims and, if so, what do they look like and where do they come from? Additionally, some observations made by scholars in France at the time on mixed neighborhoods and mixed classrooms resembled my own observations in Berlin.[6]

I knew that antisemitism in Europe is not only a problem on the fringes of society and also that antisemitism among Muslims is just a small part of the overall picture of European antisemitism. However, some young European Muslims have emerged as a new group of bigots, and no research had focused on that issue, which led me to focus on patterns of antisemitic argumentations among youths in Europe of Arab or Muslim background. In the course of my study, I learned that the Muslim identity is important for all participants and, therefore, I describe them as "European Muslims."

I also made some observations on possible influences of antisemitic attitudes among young Muslims and had assumed that Islam or Islamism is only a minor factor. I noticed that only a few students in our workshops were familiar with antisemitic Islamist media, such as the Turkish newspaper Vakit[7] or the antisemitic Arab TV channel Al-Manar.[8] Students who were engaged in Islamist-fundamentalist organizations were the exception. However, Islamist organizations have disseminated antisemitic literature in bookshops, at an annual local Islamic book fair, and at the local market.[9] I suspected that antisemitism in Islamist discourses has influenced a few students indirectly because some of the local mosques are influenced by Islamist organizations. But I also was aware of the fact that many young Muslims do not regularly pray or attend mosques and that notions of Islam are very different between communities. At the time, I was living in Berlin-Kreuzberg, close to a Cem, an Alevi house of worship, and a Sunni mosque affiliated with Milli Görüş.

I also had assumed that many young Muslims identify with Palestinians and would thus tend to one-sided views on the Middle East conflict, resulting in possible demonization of Israelis and Jews. However, I already held some doubts about this thesis as the main explanatory factor for antisemitic attitudes due to my experiences with students of Turkish origin who explicitly rejected such identifications with Palestinians, partly because of feelings of animosity between people with Turkish and Arab backgrounds.

Since my early school years, I have been aware of racism and of the refusal to accept "foreigners" as an integral part of society in Germany. I assumed that this societal rejection of foreigners might lead to a stronger Muslim identification. As some believe that enmity against Jews is part of a Muslim identity ("Muslims don't like Jews") and as a strong Muslim identification facilitates Islamist interpretations of Islam, I assumed that exclusion was at least an indirect factor influencing antisemitic attitudes among those who feel rejected.

I was interested primarily in discovering what antisemitism looks like among those who have negative feelings toward Jews. My main interest was not to highlight Muslim antisemitism as a political problem, and thus the percentage of young Muslims who harbor antisemitic resentments was not my primary concern. I knew that there are some young Muslims with antisemitic feelings and others without them. I was convinced that even if this is only a problem that pertains to a small minority, it is worth spending a significant amount of time to understand how these dangerous ways of thinking work.

To summarize, the research project was designed to gain a better understanding of both antisemitic stereotypes and patterns and ways of thinking among students with Arab and Muslim backgrounds. The main question of the project asked what kinds of rhetoric and reasoning are used to justify negative views of Jews. I also expected to find some clues on sources of antisemitism.

Data Collection Method and Context

I chose a guided, semi-structured, face-to-face interview as my investigative method to produce data, including the respondents' individual views and patterns of argumentation.

Interviewees were approached outdoors[10] in Tower Hamlets and Finsbury Park in London, Belleville and Barbès in Paris, and Kreuzberg and Neukölln in Berlin. These districts, traditionally inhabited by many economically disadvantaged immigrants, have in the recent decades mainly been inhabited by individuals from countries with Muslim majorities. These inhabitants have built a diversity of immigrant communities of Muslim cultural and religious backgrounds, with corresponding immigrant organizations. All these neighborhoods are relatively close to the city centers. Some neighborhoods were partly influenced by Jewish immigration in the past, as was the case for Tower Hamlets, Belleville, and Kreuzberg. Today, there is a synagogue in Kreuzberg and Tower Hamlets, but Jewish life is most visible in Belleville. Some parts of these rather economically disadvantaged districts are increasingly popular with students and artists, who contribute to a more mixed sociocultural background.

While these districts are comparable in many ways, the ethnic backgrounds of Muslims living in them are quite different. The ethnic backgrounds of Muslims in each of the three countries consist of mostly Turkish in Germany, mostly Maghrebian in France, and mostly South Asian in Great Britain.

Largely for practical reasons, I had to restrict the participants to male interviewees. Young men are easier to contact spontaneously on the street, both because they are more numerous than women and more willing to grant an interview. Also, most perpetrators of antisemitic incidents are young men.[11] However, gender might influence rhetoric and attitudes toward Jews. The findings should not be transferred to Muslim women without further research.[12]

Interviewees were approached randomly on the streets in quiet areas. They were asked if they were willing to (anonymously) give their views on their neighborhoods, experiences of discrimination, and general political matters. They were told that the interviews were for an academic study of young people's views in Germany, France, and Britain. The interviews started off with views on the interviewees' life in the neighborhood, their occupation and interests, and their experiences of discrimination and possible conflicts in the neighborhood between ethnic or religious communities. The interviewees were given freedom to express their views and experiences and to talk about whatever issues they wanted. The interviewer merely directed the conversation and tried to ensure that participants give some biographical data and comment on perceived discrimination, the Iraq war, the terror attacks of September 11, 2001, and the Middle East conflict. At the end of the interview participants were asked, if they had not already talked about these matters earlier,[13] if they could befriend or marry a Jew, what they thought of the belief that Jews are rich, and what they thought of equating the sufferings of Jews at the hands of the Nazis with the sufferings of the Palestinians via the Israelis. The interviewers tried to ask questions as outsiders, not judging the interviewee, but also not necessarily hiding their own point of view.[14] The interviews were conducted in the language of the country.[15]

The interviews were only held if the person fell into the following subject group: 14–27 years old, male, and self-identifying as Muslim.[16] Most of interviews were conducted with one person at a time, though friends standing by were allowed to participate, which led at times to interviews with two or more respondents. Altogether, 117 young male youths in Paris (40), London (40), and Berlin (37) who consider themselves Muslim were interviewed from 2005 to 2007. This number includes only those who answered most or all of the questions. Group interviews consisted of two to four respondents, most in pairs of two interviewees, which enabled discussions with individual interviewees. The group interviews are particularly interesting for an analysis of some of the group dynamics among young people. The average length of an interview was about forty minutes.

The interviews were recorded and transcribed according to transcription guidelines designed for qualitative interviews by Heiner Legewie and Elke Partzold-Teske.[17] The investigators' observations were also recorded.

Reflection on the Interviewers and the Investigator

I conducted most of the final interviews myself, but pre-tests of data collection involved one female and one male interviewer of Turkish Muslim background, and one female and one male interviewer of German Christian background, all of whom were 20–35 years old. Ten interviews with different combinations of interviewers were analyzed in terms of the influence of the interviewer's background on the interview. There was no significant difference in the openness of the interviewees regarding the main topics, and all interviewers established a good level of rapport with the interviewees. However, some of the interviewees made sexual allusions toward the female interviewer of German Christian background.

The interviewers' non-Muslim background helped them, as outsiders, to probe for more detail. However, it has been argued that interviewees hold back socially unacceptable views such as antisemitic attitudes when with outsiders.[18] Although this has not been observed in the pre-tests, some interviewees might harbor stronger antisemitic views than the views they actually expressed during the interviews.

After the pre-tests, I, as an interviewer of German Christian family background (I converted to Islam for marriage-related reasons in 2003), conducted most of the interviews in Berlin and all of them in London and Paris. In London and Paris my position as an outsider was even stronger, as I was seen as a foreigner, which helped to disperse the initial suspicions of a few interviewees about my possible collaboration with the police. However, in analyzing the interviews, I kept in mind that the responses of the interviewees are a reaction to the interviewer and also a kind of self-presentation. As the interviewers did not hide their disagreement with anti-Jewish attitudes, one might think that the interviewees could be partly influenced by what they thought the interviewer wanted to hear. However, interviewees did not show reluctance in voicing biased views and these views were not presented in a provocative way. The atmosphere during the interviews was generally calm and friendly.

The research process was accompanied by self-observation through weekly reports in a research diary and reflections on the analytical process with experts in the field. In some cases, I was profoundly shocked after some respondents voiced hatred and the intention to harm Jews while I was having a friendly and open conversation with them. The interviews were then coded and analyzed with an emotional distance a few months later.

Analytical Strategy

Interviews were analyzed from the beginning of the project, and additional data was collected until various antisemitic arguments and perceptions of discrimination were only repeated in new interviews and no additional stereotypes or views were expressed in new interviews. The sample was thus "saturated" across the three cities.[19] The goal was to find a topology of argumentative patterns as opposed to a topology of individuals, which is particularly relevant for the question why young Muslims say they dislike Jews.[20]

The initially targeted size of the sample was extended from 60 interviewees to 117 to achieve, in a constant comparative analysis, a saturation of patterns of argumentation and an equal distribution in the number of interviews among the three cities. It turned out that the majority of interviewees in Germany were of Turkish origin; most interviewees in France had a Maghreb background, and in the UK most originated in South Asia. Thus, the ethnic backgrounds largely represented those of Muslims in each country. This country-specific ethnic representation, and particularly the fact that the arguments were repeated in all three cities despite the different contexts and interviewees' ethnic, educational, and cultural backgrounds, are strong indications that these arguments can also be found among other young (male) European Muslims.

The analytical strategy is based on a five-stage method of qualitative content analysis:[21] open initial coding of eighteen interviews; development of a coding guide; coding all interviews; production of case overviews of all interviewees; and in-depth, single-case analysis.

In the first stage, codes for the analysis were set up in response to the material from six interviews per country in open coding (inductive coding) and were partly pre-set for basic data, such as biographical information. Open coding is understood as generating theme lines from text fragments. In a procedure of inductive category formation,[22] similar theme lines were put together as codes, which were then grouped in categories. Despite the openness in the coding process, the aim was to analyze the interviewees' views about Jews and perceptions of discrimination against themselves. Thus, the analytical approach was goal-oriented toward a description of particular phenomena (what and how) and an analysis of possible factors that influence anti-Jewish attitudes (why).

In a second step, these codes and categories were defined and brought together in a coding guide, which included a definition for each code that was tested and revised. These first two steps were enacted for each of the three countries separately. It turned out that the three coding guides could be synthesized into one coding guide with only minor adaptations.

Third, using the coding guide, all interviews were coded and the framework of codes and categories was further adapted in an iterative process, that is, new codes were applied to all previously coded interviews. The categories were further differentiated, progressively given empirical content, and modified accordingly. Relations between the codes and the categories were examined and described in memos. The data was coded using the software Atlas.ti.[23] By the end of the coding process, the codes and categories and their relation to each other reflected the data. The coding guide in fact evolved into an analytical framework. The description of categories and their properties are the main results of this study.

Four patterns of argumentation for negative views of Jews emerged: (1) "classic" antisemitic stereotypes and conspiracy theories; (2) negative views of Jews with regard to Israel; (3) negative views of Jews related to religious or ethnic identity; and (4) negative views of Jews without any form of justification or rationalization. Two main categories emerged on the issue of discrimination and exclusion: perceived discrimination and identification (or non-identification) with the nationality of the country of residence.

Fourth, case overviews of all interviewees were produced and compared. A short summary of biographical data (age, ethnic background, country of birth, education/occupation, nationality), and relevant views (on Jews, discrimination, and Islam) was produced for each interviewee. Special attention was given to comparisons within groups of interviews from each country and to comparisons among the three countries. The focus of the comparisons was on the categories referring to discrimination and views of Jews. The case overviews helped to contextualize quotes from individual respondents within the respective interviews, and were used to select individual cases for in-depth, single-case analysis in the fifth stage, selecting those who reject antisemitic arguments.

I use Helen Fein's definition of antisemitism from 1987 and the Working Definition of Antisemitism[24] as a guideline to determine whether to label particular remarks as antisemitic. Fein defined antisemitism "as a persisting latent structure of hostile beliefs toward *Jews as a collectivity* manifested in *individuals* as attitudes, and in *culture* as myth, ideology, folklore and imagery, and in *actions* – social or legal discrimination, political mobilisation against Jews, and collective or state violence – which results in and/or is designed to distance, displace, or destroy Jews as Jews."[25]

The Working Definition of Antisemitism was formulated in 2005 by the European Monitoring Centre on Racism and Xenophobia (EUMC), now the European Union Agency for Fundamental Rights, with the assistance of a number of organizations. It fits Fein's definition in its general definition: "Antisemitism is a certain perception of Jews, which may be expressed as hatred toward Jews. Rhetorical and physical manifestations of antisemitism are directed toward Jewish or non-Jewish individuals and/or their property, toward Jewish community institutions and religious facilities." Additionally, the Working Definition of Antisemitism provides a number of examples, including distinctions between criticism of Israel and antisemitism with reference to Israel. The full Working Definition is included in Appendix A.[26]

However, the Working Definition emphasizes that one must take into account the overall context of particular statements. I leave it to the reader as much as possible to decide if particular views are antisemitic or rather only particular opinions on Jews and other issues. I focus on the analysis and presentation of patterns of argumentations for negative views of Jews.

I present as many excerpts from the original data as possible, rather than attempting to reconstruct the general sense of what participants said, in order to further enhance reliability.[27] I have marked all changes to the original text, such as deletions, additions, and supplementary comments, by enclosing them in square brackets, except for deletions of hesitation or filler words (such as "uh," "um," or the equivalent), and immediate repetition of the same word or words ("I went went" was changed to "I went"). Obviously, the selection of quotes also implies subjective and analytical decisions. Therefore, I also present and discuss quotes and findings that contradict one another. Methodologically, these discussions and also the in-depth case studies of interviewees who reject antisemitic arguments (presented in chapter 11) comprise negative case analysis and further add to the reliability of the findings.

WHO ARE THE INTERVIEWEES?

The analysis is based on interviews with 117 young male youths in Paris (40), London (40), and Berlin (37) who stated that they are Muslims. On average, the interviewees were 19 years old at the time of the interview: 17 in Berlin, 18 in Paris, and 20 in London. The table of interviewees in Appendix B provides an overview of all 117 individuals, including information on their level of education, age, and ethnic background.

Education

The level of education among interviewees varied widely. Many respondents were enrolled in or intended to apply to vocational/technical colleges,[28] while others were qualifying for further studies in university. In all three cities (between ten and fourteen interviewees total) there were some who had no formal qualification and had dropped out of the educational system altogether. Nine participants were studying in university or had graduated already. In comparison to the general population, the interviewees had a lower level of education than average.[29]

The German, French, and English educational systems are very different. In order to compare the educational level of the interviewees of different ages in different countries, I created five categories of educational levels.[30] Category 1 refers to the lowest level of education, meaning interviewees had dropped out of normal education and had no formal job qualification. Category 2 indicates a basic form of job qualification, one already achieved or to be attained in the future because the interviewees were attending vocational schools. In Germany, this means an educational orientation with the goal of the qualification "Lehre." In France, the equivalent is a "Certificat d'aptitude professionnelle" (CAP), the "Brevet d'études professionnelles" (BEP), or similar qualifications. For England, I used the vocational/technical colleges as an equivalent. Category 3 stands for people who intend to pass the "Abitur," "baccalaureat,"[31] or "A-levels." Category 4 represents those who had passed the qualification "Abitur," "baccalaureat," or "A-levels" for further studies at the university level. Category 5 stands for university students and graduates. In some cases, interviewees provided unclear data on their educational background. In category 1, there were ten to fourteen interviewees. Most fell into categories 2 and 3. Five to six were in category 4, and nine participants were in the last category. Overall, the mean for participants' category level was 2.5, slightly lower in Berlin (2.3) and Paris (2.3) and somewhat higher in London (2.8). The majority of interviewees in all three cities have or were going to receive a vocational or technical form of qualification. Some have aspirations for higher education, and a few have achieved it.

Economic Situation

The interviewees' economic background is predominantly working class. Almost all interviewees grew up in the district in which they were interviewed, which are classified as disadvantaged areas. At the time of the interview, most lived with their parents, sometimes in cramped premises or public housing. A few others lived only with their mothers because their parents are divorced or separated.[32] Some older interviewees lived on their own or with a partner.

Some interviewees decried their economic situation, but most stated that they have enough money to get by. This might be partly due to the fact that many are supported by their parents. Likewise, most interviewees in Berlin and London do not have a grim picture of the future and of future job prospects for themselves, even if some, objectively, have slim chances of earning a living above the minimum wage due to poor qualifications.

One explanation for some of the relatively optimistic attitudes is that interviewees are confident they will find a job through family connections. In France, attitudes toward the future are more negative; in particular, some interviewees with lower levels of qualification in categories 1–3 showed frustration about their job prospects. Indeed, the particularly high unemployment rates in France and Germany among young people with lower qualifications make it more difficult for these youths than for their peers in Britain to find a job.[33] Interviewees from Paris in particular stated that their ethnic background presents an obstacle to finding work. By contrast, in London, many expressed the opinion that if they work hard and make the right decisions, they will able to get a good job.

Everyday Life

Most interviewees spent most of their time in college, a few in university, while some had a job, full-time or part-time. Others were out of work, waiting for training programs, or applying for jobs. Many said they played sports, such as soccer, and spent time with friends in public places in their neighborhood, in youth clubs, and at home, or chatting with friends on the internet or over the phone. Some interviewees help out their parents in small family businesses or work part-time jobs. Many are familiar with marijuana or other "soft drugs," petty crime, and violence, which they have witnessed in their area. A few have even been perpetrators and/or victims. Particularly in Paris, but also in London, many interviewees are frequently stopped and controlled by the police on the street. Many interviewees rarely leave their districts, though some are more mobile within the city and a few have traveled abroad without their parents, often with a soccer club or school. However, most interviewees go on vacation in the country of their parents' origin, though usually not every year.

Sources of Information

A primary source of knowledge and information that was cited for interviewees is school, which was also generally regarded as the most reliable. Other sources include media such as TV, the internet, and newspapers, family and friends, and, for some interviewees, mosques, particularly on religious matters. Only one interviewee, Tayfun,[34] said that he is a member of an Islamic organization, the youth group of his local mosque that is affiliated to Milli Görüş.

Most interviewees watch predominantly German, French, or British TV, respectively. However, many are also influenced by foreign channels through their parents' watching habits. Arab news stations, such as Al-Jazeera, are popular among some participants, even though they often do not understand the Standard Arabic that is spoken on these channels. Some interviewees in London occasionally watch the English edition of Al-Jazeera. Most interviewees usually do not buy newspapers but do read their parents' papers or free ones, such as those in Paris or London.

The internet is primarily used for chatting and social networking but also for searching for work or internships, games, music, pornography, sports results, politics, and religion. Some interviewees reported having internet access at home or in school, while some patronize cyber cafés and others hardly use the internet at all.

Experiences of Discrimination

The majority of interviewees reported experiences of discrimination or of being subjected to negative stereotypes and prejudices against their ethnic or religious community.[35] However, there are a number of country-specific and ethno-specific differences. Additionally, the perceptions of exclusion, which are reflected in self-identifications as German, French, or British, are fundamentally different in the three countries.

Interviewees reported hostile looks, threats, and even physical attacks, the latter particularly in Germany. Others reported that native-born people are often afraid of groups of Arabs or blacks and therefore do not openly show prejudices, but they inwardly stereotype Arabs as thieves and blacks as aggressive. Many interviewees from France sense discrimination in the job market due to their skin color and Arab-sounding names. Discrimination based on one's social background and district of residence is also particularly felt in Paris.

Interviewees in all three cities feel they are discriminated against on "racial" or, to a lesser extent, religious grounds. The latter is more common in Great Britain than in France and Germany.

Interviewees also reported discrimination based on prejudice against their social background, their neighborhood,[36] or status of residence. Many interviewees, particularly in Britain, feel that there is prejudice against Islam and Muslims. A few feel indirectly affected when

Muslims in other countries are attacked. A prominent opinion is that there has been a rise in discrimination against Muslims since the terrorist attacks of September 11, 2001, in the United States and July 7, 2005, in London.

However, some participants said that they do not feel discriminated against at all, particularly in everyday life in their neighborhood. "*Everything is perfect here. There's nothing here, no racism, nothing*" (Orhan, Berlin), stated one, while another insisted, referring to Tower Hamlets, "*There's no racism, man [. . .]. It's just the police*" (Gourab, London). Respondents from France exhibited similar views but often immediately added that there is discrimination outside the own district: "*It doesn't feel like there's discrimination here. It's really cosmopolitan here. There isn't any here, but as soon as you go away from here . . .*" (Haroun, Paris).

This perception can stem from many factors. It might be that the negative effects of stereotypes and prejudices about their community are indeed very low in everyday life in the neighborhood. After all, interviewees frequently said that there is no discrimination in the neighborhood because most residents are from their own community. Even so, interviewees may not have revealed all their experiences and feelings of discrimination or they might not have been aware of the forms of biases they faced. In addition, some interviewees were reluctant to portray themselves as victims. This may have led to a suppression of feelings of discrimination. Some preferred to ignore or downplay discrimination against them. Racist expressions, such as "sale Arabe" (dirty Arab), were seen by some participants as having been made in jest.

A few interviewees have experienced physical attacks or threats that were motivated by prejudices, most of them in Germany. In Britain, some violent conflicts with members of other ethnic minorities, such as black people or Hindus, were also perceived as racist.

Verbal abuse and insults are common forms of discrimination reported by interviewees. Insults often relate to ethnic background, or rather to what the insulters think their target's ethnic background is. In Germany, common insults reported by participants are "scheiß Türken" (shitty Turks) and "scheiß Ausländer" (shitty foreigner), while "sale Arabe" (dirty Arab) and "sale noir" (dirty black) are common in France. In Britain, the most common insult for people of South Asian background is "Paki," derived from the word Pakistani, regardless of the targeted individual's actual ethnic background. "Fucking terrorist" and "Muslim terrorists" are also insults reported by a number of interviewees, again, mostly from London. These insults reflect the different ethnic backgrounds of the largest ethnic minorities of Muslims in each country and indicate the particularities of the three countries, such as the "othering" of "Ausländer" (those who are perceived as foreigners) in Germany and the suspicion of Muslims' involvement in terrorism in Britain, particularly after the bombings in London in July 2005. However, only a minority reported that they had been victim to such insults and other generalized accusations related to their Muslim identity; instead they reported hearing of such incidents. For example, one British respondent said, "*No one has said anything to me yet. But I'm hearing stuff [. . .] from friends, from other people, they say, people come and they say: 'You did this, you done that, you bombed*'" (Baru, London). The knowledge that other members of one's own community have been victimized adds to their feeling of discrimination, particularly if they live in similar circumstances, and shows them that they could also be targeted. Others pointed out that they had been insulted themselves, some on a regular basis: "*They say, 'dirty Arab' for example [. . .]. This is really every day that you hear it*" (Massoud, Paris).

The most serious attack was described by Kassim, of Lebanese background, in Berlin, and was vividly recounted even though it happened twelve years prior to the interview. Kassim lived in Berlin-Lichtenrade, a West Berlin district, until the age of six. Multiple Arab families including his own were attacked in their homes by neo-Nazis, who painted swastikas on their houses and shouted slurs saluting Hitler. An arson attack had to be extinguished by firefighters. According to Kassim, the attackers were chased away by armed relatives and were eventually arrested by the police. Many of the other reported attacks and threats occurred on public transportation. Murat, of Turkish background, recalled an attack on a train to Erkner, a town in Brandenburg that is close to Berlin, in which he and his friend were assaulted. Umur described a situation in which he had feared being seriously attacked by a group of skinheads in Berlin-Rudow, also on public transportation. In both cases the victims did not count on help by train staff or other passengers.

For some interviewees from Germany, racist violence and the feeling that they were under threat were reason enough to avoid certain areas.

In France, too, some interviewees tried to avoid certain areas. Two black interviewees, Kassi and Diaba from Paris, were on their way to work at a soccer stadium situated between the districts of Boulogne and Auteuil in the outskirts of Paris when they were spit at and pelted with cans and bottles. They identified the perpetrators as white racists. Among their friends, the area is known to be dangerous for black people, but they had to pass it, they said, to go to work. Another interviewee from Paris, Aswad, of Egyptian and Algerian heritage, had a similar threatening experience at the same place: he was also on his way to the stadium where "skinheads" and "crânes rasés" wanted to beat him up in an area he described as rich and where no Arab or black people live. The perpetrators shouted slogans hailing the ultra-nationalist politician Jean-Marie Le Pen, he said.

Kashi from London was assaulted as a Muslim. He was threatened on public transportation, like Murat and Umur from Germany. But in contrast to the interviewees from Germany he felt that he could rely on the authorities and CCTV (surveillance cameras) to give him some protection from violent assault.

Cross-national comparisons of the perception of otherness prove interesting. Generally, interviewees in Germany feel that there is discrimination against "foreigners" (who might have German nationality) based on skin and hair color, and they described themselves mostly as foreigners. In France, the impression is that discrimination focuses foremost on "Arabs" and "blacks," based on skin color, Arab names, and places of residence. In Britain, many respondents think that discrimination is based on skin color, too, but others believe that anti-Muslim prejudices prevail.

Nationality, Ethnic Background, and National Self-identification

All interviewees have experienced immigration directly or indirectly, that is, either they themselves or one or both of their parents were born outside the country. Most interviewees, however, were born in Germany, France, or Great Britain. Nevertheless, at least twenty-four interviewees do not hold German, French, or British nationality (fifteen in Berlin, six in Paris, and three in London), reflecting to some extent the different national immigration policies and immigration history.

The interviewees in each city roughly represent the predominant ethnic minority groups in the respective country.

In Germany, the majority of interviewees are of Turkish origin and identify as Turkish, although some interviewees of Turkish Kurdish background see themselves as predominantly Kurdish. Arab interviewees in Germany are predominantly of Lebanese or Palestinian origin. They stressed their Arab and Lebanese or Palestinian identity, although many possess German nationality. Interviewees explained that their reluctance to identify as German was due to a lack of acceptance as Germans and their attachment to the culture and values of their parents' ethnic background.

In France, almost all interviewees or their parents come from a former French colony, primarily Algeria, Morocco, or Tunisia. Others stem from Guinea, Ivory Coast, and Turkey. Some are products of mixed marriages, notably Algerian Moroccan. At least one interviewee of Moroccan background feels strongly about his Berber and Maghrebian background and distances himself from an Arab identity. However, most interviewees of North African background emphasize their Arab background. Generally, interviewees in Paris who were born in France consider themselves to be both French and members of their parents' country of origin. However, they are conscious of not being regarded as "real" French citizens within French society, especially by the police.

Interviewees from London are predominantly of South Asian background, originating mostly from Bangladesh and Pakistan. Others have Egyptian, Moroccan, Algerian, Somali, or "Black African" backgrounds. In London, only one interviewee reported having parents from two different nationalities, that being Bengali British. The question of self-identification as British shows some similarities in the French interviewees' answers. Most who were born in Britain were not reluctant to say that they are British, but often tacked on an attribute like British Asian or, in some cases, British Muslim.[37] Some highlighted their identity as "Londoners." Some feel that they are not regarded as British by the police and often referred to "their community" as Asian, Bengali, and so forth.

"Back home" is an expression many used to refer to the country their parents or grandparents had emigrated from.

Muslim Identity

Most interviewees identify strongly as Muslim, with the exception of a number of Alevis of Turkish or Kurdish background from Germany and Berbers from France. These people give less importance to their religious identity but they, too, consider themselves Muslim. The interviewees demonstrate major differences in their level of devotion and religious practice, their knowledge about the Qur'an, and their attendance of mosques and Islamic schools (*madrasas*) when they were younger. Some rarely visit mosques or do not fast during Ramadan, while most participants visit mosques on important occasions like Eid Al-Fitr and Eid Al-Adha, and most try to do at least some fasting during Ramadan. Others show greater religious practice and visit mosques more regularly. The interviewees' cultural background and social circle seem to be two major factors contributing to their religious practices, which are also influenced by Muslim organizations and mosques. Many interviewees stated that what is said in mosques is very important to them. Their Muslim identity often implies a feeling of solidarity with Muslim communities from other countries to some extent. Many wish to become more religious, as defined by a stricter following of religious rules. The motivation for becoming more devoted and more attached to a Muslim identity varies widely. Most participants quoted their parents and social circle as responsible for giving them a basic knowledge of Islam; many added *madrasas,* which they had attended regularly around the ages of 10–14, as a source of knowledge about their religion. This basic knowledge usually implies the wish to follow religious rules, such as praying five times a day, going to the mosque at least every Friday, fasting, and going on a pilgrimage to Mecca. The corresponding valorization of religious observance among their social circles is a constant incentive to become more religious. Devoted Muslims are generally well respected. The young Muslims often discuss Islam with their friends and also use the internet and Islamic websites to learn more about Islam and keep up with religious trends.

Of course, individual participants have different concepts of religion. Many have a literal understanding of the Qur'an and of Muhammad as a role model for today, and attempt to take both as direct guideposts for everyday life. This aspiration goes together with an emphasis on demands and punishment in religion. But others put particular statements of the Qur'an and Islamic scholars in perspective and have a less authoritarian understanding of religion. Some participants show a more mystical and somewhat superstitious understanding of Islam.

FOUR

Patterns of Antisemitism among Interviewees and Beyond

EVEN THOUGH IT IS NOT THE GOAL OF THIS BOOK TO EXAMINE the scale of antisemitic attitudes, the pervasiveness of various forms of antisemitism that were voiced during the interviews was striking and upsetting. However, it should be stressed that antisemitic attitudes were not expressed by all participants: some respondents showed no signs of antisemitic attitudes at all and none were part of an antisemitic group or intended to start one or join one.

The goal here is to examine qualitative aspects of antisemitic thought and verbal expressions. What kind of images do young European Muslims have about Jews and how are negative views justified?

The study shows that most antisemitic argumentations are fragmented and multifaceted among a large sample of ordinary young Muslim men across Germany, France, and Britain. Antisemitic argumentations among Europeans Muslims can be reduced to neither hatred against Israel nor to an expression of Islamism, Islam, or Muslim identity.

Even so, the majority of interviewees displayed some antisemitic views in at least one of the categories described below. Some forms and sources of antisemitic expressions are similar to those of youths of other backgrounds in the three countries.[1] Jews are commonly thought of as a unitary category[2] and generally as a malevolent group of people, even if they are partly admired.

A small minority of interviewees, especially in Germany and France, directly and physically threatened Jews in the past and still pose a threat for Jews if they have not changed their attitudes. In Britain, a few interviewees described threatening behavior of peers they know. The interviewees who pose a physical threat to Jews do not seem to be isolated among their peers. Their aggressive forms of antisemitism are usually not shared but are nonetheless tolerated within their social circles.

Antisemitic attitudes and their forms of expression, and ways to justify anti-Jewish sentiments, vary considerably. Among young European Muslims they can be classified in four patterns that were surprisingly similar in all three countries: "classic" antisemitic attitudes, which include stereotypes of Jews and conspiracy theories; anti-Jewish attitudes with reference to Israel; anti-Jewish attitudes with reference to Islam, Muslimhood, or ethnic identity; and anti-Jewish attitudes without rationalization. These four patterns can be voiced independently of each other, but also are interconnected in two ways. Some topoi overlap; for instance, the topos "Jews kill children" comes from the "classic" antisemitic trope that Jews allegedly kill Christian children for ritual purposes. The same charge is linked to anti-Jewish attitudes with reference to Israel in descriptions of the Middle East conflict. Second, individuals usually use more than one pattern to express antisemitic resentments and combine different arguments.

In the next chapter, I describe and illustrate the four patterns by placing the voices of the interviewed people at the center of the analysis. Not all statements are clearly antisemitic by the standards of Helen Fein's definition and the "Working Definition of Antisemitism" that I use here.[3]

It is generally difficult to draw conclusions about resentments on the basis of relatively short statements. When is somebody to be considered an antisemite? Is it when that person adopts antisemitic stereotypes occasionally, or only if he or she is obsessed by hatred of Jews and has an antisemitic worldview? Antisemitic action, on the other hand, can also be taken by those who do not have a coherent antisemitic worldviews. Answers to these issues are left to the reader to decide, based on the descriptions and numerous examples that follow. The focus here is on a presentation of arguments, however fragmented, of participants' explanations as to why they dislike Jews.

In any case, a precondition of these patterns of antisemitism is the notion of Jews as a unitary category. Individual Jews or different groups of Jews were rarely differentiated. Many interviewees emphasized this perceived "oneness" of Jews by using the definite article "the Jews," with its notion of "*how the Jews essentially are*" (Adnan, Berlin). This perception can include the belief in a common interest and joint identity among "the Jews" of the past, present, and future.

GENERALIZABILITY

The question in qualitative studies is not representativeness but generalizability: in which other contexts and to what other groups do the findings apply? This study shows how young Muslim men, randomly approached in areas with a high percentage of Muslims in Berlin, Paris, and London, explain their views to a stranger in face-to-face interviews. Gender might influence rhetoric and attitudes toward Jews.[4] The findings should not be transferred to Muslim women without further research.

The three cities in three different countries, and also the different ethnic backgrounds, represent significant changes in context; the sample was large enough that patterns of argumentation were only repeated in additional interviews; and the respondents' views of Jews in the three countries were very similar.

This indicates generalizability beyond the sample. The fact that the interviewees' ethnic backgrounds are largely representative of Muslim ethnic backgrounds in each country further enhances the generalizability of the qualitative results for young male Muslims in Germany, France, and Britain.

It is thus reasonable to conclude that the four main patterns of antisemitic argumentation can be found among other young male Muslims in these countries, and possibly in other European ones.

Additionally, some findings on possible sources of antisemitic attitudes presented in chapter 10 can be generalized. The observation that discrimination is not a relevant factor for antisemitic attitudes among interviewees proves that, generally, discrimination is at least not a necessary factor for antisemitic attitudes among European Muslims. Nevertheless, perceptions of discrimination that include conspiracy theories such as the widespread belief in a "war on Islam" can be associated with animosity against Jews and the belief that they are enemies of Islam.

The fact that some perceptions of Muslim and ethnic identity include anti-Jewish attitudes, described in detail in chapter 7, is also valid beyond the sample, as is the observation that most participants use several different rationales that are not necessarily related: antisemitic views often do not constitute one coherent whole. This explorative study demonstrates multifaceted and diverse antisemitic argumentations and influences. Single-sourced explanations, such as blaming discrimination, the Israeli-Palestinian conflict, or Islam in general for young European Muslims' hostile views of Jews, are proven to be false.

Three main findings can be generalized regardless of ethnic or religious backgrounds. First, the study demonstrates that individuals can choose to position themselves against antisemitism despite antisemitic influences from friends, family, and the media. Individuals have a choice (within social restrictions) to adopt or to reject antisemitic attitudes and thus bear responsibility. Second, patterns of antisemitic argumentation are often fragmented and those who use them are usually not bothered by the contradictions in their argumentations. Third, such individuals can pose a direct threat against Jews even if their antisemitic views are not coherent.

FIVE

"Classic" Modern Antisemitism

RESPONDENTS EMPLOYED TROPES OF MODERN ANTISEMITISM that can be described as "classic": namely, conspiracy theories that fantasize immense "Jewish influence" and "Jewish power" in politics, business, and the media. Participants also stereotyped Jews as rich, clever, stingy, treacherous, and clannish, or, more rarely, ascribed physical attributes to Jews such as a big or hooked noses. The most common tropes involve allegations of conspiracies and the linking of "the Jews" to money and business and stinginess.

CONSPIRACY THEORIES

Conspiracy theories were often expressed in fragmented ways, and many respondents were doubtful about various details. "Rumor" is an apt description of this phenomenon.[1] Not all conspiracy theories accuse Jews alone of conspiring – even if most do. "The Americans" or the American president or government, and occasionally, politicians of other countries, such as former British prime minister Tony Blair, have also been accused of being engaged in conspiracies. Some respondents mentioned allegedly influential Freemasons, who are often thought of as conspiring in alliance with Jews. Therefore, conspiracy theories about Freemasons may be regarded as coded forms of antisemitic conspiracy theories.

Common themes for antisemitic conspiracy theories are "Jewish power" in the world, "Jewish influence" in the United States, the terrorist attacks of September 11, 2001, the Holocaust, the media, suicide attacks, the Middle East conflict, the alleged war against Muslims, and, occasionally, topics such as AIDS and tsunamis. Jews are accused of being either the masterminds of such events or of using them for "their interests."

All antisemitic conspiracy theories include the notion of a common "Jewish interest" behind the alleged conspiracies. Another study, based on interviews with twenty-five young Muslim men and women in Berlin in 2009, found strong beliefs in conspiracy theories about September 11, the Iraq war, and the media, particularly in relation to the coverage of the Middle East conflict.[2]

There are many reasons why people want to believe in conspiracy theories. A central rationale among interviewees seems to be the wish to explain and personalize complicated processes. "*For everything that must happen, there is a reason,*" declared one after stating, "*It's obvious now, that there is someone, and not just someone, but a group of people [. . .] like a ruling class we hardly see*" (Neoy, London). This is a textbook illustration of the tendency to seek out simplistic worldly explanations.[3] The same interviewee holds conspiracy theory beliefs about the terrorist attacks of September 11, the Holocaust, Israel's power, and his assumption that "*all these other big channels they are owned by Jews and they control the majority of the media.*"

Jews Rule the World

Conspiracy theories about Jews ruling the world can focus on the present, the past, or the aims of Jews for the future, exemplified in the following three statements, respectively: "*At the moment, who are the leaders of the world? [. . .] The matador from America, he's a Jew*" (Abhijt, London); "*They had ruled certain parts of the world*" (Malik, London), and, "*They want to dominate the world*" (Aswad's friend, Paris), all referring to "the Jews'" or "the Jewish people's" domination of the world. This belief can also be expressed indirectly, for example, by stressing the influence of the Israeli secret services on world politics. Many interviewees backed up their allegations with examples of alleged "Jewish control" of the business sector. The stereotype of rich Jews is often directly associated with power: "*They own a lot of businesses and [. . .] they do have a lot of power 'cause finance obviously brings you power*" (Bahaar,

London). The tropes of "Jews rule the world," "rich Jews," and "Jewish control of businesses" are often intermingled. One British interviewee combined these three tropes:

> *Well, obviously if you can see that Jewish are the rich ones around nowadays. They are the one [sic] who control everything [. . .] even Britain because if you see Sainsbury's, Tesco, Iceland,*[4] *it all belongs to them. They are the rich ones. They're the ones who're controlling the country and the world right now.* (Nirmal, London)

Nirmal does not distinguish between economic and political power. Wealth is equated with power and influence. He cited major supermarket chains that have shops in his area as evidence of the prevalence of rich Jews by saying that the shops are owned by "the Jews." Real or imagined rich Jews and Jewish business leaders are seen as evidence of "Jewish control." Consider the three examples below, one for each city.

> *They're the richest. Almost everything belongs to them, the Jews [. . .]. Everyone can see that, the Jews are always at the top of everything [. . .] for example, like, the companies, everything belongs to them, everything, everywhere where money is made, there's a Jew behind it.* (Suleiman, Berlin)

> *It's them who have all the banks there, the millionaires, it was the Jews.* (Bilal, Paris)

> *You see these companies man, all these companies like the majority in big companies in West End and so they're owned by Jews, innit? [. . .] Anything like supermarkets and stuff [. . .]. It's a Jew man running it at the end of the day. He's got all . . .* (Rajsekar, London)

In all three statements Jews are not only stereotyped as rich; the statements also imply that Jews control the economy. "Evidence" was readily added by naming companies which are allegedly owned by Jews, "*like McDonald's, there's so many around the world, but when you actually go to the main group, yeah, that owns it, the whole thing, it's Jews*" (Bashkar, London), or, more locally, "*Barbès Boulevard, half of the mobile stores are run by Jews*" (Sabri, Paris). The belief in "Jewish influence," even if it is not accompanied by the direct allegation of Jews ruling the world, is a conspiracy theory in itself: this belief implies that all Jews have a common agenda which is often undefined but is understood as sinister.

In contrast to the examples above, some interviewees' stereotypes of Jews as being rich are not necessarily associated with power. One respondent asserted, "*No, they don't have power. The only thing they have is money . . . Power, I say the ones who've got power is Muslim people. Who, us lot we've got the power, but they've got all the money"* (Baru, London). Baru sees his own community as more powerful.

The belief of "Jewish power in the world" is not always negative but can imply some form of admiration. "*The Jews have more power because they're the ones who make everything, they're the ones who invent everything, they're the ones who are the most rich, and who are the most intelligent [. . .]. God gave them the power. They have the money"* (Kaba, Paris), proclaimed one man of Guinean origin. He even explained that powerful, rich, and clever Jews existed because of a divine gift. Power through clannishness can also be praised:

> *I like the way they work [. . .]. That bonding around themselves, if someone is [. . .] on the other side of the world, and there's a group on this side of the world, they would help each other. So, that's how the power rises, isn't it? I mean that's why maybe most people think that the majority, I mean, the power belongs to Jews, at the moment, at this stage.* (Abhijt, London)

Evidence of "Jewish power" is not restricted to allegedly Jewish international companies or world politics, but is sometimes seen locally: particularly in France, interviewees pointed to local Jewish businesses such as mobile phone shops in their neighborhood, or took a Jewish school as evidence of Jewish power and influence.

Jews Control the Media

The antisemitic trope of Jews controlling the media is voiced in different ways in the three countries. Respondents in Germany mainly said, rather allusively, that Jews manipulate the media to conceal Israel's atrocities. Adnan, of Palestinian background, was told by the interviewer that in some European countries the TV channel Al Manar might be prohibited. He commented:

> *They must have something to do with it, somehow, a little [. . .], the ones who want to ban it, so that they don't see what Jews are really like. So they only want to show the things that the Palestinians do, but what the Jews do, they barely ever show that actually [. . .]. What you see on the German TV shows and on the Arab ones you see a lot more about the Palestinian things that happen [. . .]. On German ones [. . .] we don't see what happened to the children and things like that.* (Adnan, Berlin)

Adnan suggested that "they" conspire to conceal atrocities committed by Jews against Palestinians, covering up "how the Jews really are." He did not explicitly say that "they" are Jews, but clearly that "they" act in the interests of "the Jews." Some perceive coverage of the Middle East conflict in the German media as generally false and biased because, they feel, it does not show pictures of atrocities against Palestinian victims shown on Turkish or Arab TV channels or on the internet. However, only a few interviewees directly said that Jews control TV.

In France, respondents often said that Jews dominate French TV, highlighting Jewish actors, TV presenters, and stand-up comedians, such as Julien Courbet, Arthur (Jacques Essebag), Alain Chabat, and Gad Elmaleh.

> *On TV, they're all over the TV; everything you see there, like Julien Courbet and all; like TV hosts, they make up 90 percent of everyone on TV, the Jews [. . .]. From TF1 to M6, I don't know about the other stations.* (Azhar, Paris)

However, the Jewish actors and presenters are fairly popular: "*Honestly, the only good films are the films made by the Jews and the Arabs,*" said one respondent (Jabar's friend, Paris), even though he stated elsewhere that he does not like Jews. Still, some see Jews' prominence in TV and movies as a sign of Jewish influence and power in the world: "*Yeah, it's true, in the United States, there are a lot of Jews in power [. . .]. Same thing in France. Arthur is a Jew, and there are a lot at TF1*" (Sabri, Paris). One interviewee focused on Jewish control of France, taking TV as only an example: "*Anyway, they're the ones who are controlling France. It's the Jews [. . .]. In all of France, they're the ones controlling everything, the television, the cinema, everything*" (Hamza, Paris). Others see Jews on TV as a sign and result of Jews being rich, powerful, and clever: "*They are clever, they are behind and in front of the camera*" (Omar, Paris).

Respondents in Great Britain see Jewish influence in American TV channels such as Fox News, Fox TV, and CNN, as well as in the film industry, as expressed in statements such as "*Most of the producers of Hollywood are Jews*" (Abhijt, London), or, as part of the "Jewish influence" in the United States: "*Jews do run American power, whatever, they are connected and all that, and media because they are in higher ranking positions of, like music companies, and film companies*" (Aba, London). Interviewees in Britain see "the Jewish influence" in terms of ownership and management rather than in the influence of Jewish actors or presenters. Sabir, of South Asian origin, stated, "*Fox TV, the manager is a Jew*" (Sabir, London), and then accused the American mainstream media, such as CNN, of not showing the sufferings of Palestinian children because he believes these to be Jewish companies. Thus, he made the same allegations as Adnan from Berlin of Palestinian background that "the Jews" cover up "their" crimes against the Palestinians with their influence in the media. As in France, participants in Britain often see "Jewish influence" in the media as a result of Jews' wealth and power, but they frequently referred to the American media, possibly because they are more familiar with it than are the French-speaking participants.

Jewish Influence in the United States

For some respondents Jews and the United States are almost identical: "*America is Jewish. Bush is Jewish*" (Sabir, London), stated one. But the perception of "Jewish influence" in the United States is usually voiced in statements stressing the influence on the economy and on the government:

> *Yeah, it's true that the biggest corporate bosses in America or the lobbyists, so, the ones who have a lot to say, that they're mostly Jews [. . .]. You can tell that when you look at how so many Jews in America have such an important influence, and one, I'd say, not exactly limited power at the moment.* (Sharif, Berlin)

Others pointed to "Jewish influence" on the American president: "*I heard, like, Jews are the people that basically controls Bush*" (Rajsekar, London). Rajsekar's statement also reveals his perception of Jews as an entity by his use of the singular form for the verb "control." Some participants see "the Jewish influence" through Israel or Zionism: "*Big people behind George Bush are, the majority are like, Zionist Jews*" (Tarak, London). Within this rationale Israel is seen as powerful, "*'cause they have an alliance with the U.S.*" (Neoy, London) and because "*as soon as the Jews are at war, the Americans have to join, it's inevitable*" (Kamel's friend, Paris).[5]

Many think that Israel and the United States are cooperating closely. One German respondent stated that Israel and the United States are working against the Arabs: "*They're all working together, that's just how it is. That's how it is. And so, Israel and America [. . .]. We, Arabs, we know that especially well, since we listen to Arab news and stuff. And America gets involved in fucking everything*" (Ahmed, Berlin). Interestingly, some believe in the "Jewish influence" in the United States but reject the idea that Jews control their country of residence: "*In France, it's not the Jews who are leading society, it's more . . . It's secular [. . .]. The United States, it's not a majority but [. . .] there, almost all of the big companies are Jewish*" (Samed, Paris). The speaker thus rejects the antisemitic trope that Jews control France and argued that the country is strictly secular, but he believes in the stereotype when it comes to the United States.

Conspiracies Regarding the Terrorist Attacks of September 11, 2001

The terrorist attacks of September 11, 2001, are a prominent theme for antisemitic conspiracy theories around the world.[6] Almost all interviewees condemned the attacks, but many questioned the responsibility of Al Qaeda and think that the American government or "the Jews" were somehow involved. Consider the statement below, in which the secret services of Israel and the United States are accused of conspiring against Muslims and staging the attacks of September 11, 2001:

> *[The] Israeli secret service is the biggest one anyway, they, what they do and everything. Of course, if you're an average civilian like me you can't understand everything or pick up on everything, but you hear here and there about all the things that they staged and stuff. They say for example that this 9/11 was a set-up that they planned, they say, 3,000 Jews weren't at work on that day. They say, that they purposefully did this 9/11 thing in order to have a reason to wage war against the East, Middle East, against the Muslim world, but in quotes 'terror.'* (Ümit, Berlin)

Vague descriptions and reference to rumors are generally typical for conspiracy theories.[7] The statement above begins with dark insinuations about the activities of the Israeli secret services. In this rationale, one depends on rumors, such as the allegation that Jews did not show up for work, to find out the "truth" and to reveal that this is all part of a conspiracy against Muslims. Both the rationale that the attacks were staged in order to have a pretext to go to war and the allegation that Jews did not go to work in the Twin Towers on September 11, 2001, are widespread among participants. The obvious, but usually unenunciated, implication is that Jews knew about the attacks and thus must have been involved. Others believe in an alleged cooperation between Bush and Bin Laden, some referring to the film *Fahrenheit 9/11* by Michael Moore as evidence. Another recurring piece of "evidence" cited was footage (on the internet) from the collapsing Twin Towers in slow motion, allegedly showing that the planes did not cause the collapse.

Some framed their conspiracy theories about 9/11 in the context of a much wider conspiracy, going back centuries. Ramzi from Berlin, for example, reported from an old "black book" in which the First, Second, and even Third World Wars and 9/11 were predicted.

In some cases, interviewees exposed the will to explain events with conspiracy theories, but not necessarily antisemitic ones. Çeto, a German participant, denounced the accusation that Jews were behind 9/11. He sees this accusation as a form of paranoia of alleged Jewish power and quoted from a survey in Germany to bolster his argument, indicating that he studied antisemitism in school.[8] But when asked who he thought was responsible for the attacks of 9/11, he responded: "*I don't know, I believe [it was] Bush, somehow*" (Çeto, Berlin), adding that there were links between the families of Bin Laden and Bush, and that Bush had the motive to find a reason to attack Iraq. Çeto exhibited relatively little antisemitism overall, which was possibly a result of his education in school and his overall liberal attitudes. However, the attraction of conspiracy theories surrounding 9/11 is stunning; many responses seem to compete for the title of most convenient conspiracy theory. Consider how Çeto balanced two such theories:

> *Well, both make sense, but I don't think that it was Jews, even though you hear that the Jews did it, so that Bin Laden, and you know, Bin Laden is a Muslim, that the Muslims get the blame for it somehow, so that America can wage war against Muslims, that maybe Muslims should be exterminated, but that's going a little too far, why would someone, like, want that? Yeah, I don't know, this theory about Bush is kind of . . . sounds more logical.* (Çeto, Berlin)

Çeto had heard of the conspiracy theory that "the Jews" planned 9/11 to draw America into a war against "the Muslims." He does not reject this idea because of its grotesque and outrageous implications – that is, the allegation that Jews acted together as one and planned the death of almost

3,000 people in order to exploit the United States for "their" interests in an alleged war against "the Muslims." He rejects this conspiracy theory because he thinks that it is "exaggerated" and that, in this case, it is "more logical" that the American president himself was involved.

Conspiracy Theories about the Holocaust

Only a small minority of interviewees voiced conspiracy theories about the Holocaust. In such cases, the interviewee cast doubt on the Holocaust, joined with an oracular belief in "*an elite who said what does and what doesn't go*" (Neoy, London) or with the belief that education about the Holocaust has been pushed in recent years "*because of the political climate in the Middle East, with Israel*" (Manoj, London). Manoj questioned the Holocaust in the form of a rumor: "*What a lot of people are saying, is did the Holocaust exist or not? A lot of things don't add up. They are saying six million Jews got massacred, but were there six million Jews in Europe at that time?*"

Three interviewees in France and one in Germany are persuaded that Hitler was himself Jewish. In Germany, one interviewee contended that Germany allegedly pays annual reparations of 200 million Euros to Israel because of a feeling of thankfulness to Jews: "*The Germans believe the Jews had killed [. . .] Hitler back then [. . .] and until now they are paying because they are so daft*" (Ramzi, Berlin). The same interviewee is convinced that "the Jews" helped Germany "in the beginning" and that Hitler then attacked "the Jews" to prevent them from taking over the country. He thus believes in Nazi propaganda about Jewish aggression against Germany. A vicious conspiracy theory about the Holocaust, which was voiced in insinuations and fragments by a few other respondents, is the allegation that the Holocaust was intentionally planned in order to create Israel. Another respondent in Germany expressed this plot in detail:

> *People also say that Hitler was a half-Jew, and that it had already begun back then, in the Hitler times, the blueprints for Israel. And how can you build a Great Israel, when you want to get to a Great Israel as quickly as possible? That you only take the richest and the ones that would, like, help you get ahead, you take, like, those Jews and you just exterminate the rest. Because, they're, like, a burden on us. The old*

and the disabled and the ones who don't contribute anything, the illiterate [. . .]. Now, the only ones who are alive, you can see today, are the rich and educated Jews. (Ümit, Berlin)

Ümit portrayed Hitler as a Jewish puppet and, in Nazi-terminology, as a "Halbjude" (half-Jew) himself. He presented the Holocaust as a project to kill those Jews who were a burden so as to lay the foundation of "Greater Israel." As evidence for his theory, he holds the antisemitic assumption that only wealthy Jews are alive today.

The Middle East Conflict as the Result of a Plot

Some see the State of Israel as the result of a conspiracy against "the Arabs" or "the Muslims." They adopt the view that Israel is responsible for the problems of Arab countries. This view is usually embedded in a Manichean view of the Middle East and the West, the latter being responsible for the creation of the State of Israel as part of an alleged war against the Arab world or against "the Muslims." One French interviewee summed up this view:

Israel is having a part in our war [. . .]. That's not by accident. It's all been planned [. . .]. By the West, by America [. . .]. All of the problems that are happening in the Arab countries are because of them, because of Israel. Israel is on that side [. . .]. Israel wouldn't exist normally [. . .]. It's America who chose, not the Jews, for them to be in the middle of the Arab countries, right in the middle of the Arab countries, why? To stir up conflict between them. (Hichem, Paris)

Hichem framed Israel as being responsible for "all problems in Arab countries," but said that Israel's existence is part of an American plan to cause mischief in the Arab world. Elsewhere, he explained that Israel is continuously expanding because "*they wanted too many material things, money,*" a value he thinks is rooted in Judaism.

Others believe that "*Zionism is synonymous with Freemasons [. . .], New World Order; it's all linked*" (Rahim, London). However, only one interviewee, of Palestinian background, voiced a theory of conspiracy that Palestinians in particular are targeted: Mousa is convinced that Israelis poison the water of Palestinians in order to sterilize them. This allegation resembles the antisemitic trope from the Middle Ages of Jews poisoning wells.[9]

Jewish and Christian Plans to Fight Muslims

Some respondents believe that Christianity, Islam, and Judaism are literally at war, struggling for world power. One contended:

> *For us in Islam, they say that we are going to conquer the world and then at some point the world is going to end, for the Christians it's certainly the same, they're going to conquer the world and for the Jews it's also exactly the same, you have to conquer the world. That's why there's this conflict between religions, and why there always will be one.* (Ümit, Berlin)

Such views of alleged eternal and destined conflicts prohibit reconciliation or hope for compromise.

Military aid from the United States to Israel is seen as evidence that Jews and Christians are fighting together against Muslims. One interviewee believes that the Qur'an predicts a holy war in which Muslims will defeat Jews, and considers the toppling of Saddam Hussein as part of a Jewish plan to weaken the Muslims:

> *This is part of the Jewish plan. They are planning it all out, 'so let's take out all the Muslims, make their side weaker,' 'cause that's what they are trying to do. Because Saddam was a super power[ful] man for us because he was a Muslim, strong, he had lot of armies, he was a good support to us. If the war came along we would definitely have his support, but now they took him away.* (Sabir, London)

The fact that it was American troops that toppled Saddam Hussein and his regime did not sway him, for Sabir believes that President Bush is Jewish.

STEREOTYPING JEWS

The trope of rich Jews is very popular among interviewees from all countries and backgrounds. Other stereotypes are related to this one, such as the belief that Jews are stingy, greedy, or exploitative. Jews were also portrayed as clannish, treacherous, and clever. More rarely, certain physical characteristics were attributed to them.

The Trope of Rich Jews

The stereotype that Jews are generally rich is so common that almost half of all respondents embraced it. But it should be noted that some of those who reject this stereotype showed anti-Jewish attitudes in other forms, including open hatred against Jews. The trope of rich Jews was often voiced directly in statements, such as "*The Jews are always the one at the head of businesses, the richest one*" (Fatin, Berlin); "*The majority, they are rich*" (Aswad's friend, Paris); "*They've got money, they've got everything*" (Baru, London); or simply, "*They are rich*" (Ahlam, Paris). Millionaires are often imagined as Jewish, and some of those interviewed cite supposedly Jewish millionaires such as Roman Abramovich, Alan Greenspan, and Bill Gates[10] to make their point. The argument that Jews are rich because they work in professions such as law and medicine was only pronounced by a few interviewees from France, such as one who said: "*They have a lot of money. Yeah, here, the government, you see the lawyers? All Jews. The judges, all Jews, the dentists, all Jews, the doctors, all Jews*" (Jabar, Paris). A few others are convinced that God gave wealth to "the Jews" or explained that Judaism teaches materialism: "*The Jews' paradise is on Earth, haven't you seen, they all have nice cars*" (Assim, Paris). This belief resembles the antisemitic trope of the Golden Calf, which accuses Jews of idolatry and worshipping money.[11]

Interestingly, the stereotype of rich Jews is common even among those who explicitly said that they do not want to stereotype and that they have nothing against Jews. Bahaar, for instance, portrayed Jews as established people who are rich and powerful because they allegedly own global businesses, but he acknowledged that Jews have been victims of discrimination, and he rejects general accusations against Jews in the same way he rejects anti-Muslim generalizations.

Big Companies, Managers, and Shops Are Seen as Jewish

Some turned the stereotype of Jews being rich around by saying such things as, "*All the richest people, they are Jews*" (Sabir, London). Many are convinced that big companies "are Jewish" or owned by Jews, or that "*almost all the big companies [in the United States] are Jewish*" (Samed, Paris). The economy – more precisely, profitable businesses, international companies, and "big money" – is associated with Jews. Some highlighted that owners or managers of a particular company are Jewish; others literally talked about "Jewish companies."

Part of antisemitic belief is that a Jewish ownership changes the character of the company or makes it part of "Jewish influence." Consequently, as shown above, the trope of "Jewish companies" is often linked to the trope of "Jewish power" and antisemitic conspiracy theories.

Jewish influence in the economy is often seen through ownership of companies in the United States, particularly by interviewees in Berlin and Paris. "*The United States, it's not a majority but there, almost all of the big companies* are *Jews [. . .]. Like, I heard that the head of* IBM *is Jewish, that the manager is a Jew*," said one (Samed, Paris), procuring the rumor that the director of IBM is Jewish as evidence for his claim that almost all big companies in the United States are Jewish. Similarly, a German interviewee stated, "*For example, in America, the biggest corporate bosses are mostly Jews*" (Sharif, Berlin). American banks are also associated with Jews: "*In the American banks there are only the Jews – who are rich*" (Bilal, Paris).

Interviewees from Paris often stated that local businesses, particularly mobile phone shops, are Jewish, or even identified a local shopping street in Paris-Barbès as Jewish. One, for example, answered the question of whether there were Jews in the neighborhood as follows: "*You go straight on and all the mobile phone shops it's from them [. . .]. There are only Jews down there*" (Hafid, Paris). His friend agreed: "*It should be called 'Feujs*[12] *boulevard,' well, boulevard of the Jews*" (Azhar, Paris). The stereotypical association of local businesses with Jews might be explained by the higher likelihood of Parisian interviewees seeing Jews in their neighborhood than interviewees in Berlin or London.

However, in Berlin, where the respondents hardly ever see Jews, some think that prestigious department stores such as KaDeWe or Karstadt are owned by Jews, or believe that Jews control the most famous shopping street in Berlin, the Kurfürstendamm (Ku'damm). In London, many interviewees labeled well-known companies, such as Marks & Spencer, Sainsbury's, Coca-Cola, McDonald's, Levis, Barclays Bank, and Tesco as Jewish or claimed that they are owned by Jews, usually to illustrate that Jews are rich or economically influential.

The underlying rationale was that major successful companies must be Jewish: "*Big companies in West End and so they're owned by Jews, innit?*" (Rajsekar, London). Some participants link this alleged Jewish ownership to sinister goals. "*Mr. Marks and Mrs. Spencer's were Jewish,*" said one (Salim, London),[13] in an attempt to explain why Marks & Spencer allegedly finances Zionists and supports Israel, to which he objects. Other interviewees, mainly from London, accused allegedly Jewish companies of funding the war against Palestinians by allotting a certain percentage of their profits to buy weapons for Israel. Consider the excerpt of the interview with two men from London who combined the stereotype of rich Jews with conspiracy theories and Manichean views of the Israeli-Palestinian conflict:

Kashi: Israel, they're rich, every single Israeli, they have millionaires, they got money [. . .]. I think most of the Jews they're rich, because, look Nike company, all the big company, most of them, they're owned by Jews [. . .]. Levis, Nike, McDonald's, all [. . .]. The main owners are Jews. They got money and everything. Those poor Palestinians, they got nothing.
Bashkar: You know why, because you know when they wanted to boycott Israel, the Palestinians, they wanted to, not Palestinians, some other Muslim groups, they wanted to boycott Israel, so they['ve] done leaflet[s] [. . .]. Imagine I buy, they said, it was written, whenever you buy a pack of Benson and Hedges, yeah, is that £4, 50p, or £5. So £5. So maybe from that £5, 2p is gonna go for the bullet, so he can shoot the Palestinian, the Israeli soldier [. . .]. It's a tax [. . .].
Kashi: Yeah, this tax money goes to the war [. . .]: a percentage. You know our tax money, some of them it goes to the government, to fight the war in Iraq, that's the way it works.
Bashkar: Tescos, Sainsbury's, Agida, just go to Sainsbury's.
Kashi: So many.
Bashkar: So many.

Bashkar and Kashi conflate Jews and Israelis. Referring to leaflets of a boycott campaign against Israel by Muslim organizations, they imagine that the economy is ruled by Jews and that companies "owned by Jews" finance weapons for Israeli soldiers to shoot Palestinians. In addition, Kashi mixes this notion up with the fact that British troops in Iraq were paid by taxpayers' money.

The accusation is that "Jewish companies" work for sinister goals with the money of ordinary people.

Imagining Local Jews as Rich Makes Them a Target for Robberies

Interviewees in London and Paris imagine Jews in those cities as "established," "very favored," coming from "good families," driving nice cars, playing tennis, and attending expensive private schools. Statements such as "*You don't really see much Jewish [sic] who are poor*" (Nirmal, London) and "*All the Jews are rich, innit? There is not a single one who is poor or who lives in the banlieue*" (Aswad, Paris) indicate that some believe that every single Jew in Paris or London is rich.

Such perceptions make Jews a preferred target for robberies. A British respondent explained: "*Because a lot of the Jewish people are rich you will find notes, 100 pound notes in their pockets. Because they're rich a lot of people go and rob them [. . .]. I've seen it a few times [. . .]. That's what I mean like them areas, Clapton and Stamford Hill, they're areas for people to get money and the way they get money is by robbing them and Jewish people won't fight back*" (Naresh, London). Although Naresh does not endorse robbing Jews, he takes it as a fact that Jews are a valuable target for robberies. Sabri from Paris admitted without regret that he stole his Jewish classmate's pocket money.

Through the lens of the belief that Jews are rich, the abduction and murder of the Jewish mobile phone salesman Ilan Halimi[14] is seen as "*a story of dough, that's all.*" "*Ilan Hamilim [sic] [. . .], they made such a big story out of it talking about Jews-Muslims, it's not that really, it's a guy who sees somebody else who has money*" (Haroun, Paris). A young Parisian of Moroccan parentage, Halimi was abducted by a youth gang in January 2006 because he was Jewish. The perpetrators had asked for an extremely high ransom, which the family was unable to pay. The leader of the "gang of barbarians" described himself as "Salafist," Islamist.[15] After being tortured for three weeks, Halimi was found naked, handcuffed, and covered with burn marks, near railroad tracks south of Paris on February 13, 2006. He died from his wounds on the way to the hospital. Haroun attempted to reduce the crime to a "story of money" and adopted the assumption that Ilan Halimi "had money."

Rationalizations and Rumors That Jews Are Rich

Some participants were reluctant to voice the stereotype of Jews as wealthy. This reluctance was expressed in phrases such as "*I've never experienced it 'live' myself. That's why I don't make any judgment about it. But I'll say this: if not even a little bit of this stuff was true, then not so many people would say it. Or it's just a stupid rumor"* (Umur, Berlin); "*There are definitely, like, clichés that they're rich"* (Tunay, Berlin); "*It's partly true and it's partly a lie, maybe"* (Samed, Paris); "*However somewhat true"* (Haroun, Paris); or "*I'm not even sure, like, if it's true or if it's like people are just saying it"* (Baru, London).

All these statements were made with reference to the stereotype of the rich Jew and show that some who repeat them are uncertain about its truth value. Others were adamant that the stereotype is true and referred to sources such as "*My friend told me"* (Nirmal, London) or "*We got that through the internet"* (Debesh, London). Vague references made to history function as even more obvious examples of self-convincing. A German interviewee believes that Jews are wealthy because "*it has a lot to do with the history, you know, that they were involved in trade"* (Sharif, Berlin). A French respondent explained, "*They have always been in trading, they are very very good businessmen"* (Haroun, Paris). Some participants, like Haroun, think that one should not be jealous of Jews. "Jewish wealth" should be seen as resulting from merit, noted a British interviewee, "*because they have worked for that and [. . .] they like to study, get knowledge and get a lot of money, get rich, so . . . they have done that over a period of time and so now they have good positions"* (Labaan, London). This perception can be manifested in a more essentialist way: "*That's what Jewish people are good at: business, finance, they were good at that"* (Hussein, London).

Respondents rarely took Jews they knew personally as evidence for their observations, probably because only a very few know any Jews. But some did reference actual Jewish acquaintances, for instance, by referring to an allegedly wealthier Jewish classmate or an allegedly stingy Jewish ex-girlfriend.

Rejecting the Stereotype of Rich Jews

Many participants, although they do constitute a minority, do not explicitly endorse the stereotype that Jews are rich, but only a few understand that portraying Jews as generally wealthy constitutes a biased stereotype. A French respondent commented on his friend's declaration that the majority of Jews are rich: "*No, look, they all live in the [council] blocks*" (Nadem, Paris). He argued that the stereotype is wrong, offering evidence of poor Jews who live in council housing in the neighborhood. He does not seem to know that wealth is an antisemitic stereotype and he also used antisemitic expressions elsewhere, for example, using "Jew" as an insult.

However, a British respondent described and critiqued the pattern of thought that financially successful people are labeled Jewish regardless of their religious background:

> *With Bengali people, like, you know, not tryin' to discount culture, it's all about money, with Bengalis, you know. And, if someone is rich, you know, they say they are Jewish. You know, successful people, like you know, like Bill Gates, or owner of Virgin, forgot his name, yeah, Rupert Murdoch, they say like they are Jewish, just because they are rich and successful, but they're strict Catholics.* (Rahoul, London)

Rahoul's rationale is presented in more detail in chapter 11 as one of the positive case studies of rejecting antisemitic thought. He demonstrated that some participants are aware of the fact that the stereotype of rich Jews is more than a false generalization.

Stereotypes of Jews as Stingy, Greedy, and Exploitative

The stereotype of Jews as being stingy is closely related to the stereotype of rich Jews and was often mentioned by the same people and in close proximity. One German respondent stated: "*There are definitely, like, clichés that they're rich, like, that they're cheapskates*" (Tunay, Berlin). Interviewees are often aware of the fact that this is a common stereotype, yet it is one in which they believe. The association of stinginess with Jews can be integrated in everyday language. The French expression "*manger en juif*" is used, as Sabri explained, to denounce someone who hides eating because he is not willing to share his food. In French, "*tu es un Juif*" (you are a Jew), and also in German, "*Du Jude*" (Jew!), is used by some interviewees as a direct accusation of stinginess in everyday life, they reported.[16] The association of Jews with stinginess is also strong among interviewees from London. Neoy, for example, insisted that the stereotype of Jews as stingy is true and backed it up with his "argument" that even religious Jews do not donate to the poor. The fact that philanthropy is an important part of Jewish tradition does not matter in the persistence of this stereotype. However, this belief may be related to the fact that he considers himself very religious and donating to the poor is often referred to as one of the five pillars of Islam. The contrast between Muslims who donate to the poor and Jews who are stingy was also made by two Muslims in London:

> *Interviewer: What does it mean, "Jew," for you?*
> *Ganesh: Jew means . . .*
> *Sakti: To be honest, if there's 1p on the floor, they will take it, you know? You know, Muslims they see 1p, they will allow it. Well, you meet Jew people, [. . .] they will take it.*
> *Ganesh: They will give it to the Mosque [. . .] for charity [. . .]. Jew people they put it on the pocket.*

Ganesh and Sakti so strongly associate Jews with stinginess that they define Jewishness essentially as stingy. The related stereotype of Jews as greedy is less common, even though one respondent directly said, "*They [the Jews] have got a lot of greed*" (Bankim, London), and others made allusions that Jews excessively desire wealth and profit.

Another related but rarely employed topos is that of exploitative Jews. Moukhtar from Paris utilized it while describing his mother's cleaning job: allegedly, Jewish employers pay less than "the French." He also sees his former Jewish boss as exploiting unpaid trainees. Another French interviewee argued in the same vein, saying that Jews would never employ a Frenchman "*because a Frenchmen here, he knows the laws, he knows how it works [. . .]. They take blacks [. . .], they exploit them, the poor guys, you see*" (Jabar, Paris). It should also be noted that both in Jabar's and Moukhtar's portrayal of Jews as exploitative, they distinguish between (French) Jews and Frenchmen.

The Stereotype of Jews Being Clever

Jews were also portrayed as clever, a portrayal which was often accompanied by a sense of admiration. Kaba from Paris of Guinean background sees Jewish cleverness as a gift of God, and one reason for the alleged success of "the Jews." A British respondent explained:

> *I was browsing under Google, and then I found something there and it mentioned quite a few people. Few of the top actors and actresses they are Jewish, but they are*

> *supposed to be the richest actors and actresses around. And it's not only that, the reason they['re] all doin' that: Jewish are clever. That's one thing I respect them for; they are clever. They know the way around things. They are extremely clever; they know how to manipulate people's minds.* (Sabir, London)

However, Sabir's description of Jewish cleverness was not without malice: Jews are clever at manipulating people. Others blend the attribute of cleverness with different negative allegations, such as being crooked or exploitative.

The Stereotype of Jews Being Clannish

Jews are thought of as being clannish: "*they stick together*" (Ümit, Berlin) and help one another. "*They don't like to mix [. . .]. The Jews, that always stays amongst Jews*" (Anis, Paris). A respondent from Berlin takes the fact that he has no Jewish friends as proof of his assumption that Jews are clannish. Some admire an alleged solidarity that they miss in their own community. Help among Jews is thought of as direct assistance for those in need: "*They help each other. That means, like, today, they have lots of stores and if they see, like, a Jew begging, then they'll pick him up and put him in a store*" (Azhar, Paris).

This perception of Jews helping each other goes hand in hand with the notion of a strong global bond between Jews. This connection is seen as a source of power: "*That bonding around themselves [. . .] that's how the power rises*" (Abhijt, London). Ümit from Berlin reasoned that the alleged clannishness of Jews results from their strong sense of community and long history of persecution.

The Stereotype of Jews Being Treacherous

The image of treacherous Jews often has a religious dimension, that is, "the Jews" are held responsible for denying and betraying prophets such as Muhammad, Jesus, and even Moses. Sabri gave an example: "*It's them, they betrayed the prophet*" (Sabri, Paris). Ümit mixed the Christian accusation that Jews denied and betrayed Jesus with the accusations that Jews denied and chased Moses and that, at the time of Muhammad, "the Jews" who allegedly pretended to be Muslims were secretly dissuading

Muslims from their faith. He believes that this treacherous character of Jews is the reason why they are persecuted until today and cursed by God. He concluded, "*They can only hurt you, and they're sneaky*" (Ümit, Berlin).

The internalization of the image of treacherous Jews may be the reason why Suleiman, of Palestinian origin, described Arab Jews as vile traitors, and Aswad's friend from Paris explained that "sale feuj" (dirty Jew) can be an insult applied to traitors. As described above, Jabar, also from Paris, accused Jewish employers of scheming and fraud while Moukhtar accused Jewish employers of cheating their employees. A British interviewee justified his generalization that Jews are untrustworthy with personal experience at work with a Jew who "*used to tell the big boss everything*" (Nader, London) and compared him to a snake.

Alleged Physical Characteristics of Jews

Particular physical features are only seldom attributed to Jews. Rather, Jews are usually perceived as looking like anybody else, though some can presumably be distinguished by special dress: "*You can see they are Jews because they have their traditional cloth*" (Labaan, London). Others said that they can recognize Jews by their haircuts, referring to Orthodox Jews, or by a necklace (in the form of the Star of David). However, those who referred to Jews as dressing in a particular way were often not clear if they believe that all Jews dress in that way, which can perhaps be explained by their perception of the Jews as a unitary group. A French respondent, for instance, asked: "*Why do Jews wear caps? The hats, and what's more, they all look the same . . . it's weird*" (Bilal, Paris). "*The big hats and long beards*" (Bankim, London) were also mentioned in London as characteristics of Jews,[17] but only a few respondents claimed that all Jews are physically different. Two friends, in France, were adamant that they can recognize Jews on TV by their looks: "*You can tell by their faces*" (Azhar, Paris). However, the old stereotype of Jews having large noses was only voiced by one interviewee (Sharif, Berlin), who is aware of the fact that it is a stereotype, but he confirmed that he knew a Jew from school who, he said, does have a long nose.

The Rejection of Jews in Personal Life

Only a few interviewees stated that they object to befriending Jews on principle. Many interviewees said, *"I wouldn't mind having a Jewish friend"* (Abhijt, London); *"Yes, why not, it's okay"* (Fatin, Berlin); *"I talk to everyone [. . .]. I don't care. I like to be friends"* (Bankim, London); *"I can have a friend, a friend of all races"* (Kaba, Paris); *"I cannot say now, 'Yes, I would never have a Jew as a friend or girlfriend.' It depends entirely on the person"* (Salih, Berlin); or even *"I'm friends with Jews, it doesn't bother me"* (Chafik, Paris). Even among those who showed antisemitic attitudes, many stated that they would befriend Jews, invite Jewish neighbors, or help Jews in need, and a few in fact have Jewish friends.

A positive attitude toward possible friendships with Jews seems to be related to a general positive attitude toward friendship and, possibly, to the aim of not emphasizing ethnic background in personal relations. Those who claimed they would not mind befriending Jews also rarely voiced open hostility against Jews. However, some interviewees were able to imagine befriending individual Jews while strongly rejecting "the Jews." The following excerpt (Halil, Berlin) is most interesting in that respect:

> *Interviewer: Would you oppose having a Jewish friend?*
> *Halil: Friend?*
> *Interviewer: Yes.*
> *Halil: Well, . . . yes, well, how should I say, if he's okay, [if he's] not such a Jew.*

The conditions Halil sets for a friendship with a Jew seem impossible: not being Jewish. The animosity against the abstract, imaginary Jew negatively influences possible relations with real Jews.

Others believe that they cannot befriend Jews because Jews would not want to befriend them, thus portraying Jews as segregated, clannish, or biased. Sometimes they accused Jews of rejecting friendship and trust: *"I'd like to, but they don't want to either. They have no trust, so we don't have trust either"* (Ahlam, Paris). Some participants voiced stronger reluctance, for example, by saying that one should beware of Jews, pointing to the belief that Jews are treacherous.

Outright rejection of the possibility of befriending Jews is found particularly among those who bluntly stated that they hate Jews. The rejection of friendship is specific with regard to Jews: Nader from London has no problem befriending Christians, but would not even like to shake hands with a Jew.

Some do not want to be friends with Jews because they expect Muslims and Jews to be enemies, because they believe that this would cause a religious problem (without being able to give further details), or because they assume that their friends or "other Muslim people" would dismiss the friendship. One respondent (Baru, London) combined all three arguments:

> *Interviewer: Could you imagine to have a Jewish friend?*
> *Baru: If I do have it, then it won't be . . . well, I can't stay, 'coz then it would be problem with my religion. 'Coz we've got a problem against them. So if I stay with a Jewish then [it would] cause problems with [. . .] other Muslim people, [they] will hate me.*

The matter becomes more difficult when it comes to the question of a hypothetical Jewish girlfriend or wife, which far fewer interviewees can imagine. However, some have no objections and a couple of interviewees from Paris even have a Jewish girlfriend. Most participants who can imagine marrying a Jewish woman insisted that their wife would have to convert to Islam:

> *If she converts, there's no problem [. . .]. She'll become Muslim and then [. . .] we'll love each other forever [. . .]. But if she [. . .] wants to stay Jewish, well then, you know very well that Jews and Muslims, it's a little . . .* (Omar, Paris)

The alleged animosity between Muslims and Jews is one of the main reasons why many interviewees said that they would object to marrying a Jewish girl. Others referred to their parents who would not allow it, their cultures which would not match, or their religion which would forbid it. Some respondents simply said, in various forms, "*I'm not allowed to marry a Jew*" (Kassim, Berlin). A few participants rejected marrying a Jewish woman or having a Jewish girlfriend directly because of their general hatred of Jews, showing strong reactions to that question. Consider the outburst of a Berlin man in response to the question:

> *Interviewer: Can you imagine having a girlfriend, a Jewish girlfriend?*
> *Naaem: Never, dude, I would pull off her head [. . .]. I hate Jews!*
> *Every Jew should, I would kill every Jew on earth.*

Some feel disgust even thinking about having a Jewish wife: "*It's disgusting [. . .] Because then everyone's going to tell you, 'ah he got together with a Jew! Ah that's nasty' [. . .] Ah, the Arabs, they don't like the Jews either!*" (Bilal, Paris). Adding to that, he explained that people from his social circle would point a finger at him because "the Arabs" allegedly do not like "the Jews." It is in this sense that an interviewee from Berlin does not want to have a Jewish wife because he feels pity for his future children: "*If my mother were a Jew, I wouldn't be okay with that, so I don't want to do that to my children*" (Ismail, Berlin). Others do not know why they would not marry a Jewish woman but insisted that it would not be possible. A British interviewee, who said he would befriend Jews, is adamant that marrying a Jewish woman is out of the question:

> *I'm allowed to marry a Christian [. . .] not a Jew, no [. . .]. It's . . . just no [. . .]. To be honest, I don't know the answer, man! [. . .] I don't know where I got it from. But I'm sure I can, I can marry a Christian, but not a Jew.* (Abhijt, London)

The rejection of intimate contact, of marrying a Jewish woman, often is specifically directed against Jews and not against other religions in general, as this example shows.

The Trope of Jews Being Alien to the Nation

Since the emancipation of Jews in the emerging Western nation-states, the view that Jews do not really belong in a country and that they are not full members of the nation has been identified as an important trope of modern antisemitism.[18] Many participants also see German, French, and British Jews not as citizens of those countries with Jewish religious affiliation, but as essentially different from Germans, Frenchmen, or Britons. Linguistically, Jews are often distinguished from Germans, Frenchmen, and Britons. A French respondent, for instance, said about employers: "*What is he, the guy? French, no! It's a Jew*" (Moukhtar, Paris). He explicitly distinguished Jews from Frenchman. This trope was expressed most commonly in the form that "their country" is seen as Israel rather than Germany, France, or Britain.

A respondent from Berlin described Jews as cosmopolitans living in many countries, but faithful to Israel: "*The [Jews] educate themselves, they make, they do, they work, they earn, whatever country they're in, but they invest of course in their own country, Israel*" (Ümit, Berlin). In his view Jews are not an integral part of their respective societies. Some made analogies to their own migrant community to point out that Jews are strangers: "*They are strangers like us, it's not their country here,*" said one (Jabar, Paris), also explaining that in Britain only British people have power, that neither Jews nor Asians do, and thus rejecting the antisemitic trope of Jewish power.

Also prevalent is the idea that "Jewish companies" or Jews in general financially support "their motherland Israel," summed up by a British respondent: "*Israel, this is the actual motherland, isn't it, for all the Jewish [people]. This is the holy place . . . this is everything to them and they always send their money to their country to fly private Apache helicopters to bomb the other, eh, Palestinians*" (Sabir, London). These perceptions are part of conspiracy theories and are often intertwined with a Manichean view of the Israeli-Palestinian conflict. Because Jews are often viewed as belonging to Israel, or as being of Israeli origin, they are held responsible for actions of the Israeli government or for killing Muslims or Arabs. "*It's their country which kills,*" said one (Bilal, Paris), referring to Jews in France.

CONCLUSIONS

A number of "classic" antisemitic tropes were exhibited openly, and only rarely in coded forms, of which conspiracy theories and stereotypes associating Jews with money figure most prominently. These tropes include characterizations of Jews as being rich, stingy, treacherous, and clannish by nature.

The tropes characterize "the Jews" as one entity with a common (sinister) "Jewish interest." The widely used terms "Jewish influence" and "Jewish companies" capture this notion. "The Jews" are portrayed as being "behind" companies, governments, or the media. The "Jewish influence" is hidden. It is claimed that well-known shops and companies are owned by Jews, not that the workers or products are Jewish.

Although "Jewish influence" is certainly seen on a national or even local level, it is largely viewed as existing on a global level and in association with the United States.

Some stereotypes and conspiracy theories were linked to the Middle East conflict or to perceptions of Islam or the Muslim or Arab identity.

Tropes of "classic" modern antisemitism were not used to justify hatred or violence against Jews directly, nor were they employed as arguments not to befriend or marry a Jew. Still, they enhance a negative and potentially threatening image of "the Jews."

SIX

Antisemitism Related to Israel

ANTISEMITIC RESENTMENTS CAN BE EXPRESSED THROUGH hostility to Israel. Scholars have debated on where the dividing line between criticism of Israel and antisemitism lies.[1] The Working Definition of Antisemitism[2] gives examples of words that can be considered antisemitic (as distinguished from criticism) and serves here, together with Helen Fein's definition of antisemitism,[3] as a guideline of the tropes I discuss. However, the extensive description of participants' perceptions gives readers the opportunity to decide for themselves whether a particular expression should be considered antisemitic or simply a critical view of Israel. The aim here is to present patterns of argumentation for negative views of Jews with references to Israel.

About half the interviewees showed hostile attitudes toward Israel to varying degrees, many in rather unambiguously antisemitic forms. However, it should be noted that for the other half, Israel and the Middle Eastern conflict are not important issues and these respondents' identification with "the Palestinians" is low.

In this chapter, I first illustrate how Jews and Israelis are conflated in various ways. Second, I show how the Israeli-Palestinian conflict is embedded in Manichean perceptions: Israel is portrayed as evil, represented by cruel soldiers, and Palestinians are seen as poor and innocent. Equations of the Palestinians' sufferings with the Jews' sufferings during the Holocaust enforce this perception. Third, I describe the use of the compelling topos of "Jews kill children," which is deeply engrained, not only among interviewees or Muslims, and central to a sharply dichotomous view of the Middle East conflict. Fourth, I analyze the way in which Israel is delegitimized and its right to exist is denied. The main argument is expressed in the topos that "the Jews" have illegitimately taken over Palestinian land. Fifth, I examine the justifications for suicide bombings in Israel. Lastly, I describe how the Israeli-Palestinian conflict is seen as part of a much wider struggle in which some participants see themselves to be involved. These argumentations are then brought together in the conclusion, where I focus on their role in enforcing hatred of Jews.

CONFLATION OF JEWS AND ISRAELIS

The conflation of Jews and Israelis is not necessarily an expression of antisemitism. But in combination with negative attitudes toward Israel, it enhances negative views of Jews. According to the Working Definition of Antisemitism, antisemitism can be manifested by "holding Jews collectively responsible for actions of the state of Israel." Werner Bergmann also noted that references to all Jews is an important criterion to be used in distinguishing antisemitism from criticism of Israeli policies.[4]

The majority of interviewees conflated Israelis and Jews living in Germany, France, or Britain at some point during the interview. Some explicitly said that they do not see any differences. The Israelis[5] were described as "the Jews" and generalizations were drawn from Israel to all Jews. European Jews were related to Israel. For most interviewees, Jews are a unitary category. Some justified their hatred against them with a conflation of Jews and Israelis: *"But we don't hate the Jews because they are Jews; no, because they are Israelis. They are occupiers. Israel has never existed"* (Youssef, Paris).

Youssef's statement is contradictory. He differentiated between Israelis and Jews, but said that he hates Jews because they are all Israelis and he hates Jews because "they are occupiers." He made it clear that he was not purely referring to the occupation of the Palestinian territories by saying that Israel has never existed. But how can there be Israelis without Israel? Youssef's contradictory rationale can be explained by his perception of "the Jews" as one entity, a category of which "Israeli" is only a part. This perception is combined with a Manichean view of the Middle Eastern conflict.

Israelis Are Seen as "the Jews"

The words "Jews" or "the Jews" were frequently used within the context of the Middle Eastern conflict in descriptions of actions by the Israeli army or government. Brian Klug, for one, has argued that these generalizations are expressions of outrage against Israeli military action and that those who use such words, in fact, are referring to the Israeli government.[6] In other words, do participants mean the Jews when they say "the Jews" in the context of the Middle Eastern conflict? Answering "no" would bring us into serious philosophical difficulties: words are directly related to terms, concepts, and ways of thinking.[7] However, also on an empirical level, a number of participants made it clear that they do mean all Jews when talking about "the Jews." Consider the excerpt of an interview with two French Muslims, Azhar and Hafid, both of Maghrebian origin:

> *Azhar: I think that with Lebanon and Israel, it's finished there [. . .]. The Jews deserve it.*
> *Interviewer: Pardon?*
> *Azhar: You're talking about the Jews here, right?*
> *Interviewer: Yes, yes, or the Israelis.*
> *Hafid: Ah the Israelis, they're Jews.*
> *Azhar: Actually, we, the Arabs, uh, Muslims and Jews don't get along.*

The interview was conducted in October 2006, a couple of months after the war between Israel and Hezbollah. At that time, Israel had withdrawn and Hezbollah had declared victory.[8] Azhar showed his satisfaction about the outcome of the war by saying that "the Jews" had deserved it. The interviewer's irritation about this generalization was met by Hafid insisting that Israelis are Jews, which, indeed, is true for 75.5 percent of the Israeli population.[9] But Azhar made it clear that he means all Jews and not only Israeli ones by using an alleged general enmity between "the Jews" and "the Arabs" or "the Muslims" as an explanation for his satisfaction of the outcome of the Lebanon war. Others made it perfectly clear that they mean Jews when they say "Jews" in the context of the Middle Eastern conflict by adding a religious category: "*How Israel does that, for example with, they kill babies [. . .]. To have no heart, those are the unbelievers. Those are the Jews! Those are the Jews*" (Ramzi, Berlin).

Ramzi took Israel simply as an example to make his point that Jews are heartless. There is no doubt that he meant "the Jews" when he said that "they" kill babies. Others see the Israeli-Palestinian conflict in an apocalyptic-religious perspective. A British Muslim expounded:

> *Do you know why Jew[ish] people get all their equipments? Because Bush is giving them equipments to get rid of all the Muslim countries [. . .]. Because in our religion it's written on the Qur'an, and it says there's a holy war coming now. They wanna kill all the Muslim people.* (Agantuk, London)

In such views of a war between religions at the end of time, in which all Jews unite against Muslims, distinctions between Israelis and Jews become meaningless.

However, the conflation of Jews and Israelis is more ambiguous in other cases. Some interviewees tried to distinguish between Israelis and Jews in some contexts but conflated these categories in others. Distinctions were made, for example, when participants wanted to express their respect for other religions but conflated Jews and Israelis when they commented on the Middle East conflict or when they described global conspiracy theories. Some participants gave the impression that they were explicitly taught to distinguish between Jews and Israelis without understanding why they should do so. Aswad from Paris, for example, explained that one should speak of Israelis rather than Jews in the Middle Eastern context but he had to correct himself several times and eventually saw "*many of these little logical connections*" (Aswad, Paris) between Israelis and Jews in France.

Jews Are Perceived as Belonging to Israel

Jews in Germany, France, and Britain are suspected of supporting Israel and having their roots there. This is not exactly a conflation but rather an underlying assumption that often meets an antisemitic trope: "Accusing Jewish citizens of being more loyal to Israel, or to the alleged priorities of Jews worldwide, than to the interests of their own nations" is one component of the Working Definition of Antisemitism. Interestingly, this accusation was often made by comparing one's own religious or ethnic community to Jews, portraying both as migrant communities and thus alien to the country of residence. A British interviewee, when asked about his view on the relation between Jews in Britain and Israel, responded:

> *Obviously they're from Israel, 'cause Jewish [people] are mostly from there [. . .]. They probably moved in here [. . .]. Not all Jewish [people] are from Israel, they can be from other countries. Like, Muslims they're from all over the world, Jewish as well they're from all over the world. Not just Israel.* (Nirmal, London)

Nirmal perceives British Jews as migrants, mainly from Israel, ignoring the fact that most British Jews have ancestors who lived in Britain centuries ago.[10] A French Muslim put it slightly differently, convinced that French Jews regularly visit Israel as their home country because "*everybody has been to his country of origin at least once*" (Bilal, Paris).

In addition, two recurring topoi about Jews are that they support Israel morally and that they send money there. Some accuse Jews in Germany, France, or Britain of being happy about Palestinian sufferings and casualties.

A few interviewees distinguished Orthodox Jews or "religious Jews" from Jews who allegedly support Israel.[11] Sharif from Berlin, for instance, praised Orthodox Jews because he thinks that their strict interpretation of the Torah prescribes Jews to live without a state. Hussein from London believes that those who "*are not practicing, who have political ideas,*" create the problems, while the "*people of the Book; they don't have a problem.*" These perceptions sometimes led to the rationale that non-Orthodox Jewish citizens were generally accused of supporting Israel.

However, a few participants demonstrated that they do not conflate Jews and Israelis, most clearly shown by a German respondent:

> *Since I've dealt with the topic [in school], I know that they have nothing to do with it, but they're often blamed; but the Jews in Germany don't have anything to do with the Jews in Israel, it's just the religion that binds them together. There are Israelis and there are Germans, yeah, all Jews. Many think that a Jew is then also an Israeli, but [it] is not like that at all.* (Çeto, Berlin)

Çeto referred to what he had learned in school, which demonstrates that education can help students to distinguish between, in this case, German Jews and Israelis.

MANICHEAN PERCEPTIONS OF THE MIDDLE EAST CONFLICT

Dualistic views of good and evil of the Middle Eastern conflict distinguish between Israel or "the Jews," on the one hand, and "the Palestinians," "the Arabs," or "the Muslims," on the other.[12] One side is portrayed as comprising evil perpetrators and the other as composed of good people and victims. Some interviewees put it bluntly: "*Jews are evil and the Arabs are nice*" (Abdullah, Berlin). Differences among various groups, both within Palestinian and Israeli societies, are not taken into account. These views are immune to opposing facts and arguments because they imply a preconceived opinion in which Israel alone is responsible for the Middle East conflict.[13] This view can be seen as antisemitic in itself through its demonization of the Jewish state.[14] If "the Israelis" and "the Jews" are conflated, then Manichean perceptions of the Middle East can lead to justifications of hostility against Jews. Israel often serves merely as an example for the evilness of "the Jews," and hostile views of Israel are used as justifications for hatred against Jews.

Soldiers against Innocent People

The image of the evil Israeli soldier versus the innocent Palestinian is a central trope in the polarization of the Middle Eastern conflict. Israelis are associated with tanks, machine guns, and threatening soldiers; Palestinians, on the other hand, are portrayed as poor, imprisoned, defenseless, and innocent, traits that are often represented through the symbol of a child. Kassim's description of the Israeli-Palestinian conflict was reduced to this image: "*The Israelis, they are warriors, they kill children, and the Palestinians are such poor people [. . .] and they come and just attack them*" (Kassim, Berlin).

Images of families brutally violated by soldiers are typical; images of stone-throwing Palestinian children against Israeli tanks and machine guns are also popular and powerful. "*Submachine guns against rocks*" (Mohamed, Paris) are part of this image, in which Israelis can get dehumanized: "*It hurts me. I see men with weapons killing kids [. . .]. Even a dog wouldn't do that. Those people are worse than dogs*" (Khalil, Paris).

This both illustrates the demonization and dehumanization of Israeli soldiers and points to an emotional attachment interviewees feel toward suffering Palestinians. Khalil declared that watching these images of violence makes him suffer in turn.

Palestinian Victimhood

The caricatural image of Palestinian victimhood is enforced by the portrayal of Palestinians as particularly poor. Adnan, a Berlin resident of Palestinian origin, described Palestinians as starving:[15] "*They are starving, they have hardly any clothes, mostly dirty or tattered things because they cannot buy clothes.*" Others stressed the inequality between Palestinians and Israelis and linked this inequity to the unfair and cruel treatment of Palestinians by Israeli soldiers:

> *They are not equal. Economically they are not equal, socially they are not equal [. . .]. They get a gun in your head and they say: "How are you feeling now? How are you feeling? Get on your knees." Bang!* (Tarak, London)

The disparity and injustice are seen in all accounts: "*They got everything, they got all the weapons, and [. . .] food supply, aid supply, everything, man. They control everything*" (Gourab, London). Some highlighted that Palestinians possess only inferior weaponry or contended that they are defenseless: "*In Palestine they have no weapons*" (Ismail, Berlin). Such descriptions of destitution make Palestinians look entirely helpless and innocent and call for alliance with "the weaker side" of the conflict.

A symbol of that perception is the image of innocent and defenseless children, which is often used as part of the topos "Jews kill children," described in detail below. Equations of the Palestinians' situation with that of the Jews during the Holocaust also contributes to the portrayal of Palestinians primarily as victims.

Equating the Sufferings of Palestinians with the Holocaust

What is the rationale of equating the sufferings of Palestinians with the Holocaust? A basis for this comparison seems to be the perception of a deep suffering of "the Palestinians" at the hands of "the Israelis" or "the

Jews." One recurrent theme was the killing of children which, in the eyes of some participants, amounts to atrocities like those committed in the Holocaust. "*It's more or less the same thing. They kill the children*" (Hamza, Paris), said a French Muslim with reference to the Holocaust and the Middle East conflict. The argument that Palestinians in the Gaza Strip are imprisoned was also used to justify this equation. Consider this statement:

> *So, I've heard that many Jews are blamed or attacked because they, you know, they went through the Holocaust and now they're doing that to the Palestinians, since they are theoretically locking them up in the Gaza strip.* (Çeto, Berlin)

In Germany, such arguments have been interpreted as a projection of guilt for the Holocaust.[16] Though Çeto might have been influenced by such tropes, as a person of Turkish Kurdish origin he is likely not motivated by this guilt.

The use of the antisemitic topos that Jews allegedly talk too much about the Holocaust points in the same direction. Another respondent in Germany of Turkish origin concluded: "*They are killing people like the Nazis killed the Jews, and so there's no difference there. And then the Jews can't complain about what Hitler did to them when they are already doing it themselves*" (Necet, Berlin). Necet not only equated the Jews with the Nazis and said that they should not complain about the Holocaust today, but he portrayed "the Jews" as one entity, merging not only Israelis and Jews but also the Jewish victims of the Holocaust more than sixty years ago and Israelis today.

Equations of the Holocaust with the treatment of the Palestinians insinuate evil intentions on the part of the Israelis. A British respondent thinks that "it" is similar "*because the idea of it is roughly the same, I mean, just killing someone because you think you're better or they're different or they're wrong*" (Bahaar, London). The Holocaust becomes a general term for many, conveying the meaning of hatred against others. One British interviewee even portrayed the Holocaust as a Jewish claim before he described the killings of Palestinians as "a present-day example of the Holocaust":

> *Before, the victims were the Jews, so they claimed, now, we see that the Jews are the oppressors because what is happening in Palestine, if you see the pictures of the Israelis,*

> *up-to-date weapons are killing these little Palestinian kids for throwing stones at them. And that is a present-day example of the Holocaust [. . .]. I think Israel is playing the role that Hitler played.* (Noey, London)

Some even stated that the treatment of Palestinians is worse than the way Jews were treated in the Holocaust: "*It's more perverse. It's really dirty*" (Khalil, Paris). He believes that "the Jews" want to kill all Muslims. A British interviewee was not sure if the intent to exterminate all Palestinians exists, but he was adamant that the Jews seek to take over Palestine and the world:

> *But obviously unlike Hitler, Hitler did it alone. They're getting their help from America and this country. They're getting more help [. . .]. I am not sure whether they want to kill all the Palestinians. But I do know that they want to take over their country. Take over the world.* (Nirmal, London)

Nirmal believes that Israel has perpetrated atrocities against the Palestinians similar to those committed in the Holocaust, "but" with help from the United States and Britain; he extends this belief, via antisemitic conspiracy theories, to a desire for world conquest.

To conclude, equations of the Holocaust with the Israeli-Palestinian conflict imply the perception of deep sufferings of "the Palestinians" at the hands of Israel, and lead to the accusation that "the Israelis" or "the Jews" harbor evil intentions. Such equations are antisemitic as such, but they are often accompanied by additional antisemitic stereotypes and tropes, such as Jews being child murderers, or that "the Jews" allegedly talk too much about the Holocaust, or antisemitic conspiracy theories.

Identification with "the Palestinians"

Many interviewees identify with Palestinians, often by stressing their common Muslim or Arab identity. The identification with Palestinians is stronger among participants of Arab background, whereas most participants of Turkish or South Asian background are reluctant to identify with Palestinians. However, identification with Palestinians is sometimes strong even without an Arab background. "*All Muslims are brothers and sisters, no matter which nationality [. . .]. Even though I'm Turkish, I'm with the Palestinians*" (Ümit, Berlin). Here, a British respondent affirms that Muslims feel connected to the Palestinians: "*Every Muslim has an opinion on that, because [. . .] if you go to the mosques you see them praying for them, you see people giving money for them, Muslims in Palestine*" (Salim, London). A man of North African background strongly identifies with Palestinians and feels involved in their struggle against "the Jews":

> *There would have been war between the Jews and the Palestinians [. . .], we would have won, we would have won, that's sure. But since there's George Bush, who gives out missions and all that, weapons and all that, it's not surprising. Now, we have rocks, you know, you've seen it on TV. We don't have weapons, we take the, they take the rocks and throw them.* (Omar, Paris)

Omar used "we" as a unitary category for "the Palestinians" and "the Muslims," including himself, but he is not sure if wants to include himself in the fight: he switched from "we" to "them" when he spoke of throwing stones. Identification with "the Palestinians" is usually found in coexistence with a Manichean view of the Israeli-Palestinian conflict. This mindset takes the conflict beyond the Middle East, because those who identify with the Palestinians do so in the name of "the Muslim" or "the Arab" community.

However, it should be stressed that many other interviewees showed no signs of identification with the Palestinians. Some even explicitly distanced themselves from them. A respondent of Turkish Kurdish origin said about Palestinians, "*They, themselves, are acting violently [. . .]. I actually don't have any sympathy for them since they only have themselves to blame*" (Çeto, Berlin). In Paris, it was striking that those who showed no signs of identification with Palestinians stressed their non-Arab identity, such as this Berber man:

> *We, we aren't Arabs, we are Maghrebians [. . .] and Palestine, those are Arabs. And Palestine, honestly [. . .], anyway, I'm a Berber.* (Masmud, Paris)

In Britain, many interviewees identify with the Palestinians "as Muslims," but others, such as a man of Bengali origin, referring to the Middle Eastern conflict, distanced themselves and showed no interest in the subject: "*Fuck this bullshit man [. . .]. Let them get along with their business*" (Rahoul's friend, London).

Non-identification with the Palestinians is influenced by an ethnic identification against Arab identity or by indifference to the Israel-Palestinian conflict. Those who do not identify with "the Palestinians" are emotionally less involved in negative views of Jews with reference to the

Middle Eastern conflict. However, as Çeto, who distanced himself from Palestinians, demonstrated with his comparison between the situation of Palestinians in Gaza and Jews during the Holocaust, this lack of identification does not prevent them from voicing antisemitic statements with reference to the Middle Eastern conflict.

THE TOPOS "JEWS KILL CHILDREN"

The recurrent topos of Israel or "the Jews" killing children in the context of the Middle East conflict resembles the medieval antisemitic stereotype of Jews murdering Christian children for ritual purposes.[17] The accusation is that children, a symbol of innocence, are killed deliberately; hence, the perpetrators must have evil motives. This stereotype adds to the profile of an evil State of Israel and, if Israelis and Jews are conflated, is used as evidence for the evilness of Jews.

This topos was employed by almost one quarter of interviewees, more often as "Jews kill children" than as "Israelis kill children." All those who said "Israelis kill children" conflated Jews and Israelis in other contexts, so that it can be assumed that the topos is used as an implicit or explicit allegation against Jews, not only against the State of Israel, Israelis, or the Israeli army. Indeed, some participants used the topos as a direct explanation for the hatred of Jews that also targets Jews in their neighborhood. Bilal, a French Muslim, speculated why Jews are hated in his neighborhood: "*Those Jews there . . . with their planes, they bombard apartment buildings where there are children [. . .]. That stirs up some hatred.*" A counterpart from Berlin used this allegation to justify his and his friends' antisemitic outbreak of screaming, "*Fucking-Jews, fuck-Sharon,*" during a school trip to the local synagogue: "*I'm angry because they kill small children!*" (Kassim, Berlin). (Ariel Sharon was the Israeli prime minister at the time.)

The topos not only demonizes Jews but also reinforces the image of "the Palestinians" as innocent and helpless. It is used to blame "the Jews" in the Middle Eastern conflict, to highlight their evilness, and to empathize with "the Palestinians." The accusation is that children are killed deliberately. "*They are like killing innocent children, and you see it on the TV [. . .] they attack little children and women*" (Kajal, London).

This comment was made with reference to the Lebanon war in 2006. Kajal, of South Asian origin, sees children as being deliberate targets of the Israeli forces rather than simply as tragic victims. The topos of Jews killing children serves as an emotionally charged argument and illustration for blaming "the Jews" for the Middle East conflict. A Turkish participant from Berlin used the topos as evidence for his argument that the Jews started the conflict and that they are to blame for it: "*The Jews are just starting it. They kill small Muslim children, they do everything, they rape small children, women, even grannies*" (Memduh, Berlin).

Memduh added the accusation of perverse rape to the topos and stressed that the children killed were Muslim, possibly because he wanted to show his identification with the Palestinians and sought to portray Muslims as victims. These strong images allow him to describe his dualistic views of the Middle East conflict in a few words. "They are killing children" can be used as a metaphor for the whole conflict:

> *The Jews are up on top with their machine guns. They shoot at them [. . .]. The little kids, they throw their stones like that. It's shameful. They have no shame [. . .]. They, what do they want? They want to crush Islam. So, after that, I don't listen to anything that they say, I don't listen to anything, I don't believe them [. . .]. They're animals, they have no shame, killing kids.* (Khalil, Paris)

Khalil also described the Israeli-Palestinian conflict in images, from the soldiers with their machine guns to children throwing stones. Additionally, he accused "them" of striving to crush Islam. Khalil is resentful: "They are animals, they are not ashamed of killing children," summing up his morally charged accusations against Jews, who are portrayed as evil and inhuman.

However, the topos of "Jews kill children" also serves as a means of empathizing with "the Palestinians." A British Muslim declared with reference to what he had read in a Pakistani magazine: "*Look at Palestine, I feel so sorry for them [. . .]. They cut the stomach and get the pregnant baby out*" (Kashi, London).

The image of a baby or a pregnant woman as a victim aggravates the accusation and was used by others in Paris and Berlin. While the complex situation and the living conditions in the Palestinian territories are mostly unknown and hard to imagine for young European Muslims, images of murdered children are more accessible to the imagination.

Some participants took the perspective of those whose family members have been killed and imagined what they would feel if they lost their little brother or sister:

"Me, I'm at home, sleeping calmly, I see my father get killed, my mother get killed, my little sister get raped [. . .]. What am I going to do? [. . .] I'm going to get revenge" (Haroun, Paris). Of Maghrebian origin, Haroun sought to explain the motivation of suicide bombers in Israel by imagining how he would react if his family were killed. He used the topos of Jews as child murderers to comprehend and justify the feeling of anger and the call for revenge against the Jews.

The media provide images of the Middle East conflict that can be interpreted as confirmation of the topos of "Jews kill children." Interviewees directly referred to such images. A key picture in this respect is the footage of the alleged killing of Muhammad al-Durah in 2000, at the beginning of the second Intifada. The young boy was filmed with his father crouching behind a block of concrete, after being allegedly shot by Israeli soldiers. These pictures were broadcast all over the world and al-Durah became an icon of Palestinian martyrdom, even after serious doubts were voiced about the authenticity of the broadcast.[18] Consider what a respondent from Berlin associates with Israelis:

> *The Israelis [. . .] kill small children, babies, they shoot them [. . .]. A small child, sitting next to his father, they give him a shot in the head, from behind [. . .], I don't like it that they murder small children.* (Kassim, Berlin)

Six interviewees referred to images that allude to the picture of Muhammad al-Durah. Such images are ingrained in their memory even if they do not necessarily remember the exact story and circumstances. Kassim recalled that a child was shot sitting next to his father. A French interviewee directly referred to images on TV:

> *They showed it on TV, they ran it for a little bit [. . .]. The kid, the poor thing, yeah, behind the rock there [. . .]. Okay, you kill the father, but why do you kill the child? It's not good.* (Jabar, Paris)

His description refers more directly to the images of Muhammad al-Durah than Kassim's, but both used it to back up their moral judgment of the Middle Eastern conflict.

DELEGITIMIZATION OF THE STATE OF ISRAEL

Different rationales were brought forward to deny Israel's legitimacy, denial which is an antisemitic trope in itself.[19] The main argument, put simply, is that Jews have built Israel on what is regarded as Palestinian, Arab, or Muslim land, and that the establishment of a Jewish state in Palestine was therefore wrong from the beginning. This is often expressed in the topos "Jews have taken over Palestinian land," which I discuss below. The suffering and oppression of Palestinians, a Manichean view of the Middle Eastern conflict, and the topos that "Jews kill children" were frequently added in statements about Israel's perceived illegitimacy but were rarely used as an argument to delegitimize Israel on their own.

However, many participants expressed themselves ambiguously: it was not clear whether they denounce the occupation of Palestinian territories or if they regard the entire State of Israel as an occupation of "Palestine." An analysis of the context reveals that interviewees who made these allegations tend to mean the latter. Similarly ambiguous are the relatively rare statements criticizing the border or "the wall" between Israel and the Palestinian territories.

A few interviewees accuse Israel of expansionism, of the wish for a "Greater Israel." Some blame Great Britain and the United States for enabling the creation of the State of Israel. Other respondents compare the creation of the State of Israel to a hypothetical invasion of Germany or France, with invaders occupying half of the country. A few others think that a Jewish state should be somewhere in Germany. The occupation of religious places, such as the Dome of the Rock, were also brought forward as arguments for the illegitimacy of the State of Israel. The refugee problem, Jewish "settlements" in the West Bank, and checkpoints controlled by the Israeli army were rarely mentioned.

The wish for the dissolution or annihilation of the State of Israel was sometimes expressed bluntly and with fervor, and sometimes ambiguously and implicitly. Ethnic background seems to be a relevant factor in determining feelings about Israel. Only a few interviewees with Turkish background openly called for the dissolution of Israel. The most aggressive expressions of delegitimization came from participants of Lebanese or Palestinian background, whose views about the State of Israel are dealt with separately at the end of this chapter in order to avoid distorting the general picture. Nevertheless, the same arguments, with less aggressiveness, were also found among participants from other ethnic backgrounds.

However, it should be stressed that a majority of interviewees believe a two-state solution is the best way forward in the Israeli-Palestinian conflict, despite their feelings of injustice both about the sufferings of Palestinians today and in the past as a result of the creation of the State of Israel.

The Topos "Jews Have Taken Over Palestinian Land"

The Arab countries have opposed the State of Israel having been founded on parts of the territory of the British Mandate of Palestine. The legitimacy of acquisitions of land by Zionists before, during, and after the creation of the State of Israel has been challenged internationally. Jewish settlements in the Palestinian territories are still controversial today. However, the creation of the State of Israel in the British Mandate of Palestine was in accordance with the partition plan ratified by the UN General Assembly in November 1947.[20] Indeed, there was less dispute in the international community regarding the formation of the State of Israel than there was for the creation of most of the other countries that came into existence after the Second World War.

About a third of the interviewees expressed, often in similar words, their assumption that "the Israelis" or "the Jews" wrongly took over Palestinian land, and all but three of those who did equated Israelis with Jews. The main argument for this topos was that historically, the territory was allegedly Palestinian land and not Jewish. "*Israel, right now are trying to take over Palestine. They're trying to say it's their country, when as you can see in the history clearly Palestine is their own country*" (Nirmal, London). A French Muslim of Guinean origin emphasized the fate of Palestinians: "*The Israelis [. . .] chased them from their land [. . .]. It's the Palestinians who were there before [. . .] and now the Palestinians end up with no land*" (Ousmane, Paris). Particular aspects of history will need further clarification and some territories are disputed between Israel and Palestinians. However, there is no doubt that Jews have lived in the region for thousands of years and that the history of the relatively recent Israeli-Palestinian conflict and the establishment of the State of Israel would be oversimplified and wrong if reduced to a one-sided story of Palestinian refugees.

Some participants, such as one in Britain, believe that establishing a Jewish state was only possible as a result of the Holocaust: "*If the Western world helped the Muslims to regain their land, for example, Palestine, it belonged to the Muslims and then through the Holocaust they came through*" (Tarak, London).

Tarak wants "the Western world" to help Muslims regain "their land." He thus considers Israel's territory to be Muslim land. A respondent from Paris even thinks that Jews should not be in that part of the world because it is a "Muslim country": "*What are they doing there, it's a Muslim country, Palestine*" (Ahlam, Paris).

In most cases, participants did not dispute the legitimacy of particular Jewish "settlements" or the border between Israel and the Palestinian territories but rather questioned the legitimacy of the Jewish state altogether. One went straight to the point when he demanded: "*We have to go to the root, and the root of the problem is they're in someone else's land*" (Hussein, London). A respondent of Maghrebian background argued that Jews had taken more and more land and unjustly created Israel: "*That doesn't exist, Israel, usually. It must not exist. They gave them a little land and they started taking more and more. Now it has become their home*" (Housni, Paris).

By charging that "Jews have taken Palestinian land," the respondents question the very legitimacy of the State of Israel.

Denying the Existence of the State of Israel

Many participants go further than not accepting the legitimacy of the State of Israel: they do not accept even the existence of the State of Israel. "*Israel doesn't exist*" (Bashkar, London). The two main arguments for this astonishing denial of reality are that the land belongs to other people and that, historically, there had been no state called Israel before World War II. This denial against the knowledge that the State of Israel is a reality today is an expression of the intense opposition to the State of Israel and a call for its dissolution.

Consider a British Muslim's expression of this denial in the context of the conversation between himself, a friend, and the interviewer:

> *Kashi: Go back a hundred years. Did Israel exist? No. Who's land was it? Palestinians'. Who took it over? Israel. Nothing happened [. . .]. They took their whole country over and nobody says nothing.*
> *Bashkar: Israel doesn't exist. It doesn't exist.*
> *Interviewer: It doesn't exist?*
> *Bashkar: Hundred years ago it wasn't there. It was Palestine [. . .].*
> *Interviewer: But now, does it exist?*
> *Kashi: No.*
> *Bashkar: Now they became an image.*
> *Kashi: [. . .] You know England; we have to believe in Israel as a country exists. But you know Saudi, Dubai, Kuwait, those Arab countries. If you go there, and you show them the passport and they gonna check which country you went to, if they say Israel, they won't let you in their country. 'Coz they don't, still, so the Arab they don't believe in Israel as a country. 'Coz that's Palestine.*

Kashi and Bashkar are both of South Asian background. Kashi referred to the fact that a number of Arab countries do not recognize Israel. He contrasted this with what he perceives as an obligation in Britain to "believe in Israel." He portrayed Israel as a state whose existence is not only unjust and illegitimate, but also only accepted by some and thus not fully recognized as a state; the denial of Israel's existence, therefore, seemed more plausible.

A respondent from France of Moroccan origin also denies the existence of Israel and added another argument saying that Jews, before the Holocaust, had no country and "*were like the Gypsies*" (Housni, Paris). He does not understand why this should have changed and was adamant that Israelis should abandon "Palestine" (including Israel). Consider this excerpt from the interview with him and his friend Omar, also of Moroccan origin.

> *Housni: I would say that if that is supposed to end –*
> *Omar: – that they share the country.*
> *Housni: Yeah, the Israelis have to leave.*
> *Interviewer: But where are they going to go?*
> *Housni: I don't know. They can figure it out, because Palestine isn't their country. Palestine is Palestine, obviously. Israel isn't normally right next to it.*
> *Omar: Palestine, is Muslim, I don't know, normally, there are only Muslims there.*

> *Housni: They go to America, I don't know.*
> *Interviewer: But you said earlier that they should share it?*
> *Omar: They'll go to America if . . . now, if the only solution is that they share it, the Israelis there, the Palestinians there, there you go [. . .].*
> *Housni: I don't agree with sharing. 'Cuz to share what? It's like if I have [. . .] something, and you, you come . . .*
> *Omar: It's like if the Americans, you know, if they came to France, they want half of France. Are the French going to agree to that? Are they going to give them half? [. . .] No. They're going to defend themselves. And that's what the Palestinians did. They wanted to take their land, that's not okay. So now there's going to be war up 'til the end.*

Initially, Omar endorsed a two-state solution. But then, possibly as a result of Housni's uncompromising views, he became more and more hostile to the idea and stated that "Palestine," including what is now Israel, should be exclusively Muslim. He then contemplated that giving half of the country to Israelis would be unjust, comparing it to a hypothetical and preposterous demand by Americans for half of France. He finished his thoughts by justifying a "war until the end" by Palestinians to fight Israel. For his part, Housni proposed that Israelis should leave the country for America.

Some participants, such as Nirmal of South Asian background, advocated tolerance of Jews on the territory of today's Israel but under Muslim rule. Malik, also of South Asian origin, believes that Islamic rule will bring a solution to the Israeli-Palestinian conflict and peace in Israel and everywhere.

Others were more ambiguous, such as Ümit from Berlin of Turkish origin. However, both solutions he suggested do not imply the existence of a Jewish state. He proposed either peaceful coexistence among Jews, Muslims, and Christians or the expulsion of everybody and thus the dissolution of the State of Israel:

> *The Jews lived there earlier, and then the Christians lived there and now we have lived there, yeah, no, there's no solution. You have to find a middleground, that people either live together, or not at all. In that case, everyone should leave that country, and build a huge fence around it and nobody should enter.*

Another way of ambiguously questioning Israel's right to exist is to formally endorse that right, but to portray the creation of the state as fundamentally wrong and unjust, and then to question the basis of Israel's national ideology. A British respondent spoke in this vein:

> *It has a right to exist, but no one talks, in the West especially [. . .] about how it came into existence. We know it's a fact, that Israel came into existence on the back of genocide and ethnic cleansing [. . .]. When we have the Palestinian conflict now, they won't teach you, that that is actually related to when Israel was first established, back in 1947, 1948. They will not say that. That's where the problem started.* (Manoj, London)

Manoj claimed it is an established fact that "Israel came into existence on the back of genocide and ethnic cleansing." Stressing that the main problem is rooted in the state's establishment is inconsistent with Manoj's initial assurance that Israel has a right to exist.

The next example shows that Israel is blamed for the conflict, regardless of the actual behavior of Palestinians or Israelis today, because Israel is perceived as being fundamentally in the wrong:

> *Lets face it, Israel is occupying someone else's home, isn't it? [. . .] So, it's them who's inciting. Maybe the figures say Palestinians have killed more Israelis, Jews, yeah? But does that matter? End of the day, you're occupying someone else's house, obviously he's going to try to fight you and get you out of there, isn't he?* (Hussein, London)

Hussein justified the Palestinian fight to get Israelis out of the country with a frequently made analogy to people who defend themselves against intruders in their own house. In this view, the fighting can only end when the "intruders," who are always to blame, leave the house.

Delegitimization of the State of Israel by Participants of Lebanese or Palestinian Background

In this section I focus on the views of the fourteen participants of Lebanese or Palestinian background on the legitimacy of the State of Israel.[21] Werner Bergmann points out that the motives for voicing anti-Jewish statements might be different among those who fear for family members in the Middle Eastern conflict compared to others who do not.[22] This might be particularly true when it comes to the delegitimization of the State of Israel. What evidence is there in the interviews for this hypothesis?

Only two of the fourteen interviewees reported the direct suffering of family members from the Israeli-Palestinian conflict. Nabil noted that his family members had to flee from the Israelis to Lebanon, the place of his birth, and that they still keep close contact through methods such as exchanging family videos. Nevertheless, he has a balanced view of the Middle East conflict and showed no signs of hatred of Israel or Jews. Ismail, on the other hand, openly indicated his wish for the dissolution of Israel and the killing of Jews and expressed hatred against Jews in his neighborhood. He said that his father had been at war *"against the Jew"* and that relatives of his father died *"because of the Jews."*

The majority of those who identify as Palestinian or Lebanese expressed a wish for the dissolution or annihilation of Israel and the expulsion of Jews from "Palestine." This was articulated in both subtle and blunt ways: *"They have just the same right to life or to a country. But it doesn't have to be where we are"* (Sharif, Berlin); *"Either they should go somewhere else and if not, they should just all rot, in my eyes"* (Adnan, Berlin); *"The Jews [should] bugger off [. . .]. They should piss off"* (Naeem, Berlin); *"I would kick the Jews out"* (Hamudi, Berlin).

Others showed sympathy for Hezbollah in its fight against Israel or expressed their wish for annihilation of Israel: *"Israel? [There] is no Israel for me"* (Mousa, Berlin). Some even called for the annihilation of all Jews: *"Then I would say [. . .] that they [. . .] give back the frontier, or whatever you say and that the damned Jews should be burnt"* (Bashir, Berlin); *"They should be slaughtered like pigs"* and *"I would eradicate all Jews, shooting them into the sea and goodbye"* (Suleiman, Berlin).

Participants like Suleiman left no doubt that they are unwilling to find a peaceful solution. He declared that he hates Jews because of their "race," but he also denies Jews their identity as a people, arguing that they come from many different countries. He said the following about "the Jew":

> *He just belongs to this race; therefore I hate him [. . .]. What kind of a people are they, black, white, brown, what kind of a people are they, they are not a people, the Jews [. . .]. There have to be original roots like that: all Palestinians and all Germans. But the Dutch, America, Germany, Russia, Poland, [. . .] they all actually come from other countries, but they build up a community of people, that doesn't exist at all. . . . [Disdainfully:] Jews.* (Suleiman, Berlin)

Suleiman's antisemitism takes a racist form here. He sees Jews as the "Gegenrasse"[23] and even without any rights to be a veritable race, the anti-race in opposition to Germans and Palestinians.

A few interviewees of Palestinian or Lebanese background made contradictory statements regarding their opinions on the dissolution of the State of Israel. In one passage, a respondent in Germany expressed the wish for peace in the Middle East and said that a two-state solution between Israel and the Palestinians was the most realistic option available. However, afterward, he referred positively to "the proposal of the Iranian president" to relocate Israel to a part of Germany: "*They also have a right to live, or to have a state. But it doesn't have to be at our place, of all*" (Sharif, Berlin).[24]

The term "Zionism" was hardly used. Sharif, the most educated interviewee of Palestinian background, was the only participant to use the argument that Zionism allegedly contradicts Orthodox Judaism and that Jews should not form a state.

Some interviewees of Palestinian or Lebanese background wore a sign of their adamant rejection of Israel around their necks: a chain with a pendant in the colors of the Palestinian flag in the shape of Israel and the Palestinian territories. This is an expression both of Palestinian nationalism as well as of the wish for the dissolution of the State of Israel.

JUSTIFICATIONS FOR SUICIDE BOMBINGS IN ISRAEL

Suicide bombings in Israel, which often deliberately target civilians, are an attack against both the Jewish state and Israeli society. Some participants justified suicide bombings in Israel and other places, such as Iraq. Justifications for such acts in European countries or in the United States were very rare. Some who approved of suicide attacks against civilians in Israel were apologetic in their argumentation and stated that the "method" is wrong. Others portrayed suicide attacks as a legitimate means of defense or, exceptionally, even endorsed such attacks to the point that they said they would consider carrying them out themselves one day. However, the desire to commit a suicide attack was only uttered by those who believe that suicide bombers are rewarded with their ascent to paradise. This indicates that hatred against Israel combined with Islamist beliefs that Jews are the enemy and should be fought leads to extreme radicalization and Jew hatred.

However, the main rationales for justification or endorsement of suicide attacks in Israel, often put forward in combination, are that suicide bombers

- want revenge for the sufferings of their families or their community, for which Israelis are supposedly responsible,
- are part of the legitimate fight for their country, land, or faith,
- gain a place in paradise, and
- contribute to the killing of Jews[25]

However, the latter rationale was used only by some of the few respondents who openly hate Jews.

It was striking that many respondents were adamant that suicide bombers must have had good reason to commit these attacks, precisely because they sacrifice their lives to carry them out. A British Muslim of Bengali origin argued:

> *Would you give your life away for anything? [. . .] No one would. I love my life. I don't want to die [. . .]. Then why on earth would one sane man blow himself up? [. . .] So we need to understand why. What is [it] that he's being affected by so much that he feels that there is no point living? He feels [. . .] in a state of destitution that he feels [. . .], "there is no point in me living, let me blow myself up" [. . .]. Maybe collective experience as well as individual experience [. . .]. Maybe they've seen their people being raped in front of them.* (Tarak, London)

Tarak did not consider the possibility that those who commit suicide attacks are indeed wrong and insane. He argued on the assumption that suicide bombers act rationally for important reasons, and he searched for possible and legitimate rationales, including collective or individual experiences such as seeing "their people being raped."

The topos of "Jews killing children" was often used in this context to stress the suffering of those who commit suicide attacks and to justify their actions. A respondent of Maghrebian background, for example, said, "*There are children dying [. . .] and then in turn there are attacks as a response to that*" (Assim, Paris). An interviewee of Turkish origin tried to put himself in the position of a suicide bomber and found that he would do the same if his children or his brother were murdered, suggesting that this is what happens to suicide bombers: "*What Palestinians, what the suicide bombers are doing, that's for sure, for me, in my opinion they are right to do that, because if they kill my little brother, or my son [. . .], I would do the same thing, that's why*" (Memduh, Berlin). Suicide attacks are seen as a legitimate form of revenge. "*They want revenge, that's normal*" (Omar, Paris). Others emphasized the allegedly terrible situation of suicide bombers' family or their countrymen as a driving factor behind the execution of these atrocities. In this context, Palestinians were portrayed as imprisoned, surrounded, and controlled by Israel without any hope of escape or prospects for a better life.

The argument that suicide attacks are a legitimate form of fighting in the Palestinian struggle often goes along with the argument that Palestinians lack other weapons and military equipment: "*Explosive belt, yeah, well [. . .]. They defend themselves any way they can*" (Hamza, Paris); "*I just think suicide bombing, even though it's wrong, they haven't got the rockets and the jet planes to fight a proper war, so that's their way of fighting the war, innit?*" (Aba, London).

A few participants see suicide attacks as an effective means of killing Jews, including civilians. "*I want a hundred Jews to blow up with me*" (Suleiman, Berlin). Ismail, also of Palestinian origin, argued similarly but added that suicide bombers fight for their country and did not say that he wants to become a suicide bomber himself. The wish to murder Jews matches the respondents' aggressive hatred against "the Jews" they showed in other parts of the interviews.

The vast majority of respondents, however, believe that suicide bombers go to hell, but a few share the ideology that suicide bombers gain their place in paradise by dying in the holy war. Three, two from Berlin and one from Paris, declared that they want to die in such a holy war themselves, believing that they will gain a place in paradise. In the next chapter on rationales with references to the religious identity, I discuss this wish in greater detail.

SEEING THE ISRAELI-PALESTINIAN CONFLICT AS PART OF A WIDER CONFLICT

The conflict between Israel and Palestinians was frequently seen as part of a wider struggle, one between "the Jews" and "the Palestinians," or "the Muslims," or "the Arabs." As shown above, some interviewees even identify with the conflict, commonly through an identification with "the Muslims." But some widen the context further and situate the Israeli-Palestinian conflict as part of an eternal war between "the Muslims," "the Jews," and "the Christians," or as part of a war of "the West" against "the Muslims." Some meld the war in Iraq with the conflict between Israel and the Palestinians, and consequently conflate the United States with Israel. Others note a symbiotic relationship between Israel and the United States in alliance against "the Muslims."

The Israeli-Palestinian conflict is framed as a war between "the Jews" against "the Muslims," as a respondent of Guinean background in France expressed: *"In Israel [. . .] the Jews, they make war against the Muslims"* (Diaba, Paris). A British Muslim shared this perception and argued that "we Muslims" fight with the Palestinians for the holy places, a struggle which he sees at the center of the conflict: *"Israel, this is the actual mother land for all the Jewish [. . .]. They wanna take over most of Palestine. That's what they wanna do. But [. . .] they have so many holy places there that we Muslims won't let that happen and this is what the fight is"* (Sabir, London).

A respondent from Paris of Maghrebian background sees Israel as part of the Arabs' and Muslims' conflict with "the West," and believes that all problems in Arab countries have been caused by Israel: *"It's all been planned [. . .] by the West, by America, because they knew, look at all of the problems that are happening in the Arab countries are because of them, because of Israel. Israel is on that side"* (Hichem, Paris). Others frame the Israeli-Palestinian conflict in the context of even more extensive religious wars allegedly prophesied in the Qur'an, or as part of longer conflict between Muslims and Jews over land far larger than "Palestine" and dating back to the time of Muhammad. A Berlin respondent of Turkish origin combines the "historical" framing of the Israeli-Palestinian conflict with the idea that Islam, Christianity, and Judaism are in an eternal fight for world primacy.

Interviewer: Do you know anything about the Middle East conflict, about the conflict between Israel and Palestine?

Ümit: This conflict has been going on for I don't know how many hundreds of years [. . .]. For us in Islam, they say that we are going to conquer the

> *world and then at some point the world is going to end, for the Christians it's certainly the same, they're going to conquer the world and for the Jews it's also exactly the same, you have to conquer the world. That's why there's this conflict between religions, and why there always will be one.*

Ümit's conspiracy theories about the terrorist attacks of September 11, 2001, are also part of this topos: it all makes sense as a plot to stage a war against Muslims. Hence, he does not distinguish between Palestinian and Afghan victims and accused the interviewer as being part of the Western world: "*You only make war against Muslims, just ordinary Muslims; you have seen on TV: Palestinian or Afghan or I don't know, with his children, defenseless, unprotected.*"

These examples demonstrate how the conflict between Israel and Palestinians is often perceived, in all three countries, as a particular instance of a far greater conflict. A general enmity between Muslims and Jews is the most common form for this larger framing.

CONCLUSIONS

Antisemitic attitudes with reference to Israel are often based on a conflation or equation of Israelis with Jews and on a Manichean view of the Middle East conflict. The attitudes can serve as a justification for general hostility against Jews, including German, French, and British Jews. These justifications of hostility can be limited to a brief allusion to the Middle East conflict, with comments such as "because of Palestine" or "because of the wars with Jews," but some interviewees fleshed out their claims by mentioning that Jews allegedly kill children or that "they" have taken away "our" land. The latter is the main argument for delegitimization of the State of Israel. The empirical evidence shows that if young Muslims express, in the context of the Middle East conflict, hostility against "the Jews" they actually mean "the Jews" and not Israelis only. The topos "Jews kill children" adds to the portrayal of an evil Jewish state and, if Israelis and Jews are conflated, of the evilness of Jews, stirring up harsh emotions. The charge that Jews are child-killers is one of the main justifications of openly admitted anti-Jewish hatred.

The extent to which interviewees justified the intensity of hostility toward Jews with the Middle Eastern conflict related to their identification with "the Palestinians" and to their ethnic background. In France, some participants of Maghrebian background justified hostility and violence against Jews in their neighborhood with the Middle East conflict. Similarly, in Germany the majority of those with a Palestinian or Lebanese background justified hatred against Jews with the Middle East conflict; some even called for violence against Jews. On the other hand, those of Turkish background did not allude to the Middle East conflict to justify hatred against Jews in their neighborhood. Interviewees of South Asian background from Britain who justify hostility toward Jews in Britain with the Middle Eastern conflict are also less radical and less aggressive in their hostility against British Jews.

Arab identity is an important additional factor that can increase hostility against European Jews by the use of justifications related to the Israeli-Palestinian conflict. This matter is discussed in more detail in the next chapter, under the section about patterns of argumentation with reference to religious or ethnic identity.

SEVEN

Antisemitism Related to Islam or Religious or Ethnic Identity

THE MAJORITY OF INTERVIEWEES ACCOUNTED FOR THEIR animosity against Jews as a function of their religious and/or ethnic identity. Often, they did so indirectly by stating that, generally, Muslims or people of their own ethnic background dislike or hate Jews. In most cases, respondents included themselves as part of this community; only exceptionally did they distance themselves from such a generalizing assumption. The perception of general animosity between Jews and interviewees' (religious or ethnic) communities was also used directly as an explanation or justification for personal negative views of Jews. As we have seen, this rationale is certainly not the only one, but, due to its implications regarding the very identity of these individuals, it is surely an important one.

Some participants argued on the basis of both their religious and ethnic identities for a "natural" enmity toward Jews: *"Really, we, the Arabs, um, the Muslims and the Jews we don't understand each other"* (Azhar, Paris). In this quote Azhar adopted the perception of general animosity against Jews, but he was not quite sure whether this enmity was rooted in his Arab or Muslim identity. Religious and ethnic identities were often blurred. When interviewees spoke about "us" with reference to their community, it was often unclear whether they were referring to their religion or ethnicity. This ambiguity was confirmed in another qualitative study on antisemitism among young Muslims in Berlin.[1]

However, the various arguments that different participants offer usually can be distinguished. I start with the presentation of arguments and justifications for the dislike of Jews with reference to Islam or Muslim identity. Religious identity was used more often than ethnic identity to justify hostility against Jews, followed by certain ethnic identities, particularly Arab, but also other specific ethnic identities, such as Algerian, Egyptian, Pakistani, Bangladeshi, or Maghrebian.

Justifications of hostility toward Jews with reference to Islam, Muslim identity, or ethnic background were sometimes linked to other "classic" stereotypes, such as those identifying Jews as rich and influential, or to resentments pertaining to the Middle Eastern conflict, but they cannot be reduced to perceptions of the conflict. Interestingly, a number of statements directly contradicted the thesis that hostile attitudes toward Jews among Muslims are rooted in the Israeli-Palestinian conflict. One interviewee from Berlin expressed this view in the most straightforward way:

> *Interviewer: And then you'd rather say that because of the [Middle East] conflict you also have a problem with Israelis?*
> *Ümit: No, not because of them. As a Muslim you have problems, not with Israelis, [but] with Jews.*

Ümit believes that Muslim identity necessarily leads to hostility against Jews, and explicitly rejected the argument that such hostility derives from the Middle East conflict. The generalizing and essentializing assumption of enmity, expressed in this statement, denies that there are different views among individuals within the community and different interpretations of Islam; it portrays Muslims as a homogeneous category with regard to attitudes toward Jews.[2]

THE ROLE OF ISLAM AND MUSLIM IDENTITY IN ANTI-JEWISH ARGUMENTATIONS

Religious rationales were intertwined with argumentations based on Muslim identity. In young Muslims' discussions about an alleged "interdiction" against befriending or marrying Jews, for example, religious reasons and pressure from other Muslims were mixed. Interviewees' references to a long history of animosity between Muslims and Jews can be related to the historical perspectives of conflicts between the two groups or to an interpretation of Islamic scriptures that highlights the conflicts between Muhammad and Jewish tribes. Direct references to the Qur'an or to the belief that suicide bombers go to paradise for killing Jews, on the other hand, are rooted in certain interpretations of Islam. References to the Qur'an have particularly strong authority as the Qur'an is regarded as the word of Allah, dictated to the prophet Muhammad, and thus seen by numerous interviewees as reflecting divine truth: *"I'm Muslim, I believe in everything that is written in the Qur'an"* (Housni, Paris).

The level of animosity against Jews with reference to Islam or Muslim identity varied. This variation in hostility also held true for those who saw similarities between Judaism and Islam or who viewed Muslims and Jews as "cousins." One interviewee said adamantly, *"Muslims are supposed to be the Jewish's worst enemies"* (Sabir, London). He saw Muslims and Jews in a global war.

Other interviewees assumed the existence of a mutual antipathy. One, for instance, showed sympathy for a Muslim police officer who did not want to protect the Israeli embassy in London[3] and justified his action by saying: *"It's known Muslims and Jewish people don't really get along [. . .]. I think it's because of religion"* (Kajal, London). However, the assumption of a general enmity between Jews and Muslims was widespread. It was expressed explicitly or implicitly and in passing, and even in seemingly unrelated contexts such as the Holocaust. One respondent in Germany wondered, in a similar vein to a couple of interviewees from France and Britain, why Hitler killed Jews when he was not Muslim:

> *Actually, I don't know, you shouldn't be happy about it, I don't know, what Hitler's objective was, I don't know that either . . . so I don't have any idea. And he wasn't a Muslim, but he killed the Jews, it's also strange.* (Beyar, Berlin)

This quote shows that Beyar assumes that there is a murderous hatred among Muslims against Jews, from which he is not ready to distance himself. He did not explain this underlying assumption but wondered why non-Muslims might hate and kill Jews, implying that it was not strange but rather normal for Muslims to kill Jews. Beyar's conviction that a non-Muslim's desire to kill Jews is strange obscured his ability to make sense of the Holocaust. He is aware of the stigma against celebrating the Holocaust, but he seems to regard the Holocaust with some satisfaction, which he relates indirectly to his Muslim identity. He is conflicted about his feelings of hatred against Jews as an expression of his Muslim identity, on the one hand, and the moral taboo against expressing happiness over the murder of six million Jews, on the other.

Whereas many participants accept and adopt the assumption that "the Muslims" dislike Jews, their justifications were often vague.

In the following section, I delineate the interviewees' arguments beginning with references to Islamic history at the time of the prophet Muhammad. Interviewees accuse Jews of betraying Muhammad and rejecting him and his message. I then demonstrate how respondents root assumptions of an eternal and predestined war between Muslims and Jews in that time. Current conflicts are taken as evidence of a predestined enmity between "the Muslims" and "the Jews." Most prominently, the Middle East conflict serves this purpose. The wars in Iraq and Afghanistan are seen as evidence of a war against "the Muslims," which is framed as a war between religions. In this notion of a religious war, Jews and Christians are seen as global enemies. I discuss two specific topoi within the notion of a war between Muslims and Jews: the perception that Jews drive Muslims from their territories and holy places and the belief that those who die in the war against Jews go to paradise. Both beliefs were cited to justify hostility toward Jews as a general group. Other patterns of argumentation with reference to Islam include direct references to God's perception of the Jews, who allegedly condemns them for their materialistic and life-affirming lifestyle. Interestingly, God was also said to have given Jews money, power, and intelligence. However, some considered it a "sin" to have an intimate relationship with a Jew. Finally, I present rationales for rejecting the widespread assumption that Muslims and Jews are enemies.

Historical Perspectives on Hostility between Muslims and Jews

Participants often referred to "Islamic history" or conflicts between Muhammad and his adherents, on the one side, and Jewish tribes, on the other, to illustrate and justify enmity against Jews. Muslims' hostilities against Jews today were framed as revenge against Jews for things "they" did in the past or as part of an ongoing historical struggle with the Jews. However, references to Islamic history were usually vague. The following French interviewee's argument is a good example. He was not sure what particular kind of mischief Jews made, but he was adamant that "the Jews" are to blame, that what they did is unforgivable, and that their actions resulted in eternal animosity between Muslims and Jews:

> *Sabri: We have a history with them [. . .], I don't know that much about this kind of thing, but, a long time ago, I think that they were the ones who betrayed the prophet [. . .]. After that, the Muslims, there's a story like that. Yeah, that's one thing, it's something that makes it worth going to war with them.*
> *Interviewer: Even now?*
> *Sabri: No, not war, but to . . . well, we don't talk to them [. . .]. It's not a war between the Arabs and the Jews, I don't know . . . it's about religion [. . .]. They did something that wasn't good, and it's unpardonable [. . .]. It's weird, you can't, everyone is obsessed about it [. . .]. They have to change. It's the Jews who did something bad [. . .]. It's too late. It was at the beginning, [and] given the way they are . . .*

Sabri emphasized that the enmity was related to religion and mentioned an alleged betrayal of Muhammad by "the Jews," but he was uncertain about this event. Even so, he insisted that whatever Jews did at the time is unforgivable and still has a strong impact today. However, he hesitated to endorse a war against Jews and eventually deemed it more appropriate not to talk to them. For a moment he considered that the relation between Jews and Muslims today might improve if "the Jews" changed, but he concluded that it is too late for change.

A British Asian participant provided more background to the belief that hostility toward Jews is rooted in Islamic history:

> *Back in those days when prophet, sallalahu 'alayhi wa salam,[4] was alive and he tried to spread Islam [. . .], the other religions they didn't want him to spread it [. . .]. That was the Jewish [religion]. Muhammad, sallalahu 'alayhi wa salam, he tried to spread it and they tried to kill him [. . .], the enemies. So in order to defend ourselves we do Jihad [. . .]. They try to take back the country that belonged to us. And that's what he did, Jihad, so he fought back what belonged to us. And just lived the life which we want like, everyone wants [. . .]. Obviously if you can see that Jewish [people] are the rich ones around nowadays, they are the one[s] who control everything [. . .]. They're the ones who're controlling the country and the world right now [. . .]. Obviously Islam and Jews we have a conflict with each other. We're enemies [. . .]. Still today they want their revenge, they want to be in control. They want to destroy it [. . .]. They believe that Arabia was their country but obviously it belonged to us Muslims and when we took it from them they . . . they've been trying to get it back ever since [. . .]. Not just all Arabia, basically the whole Middle East. The whole main Islamic headquarters. Basically the bits are Arabia, Iraq, Palestine . . . as you can*

> *see Israel, right now are trying to take over Palestine. They're trying to say it's their country, when as you can see in the history clearly Palestine is their own country.* (Nirmal, London)

Nirmal identified those who tried to kill Muhammad as Jewish and as "the enemies." His concept of Jihad included the defense against these enemies who are Jewish and all those who threaten Islam or hinder its spread. He also portrayed Jews as those who hinder "everyone" and live "the life which we want." Antisemitic stereotypes of Jews as rich and controllers of the world served to help him maintain that Jews are still a threat. Nirmal transferred the "defense" against Jewish tribes at the time of Muhammad to the present day and included himself in this fight, saying that "we are enemies," and the fights are about territories that "belonged to us Muslims." He believes that Jews carry on the conflict between Jewish tribes and Muhammad and now want "revenge" for their alleged loss of "Arabia" centuries ago, hoping to take control of "Arabia, Iraq, Palestine." This is the context in which he embedded the Israeli-Palestinian conflict. Nirmal's rhetoric implies a perception of Jews and Muslims as unitary categories over space and time.

Others applied similar rationales more directly to contemporary wars "against Jews," some with reference to the Qur'an. One respondent praised Hezbollah for being in the tradition of fighting the infidels as prescribed in the Islamic holy book:

> *That's just how it is, the Hezbollah, they're actually really the only, [. . .] who, our prophets, that's what it says in the Qur'an, who are continuing our centuries old prophets' fight against non-believers [. . .]. That's just how it is, there are too few of them.* (Ahmed, Berlin)

Betrayal of Muhammad as Source of Hatred against Jews

Interviewees from all three cities accuse Jews of betraying the prophet. Some base their assumption that "the Jews" betrayed Muhammad or tried to kill him on the Qur'an. Omar from Paris, for instance, recalled a story, allegedly from the Qur'an, in which Muhammad was saved by a spider's web from his detractors, who he suggested were Jewish and wanted to murder the prophet.[5] But only one interviewee stated that "the Jews" actually succeeded in killing the prophet. He put this in context with the rejection of the prophet Muhammad and his message by "the Jews."

God sent something for everybody in order to explain something to everybody, it wasn't so that they'd get into a war with each other [. . .]. In the Qur'an, it's written that those people [the Jews], they killed the prophet. (Hichem, Paris)

His conviction that the Qur'an states that Jews killed Muhammad obviously contradicts the belief that every word of the Qur'an came through Muhammad as a messenger, since the prophet would have to have been alive to convey his message. Stressing that God sent a message to all people that they should not be at war with each other suggests that Hichem blames the Jews, who allegedly rejected God's message, for the hostility between Muslims and Jews precisely because they do not accept Muhammad as God's messenger. Further, Hichem does not distinguish between Jews at the time of Muhammad and Jews today. When he said that the Qur'an reads that "these people" killed the prophet, he was referring to Jews in general, including those living today in North Africa, Israel, and France.

Jews' Rejection of Muhammad and Allah's Condemnation of Jews as an Argument for Hatred against Jews Today

The accusation that Jews reject God's messenger and are condemned by God was a recurrent topos among our interviewees in all three cities. Consider these examples:

Muslims are supposed to be the Jew's worst enemies [. . .]. It's from religion as well as history, because, the way it goes, the Jews and the Muslim, once upon a time we all started together, we were all the same group. But as it came along, Jewish [people] stopped on a level when one prophet came along and Muhammad, Sallalahu 'alayhi wa salam, came along as the messenger of Allah and they did not follow him, they stopped there [. . .]. Same goes for Christianity [. . .]. The reason bein' enemies, they are changing, because Islam came along and it forbidded so many things due to the time. For example, back in the years, you were allowed to drink [. . .], but as Islam came along it started pointing out: drinking is not good. The reason bein' because once you get drunk you can rape your own mother because you don't know what's happening. You go senseless and that's not right. And that's how these regulations came along that we abided by and they have stopped [. . .]. This is where the conflicts come along. (Sabir, London)

Sabir, of South Asian background, wants Muslims to be the Jews' worst enemies and believes that a holy war against Jews is approaching. He bases this hostility on history and religion, portraying Jews and

Muslims as a group who split because Jews, as well as Christians, did not follow the prophet Muhammad. He also focused on the prohibition of alcohol in Islam and believes that this is another factor involved in Muslims' hostility toward Jews (and Christians). Not abiding by the prohibition of alcohol becomes immoral and evil in Sabir's depiction, so much so that he mentioned raping one's own mother as a possible result of drunkenness. Conflicts with Jews are, according to this rationale, a logical consequence and a moral obligation rooted in religious differences. The same logic applies to Christians, as he also noted, though his focus was on Jews.

A French interviewee explained that his negative perception of Jews is based on their rejection of Muhammad as God's messenger. He views them not for what they do or "show" but associates them with "the Jew in history," in the singular form, at the time of the prophet Muhammad:

> *We, when we say Jew actually, in a way, it's because they showed us, because you know, that normally, the Jew in history, during the time of the prophet, they were the people who were preferred by God. I swear, they were better than us Arabs [. . .] and since the prophet, when he was born, they didn't actually want to acknowledge that, you know, they didn't care about the prophet [. . .]. And so that's why . . . , but, apart from that, there are Jews that are good.* (Jabar, Paris)

Jabar conflates Jews of the past and present to "the Jew." He believed that Jews were once a people preferred by God until they rejected his prophet. This is why he, and according to him Muslims in general, see Jews in a negative light, though he pointed out that there are some good Jews, implying that the others are not.

Another aspect of hatred of Jews with reference to Islam was articulated by Kaba, of Guinean origin. He too accuses Jews of rejecting Muhammad as God's messenger, but he believes that they did so because Muhammad was, in contrast to previous prophets, not Jewish but Arab; he thereby accuses Jews of being prejudiced or racist. A respondent in Germany of Turkish origin concluded that Muslims dislike Jews because they are cursed by God: "*In general Muslims have a problem with the Jews. Because they have been condemned by God*" (Ümit, Berlin).

Allusions of Jews being on the side of the devil can be interpreted as part of the perception that Jews are condemned by God. But such allusions were only made in indirect and superstitious ways, for example, by rumors of a "haunted" local synagogue or by allusions that Freemasons are devil worshippers and somehow related to Jews.

Another form of the accusation against Jews that they rejected Muhammad and God's message is that their holy scripture was falsified. "*Torah [. . .]. This isn't good. The Qur'an stayed [. . .] as it was, nobody ever changed it – and the Thora [sic] – there were some who took it*" (Mohamed, Paris). Similar accusations that the Torah and the Bible are falsifications of the Qur'an or of other "original" versions of the Holy Scripture were made in all three countries. The contradiction between the religious assumption that the Qur'an is the only valid and true divine scripture and the belief that it is the same God who gave Jews, Christians, and Muslims their scripture is resolved by the accusation that Jews and Christians have falsified their scriptures.[6]

Assumptions of a Predetermined War against Jews

The perception of hostility or even war between Muslims and Jews is sometimes based on references to the Qur'an, which allegedly predicts religious wars on a global scale between Muslims, Jews, and Christians. Two British interviewees, who did not know each other, expressed this in almost the same words: "*In the Qur'an it says there will be a holy war. One solid war that will end the world*" (Sabir, London); "*It's written on the Qur'an and it says there's a holy war coming now*" (Agantuk, London). Both are sure that Islam will be victorious. Agantuk is convinced that tsunamis, tall buildings, and Muslim girls in mini-skirts are signs of an approaching apocalypse and a holy war at the end of time, both of which are predicted in the Qur'an. He combined his belief of a war between Muslims and Jews with the accusation that President George W. Bush wanted to kill all Muslims, in cooperation with Jews, and with an apocalyptic vision of a holy war "wiping out" England:

> *In our religion, it's written in the Qur'an and it says there's a holy war coming now. They wanna kill all the Muslim people, they're doing it in [front of] the TV. But after that the big barriers are gonna open, and they're going come in. They [the Muslims] are going to take, wipe out England.* (Agantuk, London)

The perception of a general war between Muslims and Jews (and Christians) is often rooted in the belief that a preordained war of religions will occur as the end of time approaches. Sabir sees a "Jewish plan" at work to weaken the Muslims in this war by eliminating the powerful Saddam Hussein, who would have fought on the Muslims' side. A respondent from Berlin believes that Muslims, Christians, and Jews all strive for dominance.

> *This conflict has been going on for; I don't know how many hundreds of years [. . .]. It will never change [. . .]. In our Islam it is said that we will conquer the world and after that at some point it will be the end of the world. For the Christians it is surely the same, they will conquer the world; and for the Jews just the same, you have to conquer the world. Therefore, there are these conflicts between religion and they will always be there.* (Ümit, Berlin)

For Ümit, wars among Muslims, Christians, and Jews are inevitable. Based on his understanding that all three religions are allegedly striving for world power, this religious conflict is eternal and will remain until the end of the world.

The Israeli-Palestinian Conflict as Evidence of Hostility between Muslims and Jews

The perception of the Israeli-Palestinian conflict in religious terms, as a conflict between Muslims and Jews, is common in all three countries and is often generalized as a war between "the Jews" and "the Muslims." Framing the Middle Eastern conflict as a conflict between these two religious groups enforces the perception of a more general war between Muslims and Jews: "*In Israel [. . .] the Jews they make war against the Muslims*" (Diaba, Paris)[7]; "It's obvious that they ['the Jews'] want to kill all the Muslims" (Khalil, Paris). The conflict can be seen as an attack against Islam, or, as a British Muslim put it: "*Their motives are [. . .] ultimately, the denunciation of Islam*" (Rahim, London), referring in that case to Freemasonry which he equated with Zionism. His view that the Israeli national ideology allegedly targets Islam and the equation of Jewishness with Freemasonry, a code word for a global conspiracy, demonstrate that, in his view, the conflict is not confined to the Middle East.

Interviewees identify themselves as Muslims when they speak about Muslim-Jewish hostility. If they have a perception of a Muslim-Jewish conflict, most feel involved in one way or another. Consider the example of a Turkish interviewee from Berlin. After he told the interviewer about his and his family's religious practices, he was asked whether he thought Muslims and Jews could live together peacefully. He responded:

> *I don't think so. They will always have war [. . .]. The Jews are just starting it. They kill small Muslim children, they do everything, they rape small children, women, even grannies. Therefore, I don't believe that we will ever be at peace with them.* (Memduh, Berlin)

He thinks that "they" will be at war forever because "the Jews" allegedly started the war and are thus responsible for terrible atrocities against Muslim civilians, probably referring to the Middle East conflict. He then switched to "we" when predicting that Muslims will never be at peace with Jews.

In the interviewees' minds, the Israeli-Palestinian conflict serves as evidence for the view that Muslims and Jews are enemies or at war with each other. Muslims are said to hate "the Jews" because "they" fight Muslims in Palestine. This generalization can hardly be expressed more succinctly than with the statement of a French interviewee of Algerian descent: "*All the Muslims, they hate the Jews because the Jews have killed Muslims*" (Bilal, Paris).

The acceptance of the rationale that Muslims are hostile to Jews because of the Middle East conflict implies both the generalization of Israelis as "the Jews" and an identification of "the Muslims" with "the Palestinians." The latter is decisive for interviewees' choosing sides; for many, it then appears to be "natural" that Muslims in Europe take part in a conflict in another part of the world because of common religious identification with one of the peoples fighting there.

The perception that there is a war between Muslims and Jews can also be transferred to views on Jews living in the neighborhood. They are suspected of supporting this war, for instance, by sending money to Israel or, as Ramzi from Berlin suggested, even by allegedly applauding the killing of Muslim babies in the Middle East conflict.

Wars "against Muslims" as Evidence of Hostility between Muslims and Jews

In addition to the Israeli-Palestinian conflict, wars in Iraq and Afghanistan are also framed as wars against Muslims; some believe that Jews are somehow responsible or involved in these wars. Furthermore, perceptions of the Middle East conflict, the Iraq war, and the war in Afghanistan are often blurry; these conflicts are seen as examples of a larger conflict between Muslims and non-Muslims, as a war by non-Muslims against the Muslim *Ummah* (community). Uriya Shavit has noticed that the imagined global Muslim nation is attractive for many European Muslims[8] and that mainstream Islamist leaders have successfully canonized theories which depict the West being at war against the Muslims.[9] In Germany and France, 33.4 and 52.5 percent of Muslims, respectively, agree with the statement "The West is out to destroy Islam."[10] It is within this rationale that the wars in Iraq and Afghanistan were also cited as evidence of a war between Muslims and Jews.

A British Muslim who sees Jews and Muslims as enemies explicated this perception of an alleged war against the *Ummah*. Referring to the Iraq war he remarked:

> *The reason why it concerns us Muslims is because in Islam we believe that we should be one. It's like we call it the Ummah, it means one nation for Muslims. So that's why. So because they're attacking the Muslims [. . .]. It's like we don't care what country you're from, what color, if you're a Muslim, you're a Muslim. And if someone are [sic] messing with you then, it concerns us.* (Nirmal, London)

Asked specifically why he aligns himself with Palestinians, Nirmal answered: "*Obviously as a Muslim I will defend Islam but obviously I can see here that the Muslims are not wrong.*" To side with the Palestinians is, in his eyes, a defense of Islam. He sees Palestinians foremost as members of the Muslim nation and thus labels them as Muslims rather than Palestinians. Ultimately, he believes, the Middle Eastern conflict and the enmity between Muslims and Jews are only one part of the worldwide conflict between Muslims and non-Muslims.

Another interviewee's enthusiastic wish to participate in the war against "the Jews" in Iraq or in "Palestine" is also telling:

> *If someone asked me to go to Iraq tomorrow to fight, me, I'd go [. . .]. Or to Palestine. Wherever there's war [. . .] against the Jews, to help the, my br[others], the Muslims.* (Omar, Paris)

It is striking that his first aim is to participate in the war against "the Jews" and then to help his "Muslim brothers," wherever they need help. He not only sees the war in Iraq as part of the worldwide struggle between Jews and Muslims, but also includes himself in it to the point that he wants to fight with his "Muslim brothers" against the Jews.

But, as some of the examples above have shown, interviewees include themselves to different degrees as Muslims in the alleged war between Muslims and Jews. A personal declaration to be ready to fight is exceptional, however.

The Topos of Jews Dispelling Muslims from Their Territories and Holy Places

The perception that "the Jews" took over or threaten "Muslim territories," including holy places, is widespread: some cited this directly as a reason for or an example of the alleged general hostility between "the Muslims" and "the Jews." This topos was often alluded to but not restricted to the Middle East conflict, and was mostly used by participants from London; it was less relevant in the other cities.

For one young Muslim from London, the burning of the Al Aqsa Mosque[11] and other mosques around the world for which he makes Jews responsible is one of the three main reasons (along with the Jews' character and their killing of Muslims) for the alleged general hostility among Muslims against Jews:

> *We always have that thing in our mentality that Jewish people are our enemy. We don't see him as an enemy, personally, but . . . the whole community, the whole religion is our enemy because they've done a lot of badness to our religion [. . .]. They're very unfair people and they've killed a lot of Muslims for no reason, they took our land away, you know, they burned Al Aqsa Mosque, that was ours, that's our holy sacred place, like before Mecca, we used to actually pray that way. That was years ago, that was centuries and centuries ago. And basically they burned mosques and they hit a lot of Muslim people around the world, and . . . them people are very unfair, to be honest with you. So we don't like them. That's the bottom line.* (Baru's friend, London)

Similarly, two interviewees, both British Asian, view Muslim animosity toward Jews as being rooted in hatred against Israel and also against America, accusing "the Jews" of taking away such Islamic holy places as the Dome of the Rock. One explained where he thinks the hatred against Jews comes from: "*It's a religion matter. You know the temple, that's old. That's like thousands of years old*" (Bashkar, London). Even more adamant is another respondent, who is outraged that "*they [the Jews] are trying to say that Al Aqsa, one of the main mosques of Islam, it belongs to them.*" He also believes that Jews want to take the "*whole Middle East, the whole main Islamic headquarters*" (Nirmal, London), and explicitly cited both to be reasons why Jews and Muslims are enemies.

By contrast, a respondent from France, Omar, cited the conflict over the Temple Mount when he tried to describe the nature of the conflict between "the Muslims" and "the Jews," but the only detail he remembered was that Jews pray on one side and Muslims on the other.

The Belief That Those Who Die Killing Jews Go to Paradise

The belief that suicide bombers or warriors who kill Jews go to paradise is bound to the perception of a (holy) war between Muslims and Jews. This view, the most radical argument for an approval of suicide bombings,[12] is shaped by religious beliefs.

This belief is shared by only a few interviewees. But three respondents from different countries and with different ethnic backgrounds not only believe that those who die in the fight against the Jews go to paradise, but also stated that they want to do so themselves. Islam is important to them, even if they are not particularly religious in practice. A respondent of Moroccan background from Paris said that if he were asked to fight in the war of "Muslims against the Jews" in "Iraq or in Palestine," he would go tomorrow. He is convinced that, "*if I take a bullet and die [. . .] during the war, against them, normally, I'd go to paradise*" and referred to the Qur'an when he said, "*When there is war you have the right to kill*" (Omar, Paris).

A German interviewee of Lebanese origin, Bashir, and a German interviewee of Palestinian origin, Suleiman, stated that they want to become suicide bombers themselves. This is what the latter revealed in the interview:

Suleiman: If someone told me "do it," I do it. I would do it. But only, not so that one dies. I want a hundred Jews to go up with me in the air. I would do it for that.
Interviewer: Don't you like to live?
Suleiman: I would have a life that's a thousand times better in paradise, a much better one, you can't even compare it to here.

This excerpt indicates that the belief that suicide bombers go to paradise has a radicalizing effect. Suleiman hates Jews, as he said repeatedly, and declared that he wants to kill them, particularly Israeli Jews. With this rationale, suicide bombing becomes an attractive option, because the afterlife in paradise is far better than life on earth.

All three interviewees who stated that they wanted to die in the fight against the Jews and believe that they would go to paradise hold deeply antisemitic views and do not differentiate between Israelis and Jews. All three justified threats or violence against Jews in their neighborhood. Declarations of the wish to fight and die in the war against Jews are an approval and glorification of suicide bombings, even if their intent to actually engage in that war is low. Such declarations are driven by Jew hatred and radicalized by perceptions of Islam that value "martyrdom" and a holy war against the Jews.

Others were less explicit but still justified suicide attacks or a war against Jews with religious convictions and might also wish to take part in it. A young Muslim from Berlin of Turkish Kurdish background, for instance, believes that there is a general animosity between Muslims and Jews. He justified suicide attacks in general, not only against Jews, as a legitimate means to defend Islam. He believes that suicide attacks are not a "sin" under certain circumstances and would engage in them for revenge. He gave two examples of legitimate situations that would call for revenge in the form of suicide attacks: the killing or violation of family members by soldiers, and the denigration of Islam, such as in the cartoons of Muhammad in Denmark in 2005. Referring to suicide bombers, he argued:

> *If the same thing happened to me, I would do the same thing. I'm not afraid of anything at all, well, other than of God. I can't stand by while people destroy our faith, our honor, we have honor you know [. . .]. We have to protect our families, our faith, that is honor. When people just, like in Denmark, when they make those caricatures and stuff of our prophets, we think that's shit. And then we have to defend our faith.* (Beyar, Berlin)

Fear of God and the concept of honor, which are more important to him than his own life, play an important role in his rationale for suicide attacks.

Most participants, however, reject suicide bombings, and some clearly denounced them as terrorist acts resulting from a distorted interpretation of Islam. The strongest condemnation of the idea that suicide attacks guarantee a place in paradise came from a seventeen-year-old British man of South Asian origin, who commented on the terrorist attacks of September 11, 2001, in the United States and July 7, 2005, in London:

> *I am a Muslim and I tell you, in Islam if you do that then you will go to hell straight away and you will never ever be able to come to paradise [. . .]. They think that by doing that they think they can go to paradise but they must be on drugs or something, because that is a really silly thing to do right, is killing yourself as well as killing other people. And in my religion you are not allowed to kill anyone. If you kill someone then you are gonna have to pay for it after you die.* (Naresh, London)

Naresh argued both in religious and moral terms against suicide attacks. For him, life is most valuable, a value judgment he also demonstrated on other issues such as crime.

Jews Love Material Things in This World Too Much

Some interviewees accused Jews of materialism and related this to their perception of religion, though often indirectly. While this is also a topos of modern (secularized) antisemitism – Jews have often been accused of being too materialistic – interviewees argued in a religious way. Two French friends consider the supposedly materialistic lifestyle of Jews as evil. "*The Jews they will go to hell*" (Mohamed, Paris), said one, while the other explained: "*The Jews' paradise is on Earth, haven't you seen, they all have nice cars*" (Assim, Paris). Another interviewee in France framed this stereotype with his perception of Islam and the Middle Eastern conflict:

> *Israel wants to take everything [. . .]. They want to take all the, you know, I mean, between Iran, Jordan . . . what's it called, Palestine [. . .], all the neighboring countries, it wanted to finally put itself at the top. Because, they, they want material things too much, money [. . .]. Even the religion explains it, they say that those people, they think about their life, because we, we are always thinking [. . .] that there's another life after death [. . .]. They like their lives today, because they are doing well today [. . .]. Because, it's written in their book.* (Hichem, Paris)

Hichem argued that the Middle East conflict is rooted in religion, because the Jews' alleged materialism makes them want to conquer the

Middle East. He explained that Jews are too materialistic because, in contrast to Muslims, they do not think about the hereafter. This is because they lead a happy life and live according to the Torah, which he regards as a falsification of the Qur'an. Judaism thus serves as the antithesis of Islam.

God Allegedly Gave the Jews Money and Power

Antisemitic perceptions of Jews with reference to Islam are not always negative. Some participants believe that God gave the Jews the gift of power, money, and intelligence, thereby linking "classic" antisemitic stereotypes to Islam. Two friends of Guinean origin in Paris are convinced that God gave the Jews these three gifts, even though they rejected the prophet Muhammad.

Kaba: In Islam, the technology, these things, everything, it's invented by the Jews [. . .].
Interviewer: Don't you think that by birth, we are all born the same [. . .]?
Saïdou: No, it's different. The mentality is different. The mentality is [. . .] there are people who are born with the mentality.
Kaba: The Jew is – it's a gift he has given, it's God. And it's God who gave them the power. They have the money. They are clever. Maybe it's them who dominate all what is done here, all what is created [. . .], all that, it comes from them [. . .]; this can be found even in our religion [. . .]; in the Islamic religion [. . .]. The Qur'an speaks of those Jews.

Saïdou believes that Jews possessed these particular traits by birth, and Kaba founds these beliefs and antisemitic stereotypes on Islam and the Qur'an. The belief that God gave Jews money and power reinforces "classic" antisemitic stereotypes. A British Asian interviewee who said that it's "*religious issues we've got against Jewish people [. . .]. We still hate them, but we're not supposed to go and kill them*" (Baru, London), was asked about the source of his assumption of general hostility among Muslims against Jews.

Interviewer: But you said that there is some hate from Muslims against Jews. Where do you know that from?
Baru: Well, it was told, in the Qur'an, my dad told me [. . .]. Every stuff what is written is in the Qur'an, whatever's gonna happen it's written there. That's why . . . it's like some people know, older people know everything what's gonna

> *happen. Even it says how the world will end. It says everything [. . .]. I just heard it from my father [. . .], Jewish people they're more, like, they're higher than us, they've got more money [. . .]. It is true, 'coz in the Qur'an it was written that God gave them everything [. . .]. They still got everything [. . .]. They've got big, big businesses, mainly whatever it is, McDonald's, Coke, things like that, it's the Jewish people [who] own it.* (Baru, London)

Baru bases Muslims' hatred of Jews and his "classic" antisemitic stereotypes on what he believes is stated in the Qur'an. Such references have a strong authority because the Qur'an is generally seen as the direct word of God. Baru is convinced that "whatever's gonna happen" is written there and is therefore the truth. He explicitly says that what is supposedly written in the Qur'an about Jews being given "everything" by God is still true today, and he cites alleged Jewish ownership of major corporations as evidence. It is worth noting that the Qur'an authority is enhanced by the authority of his father who, he said, told him what the Qur'an says about Jews as part of his religious education.

A "Sin" to Associate with Jews

A number of interviewees stated that they do not want to have anything to do with Jews and related this aversion directly to Islam or their Muslim identity, especially but not exclusively when asked if they would mind having a Jewish girlfriend or marrying a Jewish woman. Of course, a rejection of a Jewish partner is not necessarily antisemitic; it can be the result of valorizing the importance of Muslim education for children, for example. But it can also be rooted in the perception of a general enmity between Muslims and Jews, and it can be seen as a sin to go out with Jews. This was how a Frenchman of Tunisian origin responded when he was asked if he would mind marrying a Tunisian Jew: "*It's a religion, the Jewish, it's a Jew – anyway it is not compatible with the Maghrebians [. . .]. It's a sin to go out with, to marry a Jewish girl in our religion*" (Sabri, Paris). Initially, Sabri was unsure about the reasons why Jews and "the Maghrebians" are allegedly not "compatible." Eventually, he resorted to Islamic doctrine, believing that it is a "sin" to marry a Jew and defined Jews in a religious sense. Other interviewees just said that, as Muslims, they are not "allowed" to marry a Jew or that Islam forbids friendship with Jews:

"I'm sure I can marry a Christian, but not a Jew [. . .]. It's a fact!" (Abhijt, London). Abhijt stressed that this ban is particularly directed against Jews, not against Christians. And a respondent from Berlin said, *"Well, there were Jews earlier too. . . . War with Muslims and stuff. That's why it's forbidden in Islam now to stay friends with Jews"* (Beyar, Berlin).

The perception that Islam forbids marrying a Jewish woman can be enforced by the family, which would try to prevent such a marriage, respondents said. This can go as far as disowning somebody who marries a Jew. A German interviewee of Turkish origin explained and then justified this idea: *"That's how it is with us [. . .]; the Islamic religion is always like that"* (Halil, Berlin). He assumed that his friends felt the same way.

Again, these examples show that Islam, Muslim identity, and the Muslim community often become blurred when they are used as justification for hostility toward Jews. Some believe that close contact with Jews is a "sin" or forbidden in Islam, a perception reinforced by people in their social circles, such as family and friends.

It should be noted that views on hypothetical Jewish neighbors are a different matter. Participants generally value positive neighborly relations, including those with Jews. Asked if they would oppose Jewish neighbors, many highlighted Muslim hospitality or stressed positive relations of Jews and Muslims under Islamic rule, for example, in the Ottoman Empire.[13] The wish to respect (hypothetical) Jewish neighbors was also voiced by some who assume general animosity between Muslims and Jews.

Rejections of the Assumption That Muslims and Jews Are Enemies

Fortunately, the perceptions of hostility between Muslims and Jews are often ambiguous, and a few interviewees showed how they break these assumptions. A German respondent of Turkish Kurdish origin clearly distanced himself: *"I think it's not okay that Muslims fight against Jews because all the religions belong together somehow,"* he said, stressing the common ground of all religions. He also distanced himself from literal interpretations of the Qur'an and criticized suicide bombings in Israel: *"They let them fool themselves by people who allegedly want to defend Islam"* (Çeto, Berlin).

The observation that hostility toward Jews exists among one's own community simply because they are Jews does not necessarily lead to an adoption of this resentment. A German Muslim of Turkish origin, Mehmet, talking about the Middle East conflict, provided an example of this discrepancy:

> *Mehmet: The Muslims cannot accept Jews.*
> *Interviewer: But why not?*
> *Mehmet: Well, I don't know, simply because they are Jews. Well, I believe that it's like this.*
> *Interviewer: Could you accept it, could you accept somebody [Jewish]?*
> *Mehmet: Yes, I could, the main thing is that he should be a human being, he should be good.*

Mehmet considers himself Muslim, but in this context he distanced himself from what he perceives as the opinion among "the Muslims." He wants to evaluate people individually and does not adopt a general opinion of many of his fellow believers. This way of independent thinking is exceptional, however. Another man of Maghrebian background gave more detailed insights into the reasons why he rejects the general assumption of Muslim-Jewish enmity. He explicitly rejects terrorism and the call for the murder of Jews, believing that extremists only give Islam a bad name and that they cannot be warranted with Islam since, he said, "Islam" translates as "peace."[14] He thereby declared that some radical interpretations of Islam are wrong and exhibited generally a perception of Islam that stresses tolerance. However, this man reported negative views of Jews from his elder brother, sister, and his parents, and felt that the perception of mutual hostility between "the Jews" and "the Arabs" or "the Muslims" is dominant in his parents' generation. But this interviewee finds ways of countering these arguments: there are good and bad people in every religion, he argued, and, according to his perception of Islam, God told us to be open to everybody. The most decisive counterargument however, seems to be that "*personally, it's like we, the young people, we are fed up with this conflict. Because of this everybody, we cannot live our lives. For example, we cannot love someone of another religion than our own*" (Samed, Paris). In his case, he blamed the recent split with his Jewish girlfriend on the impact of the perception of an eternal conflict between "the Muslims" or "the Arabs" and "the Jews." He personally has suffered from the widespread assumption of an enmity between Jews and Muslims.[15]

ANIMOSITY TOWARD JEWS JUSTIFIED WITH ETHNIC IDENTITIES

An essentializing concept of ethnic identity, of "us" and "the Jews," is a precondition for a justification of negative views of Jews as part of one's own ethnic identity, and with assumptions of general animosity between one's ethnic community and Jews. Such argumentations ascribe antisemitic attitudes to a hereditary ethnicity, particularly an Arab identity but also others, such as Algerian, Egyptian, Pakistani, Bangladeshi, and Maghrebian, were explicitly used. But justifying enmity against Jews as part of one's ethnic identity was less frequent than doing so as part of one's identification as Muslim.

Arab Identity

It has been argued that anti-Zionism and antisemitism are part and parcel of Arab nationalism or pan-Arabism.[16] Does this ideology of Arab nationalism influence the perception of young Europeans of Arab background of their own (Arab) identities, and thus also their attitudes toward Jews? Many participants of Arab background do believe their Arab identity encompasses negative views of Jews (while others reject such views). This underlying assumption is often uttered in passing, as from an interviewee of Algerian origin: "*In any case, we, the Arabs, we never get along with them [the Jews]*" (Hafid, Paris).

There are two main rationales for a justification of hostility against Jews as part of Arab identity, excluding religious justifications. It is either argued that such hostility is a reaction to the alleged hatred of Jews against Arabs, or the Middle Eastern conflict is used to argue why Arabs allegedly dislike Jews.

"*The Jews hate the Arabs [. . .]. I don't like them. Yes, but they hate us, that's why I don't like them*" (Ali, Paris). This man of Maghrebian background contrasted the "hatred" of Jews with the antipathy of Arabs, presenting the latter as a result of the Jews' hatred of them. A Lebanese participant from Berlin justified and generalized his hatred against Jews more confidently and aggressively: "*The Jew, he hates Arabs and so on, too. That's why we also hate, we really hate Jews very much, we hate Jews the most*" (Abdullah, Berlin). Note that he used "the Jew" in singular form when he said that "the Jew" hates Arabs and "the Jews" in plural when he expressed his hatred against them. This wording is an indication that the abstract perception of hostility between Jews and Muslims translates into hatred against (real) Jews.

Others voiced their assumption of an animosity between Arabs and Jews in milder terms. Sharif, who is of Palestinian origin, refrained from open hatred against Jews but assumed an enmity between them and Arabs when he stated that Arabs would take it as an insult to be labeled "Jew" and, reciprocally, Jews would take it as an insult to be labeled "Arab."

A German participant of Palestinian background put the hatred of "the Arabs" against Jews in a context of their (and his) additional hatred of Americans and British people: "*The Arabs, man, we all hate the Jews, the Americans and the English. Everybody. But not everybody wants to say it in public.*" Asked how he defines a Palestinian, this interviewee answered: "*Yes, somebody who is against Jews, joke, no [laughs]. A Palestinian, yes, an Arab, man. They are strong, the Palestinians, they are not afraid of death. Yes and the, a Palestinian, he wants to die in his country, not here*" (Mousa, Berlin). He initially defined a Palestinian as someone who is against Jews before amending his definition to an image of a strong and fearless Arab who wants to die in his country. Either way, his description of Palestinian ethnic identification is, at least as a spontaneous reaction, connected to hatred against Jews.

A French participant of Algerian origin provided an example of how the assumption that Arabs hate Jews is justified with allusions to the Middle Eastern conflict, explaining how the hatred is directed both against "the Jews" in an abstract way and against Jews in the neighborhood. He made the generalizing statement, "*The Arabs don't like the Jews [. . .]. Because it's like, Palestine it's an Arab country . . .*" (Bilal, Paris). He then justified his belief that Jews in his neighborhood should be afraid of Arabs by alluding to the Middle East conflict: "*They kill.*" The interviewer failed to follow this rationale, which led Bilal to say: "*If you were Arab [. . .] you would react differently from the way you do now . . . you would feel some hatred.*" This response shows that he naturally associates the Arab identity with hatred of Jews through identification with Palestinians, who allegedly suffer from "the Jews."

A French respondent, also of Algerian origin, positioned himself against "the Jews" in a potential war: "*I respect [the Palestinians] because they are Arabs like us. If there is war tomorrow against the Jews then I will not side with the Jews, sir.*" He also commented on Arabs and Jews living in his neighborhood, and assumed that they dislike each other: "*The Jews who are here and the Arabs who are here, they hear the talking; they know what's going on. Thus the Jews dislike the Arabs and mutually, they dislike each other, the two of them*" (Assim, Paris). Note that the phrase "the two of them" underlines the perception of both Jews and Arabs as each comprising one entity.

Ahlam from Paris added a different argument: "*Sometimes we ask them just one thing. They are frightened, they say, 'he will rob me'. I don't know . . . this is why the Arabs they don't like the Jews, too.*" The fear that Jews in Paris have of being mugged by young Arabs is a reason for him to dislike Jews.

Some participants of non-Arab backgrounds had also observed Arab hostility against Jews and assumed a general enmity. A respondent from Berlin of Turkish origin, for example, stated, "*Most Arabs hate the Jews because, now, Israel and so on*" (Necet, Berlin), vaguely mentioning Israel as a reason, while his friend does not understand the reasons: "*I don't know it myself, why they hate them. I don't understand, either*" (Ömer, Berlin). Similarly, another man of Turkish background reported this about his Arab friends: "*The Arabs, my friends, they always talk like that. 'Fucking Jews, fucking Jews,' always*" (Orhan, Berlin).

However, other participants of Arab background explicitly distanced themselves from the hostility toward Jews that they have observed among other Arabs. Haroun of Maghrebian background, for instance, acknowledged that there are "blacks and Arabs" who would say that they do not like Jews but, he argued, they are ignorant and influenced by television. Another respondent of Maghrebian origin, who lives in Paris and has a Jewish girlfriend, explained that he has overcome such prejudices that have led to a general enmity between Arabs and Jews – prejudices which, he believes, can be observed in the media:

Tariq: You only have to watch the media. The Jews don't like the Arabs and the Arabs don't like the Jews.
Interviewer: Yes, but these are stereotypes.
Tariq: Yes, well, but the people believe it. I left that all behind and here we go, it's been five years that I am together with the same girl.

Even though Tariq has a Jewish girlfriend and he rejects a general enmity between Arabs and Jews, he believes in a number of antisemitic stereotypes, such as that of Jews being rich and untrustworthy.

To conclude, most interviewees of Arab background have heard of the notion that Arabs dislike Jews and adopt such views; only a few reject them.

Maghrebian, Algerian, and Moroccan Identity

For most interviewees, their Maghrebian, Algerian, Moroccan, Tunisian, Lebanese, or Palestinian identity is almost inseparable from their Arab identity. The only interviewee who rejected an Arab identification despite his Maghrebian background identifies himself as Berber and Maghrebian. Asked about a potential identification with "the Palestinians" via an Arab identity, he stated: "*We are Maghrebians [. . .] and Palestine, those are Arabs. And Palestine, honestly . . . I dunno [. . .]. And then, anyway, I'm a Berber*" (Masmud, Paris). Masmud's rejection of an Arab and a Palestinian identification might influence his views on Jews, as he also rejects open hatred against Jews.

However, others related animosity toward Jews directly to their Maghrebian identity. In the context of discussing a potential marriage between him and a Jewish woman, a French participant of Algerian origin, for example, is convinced that Jews and Maghrebians are not "compatible," even though he relates this incompatibility vaguely to religion: "*It's a religion, the Jew, it's a Jewish girl, anyway, that's not compatible with the Maghrebians*" (Sabri, Paris).

Interestingly, some relate hostility against Jews to their particular country of origin with which they identify. A French interviewee reported, without sadness, the expulsion and murder of Jews in Algeria in his parents' village:

Bilal: In Algeria, in my street, there were Jews before, in the years when the French were there. They asked them to leave Algeria. [If] they didn't want to,

> *they were shot. On top of that, it's the only country that doesn't have any relations with Israel, Algeria.*
>
> *Interviewer: And what do you think about that?*
>
> *Bilal: Frankly, what is it good for to have relations with Israel?*

Bilal was referring to the early 1960s. The new Nationality Code of independent Algeria, promulgated in 1963,[17] granted citizenship only to Muslims, and Jews were driven into exile. He added, wrongly, that Algeria is the only country without any (diplomatic) relations to Israel. Few Muslim countries, in fact, have official diplomatic relations with Israel. When asked what he thinks about his own report of the expulsion of the Jews from Algeria, Bilal responded only to the last aspect of lacking relations to Israel, with which he agrees. The lack of any signs of disapproval of Algerian policies toward Jews and the open hostility toward Jews he showed elsewhere are evidence that he accepts or approves of the hostility toward Jews and Israel from his country of origin, as well as the expulsion and murder of Algerian Jews in his parental village. And, conversely, the fact that Jews were murdered in his parents' country, which has not been the issue of a widely accepted self-critical debate in Algeria,[18] might make him more comfortable in accepting and endorsing murderous Jew hatred.

A respondent from France of Moroccan origin who believes that Arabs dislike "the Jews" presented a similar opinion of Jews in Morocco who, he said, have a low status: "*They came to do business in our country. For me, personally, I think they have no place in our country. I didn't go to Israel. Why do you come to me?*" (Moukhtar, Paris). He thereby made clear that he considers Moroccan Jews alien to Morocco, which he considers his country.

The perception that Jews are not, and should not be, an integral part of society in the interviewees' countries of origin reinforces negative views of Jews.

Egyptian Identity

A respondent of Egyptian Maghrebian background related his hatred against Israelis to the history of war between Egypt and Israel and to the killing of his great uncle in one of the Israeli-Egyptian conflicts:

> *I am of Egyptian origin and the Israelis they went to war against Egypt and I, my grandmother, she lost her brother in the war and all. There are these little things. For example, in Egypt, they hate the Israelis, not the Jews, the Israelis.* (Aswad, Paris)

Aswad is one of the few interviewees who emphasized a distinction between Jews and Israelis. At times, though, he used the term "the Jews" when talking about the Middle East conflict as, for example, when he said, "*It's the Jews who bomb*" (Aswad, Paris). What he said about Egypt, that people hate Israelis, but not Jews, matches his own perception: "*We have something against the Israelis but not the Jews. We respect the Jews because it's a religion.*" Aswad's views are further evidence that discourses in one's country of origin or, more precisely, individuals' perception of these discourses, are relevant for European Muslims' attitudes toward Jews and Israelis.

Pakistani and Bengali Identities

Some interviewees of South Asian background also related feelings of hatred against Jews to their ethnic background. This was either done with reference to a particular ethnic community that allegedly all dislike Jews or to common hatred against Jews in the county of origin. One respondent referred to his community of Bengalis to elucidate his negative but ambivalent perception of Jews:

> *Jewish people, it's like basically they're stingy, man, you know? It's like they're good person[s], but they're stingy [. . .]. How shall I explain it? [. . .] They're racist to Bengali [. . .] that's why Bengali people hate them.* (Sakti, London)

Sakti had difficulties explaining his negative views and why Jews are allegedly stingy while also being "good person[s]." Just before this statement he talked about racist violence from different ethnic groups. He tied this in with the topic of racism by claiming that Jews are racist to Bangladeshis, without giving further evidence. As a result, his conclusion appears to be a reaction to Jews' stinginess and racism: allegedly, not only he, but all Bengali people, hate Jews.

Another man, who had come recently from Pakistan to study in Britain, first described antisemitic conspiracy theories that "most people in Pakistan believe," affirming that he also believes in them, and continued talking in the "we believe that . . ." vein, blaming the Jews for the attacks of 9/11:

> *Most of the people in Pakistan believe that Taliban wasn't behind the 9/11 attempts. It was actually the Yahudis [Jews] who were behind, they say that [. . .]. I think the same [. . .]. Because we believe that, they have had that [. . .] insurance of that property, all that World Trade Center and everything [. . .] and after that they claimed that money back and they, for doing all this they put all this on Afghanistan and Taliban, but actually it was the Jewish people who did all this.* (Malik, London)

He tried to add legitimacy to his antisemitic conspiracy theories by presenting them as beliefs of Pakistanis: if most believe it, there must be something legitimate to it and criticizing this belief would mean criticizing most Pakistanis.

To conclude, reference to ethnic identity as justification for animosity toward Jews can be used both to voice one's opinions with the backing of one's community and can be the result of observations of prevalent discourses within one's community or the country of origin. Those who identify strongly with their ethnic background and country of origin are likely to adopt discourses about Jews that they believe are prevalent in their community.

CONCLUSIONS

Many participants, including some of those who see similarities between Judaism and Islam, adopt the belief of a general enmity between Muslims and Jews.

Interviewees gave a wide range of arguments for negative views of Jews with reference to Islam or their religious or ethnic identity. But their perceptions of Jews often originate from the widespread assumption and adoption that "the Muslims" or "the" people of one's own ethnic background dislike Jews. Then, interviewees looked for supporting arguments in Islamic history, the Qur'an, the Middle East conflict, or the wars in Afghanistan and Iraq. Others argued that there is a mutual hatred, that Jews do not like Muslims or their ethnic community or that Jews are at war with Muslims or Arabs. Thereby, Jews are blamed for the alleged reciprocal hostilities.

A closer look into the belief that suicide bombers and warriors against the Jews go to paradise shows that this religious belief is an argument for, but not the primary motive of, support for killing Jews. It is a justification of the methods and is used as a kind of divine sanction, but the motive is hatred against Jews. The same goes for the perception that it is a sin to spend time with Jews. However, the religious justification fosters and radicalizes the hatred.

In sum, rationales for Jew hatred, including the ones mentioned here, are chimeric. They are not a valid reason to hold antisemitic attitudes but are expressions of pure fantasy and have very little to do with how Jews actually conduct themselves.[19]

EIGHT

Antisemitism without Rationalization

THE PHILOSOPHY OF THE ENLIGHTENMENT HAS MADE IT explicit: all people are equal, and differential treatment and attitudes toward groups of people are not to be accepted as God-given. They have to be justified on an individual basis. Antisemitic attitudes cannot, by definition, be justified. They are irrational in two ways. The first is shared with other social prejudices such as racism. There is no "reason" to hate "the Jews." Antisemitism is not rooted in any allegedly negative characteristics of Jews, in particular actions of Jews, or in conflict with Jews. However, as shown in the description of the three previous categories of argumentation ("classic" modern antisemitism, references to Israel, and references to Islam or one's religious or ethnic identity), participants often try to justify their hostile attitudes toward Jews by claiming negative assertions about them to be true or by extrapolating particular traits or behaviors of some Jews to all Jews. Such justifications are used to present anti-Jewish sentiments as more rational and legitimate. Second, antisemitism today is largely irrational in that it is chimeric: it is not rooted in overgeneralization or in a conflict with some Jews. As Bernard Harrison pointed out, "There is not a shred of truth" in assumptions that the Jews strive for world domination and conspire against the world: "The 'Jewish Conspiracy' has no members."[1] Antisemitism also does not serve the antisemites in a materialistic sense. Contrary to racist or misogynist beliefs, antisemitism does not legitimize a certain hierarchical social order.

However, this fourth category of antisemitic patterns captures the remarks that show that interviewees believe negative perceptions of Jews do not have to be explained or justified; in the minds of participants, they are self-evident. It shows the irrationality of antisemitism more openly than the other rationales.

Hatred of Jews because they are Jews was bluntly expressed in some statements. Individuals portrayed such hatred as personal opinions and claimed the right to advance their views with no need of justification. Others adopted the notion that negative attitudes toward Jews are common sense. The use of "Jew" as an insult is an example of how such an understanding can become embedded in language. Banalizing and accepting negative views, hatred, and violence against "the Jews" as a general group is irrational in itself. In addition, some even endorsed indiscriminate violence against Jews in their neighborhood or in the past. The Holocaust comes to the fore in two opposing ways: that it even occurred is denied by some respondents, an obvious form of irrationality and antisemitism, while others indicate their approval of its occurrence, a view which, though it might be a natural result of avowed antisemitism, is in its monstrosity even more irrational.

HATRED AGAINST JEWS BECAUSE THEY ARE JEWS

The "argument" of hating Jews because they are Jews points to the essence of antisemitism: its irrationality. Antisemitic resentments do not stem only from learned stereotypes but also from unconscious projections onto Jews, the actual behaviors or lives of whom may shape only the nature of antisemitic *expressions*. The argument of hating Jews because they are Jews is rarely bluntly voiced, but this irrational "cause" often shines through when hatred against "all Jews" is justified with accusations for which clearly only some Jews can possibly be responsible. However, a few interviewees do express this irrational sentiment frankly and insist on it. Consider one man's words, particularly the last sentence of the following excerpt:

> *Bashir: [I] would [. . .] say, [. . .] that the damned Jews should be burnt [. . .]. Maybe there are Jews who are kind or something, I don't know.*
> *Interviewer: And those who are kind, should they be burnt, too?*
> *Bashir: Yes.*
> *Interviewer: Why?*
> *Bashir: Because they are Jews nevertheless. Jews are, a Jew is a Jew anyway.*

A Berlin resident of Lebanese background and German nationality, Bashir acknowledged that there might be kind Jews, but he insisted on his wish to exterminate all Jews, because, as he summed it up, a Jew is still a Jew. For another German respondent, simply being Jewish is reason enough for being targeted by his hate. Toward the end of the interview, when he was asked if he could imagine having a Jewish girlfriend, he exclaimed that he hates Jews and even uttered that he would like to kill every single one himself.

Interviewer: Can you imagine having a girlfriend, a Jewish girlfriend?
Naeem: Never, dude, I would pull off her head.
Interviewer: Really? Let's say she was very beautiful and very nice.
Naeem: Even so. I hate Jews! Every Jew should, I would kill every Jew in the world.
Interviewer: But you said that for some it's not their fault, what's with them?
Naeem: Even so.
Interviewer: Even so?
Naeem: Yes.

For Naeem, imagining intimate contact with a Jewish woman evoked violent fantasies against all Jews in equal measure, regardless of their deeds. The interviewer was left speechless upon the adamant statement that, for him, it makes no difference whether or not Jews are personally guilty of anything. A third German interviewee, of Palestinian origin, who was quoted many times above for his clear and hateful comments, was asked why he hates the German Holocaust survivor who visited his school. He responded: "*Here, because he is a Jew. That's the only reason. Just because he is a Jew*" (Suleiman, Berlin). The Jewish identity of somebody was reason enough for Suleiman to hate this person, as he openly stated. In another context, he commented that he hates all Jews, explicitly including those in Berlin who have no responsibility for the Israeli-Palestinian conflict in any way. As he "explained": "*He simply belongs to this race ['Rasse'],*[2] *therefore I hate him. I hate the person who belongs to this race ['Rasse'], I hate him.*" Suleiman's accusation against all Jews is ultimately about being Jewish, which he interprets as a racial identity. He does not qualify any reasons why he hates the Jewish race.[3] Racist forms of antisemitism were part and parcel of Nazism and nationalist antisemitism in the nineteenth and early twentieth century. However, the "Jewish race" in a racist sense was imagined to have inherited specific characteristics for which it was despised. Suleiman's perception is a caricature of that mindset. He does not even bother to affiliate negative traits to the "Jewish race."

Most, but not all, blunt statements of hatred against Jews because they are Jews come from interviewees of Palestinian or Lebanese background. These unvarnished expressions of antisemitism are more likely to be made by those who feel that their negative feelings toward Jews can be accepted without any explanation and who do not care or do not know about the public discourse in which such blatant statements of hatred against people's identity are unacceptable. However, the same argument of hating Jews because they are Jews was put forward by Ganesh, an interviewee from London of South Asian background, but his statements do not include the explicit wish to kill Jews: "*Jewish people are Jewish, that's why we don't like them [. . .]. It's a hate, like [. . .] meaning Muslim hates Jewish, Jewish hates Muslim.*"

Despite the bluntness of the statement, Ganesh related his argument to his Muslim identity and to an alleged mutual hatred between Muslims and Jews in an attempt to add some legitimacy to his blunt confession of hatred for no other reason than a Jewish identity.

Similarly, in France, another man's explanation for the alleged hostility between Muslims and Jews boils down to this: "*We don't understand each other, because!*" (Omar, Paris) – this, even though he declared a second earlier that "*normally, the Muslims and the Jews, they are brothers.*"

Another interviewee, of Turkish origin and living in Berlin, revealed negative attitudes toward Jews in general and indirectly threatened "Jews who are Jews" when asked if he could imagine having a Jewish friend:

> *Interviewer: Would you be against having a Jewish friend [. . .]?*
> *Halil: Well, . . . yes, well, how should I say, if he's okay, [if he's] not such a Jew [. . .] then I wouldn't do anything.*

In Halil's response, his inner conflict about his general valuation of friendship and his rejection of Jews as Jews comes up. The dislike of any group of people for their collective identity itself, not for alleged particular traits or characteristics attached to this identity, does not stand up to scrutiny, and the resulting contradictory statement is not surprising. Nevertheless, the belief that it is Jewish identity itself that is detestable seems to have a highly aggressive potential. It should be noted that "justifying" hostility against Jews simply because they are Jews is combined by Suleiman, Bashir, and Naeem with the explicit call for the Jews' extermination. And, indeed, the call for exterminating all Jews is the result of this irrationality of hatred of Jews for being Jews. Jean-Paul Sartre said about the antisemite: "What he wishes, what he prepares, is the *death* of the Jew."[4]

Another form of hating Jews for their very identity was expressed by a respondent from Paris, who considers all Jews to be Israelis and who stated, contradictorily: "*They are our cousins, the Jews! [. . .] But we don't hate the Jews because they are Jews; no, because they are Israelis. They are occupiers. Israel has never existed*" (Youssef, Paris).

Youssef's extraordinary statement might be seen, prima facie, as functioning to establish a distinction between Jews and Israelis. He declares that Jews and Muslims are cousins and that therefore there is no hatred between them; his hatred is directed against Israelis only. But this is not, in fact, what he said. For Youssef "the Jews" *are* Israelis. His linguistic distinction between the words "Jews" and "Israelis" does not make any sense because he conflates them, and he detests "the Jews" even though he perceives Jews and Muslims as cousins. His argument is related to Israel but in a manifestly irrational way.

CLAIMING THE RIGHT TO HAVE ANTISEMITIC ATTITUDES AS A PERSONAL OPINION

Some interviewees openly exhibited their anti-Jewish feelings and hatred. They claimed the right to hate or dislike Jews for being Jews. A few portrayed this as a personal opinion, such as one who declared that he hates all Jews and responded when asked for his reasons: "*I just hate them, I hate them. Am I not allowed to?*" (Suleiman, Berlin). He sees no need for justification, he "simply" hates Jews, he said. The interviewer's attempts to find reasons were fruitless:

Suleiman: Is it forbidden to feel hatred against a people? I just hate this people. I hate it.
Interviewer: I just try to understand; if you say . . .
Suleiman: Simple . . . I can't stand them [. . .]. Hitler did not like them, too.

> *Interviewer: And you think that this has something to do with the fact that you are Arab, that you cannot stand them?*
> *Suleiman: Man, the Jews have been persecuted since how long? Thousands of years [. . .]. And they were certainly enemies with the Muslims earlier on, that just comes like this, I just hate Jews.*

Suleiman claimed a right to hate a people, and he regards Jews as a people worthy of his hatred. Furthermore, he linked his hatred to that of Hitler. Even then, the interviewer tried to offer a more plausible explanation, asking if Suleiman's hatred had anything to do with the fact that he is Arab. But Suleiman refused this rationale and came back to what he said initially: "I simply hate Jews." It is difficult to imagine a clearer way of rejecting any attempt to rationalize hatred against Jews. His statement that Jews have been discriminated against for a long time and that Muslims and Jews have long been enemies is no explanation, and he did not portray it as an explanation; rather, Suleiman simply joins the ranks of people who hate Jews, today and in the past.

A German interviewee of Turkish background is far less radical; he did not say that he hates Jews. Still, he did not feel that he should explain his antisemitic equation of Israelis' treatment of Palestinians with the Nazis' treatment of the Jews. He too insisted on his personal opinion: "*Well, I don't know the reason, for me personally it's the same*" (Ömer, Berlin).

A British respondent declared that he has "*a little fear of Jewish people*" and "*this little cold feeling from them*" but cannot explain why: "*I don't know, it's weird. Maybe it's just me*" (Hussein, London). He thereby also resorted to personal opinion that does not need to be supported by a reasonable argument. A French interviewee exclaimed, "*It's inevitable that there are those who dislike them [the Jews].*" But when he was asked for his reasons, he simply replied: "*I don't know, everybody has his reasons, everybody has his reasons*" (Nadim, Paris).

A PERCEPTION THAT NEGATIVE VIEWS OF JEWS ARE COMMON SENSE

Some interviewees perceive it to be natural, even common sense, that Jews are despised or stereotyped. The perception that certain attitudes toward Jews are widespread is taken as a justification for them, not as a sociological phenomenon. Participants feel no need for further arguments; they accept such assumptions as facts. A British respondent of South Asian background bases antisemitic stereotypes on the general notion of "common sense":

> *Nirmal: They're rich, one way or another . . .*
> *Interviewer: Where did you hear about that? [. . .]*
> *Nirmal: It's kind of common sense.*

Nirmal's reference to "common sense" expresses his perception that the stereotype of rich Jews is widespread and he believes in it. He showed similar bias elsewhere. Others referred to a general dislike of Jews in their community and did not feel the need to explain it or to accuse the Jews of anything specific. A veritable norm of hostile attitudes toward Jews was revealed in some cases. The irrationality here is not hidden, and what is taken to be the norm and "common sense" replaces any attempt to make a case for hating Jews. Another British participant explained: "*We always have that thing in our mentality that Jewish people are our enemy. We don't see him as an enemy personally, but the whole community, the whole religion is our enemy*" (Baru's friend, London).

He perceives the hostility against Jews by his community as something rather impersonal that does not necessarily target individual Jews. His friend had reported that "*other Muslim people will hate me*" (Baru, London) if he were to befriend a Jew. This points to an antisemitic norm within some social circles in which sanctions are applied toward those showing sympathy with Jews.

A German interviewee, of Palestinian background, also made it clear that hostility toward Jews is the norm among his friends. When asked what he would do if they assaulted a Jew, he responded, "*I can't stop my friends; if I did, they would start to make fun of me*" (Ismail, Berlin). He also stated that he would not marry a Jewish woman out of concern for his children, who would then have to live with a Jewish mother. Similarly, a respondent from Paris of Maghrebian background stated that parents would not allow a marriage with a Jew: "*Starting with the parents; they will never agree.*" He added, "*If someone grows up here [. . .], he will never marry a Jew*" (Housni, Paris). Housni thereby related the rejection of marrying a Jewish woman to the local community, without giving further reasons.

Another interviewee from France, of Maghrebian background, is convinced that Jews and Muslims or Arabs dislike each other, but he is not able to give reasons for his views, eventually just confirming his hatred: "*Honestly, I don't know. I don't know who [. . .] started it but frankly, that goes back to before our grandmothers and before our grand-grandmothers, all that. But frankly, we do hate each other, they hate us and we hate them. That's how it is*" (Azhar, Paris). Azhar only vaguely referred to a tradition of animosity but eventually argued that "that's how it is."

Others referred to the country of their or their parents' origin when stating that hostility against Jews is a normal attitude. Nadim, who was quoted above, said that everybody has his own reasons to dislike Jews, and he had a ready answer when he was asked whether he sides with Palestinians or Israelis in the Middle East conflict:

> *Nadim: Against the Jews!*
> *Interviewer: And why is that?*
> *Nadim: Because. This is what I've learned [. . .]. I've learned in my life, in what I've seen, what I was [. . .] in my village, just like this, people in the street.*

Nadim did not give any reasons why he is so against "the Jews" in the Israeli-Palestinian conflict, but referred to the people in the street in his parents' village who apparently taught him these feelings.

Expressing negative feelings against Jews in the form of a common "we" or reference to the community in the country of origin links these antisemitic feelings to the collective identity and lends them more authority. Questioning them would mean to question the whole community of those who are described as "we." This phenomenon strongly relates to the third category of antisemitic argumentations presented above that relate negative views of Jews to the religious or ethnic community. However, the observation that there is, among one's own community, animosity against Jews because they are Jews does not necessarily lead to an adoption of this sentiment. One man, for example, reported, "*I know many people who don't like the Jews*" (Samed, Paris), thereby portraying hostility against Jews as a normal attitude, though he did not generally adopt this attitude and spoke out against such views.

Samed's rationales are described in detail in chapter 11 as one of the positive examples.

Other interviewees from all three cities harbored vaguely negative feelings toward Jews without being able to explain them. They insisted on the right to possess such feelings. This was often the case when they were asked if they could imagine having a Jewish girlfriend or marrying a Jewish woman, possibilities which they rejected without being able to explain why. Take one British interviewee who tried hard to think why he would not marry a Jew and could not find any answer. Nevertheless, he remained convinced that "it's a fact" that he is allowed to marry a Christian but not a Jew. Instead of questioning this assumption, he promised to investigate valuable reasons for it:

Abhijt: Yeah, they are also people of the book, but to be honest, I don't know the answer, man! [. . .] I'll find that for you [. . .]. To be honest, you know, I don't know where I got it from. But I'm sure I can marry a Christian, but not a Jew [. . .]. I never thought about that. I can't remember where I got it from [. . .].
Interviewer: But you seem to be pretty sure, that it's a fact.
Abhijt: It's a fact! Yes, it's a fact.

The question of marrying a Jewish woman is one of a number of contexts in which vague negative feelings against Jews surface, a general sense that they are to be despised, without being able to further explain why. However, a vague feeling of rejection of Jews might simply be an expression of uncertainty over what to think of them against the background of widespread antisemitic notions. Some participants just have vague feelings that Jews are disliked and accept their rejection even if they do not believe in it. They may correct themselves if they are questioned about it. Consider the excerpt of the interview with two young men of Turkish background in Berlin:

Orhan: I'm a fan of Xavier Naidoo and he also is Jewish.
Umur: He is Jewish?
Orhan: Yes.
Umur: Yeah, you see. I didn't even know it. Yeah, wait, I have to delete [it from my phone], I have to.
Orhan: He is Jewish and I have so many of his songs. This is a small example now but anyway.
Interviewer: What do you mean? You have him on your mobile?
Umur: No, I just said it as a joke, "Yeah, wait, I have to delete [it]," yes I've had music by Xavier Naidoo on it. That's good music, stuff it.

Orhan stressed that he is a fan of a musician whom he wrongly believes to be Jewish, possibly with the intention of demonstrating to the interviewer that he is not biased. Umur, however, was surprised to learn of the alleged Jewish identity of the singer, and his spontaneous reaction was to express the intention to delete his songs from his mobile phone, though he added that the comment was said in jest. His remark, that this is good music "anyway," suggests that he still likes the singer despite his alleged Jewishness. Even though he showed in effect an initial rejection of the allegedly Jewish singer, he did not insist on his rejection but seemed to realize that being Jewish is not an obstacle for producing good music.

"JEW" AS AN INSULT

The words for "Jew" ("Jude" in German; "Juif" and "Feuj" in French) are used as insults or otherwise in a pejorative way by interviewees in France and Germany.[5] (Such usage appears to be less frequent in Britain today.)[6] Almost all interviewees from Paris and Berlin are familiar with the pejorative use of the terms "Jude," "Juif," or "Feuj," and some admitted using it themselves or even used these words during group interviews. Their frequent usage leads to habituation and to the perception that there is nothing scandalous in this use of the term. None of the interviewees were shocked by this form of antisemitic language, even if not all agree on using it and many know that it is offensive. This language normalizes the perception of negative connotations implicit in the word "Jew." In fact, the word can only function as an insult if there is a general understanding that "Jew" is something negative. Then, negative attitudes do not have to be justified or rationalized; they are accepted and even expected as such. Didier Lapeyronnie describes how difficult it is to escape the impact of such language once it is used.[7] The derogatory use of "Jew" in everyday language contributes to the association between Jews and negativity. Consider the statements of these two friends in Berlin:

> *Umur: Well, like, "You're a Jew." But you hear that expression everywhere.*
> *Orhan: Yes, you hear it everywhere and everybody uses it. But that doesn't mean now that everybody hates Jews.*

Frequently, participants consider the pejorative use of the terms for "Jew" as "nothing serious"; they trivialize it as being "a little joke" and "just for fun." On the other hand, some interviewees are not aware of the offensiveness of this kind of vocabulary because they believe the underlying stereotypes to be true, and thus do not understand why someone would be shocked regarding the use of "Jew" as an insult, because for them, "Jew" is unambiguously understood as negative. Rather, they expect that the (non-Jewish) person labeled as such will be offended by this grave insult. Bilal explicated:

> *Bilal: Even between us; if there is a guy with some cookies and he doesn't share, we tell him, "Fuck, you are a Jew."*
> *Interviewer: But doesn't that make you mad, do you think that this is normal?*
> *Bilal: No, but if somebody says this to me I just tell him: "Get lost, stop calling me like that."*

The pejorative use of "Jew" can be so ingrained in language that it serves as a substitution of negative attributes. A German respondent explained that, instead of a longer expression or a "paraphrase," it is easier and shorter to use the term "Jew":

> *That's just always the images that you have of Jews: that he, I don't know, has a big nose, that he always has a lot of money, that he's stingy. And so that's what is meant by it in the end. You can paraphrase it, but "Jew" is said at the end of it.* (Sharif, Berlin)

Another example of the substitutive use of the term "Jew" was given by a French interviewee. In his example, the stereotype of the stingy Jews is central:

> *Sabri: Eating Jewish, that means hiding while eating [. . .]. That's an expression that the Jew doesn't want to share [. . .], the misers. Often the miser, it's a Jew, "Ah, you are a Jew, share it!" you see? [. . .] There are often little connotations to Jews like that.*
> *Interviewer: And do you think that there is something true to it, in that?*
> *Sabri: Sure . . . I don't know.*

Sabri reports the common use of the term "Jew" in relation to eating and stinginess – without direct relation to Jews. Thus the stereotype is used in everyday language, but Sabri also adopts it because he believes that there is something to it and thereby retrocedes the pejorative use of the term "Jew" to Jews.

The trivialization of antisemitic language and its frequent usage can lead to a norm of open antisemitism through consensual validation and repetition. A norm of antisemitic language is accompanied by antisemitic prejudices and the establishment of a social order that labels others as "Jews."[8] The threat of exclusion is a crucial part of establishing social order. Nabil from Berlin remembered that labeling someone as "Jew" had been used to exclude a student in his school: *"At our school, in the class, but that was only [used] like, to have fun: 'Oh, yeah, he's a Jew, don't talk to him.'"*

The threat of exclusion, through labeling someone as a "Jew," can also be observed in some group interviews. In one, the conversation turned to Jewish pupils in schools. Asward's friend stated that there are no Jews in his school in France. This comment was used by another participant to label Asward's friend as a "Jew." He then had to assure the group that he is not Jewish and that he has the same ethnic (Arab) identity as the other group members.[9] Only then was he reacknowledged in the group and the interview could continue.

Asward's friend: In our school there is none.
Nadem: You, you are a Jew!
Asward's friend: No, I'm not a Jew.
Nadem: What are you?
Asward's friend: I'm an Arab!
Nadem: Ah, okay.

However, the negative connotations of "Jew" are trivialized and banalized to such an extent that one might think that the term for "Jew" and its negative meanings have nothing to do with real Jews, and thus its use is not antisemitic. The use of "Jew" might be regarded as only a metaphor. But the choice of the metaphors we use is far from meaningless: as George Lakoff and Mark Johnson have shown, the metaphors we use both reveal and shape the way we think.[10] Therefore, the pejorative usage of word "Jew" cannot be separated from the general meaning of the term "Jew" and thus both reveal and convey antisemitic attitudes.

We can add another argument if we follow Monika Schwarz-Friesel's and Holger Braune's approach. They apply the cognitive theory of the text-world model used in linguistics to analyze conceptualizations of Jews in texts.[11] The model allows the analysis of the implicit potential of inferences of information in texts or statements drawn by the recipient. According to them, a univocal antisemitic conceptualization of Jews in a text-world is conceptually closed. It does not allow inferences that oppose the patterns of thinking and worldview of the author.[12] The use of the word "Jew" as an insult or in a pejorative way does not allow positive inferences. Moreover, the pejorative use of the words for "Jew" is connoted to the terms for "Jew." The conceptualization of Jews in a pejorative use of the word "Jew" is therefore closed and is thus univocally antisemitic.

To conclude, the pejorative use of the term "Jew" enhances a Manichean perception of Jews and non-Jews, in which Jews and those labeled as such are regarded as negative or evil. Negative connotations about Jews are disseminated by framing them as self-evident and adopting them into everyday language through consensual validation and repetition, even if those who share this language are not necessarily fervent antisemites. Rationalizing antisemitic prejudices becomes obsolescent; the generally accepted negative connotations of the term "Jew" are sufficient to justify hatred against Jews: *"A Jew is a Jew anyway"* (Bashir, Berlin). In addition, the word "Jew" functions to promote exclusion and degradation, and to establish a social order within youth groups that impedes opposition to it, particularly if an antisemitic norm of communication has been established within the group. The exclusion and defamation of those who are, albeit temporarily, labeled "Jews" effectively lead to the exclusion and defamation of Jews. These findings confirm and add to results of previous studies from France and Germany that note the antisemitic use of the term "Jew" and its functions within youth groups.[13]

BANALIZING HATRED AND VIOLENCE AGAINST JEWS

Hatred and violence against Jews in general as opposed to Jewish individuals is clearly unjustifiable to common standards. Its acceptance or banalization openly neglects these common standards. On the contrary, banalizing hatred and violence against Jews facilitates antisemitic violence as a norm.

Some interviewees accept highly irrational manifestations of hatred and violence against Jews in their neighborhood. For example, a German Muslim of Turkish background noticed a general hatred of Muslims against Jews. He reported that his friends and others use anti-Jewish slurs frequently and that he had observed that Muslims had beaten up a Jewish woman in his neighborhood. Thereupon he stated: *"I don't care, I mean, I honestly can't be bothered, okay, I don't think it's right, but I'm not interested in it, am I a Jew? No. So, I don't care, it's also not meant so seriously, people just say, like, 'you Jew', to annoy someone, but that's not important to me"* (Fatin, Berlin). He does not endorse the hatred but also does not feel concerned about it, because he is not Jewish.

A respondent from Paris took a similar stance when he commented on insults against Jews: *"That's normal. If nobody's annoying me, I'm easy"* (Ismet, Paris). He just does not want to be bothered. Another interviewee from Paris perceives dislike of Jews as normal and "inevitable": *"That's for sure, it's inevitable that there are those who dislike [the Jews] [. . .]. Everybody has his reasons"* (Nadim, Paris); Nadim almost claims a *right* for everybody to dislike Jews.

Some interviewees trivialize violence against Jews in the neighborhood, regarding it as somehow normal or acceptable where it would be appropriate to be outraged. Often, they do not even feel the need to justify why they accept it. A German interviewee witnessed an assault on a Holocaust survivor who visited his school in Berlin-Kreuzberg; some of his friends were involved in the incident. His account is "neutral," lacking a condemnation of this outrageous attack. Consider his description of the incident:

> *I saw once how [. . .] a group of kids made fun of a Jew. He came to our school, here at Ferdinand,*[14] *he wanted to tell the history of the Jews, and they all spat on him, and he left [laughing slightly] [. . .]. Suleiman was also there, and Mousa, the twin [. . .]. A lot happened [. . .] on the jacket, all wet and spit, and a lot yelled 'Fucking Jew!' and everything [. . .]. I was there, but I didn't yell anything.* (Ismail, Berlin)

Another participant in Germany went one step further and declared that he does not care about Jews in his neighborhood, and explained that he thinks his friend's declaration that he will kill Jews if he sees them is his own business:

> *And even if I see a Jew, yeah, okay. I don't care at all. That's also for sure a human being, he lives in Germany, he has his own religion and has nothing to do with the war. I can't be bothered about him, and he not about me. I'm just taking care of myself. What am I supposed to start up with him? Am I supposed to, for example, kill him*

dead on the street or what am I supposed to do with him? It doesn't make any sense! [. . .] There are a lot of real troublemakers here, also Arabs [. . .]. I have, for example, a friend here, his father was killed in the war because of the Jews. And so what he says, for example: "If I see a Jew in front of me, I'll destroy him. He's gone, seriously, take his head off." For example. He's really one of those. He's a real Palestinian, original Palestinian for example and he would seriously do that. But, seriously, I don't care. That's his thing and I have my thing. (Ramzi, Berlin)

Ramzi considers himself Palestinian, as he said elsewhere, but associates a "real Palestinian" with somebody who would attack Jews on the streets of Berlin. In fact, some minutes before this statement he declared that he had once wished to kill a Jew whom he had seen on the street, which gave way to his endorsement of antisemitic violence.

Another respondent even openly endorsed antisemitic violence and stated that he would transform his hostile attitudes toward Jews into action against Jews in Berlin. He considers beating up a Jew in Berlin as a contribution to solving the Middle East conflict:

Interviewer: What do you think that people could do to solve this conflict between Israel and Palestine?
Abdullah: No idea . . . for me, if I see a Jew and he starts something with me then I would beat him up, and then I say, "Who do you think you are?"

Even though Abdullah added that he would beat up a Jew if the Jew provoked him, he would question the Jew *after* beating him up and thus beat him up for being a Jew, not for his stance on the Middle East conflict. This is obviously no contribution whatsoever to solving the Middle East conflict, but, rather, an openly irrational statement of hatred against Jews triggered by a question on possible solutions to the conflict.

A British respondent said that there are many people who hate Jews and then gave an example of somebody who even wants to kill a Jew before he dies:

Bashkar: After [the] Afghanistan war, that guy, he was young, was only about 22, he was a body-builder, Pakistani guy, [. . .] he goes, "Before I die, I'm gonna kill one Jew before I die." [. . .] You know in Iraq, yeah, they're not my family, I'm from Bangladesh, but because we're Muslim, I feel hurt, know what I mean? Afghanistan is not my country, but if anything goes wrong I feel hurt, I'm a Muslim.
Interviewer: In Palestine as well?
Bashkar: Palestine I don't feel hurt because my, well, look I'm not Palestinian, I'm Bengali, and I'm British. Me and Palestine; no connection. The only connection is religion, that's the hurt I feel.

Bashkar did not endorse the radical statement that he quoted, but he tried to justify it with the hair-raising logic of placing the call for murdering "a Jew" in the context of the wars in Afghanistan and Iraq, where fellow Muslims get hurt, even though these wars have nothing to do with the Israeli-Palestinian conflict. Interestingly, he did not even make the link to "Palestine" and only reluctantly sees a connection. His description illustrates how young European Muslims can feel drawn into the wars in Iraq and Afghanistan via their Muslim identity. His account also shows how a link can be established to a war against Jews even without an identification with Palestinians. It seems evident to Bashkar that the wars in Afghanistan and Iraq can be used to justify violence against Jews. He is not bothered by the obvious contradiction.

In Paris, a few interviewees reported that they had witnessed assaults on Jews in their neighborhoods. Bilal, of Maghrebian origin, reported an assault he had witnessed but did not react to or condemn. He is convinced that the Jews wearing characteristic hats in his neighborhood easily become target of attacks. He does not express anguish over the attack, but rather seems to perceive hostility as normal, even accusing Jews of wearing those hats in which they allegedly look all alike. Two other interviewees, of Maghrebian background, know that the Jewish school in their neighborhood in Paris is protected heavily by the police. The interviewer wanted to know if the fears of Jewish students are justified. Housni answered this by justifying the aggressions that trigger these fears:

Interviewer: The [Jewish] school is protected. Is that because they are scared?
Housni: They are scared, yeah.
Omar: They are scared; they have cameras all over the place [. . .]. There are two policemen with bats [. . .].
Housni: They are right to be scared because the other Jews; they do, um, they kill Muslims. This is why they are expecting this.

Housni thought that Jews should indeed be scared in his neighborhood. After some hesitation, he felt compelled to justify the threat against Jews and came up with "they kill Muslims," knowing that the Jewish schoolchildren who are scared in the neighborhood do not "kill Muslims." Justifying aggressions against Jewish students because other Jews are thought to kill Muslims elsewhere calls for an additional explanation of the connection between these facts. Housni fails to offer this explanation. It seems evident to him and perfectly normal that Jews in his neighborhood are attacked for something that others allegedly do.

In a French interviewee's account of a violent assault on a rabbi, the victim is portrayed as the perpetrator, which results in the respondent's minimization or even endorsement of the antisemitic violence. Remarkably, he recounted this incident as an example of the racism that he and his community have to endure.

> *Interviewer: How does it show up in other ways, racism? Are there fascists, or looks?*
>
> *Jabar: Yeah, it's the looks, you get the looks. These looks – two days ago there was, did you see this guy who battered the rabbi in the metro? At the Gare du Nord. He smashed him. You see, the rabbi, it's a Jew, the rabbi. This rabbi of the Jews [. . .]. The day before yesterday he was battered by a boy in the metro at Gare du Nord. [I swear] on the Qur'an, he broke his jaw [. . .]. He came into the corridor and the rabbi looked at the boy. But you know, you could see, it the look was mean. The other one, he told him, I don't know, "Why do you look at me?" The other insulted him – the rabbi. So the boy caught him. He crushed him. And now he is in a coma. Yes, oh, they didn't get the guy [. . .] [If] they catch him, it's death for him. You know, here, the power, who has it? It's the Jews.*

Jabar seems to agree with the rationale of the perpetrator of the assault. The perpetrator was quoted in *Le Monde* as saying, "*Dirty Jew, you look at me, I will beat you up,*" before he actually punched the rabbi.[15]

These examples have demonstrated how some young Muslims banalize, accept, and even endorse hatred and violence against Jews in a way that defies ordinary standards of logic. Hating Jews because they are Jews only becomes an "argument" in itself if it is accepted by a wider social circle as a certain normality.

Holocaust Denial and Trivialization of the Holocaust

Given widely available evidence of the Holocaust, any outright Holocaust denial is irrational. There might be reason for disbelief in the Holocaust out of horror for the atrocities, but there are no rational reasons for a denial of the well-documented murder of about six million Jews by the Nazis and their collaborators. However, a respondent from London, of Maghrebian origin, doubts the Holocaust and demands impossible "evidence":

> *We heard that Hitler used to barbecue Jewish people, used to put them in a oven [. . .]. You hear Hitler was nasty, was a killer, was bad, but we don't know. I can't tell you he is a killer, because I wasn't with him. I wasn't there sitting down with Hitler having a tea and now he tells me about his story!* (Nader, London)

Nader argues from the posture of doubting anything that does not come from his direct experience, so that he can only judge Hitler's actions if he hears Hitler himself. However, what he would accept as evidence, Hitler's personal confession to him while having tea, adds to the absurdity of his "rationale." Moreover, the way he speaks about the systematic murder of Jews banalizes the Holocaust. An interviewee from Paris of Maghrebian origin framed his denial of the Holocaust only slightly more convincingly by referring to a political or historical debate he saw on TV that focused on typhus as the main reason of the Jews' deaths.[16] However, he felt that he should take the posture of disclosing a secret and labeled the Holocaust as a "state secret," a posture often used in the context of conspiracy theories. Another interviewee, Neoy from London of South Asian background, is well aware of the fact that the Holocaust is widely acknowledged but insisted that "only" close to one million Jews were killed rather than millions, referring to a non-identified journalist and vague conspiracy theories. His and other interviewees' perceptions of the Holocaust are presented in chapter 9.

Uncontrolled Eruptions of Hatred and Antisemitic Insults

Some interviewees voiced spontaneous and vivid antisemitic reactions without providing rationalization. In social psychology, spontaneous, strong reactions are regarded as an indicator of strong attitudes.[17] Asked whether he sides with Palestinians or Israelis in the Middle East conflict, a French respondent of Maghrebian background, for example, shouted twice: "*Against the Jews! Against the Jews!*" (Nadim, Paris).

Antisemitic remarks that were made completely out of context are further evidence of strong irrational feelings against Jews. For instance, a participant from Berlin incoherently inserted an insult against the former Israeli prime minister Ariel Sharon, "scheiß Sharon" (shitty Sharon"]) in a complaint about German police. Or consider this self-description from another respondent in Berlin:

Interviewer: Do you feel in some way like a German, or a Turk, or a Kurd, or . . . ?
Beyar: Well, it doesn't matter, actually; well, I am a Kurd. For me, the main thing is not to be a Jew or whatever.

Some gave the impression that they have to impulsively give voice to their antisemitic resentments, such as one man who briefly joined the interview with his friend and intervened saying, "*Hey, can I quickly insult the Jews?*" (Jabar's friend, Paris), or another who said: "*I can say what I want? Okay, then I say I hate all Jews*" (Ismail, Berlin).

Antisemitic insults are another form of clearly unjustified and unrationalized hatred against Jews. Some interviewees reported that they have heard anti-Jewish abuses, and some insulted Jews themselves during the interview. Orhan, for example, said that some of his friends frequently insult Jews as "scheiß Juden" (shitty Jews), and Kassim admitted without regret that he has used such insults himself. A German respondent insulted Jews as "*these damned sons of a bitch*" and declared that "*the damned Jews should be burnt*" (Bashir, Berlin). Another likened Jews to pigs in his call for murder of the Jews: "*They should be slaughtered like pigs*" (Suleiman, Berlin). It is not clear if he made reference here to the allegation that Jews are descendants of "apes and pigs," which is common in some Muslim circles and has some roots in the Qur'an.[18] However, only two interviewees referred to Jews as pigs and none to Jews as apes.

Similar insults were voiced in France, where a number of interviewees admitted that they have used the terms "sale Juifs" (dirty Jews) – some directly against Jewish students. One exclaimed: "*It stinks, the Jew!*" (Farouk, Paris), when reporting of a violent encounter with Jewish youths. Jabar insulted the Jewish singer Patrick Bruel as "*son-of-a-bitch*" and generalized, "*The Jews, you see, they are idiots.*"

In London, interviewees rarely mentioned the use of antisemitic insults, such as "Yiddo," but Gourab, a British respondent of South Asian origin, described Jews as "*fucking Yids*" when asked if Jews and Muslims can live together.

These insults and eruptions of hatred against Jews are never explained or rationalized. Rather, they are manifestations of impassioned resentments against Jews.

Open Endorsement of Antisemitic Violence against Jews

Endorsing indiscriminate violence against Jews in the neighborhood is in itself another expression of irrational hatred. Moreover, a small minority of interviewees in Germany and France pose a direct threat to Jews in their neighborhood. They uttered the wish to attack Jews physically, reported on the use of violence in the past in this and other contexts, and showed clear anti-Jewish attitudes. In Britain, some interviewees know of peers who are a physical threat to Jews. A number of interviewees do not consider their neighborhoods safe for Jews.

Some voiced direct or indirect threats themselves against Jews and endorsed violence in general. They gave reasons to believe that they would attack Jews under certain circumstances. One interviewee from Paris (Hamza) and one interviewee from Berlin (Kassim) reported that they were actively involved in violence against Jews.

In addition, a few participants uttered the wish that Jews be killed, often with reference to Jews in Israel or "Palestine." However, as shown above, participants usually do not distinguish between Israelis and European Jews, and some explicitly included people in their neighborhood in their wish that "the Jews" should be killed.

Endorsing violence against "the Jews" in the Middle East is discussed separately in chapter 6 and endorsing violence with religious justifications is discussed in chapter 7. However, no interviewee related the belief that violence against "the Jews" is religiously justified with respect to Jews in their neighborhood.[19] In the following section I outline reports of violence in which Kassim from Berlin and Hamza from Paris were involved.

Kassim, of Lebanese background, reported two incidents in which he took violent action against Jews and two in which he verbally assaulted and threatened Jews. According to his accounts, he assaulted a young man in the subway who wore a Star of David attached to his necklace. His aim was to tear off the necklace and thus destroy this symbol of Jewishness. His account cannot be verified, but similar attacks on people wearing the Star of David or a *kippah* (skullcap) have been reported in local newspapers.[20]

Kassim had also participated in a large pro-Palestinian rally in Berlin, likely in April 2002, when he was fourteen years old. There, he reported that he had thrown stones at Jews. Reports confirm violent escalation by Palestinian youths against pro-Israeli opponents, including members of the Jewish communities in Berlin, and the throwing of stones and bottles against the British Embassy.[21] Kassim also reported that he and his friends tried to provoke a fight with the security guard of the Jewish Museum in his neighborhood, Berlin-Kreuzberg. He showed no sign of regret in being involved in these incidents. A school trip to the local synagogue ended with him and his friends being thrown out of the synagogue. But he justified his antisemitic outburst in the synagogue:

Kassim: My teacher persuaded me. I said, "No, I'm not going in there. If I go in there, I'm going to fight [. . .], if I see that he's wearing the Jewish star." [. . .] I mean, how am I supposed to stay calm? Look at the Jews, they go to Palestine and make war.

Interviewer: But you just said that some Jews also want peace?

Kassim: Yeah, I meant Sharon's things, they go [to] Palestine and make war.

Interviewer: But when they're here in the Synagogue, then they're not going to Palestine, are they?

Kassim: No.

Interviewer: Why are you angry at them?

Kassim: Because [. . .] on that day [. . .] a little boy was murdered with his father. The son was murdered [. . .]. Then I got mad. All of my friends, there were three of us, a Lebanese, I was the Lebanese one, Palestinian, Palestinian, we wanted to go in. We almost started a fight in there. Then the police came, security, they threw us out.

Interviewer: What did you guys say in there?

Kassim: We said, "Fucking Jews, fucking Sharon" and stuff.

Interviewer: But, if I understood correctly, you just don't like Sharon? What about the Jews then?

Kassim: Yeah, but Sharon is Jewish.

Interviewer: Okay, but are all Jews Sharon?

Kassim: I meant Sharon's army, I meant, we yelled, "Fuck Sharon and fuck Sharon's army."

Interviewer: But when you say "Fucking Jew"?

Kassim: Fucking Jews.

Interviewer: Or "fucking Jews," but look, the ones in the synagogue, the ones who live in Berlin, they can't be in Palestine at the same time, can they?

Kassim: No.

Interviewer: But you're still mad at them, how's that?

Kassim: Yeah, I'm mad. Because they kill little children.

Interviewer: But they do too?
Kassim: Un-uh [negating].
Interviewer: Then why at them?
Kassim: Not at them, at those who still want war, I'm mad at them. The ones that don't want war, I'm not mad at them.
Interviewer: But [when they] go and pray in the synagogue, do you know if they want war?
Kassim: I don't know, who knows?
Interviewer: But you're still mad at them?
Kassim: I almost fought with them.

All four incidents show that Kassim's antisemitic actions are not directed against Israel or Israelis but against "the Jews" in his neighborhood, although some justifications he put forward are related to the Israeli-Palestinian conflict. He contradicted himself, most obviously in the accounts of his antisemitic outburst in the local synagogue. He stated that he particularly hates Sharon and those who support war against the Palestinians, but acknowledged that Jews in Berlin are not responsible for the war and that he cannot know if the Jews in the local synagogue support or oppose the war. However, he still showed no regret for his verbal assault on "the Jews" and for insulting them, insisting on the plural in his insult of "*scheiß Juden*" (shitty Jews), directed against all Jews. The excerpt demonstrates the irrational way Kassim responded to the interviewer who tried to make sense of his hatred and attacks against Jews.

Similarly, a Parisian respondent of Maghrebian background did not differentiate between Jews and Israelis in his account of his own involvement in antisemitic violence after a soccer match between the French team Paris Saint-German and the Israeli team Hapoel Tel Aviv on November 24, 2006.[22] Hamza admitted, also without regret, that he took part in the violence against "*the Israelis, the Jews, yeah.*" The heated atmosphere among soccer fans after a match, and the likelihood of French Jews supporting the Israeli team, might lead to a temporary conflation of Israelis and Jews, but Hamza's opinion does not seem to be only temporary. The interview took place five months after the match when he stated, "*It's the same thing, now it's the same thing, as soon as we hear Jew, it's Israeli.*" Hamza still endorsed violence against Jews in Paris without providing any justification other than a conflation of Israelis and Jews. Cherif, also from Paris, reported a dispute over a soccer pitch with students of a local Jewish school. He admitted that he and his friends insulted the Jewish students as "sale Juifs."

In Berlin, directly threatening remarks against Jews, including Jews living in their neighborhood, were made, particularly by participants of Lebanese and Palestinian background. But some indirect forms of threats came from participants of Turkish background, too. One of Halil's friends, for example, said in a threatening tone that it would not be good for Jews to come to their neighborhood, which Halil then confirmed.

Approval of the Holocaust

One of the most appalling forms of antisemitism is the approval of the murder of European Jews by the Nazis and their collaborators. The annihilation of European Jewry was a crime against all rationality, as is its ex-post-facto endorsement. Some interviewees from all three countries endorse the mass murder of Jews, some unambiguously and others reluctantly. Perceptions of the Holocaust, including approval of the Holocaust, are dealt with in the next chapter. The examples show that some participants do not care about moral taboos in their societies against approving of the Holocaust. They also show that approval of the horrors of Auschwitz is highly irrational as well as hateful.

CONCLUSIONS

Negative views of "the Jews" cannot be justified, but they are rarely rejected as completely irrational. Many participants want to find true reasons for anti-Jewish attitudes. A British respondent, for example, asked himself: "*Why didn't Hitler like the Jews [. . .]? Why Jew people? What's wrong with them you see?*" (Rajsekar, London). And others simply accept hatred against Jews, often overtly endorsing this irrationality, insisting on it even if its internal contradictions become obvious. They hate Jews because they are Jews or they adopt negative views of Jews as "common sense" and normal, sometimes referring to their community. They adopt these views even if their argumentation becomes clearly inconsistent and irrational. These young Muslims feel no need to justify negative views of Jews by holding them responsible for negative deeds. Jewish identity in itself is considered reason enough to be despised.

This strong bias translates into language. In French and German, the very term "Jew" is accepted among participants as carrying negative connotations. Prejudice can also lead to an open endorsement of violence against "the Jews" and against individual Jews, whether today in the neighborhood or in the past, during the Holocaust.

Links to other patterns of argumentation such as conspiracy theories, references to Israel, and references to ethnic or religious identity indicate that these arguments only appear to be less irrational and inconsistent. In fact, scrutiny of these arguments reveals their untruth and irrationality.

NINE

Perceptions of the Holocaust

PRIVATE PERCEPTIONS OF THE HOLOCAUST DIFFER FROM PUBLIC discourses of the Holocaust. What are sources of knowledge about the Holocaust for young European Muslims? What is the role of their ethnic or religious background? What do they know about the Holocaust, what are biased attitudes they may hold on the subject, and how are they voiced? What are the rationales? How are their views related to general perceptions of the Holocaust in European countries? What distortions of historical facts influenced by cultural pressures and values emerge?[1] This chapter focuses on interviewees' perceptions of the Holocaust. The wider context is dealt with in detail in the edited volume *Perceptions of the Holocaust in Europe and Muslim Communities: Sources, Comparisons, and Educational Challenges.*[2]

It can be assumed that European Muslims see the Holocaust as less central to their history. Similarly, the discourses within Muslim families are generally less influenced by their own history and by a collective feeling of guilt as compared to Europeans whose families lived in Europe during the Second World War. Most European Muslims come from countries that played only a minor role in the Holocaust and from which relatively few Jews, if any, were deported to German death camps in Eastern Europe.[3] However, in many European Muslims' countries of origin, Holocaust denial is widespread; the Holocaust is often portrayed as a tool used by Israel; conspiracy theories about an alleged Nazi-Zionist collaboration are widespread; and Israel is equated with Nazism.[4] There is a level of open Holocaust denial in some mass media in Muslim-majority countries that is not seen in European countries. The

Turkish daily *Vakit*, for example, was printed in Germany for its readers there until 2005, when it was banned by the German authorities for its denial of the Holocaust, as well as for antisemitic and anti-Western propaganda.[5] Other publications, such as the Dutch Turkish journal *Doğuş*, affiliated with the Islamist organization Milli Görüş, have been printed in Europe unchallenged for years despite their outright Holocaust denial and blunt conspiracy theories.[6]

The reluctance of European Muslim organizations to participate in Holocaust commemorations, or their outright rejection of them,[7] and the difficulties schools often have in teaching about the Holocaust to Muslim students highlight the problematic views that some European Muslims hold.[8] However, in the Netherlands, a survey of teachers reveals that diminishment of the Holocaust is widespread. In 2004, 50 percent of the polled teachers said that their students diminished the Holocaust at least once during the past year, though this number was down to 25 percent in 2013. Trivialization of the Holocaust and antisemitism is more frequent in schools with large groups of Turkish and Moroccan students.[9] In Germany, *Die Zeit* published a survey on views of the Holocaust of 400 people of Turkish origin in January 2010. Sixty-eight percent admitted that they knew little about the Holocaust and 40 percent said that people of Turkish background living in Germany should not be concerned with studying the subject.[10] A poll on Muslims in the United Kingdom from 2006 shows that only a third believed that the Holocaust happened as history teaches, and 17 percent thought that it has been exaggerated.[11]

What do participants interviewed for this study think about the Holocaust? In the following sections I first give a brief description of the basic knowledge most interviewees have about the Holocaust and their sources of knowledge. Second, I present participants' doubts and conspiracy theories about the Holocaust. Third, I discuss contextualizations and comparisons of the Holocaust with other atrocities; some are biased, such as equations of Israel with the Nazis and the suffering of Palestinians with that of Jews in the Holocaust. Finally, I examine their emotional reactions to the Holocaust, ranging from condemnations of the perpetrators and empathy with the victims to approval of the Holocaust based on Jew hatred.

SHARED BASIC KNOWLEDGE OF THE HOLOCAUST

Interviewees often did not know the meaning of "Holocaust" or "Auschwitz" at first but, as the proceeding conversations revealed, most had heard of the term Holocaust and some mentioned Auschwitz spontaneously.[12] Few are familiar with the Hebrew word for Holocaust, "Shoah." Many do not know the exact year the Second World War started and ended, and some mix up historical events as different as the Second World War and the fall of the Berlin Wall in 1989. A flagrant lack of knowledge also emerged occasionally with the surmise that the National Socialists killed Jews for religious reasons or with questions such as, "*Was it a tough [. . .], equal fight?*" (Malik, London). But most interviewees did have some basic knowledge about the historical fact of the murder of the European Jews by the Nazis, including that Jews were persecuted and killed in Germany in vast numbers during the Second World War.[13] The Nazis and, particularly the dictator Hitler, were identified as the perpetrators. The fact that many Jews were gassed and burnt in concentration camps is also widely known. However, knowledge about the Holocaust is often vague and not important to participants.[14] Bashkar from London has very limited knowledge of the Holocaust, although he did remember important aspects such as the killing of many Jews in gas chambers. But consider his initial reaction to this question:

Interviewer: Do you know the word "Holocaust"?
Bashkar: Holocaust, yeah. It's that place, innit?
Interviewer: No, it's not a place.
Bashkar: Oh yeah, it's the Jews, they were killed, innit? [. . .] Millions.

Bashkar's knowledge of the Holocaust is not easily accessible, a sign, according to social psychology research on attitudes, that it is not an important issue for him.[15] Many other interviewees have much more detailed knowledge of the forms of persecution and killings of Jews, the racist ideology of an "Aryan" race, and the Second World War. Many also know details about Adolf Hitler, including his Austrian birth, his unsuccessful career as a painter, and his suicide. And, of course, interviewees know of Hitler's distinct moustache. Some put the Holocaust in the context of a long history of discrimination and persecution of the

Jews, such as being blamed for the Black Death or the murder of Jesus Christ. Very few interviewees were explicitly disinterested in the history of the Holocaust.

SOURCES OF KNOWLEDGE

Interviewees referred to school as their most important source of knowledge about the Holocaust, saying that in addition they had visited memorial sites with school groups and met Holocaust survivors.[16] However, the ideological driving forces for the extermination of Jewry are often reduced to prejudices and intolerance in general. Bahaar recalled what he had learned in school in London about the reasons behind the Holocaust: "*In lessons I learned that it's just basically a process where lots of Jews got killed because of the reason that they were different and that they didn't want them there.*" This generally widespread perception ignores the fact that well-integrated Jews and even people who did not consider themselves Jewish at all were made "different" and were also indiscriminately killed in the Holocaust. What is more, modern antisemitism goes well beyond xenophobic attitudes: it is less about exclusion of foreigners than about a global hatred of Jews wherever they are.[17]

Another frequently cited source of knowledge is television, through which interviewees learned particularly about the Warsaw Ghetto, Hitler, the persecution and murder of Jews, and the Second World War. It is noteworthy that one interviewee from Berlin visited the former concentration camp Sachsenhausen with the youth group of the local mosque. Friends and relatives, books, films, and the internet were only occasionally mentioned as sources of knowledge on the Holocaust. However, these sources, including vague references to "what they have heard," can have an important impact on questioning public narratives of the Holocaust, such as what is taught in school.

Of course, the way knowledge is presented is related to various interpretations and explanations of the Holocaust. Salih from Berlin, for example, gave a simplifying account of the Holocaust in a nutshell: "*Hitler became politician and when times were bad he lay all the blame on the Jews and then he just started to kill them all, to gas them.*" He portrayed Hitler as the only responsible perpetrator and used the theory that Jews were made scapegoats for explaining their subsequent murder. Both are prominent views on the Holocaust in Germany.[18]

DOUBTS, DENIAL, AND CONSPIRACIES ABOUT THE HOLOCAUST

Some interpretations, explanations, and beliefs about the Holocaust amount to diminishing or even denying the Holocaust. This often contradicts what interviewees have learned in school. Three interviewees explicitly depicted the Holocaust as a myth or said that far fewer than six million Jews were killed. Haroun, for example, is aware of the disparity of his beliefs and the narrative he was taught in school in France:

> *They are saying the Jews were killed and that. I don't know if that's true. This is what I was taught in school that they were deported, killed, some things. But I was told something else that there was an illness called typhus which spread everywhere and that's why they were burnt.*
>
> *[...]*
>
> *Anyway, I've heard in a political debate, they said that this was because of a strange disease, the images which were filmed, at least some of them [...] that was because of the disease which was called typhus [...] which spread across Germany at a certain time. Everywhere, a bit everywhere, well, there was in the concentration camps, I don't know, around the camps, or in the train or.... Everybody got this disease, this people had to be burnt.*

Haroun, a Frenchman of Algerian descent, doubts that Jews were killed systematically and labels the Holocaust as "nonsense" and a "state secret." He thinks that Jews and others had to be burnt because of typhus. Haroun refers to two narratives: the one he has learned in school (which he doubts) and another one which he "was told" and which he feels was confirmed in a political debate, probably on French TV, about typhus in concentration camps.

Aban, of South Asian origin from London, is another example of someone who denies the Holocaust. He is convinced that "*Hitler did not kill six million Jews [...]. He killed about six hundred thousand.*" He doubts the information he learned in school, saying that pictures of shaven-headed people in "*those jackets*" in concentration camps could be staged and that the information students get in school is probably biased. Aban gave three arguments for his doubts on the number of six million. His first argument is that there are so many Jews today that he cannot believe that, as he said, more than half of the Jews were killed.[19] This argument hints at a widespread overestimation of the number of Jews alive today. The world's Jewish population is less than 14 million (0.2 percent). However, 38 percent of those polled in the worldwide 2014 ADL Global 100 survey believed that the global Jewish population is bigger than 10 percent. Second, Aban used the film *Schindler's List* as evidence that many Jews were saved, which confirms that a film about the Holocaust focusing on the rescue of Jews can be the basis of a misconception about the Holocaust given that, in fact, only a relatively few were rescued.[20] And Aban's third argument is that "*to deal with six million Jews, and then the rest of the world. He can't [. . .]. It would take more than the population of Germany to do that.*" This seems to be a result of sheer disbelief regarding the scale of the murderous enterprise or a biased overestimate of the power of these six million Jewish civilians. Interestingly, he claimed that he has found out this "truth" by himself through "common sense." He thus presented himself as someone who has made up his own mind and who has revealed the truth against the official, allegedly biased narrative from school and TV. This is a typical element of conspiracy theories.

Neoy, another interviewee of Asian background, knows about Holocaust Memorial Day, but he is convinced that "only" close to a million Jews were killed, referring to a book by a "*journalist that actually investigated the killing*" and to "*official statistics,*" possibly mentioned in that book.[21] Most interestingly, he stated in that context: "*I think there is an elite who says what does and what doesn't go.*" He thus believes that public discourse on the Holocaust, including Holocaust Memorial Day, is dictated by a small group which he did not name. He can explain the discrepancy between public discourse and his "sources" with the help of this conspiracy theory.

A few others voiced doubts about the Holocaust, which can also be seen as a form of Holocaust denial.[22] Manoj from London of South Asian origin, however, voiced such strong doubts that he portrayed the Holocaust as a fictitious narrative:

> *What a lot of people are saying is, did the Holocaust exist or not? A lot of things don't add up. They are saying 6 million Jews got massacred, but were there 6 million Jews in Europe at that time? [. . .] So that's why they are teaching [. . .]. They want*

to make it so that people believe the Holocaust really did happen. And there's not a shadow of doubt in that. That's why they're teaching everyone from school.

Manoj tried to present the results of research on the Holocaust as contradictory by casting doubts on well-established facts. In order to back up his doubts he referred to "what people are saying," similar to Haroun from Paris quoted above. Manoj believes that "they" have an agenda of teaching the Holocaust in school.

Nader, a British citizen of North African descent, also had his doubts both about Hitler and the Holocaust. He claimed that nobody knows if and how Hitler died and referred to a narrative from "back home," meaning Morocco. Thus he is aware of a discourse in Morocco about the Holocaust which he values and which differs from, and even contradicts, the discourse in Britain. The fact that Jews were burnt was something he distanced himself from, both by indirect speech, portraying it as a rumor, and also emotionally by using vulgar language: "*We heard that Hitler used to barbecue Jewish people.*" He then added another fundamental argument for the disbelief of what happened during the Shoah: "*I can't tell you he is a killer, because I wasn't with him. I wasn't there sitting down with Hitler having a tea and now he tells me about his story!*" Nader thereby claimed that one can only be sure of historical facts if the events are of direct experience (or related face-to-face by those responsible for historical developments) and that all other accounts of history are to be doubted.

These examples indicate that it is not a lack of knowledge which leads to doubts or denial of the Holocaust. The interviewees are aware of the fact that public discourse contradicts their beliefs, but they do not accept public discourse on the Holocaust. They choose to believe in a narrative of denial which they have encountered on TV or in a book, or they believe in a rumor or something they heard from "back home," or they claim that "common sense" in the search for truth has brought them to their conclusions. Casting doubts on one aspect of the Holocaust calls into question the Holocaust as a historical fact altogether. In order to bridge the gap between the public discourse and their own narratives, interviewees believe the public discourse to be biased or staged and revert to conspiracy theories.

Rumors that Adolf Hitler was Jewish or had Jewish ancestors are a recurrent trope.[23] They are referred to as rumors ("what people say") but also as what they have learned in school: "*He's an Austrian. His mother – she is Austrian and Jewish [. . .] and he wants to take revenge [. . .]. This is what they told us in school*" (Bilal, Paris). We cannot know what exactly Bilal was taught in school. But what he has learned, and what he refers to as knowledge from school, is that Hitler's mother was Jewish and that Hitler wanted to take "revenge," for what we do not know. Portraying Hitler as being related to Jews, however, suggests that he knew Jews well and had his reasons for his Jew hatred, or even that there was a collaboration between Hitler and Jews. The latter interpretation is promoted by Ümit from Berlin, of Turkish origin. He believes that Hitler was "Halbjude" (half-Jewish) and collaborated with those who wanted to establish "a Greater Israel." He portrays Hitler as a "weapon" for this goal, eliminating all the weak and poor Jews who were "useless" for the establishment of a "Greater Israel" and not killing the educated and rich. And he takes his perception that there are mostly rich and influential Jews today who stick together and try to advance "Greater Israel" as evidence for his theory. Hence, he accuses an alleged leadership of Jews and Israelis for the Holocaust and portrays Hitler as a victim of this conspiracy. It should be noted that Ümit uses Nazi terminology, such as the word "Halbjude," and accepts the view of the National Socialists that "those who were gassed, they were simply good for nothing."

COMPARING THE HOLOCAUST TO OTHER ATROCITIES

Equating the Holocaust to the Israeli treatment of Palestinians is an antisemitic trope.[24] Some surveys have used it as an item for contemporary antisemitic attitudes.[25] How did interviewees compare the Holocaust to other alleged and real atrocities? Many equate the Holocaust to other historical events or draw inappropriate analogies of the Holocaust. In addition to equating the sufferings of Palestinians with those of Holocaust-era Jews, interviewees also drew parallels between the Iraq war and the Holocaust, equating Bush with Hitler. Some also compared the

Holocaust to today's persecution of Muslims or foreigners, as well as to slavery, AIDS, and the colonial history of France. The ways these analogies are drawn significantly diminish the Holocaust as demonstrated below. Deborah Lipstadt described this as a form of antisemitism and "soft-core Holocaust denial."[26] The analogies also show that the term Holocaust is often used merely as a reference to atrocities in general, despite knowledge about the murder of six million Jews.

Equating the Sufferings of Palestinians with the Holocaust

What is the rationale of equating sufferings of Palestinians with the Holocaust? One precondition seems to be the perception of a deep suffering of "the Palestinians" in the hand of "the Israelis" or "the Jews." A recurrent theme is the killing of children, which, in the eyes of some participants, amounts to atrocities like those committed in the Holocaust. "*It's more or less the same thing. They kill the children,*" said Hamza from Paris. Ismail from Berlin, however, acknowledged that Palestinians are not gassed but emphasized the allegedly equally cruel abuses that Palestinians have to suffer, for which he referenced Arab news channels. The argument that Palestinians in the Gaza Strip are imprisoned is also used to justify an equivalence: "*Well, I have heard, that many Jews are accused or attacked because they went through the Holocaust and now they do it with the Palestinians by blocking up the Gaza Strip, theoretically*" (Çeto, Berlin). The allegation that the Jews today are the perpetrators of similar atrocities like those of which they were victims in the Holocaust has been described as a projection of guilt within the German context.[27] However, this cannot be Çeto's motivation because he does not consider himself German. His claim that he has heard this allegation hints to the influence of this context in Germany on his perception of the Jews and the Holocaust. The use of the antisemitic topos that Jews allegedly talk too much about the Holocaust points in the same direction. This topos can be related to the wish not to be reminded of the responsibility of Germans[28] or other Europeans. As another interviewee concluded: "*They kill the people like the Nazis killed the Jews, there are no differences. So the Jews cannot complain about what Hitler did with them when they do it themselves*" (Necet, Berlin).

Such patterns, from a discourse of secondary antisemitism as an unreflected rejection of guilt feelings, are endorsed mostly by participants from Germany. It demonstrates the influence of this discourse also on people with migrant backgrounds who have no feelings of collective guilt vis-à-vis the Holocaust. Another recurrent aspect of Necet's view is that "the Jews" are seen as one unity, conflating not only Israelis with Jews but also the Jewish victims of the Holocaust more than seventy years ago with Israelis today.

Equations of the Holocaust with the treatment of the Palestinians insinuate evil intentions on the Israeli side and misrepresent the Israeli-Palestinian conflict. Sharif from Berlin, for example, thinks that the methods of the Holocaust and the Israeli-Palestinian conflict are different but that the underlying attitudes of disrespect and dehumanization are the same: "*Regarding the disrespect or the disdain it is just the same. Just as the Nazis at the time didn't regard Jews as human beings, the Israelis don't really regard the Palestinians as human beings.*" Similarly, Bahaar from London thinks that "it" is similar "*because the idea of it is roughly the same, I mean, just killing someone because you think you're better or they're different or they're wrong. . . .*" "It," referring to the Holocaust, becomes a general term that implies hatred against others.

Aba from London, of Ghanian English origin, is somehow more cautious in his comparison. He said: "*I don't know if it's as blatant as it was during the Holocaust, but [. . .] it is kind of similar [. . .]. Can't just straight up say it's another Holocaust.*" For him, it is a question of the degree of blatant hatred; he does not see the particularity of the Holocaust. And thus he said about an Israeli politician whose speech he read: "*He's just trying to evoke an emotional response in the people, like saying how the Palestinians have bombed our women and children, like the typical stuff that I studied in history, like when Hitler would say certain things to evoke an emotional response.*" He made no distinction in principal between delusional Nazi propaganda about Jews allegedly threatening the Germans and a speech by an Israeli politician pointing out real threats of terrorism by Palestinians. What is more, the Holocaust becomes an empty metaphor, unrelated to the systematic murder of European Jewry. This lack of understanding of the Holocaust enables equations with very different phenomena.

A confrontation with the fact that six million Jews were murdered can be met by an attempt to diminish the Holocaust. Bilal gave such an example when he explained why he believes that what the Israelis do with the Palestinians is the same as what the Nazis did to the Jews:

Bilal: Because [. . .] in Palestine they are still there the Israelis, they are beating [. . .] and there are always dead bodies, sometimes the guys are 14 years old, 13 years, they die there [. . .]. Even kids are dying.
Interviewer: You said that the Nazis killed 6 million Jews.
Bilal: Yeah, there are not only Jews, too.

His main argument for this equation is that Israelis are still in Palestine and that they hit and kill Palestinians, including children. The interviewer's objection that six million Jews were murdered in the Holocaust is met by diminishing the Holocaust. Noey from London even portrayed the Holocaust as a Jewish claim before he described the killings of Palestinians as "a present-day example of the Holocaust":

Before, the victims were the Jews, so they claimed, now, we see that the Jews are the oppressors because what is happening in Palestine, if you see the pictures of the Israelis, up-to-date weapons are killing these little Palestinian kids for throwing stones at them. And that is a present-day example of the Holocaust [. . .]. I think, Israel is playing the role that Hitler played.

It should be noted that Noey's presentation of "the Jews" as perpetrators today and Hitler alone as the perpetrator of the Holocaust is a recurrent theme, as is the image of modern Israeli soldiers fighting and killing Palestinian children, both among interviewees and the wider population.

Some interviewees even stated that the treatment of Palestinians is worse than the Holocaust. Khalil from Paris believes that "it" is worse because, he argues, "the Jews" want to kill all Muslims. Nirmal from Britain is not sure if the Jews intend to exterminate all the Palestinians, but he is adamant that the Jews want to take over Palestine and the world:

But obviously unlike Hitler, Hitler did it alone. They're getting their help from America and this country. They're getting more help [. . .]. I am not sure whether they want to kill all the Palestinians. But I do know that they want to take over their country. Take over the world.

Again, "the Jews" are accused of atrocities but Hitler is seen as the only perpetrator of the Holocaust. Nirmal's perception of Israel perpetrating atrocities like the Holocaust with help from the United States and Britain is clearly tainted by antisemitic conspiracy theories.

Abhijt from London raises the antisemitic stereotype of the wandering Jew who has his place nowhere.[29] He insists that "whatever Hitler did" to Jews was very different from how Palestinians are treated by Israel. He argues that while Hitler only "took out" the Jewish minority, Jews "kick out" the majority living in Palestine:

> *It's not the same, because initially Jews then [did not belong] to German[y] [. . .]. They initially came from Egypt, right? Or the Middle East [. . .]. But whatever Hitler did [. . .] the majority were non-Jews [. . .]. And he was tryin' to take out the minority out of that area, or off that state. But at this place, the impression I'm having [. . .] is that, the minority Jewish, that came to stay in a place for temporary basis which is Israel, which is not their home, are tryin' to kick out the landlords. In other words [. . .] they are tryin' to kick out the people, who actually own the place. See, it's a different thing.*

Abhijt accepts the notion of the National Socialists that Jews do not belong to Germany. He believes that "the Jews" came from Egypt or the Middle East, but he also sees Jews in Israel as strangers in a place owned by other people and thereby alludes to the image of Israel as a colonial state and to the image of the wandering Jew, belonging nowhere.

To conclude, equations of the Holocaust with the Israeli-Palestinian conflict imply the perception of deep suffering of the Palestinians in the hands of the Israelis or "the Jews" who are accused of evil intentions. Such equations often come with antisemitic stereotypes and tropes, such as Jews as child murderers, Jews talking too much about the Holocaust, the image of the wandering Jew, and antisemitic conspiracy theories.

The meaning of the Holocaust, the systematic murder of European Jewry, is neglected, while the term is used instead as a metaphor for all atrocities. Equating the Holocaust with the plight of the Palestinians is rooted in hostile attitudes toward Jews and an emotional attachment to the struggle of Palestinians against Israel rather than in a lack of knowledge. Hostile attitudes toward Jews are a motive to diminish the Holocaust. The emotional attachment to "the Palestinians" serves to exaggerate sufferings of "the Palestinians" and to see them as only victims. Together, this facilitates an equivalence of the Holocaust and the Israeli-Palestinian conflict.

The Topos of Jews Taking Revenge for the Holocaust on the Palestinians

Some participants from all three countries used the topos of Jews taking revenge for the Holocaust on the Palestinians. This rationale acknowledges the suffering of Jews at the hands of the Nazis, assumes that this suffering led to a collective trauma, and accuses the Jewish people today of taking this trauma out on Palestinians. This topos alludes to the antisemitic trope of a "Jewish revenge."[30] A psychological explanation seems plausible: one's own suppressed desire for revenge on various issues is projected onto Jews. The topos often comes with equating the Holocaust and the sufferings of Palestinians. Consider the three examples below, one each from France, Germany, and Britain, which illustrate the three main patterns within this topos:

(1) The Holocaust as an explanation for the evilness of Jews.
(2) The accusation against Jews that they have not learned from their own history of persecution but are looking for revenge.
(3) The transference of alleged psychological mechanisms of individuals to a people.

Nader from London said that the Holocaust and the suffering of Palestinians are comparable and argued thereupon:

> *[They are] trying to [take] revenge. Because as you are going to kill innocent kids and his family, that's what happened back with the Germans as well, Hitler. Why are you going to do that? Why are you going to bring the history back? [. . .] They still got that black dot in them heart.*

Nader thus explained the evil of Jews killing children and their black-heartedness with the collective trauma, presenting it as the impossible attempt to "bring back history." The Holocaust becomes the reason for the evil of Jews. Massoud from Paris deplored the fact that Jews have not learned from their own history of persecution but are looking for revenge:

> *One could have hoped that it served them as a lesson [. . .] what the Germans did to them, to the Israelis. But in fact, what they are looking for, it's vengeance.*

The argument is contradictory in itself because the purported "vengeance" targets the Palestinians and not the Germans. Note that he blurred Israelis with Jews when he used the term "Israelis."

Ismail from Berlin took a different approach and drew an analogy to the education of children, assuming that violent patterns in families are repeated from generation to generation. He thus portrayed it as a natural mechanism for the Jews to allegedly treat the Palestinians the way they were treated themselves:

> *Well, because the way they were treated – for example, if my father constantly beats me, then I will also [. . .] beat my children [. . .]. And that is the same with the Jews, the people was treated that way and now they treat the Palestinians like that.*

Ismail gave the clearest example of transferring alleged psychological mechanisms of individuals to a people. It shows that the perception of Jews as a unitary category is part of the rationale of this topos.

Analogies between the Holocaust and the War in Iraq and Equations of the U.S. President with Hitler

Comparisons and equations are not limited to the Israeli-Palestinian conflict. Interviewees drew parallels between the Holocaust and the war in Iraq, also comparing Bush with Hitler. This is further evidence that the Holocaust serves as a metaphor for atrocities such as despicable killings of innocents in war while ignoring historical differences. Additionally, it demonstrates that such distorted views are not limited to perceptions of the Israeli-Palestinian conflict.

Some relate the war in Iraq to an alleged war against Muslims. The portrayal of one's own group as victims is another motive of such equations. For Haroun from Paris, for example, Bush is a concealed racist, which adds to his claim that Hitler is like Bush:

> *Hitler is like Bush. It's the same [. . .]. In forty years we will step back and say, "Ah yes, that was more or less the same thing [. . .], just that there were planes and tanks." [. . .] It's the same, you see, now there are just missiles, that's all, they go to Iraq and they are killing [. . .]. It's a so-called not-racist racist.*

Kashi and Bashkar declared that both Bush and Blair are today's Hitler because they are responsible for bombings: "*They're killing mil-*

lions of Muslims, but they'll never say we did it" (Kashi, London). Noey, quoted above saying that that there is *"a present-day example of the Holocaust"* in Palestine, also claimed that there are similar concentration camps to those of the Nazis in Afghanistan and Iraq in which they hold prisoners, operated by the Americans. He even went one step further and accused the Americans of trying to annihilate the people in Iraq: *"The obvious conclusion is that [it] is their plan to wipe them all out. They're killing children every day. And, for example, when 1,000 Iraqis got killed, the [. . .] Secretary of State [. . .] said, 'That's the price we're paying.'"* Taking the tragic killing and death of many Iraqi children as evidence for the attempt to annihilate a people just as in the Holocaust is delusional and demonstrates that those who make such equations are not interested in an analysis of reality, neither historically nor today.

Analogies between the Holocaust and Persecution of Muslims

The argument that Muslims today suffer from prejudices similar to the prejudices that led to the persecution of Jews has been discussed widely.[31] It has been publicly claimed that Muslims are the Jews of today's world.[32] However, only a few interviewees directly compared the persecution of Jews to hostility against Muslims today, almost all of them hailing from London. That argument implies an acknowledgment of the sufferings of Jews in the Holocaust, but, again, the Holocaust only stands as a metaphor for suffering, abuse, and the killing of many innocent people. As one summed it up:

> *A few hundred [years] back it was the Jewish people. Because they were treated very badly and given bad names and now it's our turn [. . .]. In a way it's the same level because every time, like 9/11, there was many people killed, innocent people. But then again, how many innocent people have been killed in Iraq, Afghanistan, other places. . . .* (Labaan, London)

Speaking about possible reasons for the persecution of Jews, another interviewee said: *"I think everyone wants a scapegoat, for whatever problem. And now, Muslims have become the scapegoat"* (Manoj, London). The perception that antisemitism and the Holocaust are a result of scapegoating is widespread and enables equations to other prejudices. However, focusing on only that aspect demonstrates a lack of a comprehensive understanding of the Holocaust. Scapegoating cannot explain why Jews were targeted, and the scapegoat theory is questionable in general as an explanatory theory for the genesis of social prejudice. Two of its basic hypotheses, the assumption that aggression is rooted in frustration and that aggression is then transferred onto a scapegoat rather than targeting the origin of frustration, have been questioned and partly disproven in social psychological research.[33]

Hussein, also from London, made the connection between persecution of Jews and Muslims today in an interesting way. Speaking about the fact that Jews were forced into concentration camps, he asked: *"And what was his [Hitler's] reason? He was giving reasons such as they were terrorists?"* Hussein seems to think that the accusation of terrorism, which is often voiced against Muslims, could have been a pretext to kill the Jews and thereby compares both.

Explicitly Rejecting Antisemitic Equations

Some interviewees reject antisemitic equations between the Holocaust and the sufferings of Palestinians in the Middle East conflict. What are their reasons or rationales? Jamil from Berlin, for example, criticized Israel's military action but distinguished between the Middle East conflict and the Holocaust, judging the latter as much worse, and showed empathy for the victims of the Holocaust. He also did not show other forms of antisemitism. Farid from Paris rejected any equation, referring to his knowledge from school about the Holocaust. He did so despite expressing biased views on the Israeli-Palestinian conflict, alluding to the image of all-powerful and cruel Jews. Others who rejected this equation did not refer to knowledge about the Holocaust but rather to their lack of knowledge and lack of emotional involvement. Tunay from Berlin of Turkish background, for example, rejects the equation and thinks that Jews and Arabs should fight their battle among themselves, and Naresh from London believes that Jews and Muslims are equally responsible in the Middle East conflict.

The above examples reveal three different rationales for rejecting antisemitic equations. First, the lack of hostile feelings against Jews opens a non-biased view on the Holocaust and empathy for its victims. Second, educational approaches with the authority of teachers who stress the differences have been accepted despite biased attitudes against Jews. And third, a lack of emotional involvement with the Israeli-Palestinian conflict or critical views about Palestinians prevents the portrayal of a Manichean picture of the Israeli-Palestinian conflict.

The Holocaust and the Creation of the State of Israel

The perception that the Holocaust led to the creation of the State of Israel is widespread. It is often voiced together with a rejection of the legitimacy of the foundation of the State of Israel and fragments of an anti-colonialist discourse (the land of the State of Israel naturally belongs to another people and not to Jews). One interviewee phrased this perception as "*Palestine, it belonged to the Muslims and then through the Holocaust they came through*" (Tarak, London). Since he considers himself Muslim, he presented the creation of the State of Israel as a process that took land away from his own community, despite his South Asian background. The emphasis that land "naturally" belongs to a people has racist or xenophobic undertones. Another participant, for example, said the following about the creation of the State of Israel: "*The Jews they just come to another land . . . the bastards*" (Suleiman, Berlin). Suleiman is also generally opposed to immigration and wants Turkish people to leave Germany. For Palestinians he sees a special right to stay in Germany, which he couples with the demand to get the Jews out of Palestine: "*The [Palestinians] have the right to live here as the Germans have sent the Jews to Palestine. I have [the] right to live here until they will get the Jews out of Palestine, until then I have the right to live here*" (Suleiman, Berlin). Jews are believed to belong to Europe; they are even denied the right of self-determination in their own country:

> *As since back as Hitler, Jewish people they had no countries, they's just spreaded all over the world. Why now you want to be reunited, and get Palestine as your own country? You can't do that.* (Nader, London)

Nader thereby used the image of the wandering Jew who has no home country[34] and who should not have one.

Another argument is that "the Muslims" or "the Palestinians" should not be the ones to suffer from the Jews who were allegedly sent to Palestine. *"I think the Jewish people should have had their place maybe in Germany or another place in Europe, because [. . .] the Muslims was not the people who was killing the Jewish"* (Labaan, London). The notion that Jews were sent to Palestine is a recurrent pattern, for which different respondents cited the Germans, the British, the United Nations, the Americans, or the Europeans as responsible. As one explained:

> *Our teacher he told us that there was the Second World War or the First War. Then, the Europeans distributed the Jews, because the Jews were persecuted by the Germans, so that they put them in a land and the English they put the Muslims also in the same land as the Jews and therefore they fought to keep their country.* (Diaba, Paris)

Diaba's account of the historical sources of the Middle East conflict is vague and reductive. However, he sees the persecution of the Jews by the Germans as the reason for the Europeans "to put the Jews" in the land of Palestine which, in his eyes, led to the Middle East conflict. Interestingly, he also said that the British sent Muslims to the same land, too, and thus portrayed both Jews and Muslims as passive and subjected to the colonial forces of the British Empire. His theory neglects the fact that Jews were struggling to get to Palestine under the British mandate and that the British government severely restricted Jewish immigration. In this view there is also no room to consider the feuding Arab groups in Palestine with their different views on Jewish immigration at the time. Another objection lies in the euphemism he used that the Jews *"were persecuted"* in the Second World War. This is even more obvious in another interviewee's statement: *"Hitler expelled [the Jews] to Palestine. And the English gave [them] the country where the Palestinians are"* (Naeem, Berlin). However, Jews were not only pursued and displaced but annihilated. Diminishing the Holocaust reduces potential sympathy and understanding for the establishment of the State of Israel.

German Guilt and Compensation Payments

The allegation that Germany makes immense compensation payments to the state of Israel is a common topos of secondary antisemitism in Germany. This allegation is often broached as a rejection of the feeling of collective guilt for the Holocaust committed by the generation of parents or grandparents.[35] It might therefore be surprising that this topos was also used by interviewees whose family background is non-German and who barely identify themselves as German.[36]

Two friends, Ramzi and Ahmed, were interviewed together in Berlin. Neither consider themselves to be German (although Ahmed is a German citizen)[37] and both show no feelings of guilt for the Holocaust. However, within the first ten minutes of an interview which began with a conversation about life in their district and the difficulties of education and the economy in Germany, and without knowing that the interview would examine attitudes toward Jews and the Holocaust, Ramzi complained about the allegedly huge ongoing reparations from Germany to Israel.

> *Germany will go down [. . .]. It's getting worse and worse [. . .]. Berlin has a lot of debts. They were so stupid [. . .], they always think when it's too late [. . .]. Go and pay your debts first [. . .], so that you will be doing better instead of still paying every year 200 million Euro to Israel since the Second World War [. . .]. Every year, Germany pays 200 million to Israel. Why? [. . .]Because the Germans think that the Jews for example killed Hitler back then. And until now they are paying because they are so stupid [. . .]. And until now they think: "If there was Hitler now, that would be bad."* (Ramzi, Berlin)

Ramzi's statement shows that he does not consider himself German. He sees the compensation payments as a result of German stupidity, claiming that "the Germans" believe that Jews have liberated them from Hitler. His friend Ahmed did not agree with this bizarre allegation and explained, "*He meant that Germany feels guilty for Hitler,*" pointing out the feeling of collective guilt in Germany. Even so, Ahmed agrees in principle that alleged compensation payments are too high, complaining that money should instead be put aside for education of youths like him: "*Who suffers from this? We young people who do not get a proper education.*"

Another interviewee from Germany, of Palestinian background, sees compensation payments as an outcome of a bad conscience of Germany and Europe, adding: "*You should not be called an antisemite, in no way. This is also a weapon that they definitely have*" (Sharif, Berlin). He thereby alluded to the image of powerful Jews who wield the accusation of antisemitism as a weapon.[38] His statement implies that he believes accusations of antisemitism are illegitimate, a typical pattern of denial of antisemitism.[39] Erol of Turkish background believes that Germany is afraid of criticizing Israel due to "mistakes" in the past, as he euphemistically labeled the Holocaust. According to him, "criticism" of Israel is taboo and immediately becomes a scandal in Germany. He referred to the scandal surrounding a politician named Jürgen Möllemann who, in fact, used antisemitic and anti-Israeli allusions in his 2002 campaign while putting himself forward as taboo breaker.[40] The details Erol provided about the scandal show that he followed the public discourse attentively.

Why do young people with migrant backgrounds in Germany use patterns of secondary antisemitism that suggest a rejection of a feeling of collective guilt for the Holocaust, a feeling they do not have? Interviewees have learned these patterns from public and private discourses in Germany and utilize them as a form of accepted antisemitism.

MORAL JUDGEMENTS AND EMOTIONAL REACTIONS TO THE HOLOCAUST

One would expect disapproval, condemnation, outrage, or sympathy with its victims as reactions to the Holocaust, and the large majority indeed clearly disapprove of the Holocaust's atrocities. But other participants are indifferent, and a few in all three countries cite "other Arabs" or "other Muslims" who take satisfaction in the Holocaust or who approve of the systematic mass murder of Jews. The Holocaust is strongly associated with Hitler, who is usually seen and condemned as a racist and evil dictator, responsible for the Second World War and racist persecutions – "only" a few show signs of sympathy for Hitler, most clearly five participants who declared that they like Hitler. However, neither the condemnation of Hitler nor knowledge about the Holocaust necessarily lead to a condemnation of the Holocaust. Equally, more detailed knowledge about the Holocaust does not lead to less antisemitic attitudes.[41] Why, and in what ways do participants condemn the Holocaust?

Condemnations of the Holocaust

The Holocaust is denounced in general terms with attributes such as "horrible," "sad," "grave," "bad," "evil." The Holocaust is also denounced in religious terms as a sin for killing "*too many people,*" as Sakti from

London said. Participants know that the Holocaust is condemned in society and usually accept this condemnation:

> *In school [. . .] and on TV you often see coverage [of the Holocaust] because the Germans often talk about it because that was one of their worst things of the past.* (Çeto, Berlin)

Çeto, who is of Turkish-Kurdish background and was born in Berlin and has German citizenship, sees the Holocaust as part of German history, not his own.[42] Even though remembrance of the Holocaust is usually not given importance by interviewees, no interviewee directly opposes the remembrance of the Holocaust.[43] One young man represented that attitude when he stated laconically: "*They've died, so obviously they should be remembered . . . to some extent*" (Rahim, London). The use of the Holocaust as a metaphor for atrocities as discussed above diminishes the Holocaust but, actually, also shows disapproval of the Holocaust. This notion is widespread, not only among interviewees.[44] Hitler, seen as the main perpetrator of the Holocaust, is usually denounced: "*[My friends] hate Hitler*" (Mehmet, Berlin); "*Hitler is my worst enemy!*" (Nadem, Paris); "*He was a maniac*" (Kashi, London); or simply, "*Hitler was a bad man,*" as one participant from Britain said – these are frequently voiced opinions on Hitler. The general assumption that Hitler was evil is not necessarily based on facts: some argued that he raped women, for example, to stress his evilness. Additionally, particularly interviewees in Germany often perceive neo-Nazis as a physical threat against themselves and some even had experiences with them. Others, however, see ideological similarities between them and neo-Nazis regarding the dislike of Jews (see below).

Condemning the Holocaust with Restrictions: Accusations of Exploitation and Emotional Distance

A recurrent feeling that comes along with the acknowledgment of the suffering of Jews in the Holocaust is the notion that the Jews have earned something with this suffering: "*They [the Jews] have earned certain things*" (Erol, Berlin). Another notion is that Jews are accused of being too sensitive because of the Holocaust and therefore often falsely accuse others of antisemitism.

> *I think Jews, after the Holocaust [. . .] would pick up on any tiny grievance, or any comment, and just straight away say: "Anti-Semitism," straight away. Only because they've been vulnerable, innit? They've been hurt by that history [. . .]. I think if you made any comment about Jews [. . .] as soon as you say it, they'd be: "Anti-Semitism."* (Aba, London)

Hamza went even further and accused Jews of portraying themselves as victims and using the Holocaust for their purposes – a notion also common in general society:[45] "*They pose as victims because of what happened then with Hitler and all that. They do it on purpose [. . .], they take advantage of it*" (Hamza, Paris).

Others showed indifference toward the victims of the Holocaust where one would expect empathy or a moral condemnation, but such statements are often inconclusive. Sharif from Berlin, for example, did not use any negative terms in his description of the Holocaust:

> *It was one of the most important things in German history, or the most outstanding. I've always found that quite interesting, the issue itself. Not that I think that it's a good thing or that I endorse it but I found it interesting.*

Sharif pointed out that he does not approve of the Holocaust but he did not denounce it, either: he finds it "interesting." He did not show empathy with the victims, similar to Bahaar from London, who described atrocities of the Holocaust and recalled that Jews were killed and burned in such numbers that "*it looked like it was snowing.*"

Empathy

Compassion for the victims of the Holocaust is shown sporadically, and is also seen in those with very little knowledge about the Holocaust. Mehmet, for example, learned only during the interview that six million Jews were murdered, but he was appalled and tried to imagine the number. Jamil compared the atrocities of the Holocaust with the treatment of Palestinians by Israelis, judging the former as much worse. The way he described the "ghastly" atrocities done to Jews in the Holocaust shows compassion for the victims, even though his description is simplistic and historically wrong in the details.

> *What Hitler did with them back then that was much more horrible. He put them in the oven, he ripped off their skin and so on. . . . Hitler was much worse, much much worse.* (Jamil, Berlin)

Those who showed empathy also displayed no openly antisemitic attitudes. A plausible explanation for this is that hatred against Jews today impedes empathy with Jews who were murdered in the Holocaust.

Approval of the Holocaust and Common Ground with Nazis

The Holocaust is not condemned by all participants; some even show approval with the murder of Jews or declare their sympathy with Hitler, such as a participant from London of Bengali origin who said, "*I like Hitler.*" Sympathy with or admiration for Hitler can be voiced as bluntly as "*Hitler was a great guy [. . .]. He killed all the Jews*" (interviewee from a group interview in London), explicitly praising the killing of Jews. Such phrases may be partly intended as provocations, but they were often followed by matching statements. Let us consider the case of an interviewee of Tunisian origin, who said that he was just joking when he approved of the Holocaust. Here is what he said:

> *Hamza: [In Auschwitz] they killed, they burnt, they gassed [. . .]. There were Jews, there were Gypsies, there were all those who were against Hitler [. . .]. They should have continued.*
> *Interviewer: Really?*
> *Hamza: No, I'm kidding.*

Hamza thus withdrew his approval of the murder of Jews and others in Auschwitz after the interviewer inquired further. But such statements, although they are later rescinded and labeled as jokes, in general serve to make such provocations speakable even if they are not accepted in public or private discourses. Other statements by Hamza show that he is indeed full of hatred against Jews. Hamza believes that Jews control everything in France and that "the Jews" kill Palestinian children. He also approves of suicide bombers against Israelis and Americans and stated that he was involved in a fight against "the Jews." Thus he may well approve of the Holocaust, even though he did not want to fully acknowledge it to the interviewer.

Kassim, another interviewee from Berlin, dislikes Hitler but nevertheless praised him for killing the Jews: "*He is not a good man, Hitler – but he did well that he killed the Jews*" (Kassim, Berlin). Some showed ambivalent feelings toward Hitler and the Holocaust, such as admiration for Hitler's power, intelligence, and "*fitness programs*" on the one hand, and condemnation that he "*killed too many people*" on the other hand (both views from different interviewees of a group interview in London). Blatant and adamant approval of the Holocaust was one of the most shocking forms of antisemitism and most clearly and insistently voiced by Suleiman from Berlin of Palestinian background and Moukhtar from Paris of Maghrebian background. Consider Suleiman's statement:

Suleiman: What should I say about Hitler? [. . .] I think, he wanted to become an artist, but there he wasn't accepted and that were, I think, Jews. Thus his hatred of them grew more and more – he held always speeches. Then [. . .], at some point, he founded a party with the Nazis so that they became then more and more. In the Bundestag [parliament of Germany today] they had started to suppress Jews, to beat them in the streets and then at some point they were more than the majority [and they] convinced the Reich president that he appointed him chancellor and then it really started with the extermination of Jews, concentration camps and everything. That was a good man, Hitler.

Interviewer: You think it is good what he did, Hitler?

Suleiman: Of course.

Interviewer: Why do you think that's good?

Suleiman: Well, this race, he almost extinguished them [. . .].

Interviewer: But I don't understand, you said that you think they're stupid, or you hate them, because they are killing people in Palestine?

Suleiman: Yes.

Interviewer: But that was all before. I mean, before this time, before the Middle East conflict.

Suleiman: It doesn't matter [. . .]. That's them! They all came to Palestine afterward, the Jews [. . .]. So that's the same people. I think it's good that he killed them. Just those who were left over, these pigs, they came to us [. . .].

Interviewer: And the ones before the founding of Israel, why are they worth hating? I still don't understand that.

Suleiman: That's just how it is, I hate Jews. Just like Hitler hated them, I hate them, too.

The reason Suleiman initially gave for his support of Hitler and the Holocaust was that "he almost exterminated this race." The interviewer then opened a way for another line of argument, relating his hatred to the Middle East conflict, which revealed contradictions because those who were murdered in the Holocaust could not be responsible for the Israeli-Palestinian conflict. But this fact did not affect Suleiman's rationale. He concluded that he simply hates Jews, "*just like that,*" without reason or justification. However, the obviously contradictory "justification" of the murder of Jews before 1945 by the allegedly negative behavior of "the Jews" today is a pattern repeated by others. Just after saying that innocent women and children are dying in the Israeli-Palestinian conflict, Bilal and his friend, both of Maghrebian origin, stated that it was better when Hitler was alive. It can be deduced from this viewpoint that they prefer Jews as innocent victims, even of the most terrible atrocities, to the suffering of people whom they consider part of their own (Muslim) community. Obviously, today's Palestinian victims are not helped by approval of the Holocaust.

However, Suleiman left no doubts about his endorsement of the Holocaust while fully conscious of the extermination of Jews. Consequently, he praised Hitler as a good person. Suleiman hates Jews, as he declared repeatedly. Despite the fact that he was born in Germany, has German citizenship, and both his parents came to Germany more than twenty-five years ago, he feels strongly Palestinian. That is why he refers to "us" when he speaks of the migration of Holocaust survivors to Palestine: "Those who were left over, the pigs, they came to us." His hatred against Jews and Holocaust survivors is clearly not limited to Israelis. In the interview he openly disdained and abused a German Holocaust survivor in his eighties who had visited his school to talk about his experiences during the Holocaust:

> *I met Jews and that didn't go well. Here, in school, there was a Jew. After that he really looked differently, because we threw him out from school [laughs] [. . .]. He came in, was spat at by the Arab students, beaten, and then he ran away quickly [. . .]. What did he do at our school? He thus provokes on purpose that there are many Palestinians. He comes in like a Jew, like a son-of-a-bitch. So I agree with them [those who chased him from school], fucking Jew.* (Suleiman, Berlin)

His friend, Ismail, also of Palestinian origin, reported the same incident. Even though he did not insult the Holocaust survivor during the interview, he said, "*I stand with those who were against him and I just didn't think about it.*" He showed no signs of remorse about the incident, but Ismail was one of the few students from that school who met again with the Holocaust survivor in a small group. Thereupon he declared: "*In the end I felt sorry for him because in the end he was crying, because he had a little case with him. There was photo on it, he was 13 years old then. He said that basically it's not his fault that he is a Jew and he is a proud Jew.*"

Unfortunately, the intervention of the Holocaust survivor did not lead to a fundamental change of Ismail's Jew hatred. He bluntly stated elsewhere on several occasions that he hates Jews. Mousa, from Germany of Palestinian origin, denounced Hitler due to his responsibility for the many deaths in the Second World War, but he thinks that the proportion of Jews to non-Jews killed in the war is too little and declared that he wishes more Jews had died. It is therefore not a general indifference toward people who were killed in the past, but specifically to Jews, whose murder engenders not only apathy but even approval.

Holocaust endorsement exists as a phenomenon among groups other than those of Palestinian background, although the most blatant examples in this study do come from that group. Among non-Palestinians, in addition to Hamza, Kassim, and Bilal mentioned above, Moukhtar from Paris of Moroccan origin openly hates Jews and applauded the Holocaust. Assim, a Frenchman of Algerian origin, spoke of the fact that six million Jews were killed: "*To be honest, I was really in favor of Hitler. Here we go, all-out for Hitler.*" He revoked this statement only reluctantly afterward, disapproving of the gas chambers and concluding that it is "*a bit hard, it's complicated.*" Consider his conclusion in his own words:

> *No, it wasn't good what they did, the gas chambers and all that [. . .]. That wasn't good, all right, but [. . .] I don't know how to explain that to you, really, it's a bit hard, it's complicated.*

Bilal, who is also French with an Algerian background, agrees with his friend that it was better when Hitler was around. Bilal accused "the Jews" of killing children in the war against Hezbollah, which he said creates hatred against them. His views are thus another example that hatred against Jews influences one's perception of the Holocaust and can even lead to approval of the Holocaust. Azhar and Hafid from Paris of Maghrebian origin directly explained the approval of Arabs in that way and only reluctantly distanced themselves from that rationale. "*I'm somewhat happy about it, but you shouldn't do it,*" said Azhar, who knows that it is morally wrong to be happy about the Holocaust. Bashkar from London of South Asian origin knows people who endorse the Holocaust, whom he labels as "some Muslims." He distanced himself somewhat more strongly than Azhar and Hafid from that position, but he did not oppose it directly:

> *I know some people, who told us, some Muslims, they told me Hitler was good, that he killed all the Jewish. "He should kill not 6 million, he should kill 30 million," that's what they said. But I said, "I don't know, that's past, history."*

Others showed approval of the Holocaust and Hitler in verbal outbursts, with no further argumentation, often partially withdrawing the statements after further inquiry by the interviewer.

In addition to the rationale that hostility against Jews leads to approval of the Holocaust, there were also justifications of the Holocaust in line with propaganda of Nazism. Ramzi, who was born in Germany but has Lebanese citizenship, justified the "attack against the Jews" (his description for the Holocaust) as an act of self-defence. He believes that the Jews wanted to take over the country. Some participants are not adverse to Nazis. Haroun from Paris of Maghrebian origin, for example, admires a neighbor who he claimed was a Nazi general and said that he was "like a grandfather" to him. Ismail, from Germany of Palestinian origin, is proud to have excerpts on his mobile phone of Goebbels's infamous propaganda speech in front of a large audience in the Sportpalast on February 18, 1943, including the question, "Do you want the total war?" (which was enthusiastically approved by supporters at the time and which is part of the recording). Kassim has a friend of German origin who considers himself to be a neo-Nazi, while Naeem declared he is a "Palestinian Nazi" himself. Common ideological grounds were made explicit and were seen above all in the common Jew hatred but also in "family values."[46] Naeem, for example, who considers himself Palestinian despite his German citizenship, stated that if he met neo-Nazis he would simply say "Palestine." Bashir, from Germany of Lebanese background, uttered the well-known National Socialist greeting "Sieg Heil" during the interview. He is torn between approval and disapproval of Hitler: "*He is one of us. He killed the Je[ws] – no, he is not one of us, he is a son-of-a-bitch.*" His attempt to count Hitler as "one of us" is a hint to his Manichean views in which the Jews configure on the evil side. This dual worldview makes it difficult for him to condemn Hitler. But again, awareness of commonalities with Nazis is not confined to those with Palestinian or Lebanese backgrounds. Tunay, a German of Turkish background, recalled an incident during a manifestation when he was praised by a neo-Nazi for his anti-Jewish attitudes that he voiced:

> *Tunay: The Nazi [. . .], "Yes," he told me, "you have a good attitude, I like you." [. . .] There were Nazis next to me and than such a Jew there, a bit further. And I said, "Look at this fucking Jew." [. . .] [Then] I gossiped about Jews. He was happy, the Nazi.*
>
> *Interviewer: Didn't you think that's strange, that you say something that the Nazi likes, too?*
>
> *Tunay: Yes, of course. I found it funny that he thought it's cool. It was okay.*

Tunay not only noticed the common hostility of Jews between him and neo-Nazis, but he seemed to be happy with it. Moukhtar from Paris of Maghrebian origin, who openly hates Jews, said the following about neo-Nazis: "*They don't like the Jews [. . .]. Still until today, they don't like them. This is that they are a little bit like us.*" Moukhtar thus sees parallels between neo-Nazis and "us." But he is not clear about who he means by "us."

The examples show that some see common ideological grounds between Nazis or Hitler and Muslims, based on Jew hatred. Others made the observation that both Nazis and Muslims hate Jews. But instead of questioning the Jew hatred, Rajsekar of Asian background, for example, wondered what was wrong with the Jews. Beyar of Turkish Kurdish origin wondered why Hitler did not like Jews, since Hitler was not Muslim.

CONCLUSIONS

Perceptions of the Holocaust and moral judgment upon it are swayed by interviewees' views on Jews. However, interviewees have only limited knowledge about the Holocaust even though they are generally interested in its history. Almost all participants possessed the basic knowledge that the Nazis in Germany murdered the European Jews and held them in concentration camps. The most important source for this information and further knowledge was school, although in some cases interviewees referred to their schools as a source of distorted or simplistic views of the Holocaust. Some discourses oppose the public discourse of the Holocaust by denial or approval of the Holocaust. This stance is often informed by rumors in the community or a discourse from "back home."

Research on social identity has shown that identification as a group member leads to adoption of (alleged) shared beliefs.[47] If young Muslims believe hostile attitudes toward Jews are common in their community, they might adopt such attitudes that influence their views on the Holocaust, even if that contradicts knowledge they have learned in school. Additionally, some express doubt about the Holocaust, referencing national TV or books. In any case, Holocaust denial (or even approval) is not rooted in a lack of knowledge, but rather in the choice to believe a respective discourse in opposition to the socially accepted discourse. To bridge this gap between the public discourse and their narrative, interviewees believe the public discourse to be biased or staged.

Comparison of the Holocaust to other incidents or tragedies in ways which diminish the Holocaust is widespread in European societies and among interviewees. The Holocaust is used as a reference for evil or for the general suffering of innocents, becoming an empty metaphor that has lost the notion of the systematic murder of European Jewry. The Holocaust is often equated with the sufferings of Palestinians, but also often to other events such as the war in Iraq. A recurrent topos is the killing of children as a symbol of innocence. The previous equations imply the perception of deep suffering of the Palestinians at the hands of the Israelis or "the Jews" who are accused of evil intentions. Such equations are often accompanied by antisemitic stereotypes and tropes such as Jews as child murderers, the image of the wandering Jew, allegations of a "Jewish revenge" for the Holocaust, and antisemitic conspiracy theories. These equations are rooted in hostile attitudes toward Jews and emotional attachment to the struggle of Palestinians against Israel rather than in a lack of knowledge about the Holocaust. Hostile attitudes toward Jews result in Holocaust diminishment. Emotional attachment to "the Palestinians" provides a motive to exaggerate sufferings of "the Palestinians" and to see them as a unitary category and as only victims. When all these factors are taken together, they facilitate an equation of the suffering of Jews during the Holocaust and the suffering of Palestinians in the Israeli-Palestinian conflict. Very few interviewees directly compared the persecution of Jews to hostility against Muslims today, but almost all of those who did live in London and reduce the Holocaust as the result of scapegoating. Some delusional equivalences, such as using the killing and death of many Iraqi children as evidence for the attempt to annihilate a people and likening this to the Holocaust, confirm that those who make such judgments are not interested in an analysis of reality. Their opinion is preconceived and they adhere to a Manichean worldview.

The notion that the Holocaust led to the creation of the State of Israel is also a recurrent pattern of argumentation. It is often voiced together with a rejection of the legitimacy of the foundation of the State of Israel and fragments of an anti-colonialist discourse, arguing that the land of the State of Israel naturally belongs to another people and not to Jews. The anti-colonialist discourse often finds its expression in the topos that "the Jews" were allegedly sent to Palestine. Interviewees use antisemitic tropes such as the wandering Jew to present the creation of Israel as illegitimate. The Holocaust is diminished to reduce potential sympathy and understanding for the establishment of the State of Israel.

Interviewees judge the Holocaust differently. One would expect disapproval, condemnation, outrage, and sympathy with its victims as reactions to the Holocaust, and the large majority do indeed disapprove of the Holocaust's atrocities. Still, some participants are indifferent, and a few in all three countries cite "other Muslims" or "other Arabs" as satisfied with or even approving of the systematic mass murder of Jews. Blatant approval of the Holocaust is made in full consciousness of the systematic mass murder of European Jewry. Approval is the result of open Jew hatred and not the result of a lack of knowledge. Approval of the Holocaust is often associated with a positive view of Nazis, a view which some participants express despite the fact that neo-Nazis also target their own community. This contradiction is manifested in views on Hitler. The Holocaust is strongly associated with Hitler, who is usually seen and condemned as a racist and evil dictator responsible for the Second World War and racist persecutions. Therefore, those who approve of the Holocaust do not necessarily admire Hitler. Nevertheless, some showed signs of sympathy for Hitler because of his Jew hatred, most clearly five participants who explicitly declared that they like Hitler. To resume, neither the condemnation of Hitler nor knowledge about the Holocaust necessarily lead to the condemnation of the Holocaust (or to less antisemitic attitudes).

A number of misconceptions of the Holocaust among young European Muslims are also widespread in their general respective European societies: Hitler is frequently portrayed as the only person responsible for the persecution of Jews, and "the Jews" are seen as a unitary category, mingling together victims of the Holocaust and Israelis today. Interviewees also use common antisemitic tropes such as the accusation that Jews use the Holocaust for their purposes and that Jews talk too much about the Holocaust. However, in contrast to some political Muslim organizations, no interviewee directly opposes the remembrance of the Holocaust.

Participants from Germany give interesting examples of influence of the national discourse: some interviewees who do not identify themselves as German use patterns of secondary antisemitism – usually seen as a form of rejection of the feeling of collective guilt for the Holocaust which they do not have. It can be assumed that interviewees have learned these patterns from public and private discourses in Germany and use them as a form of accepted antisemitism.

Thus, misconceptions and biased views on the Holocaust can be informed by discourses in the respective European societies and by discourses in the religious or ethnic communities (and countries of origin). The latter can have a dominant impact if the collective identification with the community is predominant.

However, misconceptions of the Holocaust are often related to a lack of understanding of history in general. Many interviewees do not understand history as an open process involving the struggle of diverse actors. Just as they understand themselves as objects of society rather than subjects, they see history as the outcome of decisions made by a few people from the ruling class on which they have no influence.

Two rationales can be distinguished that allow for rejection of antisemitic views of the Holocaust and equating the Holocaust with other sufferings that result in the Holocaust's diminishment. First, the lack of hostile feelings against Jews enables a non-biased view of the Holocaust and empathy for its victims. Second, educational approaches that point out, for example, the differences between the Holocaust and the Israeli-Palestinian conflict can be accepted with the authority of teachers or others despite biased attitudes against Jews.

TEN

Sources of Antisemitic Attitudes

THE FORMATION OF ANY ATTITUDE IS A MULTIDIMENSIONAL process,[1] and this proves to be even more true of antisemitic views. This study identifies some factors of influence, but no factor in and of itself necessarily leads to antisemitic attitudes. A focus solely on any single factor would be misleading.

The genesis of antisemitic attitudes among European Muslims cannot be reduced to religious beliefs or affiliation. Such attitudes are not a *necessary* result of belief in Islam, Muslim identity, or deprived living conditions, although some perceptions of Islam and Muslim identity include hostile attitudes against Jews.

Exposure to antisemitic remarks, media, or propaganda enhances antisemitic beliefs, but exposure does not necessarily lead to antisemitic attitudes, as shown by some interviewees who ultimately reject antisemitic views despite these factors. The eventual adoption of antisemitic stereotypes and ways of thinking is a choice made by individuals.[2] Along with a number of other factors of influence, antisemitic attitudes are related to worldviews and individual psychological processes and mechanisms.[3] The interviews provide only limited data on the latter. Therefore, I concentrate on those factors which interviewees mentioned directly as sources for their antisemitic beliefs: anti-Jewish views by friends and family, as well as perceptions of religious and ethnic identities, conversations in mosques, the influence of media such as television, internet sources, music, books, and newspapers, and, in some cases, schools. Here, my findings match the results of a recent study based on interviews with social workers who work with Muslim youths[4] and with another study based on interviews in Berlin with twenty-five Arab and Turkish young Muslim men and women: "Primal factors of influence on antisemitic attitudes are, next to the media, particularly contexts of socializations, notably peer groups, school and religious orientations."[5]

I also examine the possible influence of education level and of perceptions of discrimination on the views people hold of Jews. In addition, I discuss some observations demonstrating mechanisms of projections onto Jews. The findings show that the genesis of antisemitic attitudes is not monocausal, which means that strategies to combat them should also be diverse.

Factors of influence were similar in all three countries, although I observed some differences among the countries in terms of the influence of media, religious identification, the perception of discrimination, and the influence of Islamist organizations.

FRIENDS AND PEERS

The opinions of adolescents and young adults are generally strongly influenced by peers.[6] Most interviewees were no exception to this rule, and many of the respondents referred to the antisemitic views of their friends and classmates, which are usually accepted rather than questioned. Some also reported social pressure from their peer group to participate in antisemitic discourse. Group interviews show how friends directly influence attitudes about Jews, with participants adopting their friends' arguments. Looking for consensus within group dynamics rather than debating controversial opinions is an important part of the culture of communication among friends in many groups. The exchange of views on such subjects as conspiracy theories, the Israeli-Palestinian conflict, and views on Jews can be tainted by group dynamics or used to establish a person's position within the group. Whether or not a particular view is shared depends more on the social position of the person expressing a certain view within the group than it does the argument itself. Antisemitic views among friends usually are taken as valuable opinions. They are generally eventually adopted or justified with further "arguments."

Interviewees reported that they often sit together with friends to discuss the topic of "Jews," a topic they sometimes then research on the internet. In some peer groups, anti-Jewish attitudes are widespread and negative views of Jews appear as "common sense," even if Jews are not a constant theme.

Antisemitism can form part of everyday language, such as the pejorative use of the term "Jew" in German and French. This usage results in negative associations with Jews and can amount from pressure of the peer group to employ antisemitic language.[7]

Some interviewees distinguished between their friends' ethnic backgrounds when they were asked about their friends' opinions of Jews. For example, Orhan, of Turkish origin, said that only his Arab friends show open hatred of Jews. But generally, antisemitism among friends is not confined to particular ethnic minorities, nor is antisemitism exclusive only to one's Muslim friends. Two respondents from Berlin, Naeem and Kassim, even have a common friend of German origin who considers himself a Nazi, who is known among peers for his outspoken hatred not only of Jews but also of foreigners. Others often quoted friends as a source of negative views of Jews related to the Middle East conflict. Bahaar, for instance, reported that his friends had been engaged in raising money for those affected by the Lebanon war in 2006; he highlighted the sufferings of women and children and blamed Israel for it. He then likened the Israeli-Palestinian conflict to the Nazis' murder of Jews. And Manoj applauded fellow students in his university who passed a resolution against the existence of the State of Israel. Bashkar admitted that his opinion on the Israeli-Palestinian conflict is influenced by video clips of wars in the Middle East, Afghanistan, and Chechnya, which he had been shown by friends. But friends were also quoted for "classic" antisemitic beliefs. Nirmal from London, for example, is convinced that Jews are rich and, according to a friend he quoted, Jews own 10 percent of British Gas and other companies. And Agantuk and his Christian friend[8] jointly constructed the wildest conspiracy theories about the cooperation between Christians and Jews against Muslims in an upcoming holy war.

Antisemitic Behavior by Friends and Peers

Particularly worrying are reports of antisemitic behavior by friends or peers, especially if they remain unpunished and if participants do not condemn these actions. Such behavior contributes to a normalization of antisemitism and violence against Jews. Antisemitic actions by peers are often trivialized or even justified. Bilal from Paris, for example, condemned a violent attack by a student in his school on a Jewish staff member because she is a woman, but he searched for justifications for attacking Jews in general, explaining the assault with what he believes to be a general Muslim hatred of Jews. He further believes that a Jew with a *kippah* (skullcap) would be attacked in his neighborhood and declared that he had himself witnessed a Jew being insulted on the street: "*Sometimes, I say it's well done.*" Bilal is accustomed to violence against Jews from his peers and partly justifies and endorses it.

Remarkably, interviewees who reported violence by peers against Jews were not shocked or outraged, even if they disapproved of the violence. One German respondent reported that he witnessed a violent assault in his neighborhood against a Jewish woman. Asked what he thought about it, he answered: "*What should I have thought of that – it's not right, what the Muslims did there, it makes our reputation get worse and worse.*" And just a few lines later, after discussing if the use of the word "*Jude*" as an insult is part of this hatred, he said: "*I don't care, I mean, I honestly can't be bothered, okay, I don't think it's right, but I'm not interested in it. Am I a Jew? No*" (Fatin, Berlin).

Others accept violence against Jews as normal, as expressed by a French interviewee for whom attacks and assaults against Jews are part of what he described as "*the law of the city*" (Azhar, Paris). The failure to condemn attacks on Jews by those who had directly observed them is striking. A German interviewee stood with his friends when they insulted, screamed, and spat on a Holocaust survivor visiting their school. No sanctions were reported: the Holocaust survivor had to leave school and came back another time, so that he could (almost secretly) talk to a smaller number of students willing to listen. Asked for his opinion about the incident, Ismail simply responded: "*I don't know. Because I didn't think about it, because I was standing with them who were against him*" (Ismail, Berlin).

The knowledge that other young people like themselves, with the same social, religious, and ethnic background, have attacked Jews further contributes to a normalization of attacks, particularly if no sanctions against such behavior are reported. Hamudi from Berlin was not surprised to hear that there had been an attack on Jews in his neighborhood and came up with the explanation that many people, including him, do not like Jews. Some participants search for justifications for violence even if they do not personally know the perpetrators. Jabar justified a violent attack on a rabbi in the subway by referencing the rabbi's allegedly hostile look. The murder of the Jewish man Ilan Halimi by Youssouf Fofana and his "*gang des barbares*" from Paris,[9] and the assumption that Jews in Paris fear Arabs, was justified by Ahlam with the simple fact that Jews inhabit the allegedly Muslim country of "Palestine." A French respondent explained the abduction and murder of Halimi with the stereotype of rich Jews and minimized the antisemitic motives of the murder: "*They made such a big story out of it talking about Jews-Muslims, it's not that really, it's a guy who sees somebody else who has money*" (Haroun, Paris).

Naresh from London and Cherif from Paris use the rationale that Jews are attacked because allegedly they are rich. Both stated that Jews are mugged and robbed because they have a lot of money, a stereotype in which they too believe. Both disapprove of these robberies and portray the attacks as regrettable, but common. Naresh reported that he had personally witnessed several times that boys had gone to areas where many Jewish people live and had robbed Jews "*to get money.*"

Others know of open hatred against Jews among their friends. Ramzi from Berlin has a friend who, he said, would kill Jews on the street if he saw them. But he thinks that this is his friend's personal business and explained the threat by the fact that this friend is Palestinian and that his father was killed "*because of the Jews.*" But Ramzi himself admitted that he once had similar murderous feelings against a Jew he saw on the street. Bashkar from London quoted someone, probably from his neighborhood, who is only a year or two older than he, saying, "*I'm gonna kill one Jew before I die.*" He disapproves of the statement but said that there are many with such views. He explained that such attitudes are based on the war in Afghanistan, which adds to the sense of communal Muslim unity and the hurt they feel if Muslims in other parts of the world suffer. Bashkar himself shares this feeling of unity among Muslims. Kassim even reported that he had engaged with friends in anti-

Jewish behavior. He accounted without regret that he and his friends had an argument with Jews in the local synagogue and had to be expelled by the police. Jamil, on the other hand, experienced the threat of antisemitic prejudices when he presented himself "for fun" as half-Jewish in front of his new classmates.[10] He thereby experienced anti-Jewish attitudes firsthand from his social environment.

The interviews show that violence against Jews by peers usually does not lead to outrage and condemnation of such incidents but rather to acceptance and normalization, even though most interviewees do not explicitly endorse such violence. Some participants are used to violence in their neighborhood in general, which is an additional factor for accepting attacks against Jews.

Antisemitic Remarks from Friends Present during the Interview

In some interviews, friends standing by also gave antisemitic comments. The interviewees mostly accepted, explained, or justified those remarks. If they disagreed, negative remarks about Jews were ignored or minimized, opposed in some cases, but never condemned, even in the case of blatant antisemitic remarks.[11] When a French interviewee talked about racism, his friend intervened, "*The Jews are worse*" and then asked: "*Can I insult the Jews, here?*" (Jabar's friend, Paris). Jabar continued talking about racism and prejudice against Arabs without criticizing his friend for his prejudices against Jews. While Jabar ignored his friend, others explained or adopted their friends' antisemitic views.

When a German interviewee was asked if he knew Jews, he denied that he did and passed the question on to his friend, who said that Jews better not come to his neighborhood. Whereupon Halil explained that, for religious and other reasons, a Jew in the neighborhood would not "fit": "*for us, something like that doesn't fit [. . .] in our area*" (Halil, Berlin). Participants were persuaded by their friends' antisemitic theories during the interview and even after initial rejection.

Another German respondent, Tunay, initially contradicted his friend who believed that the attacks of September 11, 2001, were part of a "Jewish war" and that therefore Jews were responsible for the attacks. But after a second friend claimed that the American president had collaborated with the attackers, he also spoke of connections between Bush and Bin Laden, and dropped his opposition to conspiracy theories of 9/11. Another example is Murat, also German, who said, after his friend's vehement opposition to the idea of having a Jewish girlfriend, that he also would rather not have one.

Social Pressure

Friends can exercise social pressure that influences others to accept or even adopt antisemitic attitudes and behavior. The use of "Jew" as an insult, which is commonplace in France and Germany, can easily lead to a situation where young people feel obliged to accept this antisemitic language or to become outcast themselves.[12] Labeling someone as a "Jew" has the function of exclusion. How do participants cope with this in a group if they or others are labeled as such? Questioning the use of the term "Jew" as an insult does not seem to be an option because it already exists as an integral part of group communication. For reintegration into the group, the pejorative use of the term "Jew" has to be accepted and only being labeled as a "Jew" can be rejected – not the respondents' use of the term as an insult in itself. In the excerpt below, a young Parisian insisted on his Arab identity after being labeled a "Jew" so as to become a member of the group again.

> *Nadem: You, you are a Jew!*
> *Asward's friend: No, I'm not a Jew.*
> *Nadem: What are you?*
> *Asward's friend: I'm an Arab!*
> *Nadem: Ah, okay.*

Peer pressure was noted by Ismail from Berlin, who stated that he would not intervene if friends threatened or attacked a Jew because he would get insulted as a "Jew" himself. Similarly, an interviewee in London, where this usage of the term "Jew" is largely unknown among interviewees, said that having a Jewish friend would not only cause religious problems for him but also "*other Muslim people will hate me*" (Baru, London). His two friends who were present in the interview confirmed that they would disapprove and would question Baru if he had a Jewish friend.

The anticipated reactions seem to be worse regarding hypothetical marriage to a Jewish girl. A French respondent vividly rejected the idea of marrying a Jewish woman because of the reaction of his social environment: "*Then everybody will say, ah, he's together with a Jew! Ah, it's disgusting*" (Bilal, Paris).

In some social circles, antisemitic attitudes seem to be valued. An interviewee in Germany observed that his friends share and appreciate strong antisemitic attitudes when he proudly told them after the end of the interview: "*I told them everything, what shit Jews are and stuff, everything*" (Abdullah, Berlin).

FAMILY

Interviewees mentioned, some approvingly, that their parents and other members of their family possessed antisemitic views, while others distanced themselves from such views. Antisemitic views from family members range from open hatred of Jews and approval of the Holocaust, as is the case for Nabil's mother (or, as with Nabil's father, the wish to send their son to an army of martyrs against Israel), to more subtle negative views of Jews, such as warnings against a Jewish friend by Samed's parents or the use of the term "Jew" as an insult by Salih's elder brother.

A number of interviewees reported that their parents would not allow them to marry a Jewish woman. Halil from Berlin is even convinced that his family would cast him out if he married a Jewish woman and believes that the reaction would be similar for his friends. Azhar and Hafid from Paris referred to their parents, who taught them that their religion forbids them from eating or sleeping in a Jewish home or marrying a Jew. They are allowed, however, to marry a Christian woman, which indicates that their rejection of a Jewish bride is not rooted in the wish to marry somebody of the same religion.

Another theme is, again, the Israeli-Palestinian conflict. Kassim knows that his father condemns Israelis, in particular the Israeli prime minister and "his army," and reported that his father denounces them as "pigs." Bashir also reported insults by his parents against Jews. Çeto said that he had heard some say that Jews do the same thing to the Palestinians as they had suffered during the Holocaust. The details his brother gave about the conditions of Palestinians in Gaza convinced him that these accusations are true. And Jamil is convinced that his father would have beaten him if he had heard that Jamil had presented him as Jewish in school "just for fun." Moreover, he argued that his father does not like Jews because "*they are at war with the Muslims*" (Jamil, Berlin). Participants also reported that their parents, especially their fathers, showed them reports on TV and newspapers from their country of origin about the Israeli-Palestinian conflict, reports which are biased. Dislike of Jews among parents and other family members is no secret, but is often expressed most clearly by those who do not share these views, like Samed who stated that "*my parents [. . .] dislike the Jews*" (Samed, Paris) and who said that his brother and sister solely blame Jews for the Israeli-Palestinian conflict. His closest family members believe in a general enmity between Jews and Muslims. Bilal's cousin, who was present during the interview, made a comment praising Hitler, whereupon Bilal just laughed. Kassim reported that he and his cousin threw stones at Jews during a pro-Palestinian demonstration.

The attitudes of family and friends play an important role in interviewees' own attitudes, and antisemitic views are often adopted. However, some interviewees disagreed with their parents' or friends' antisemitic attitudes, which demonstrates that some have independent opinions. In those cases, most are influenced by a close friend or relative. Jamil, for instance, has been influenced positively by his cousin, and Samed by his Jewish friend and his Jewish girlfriend, who challenged these attitudes. Others who rejected antisemitic attitudes among family and friends are influenced by a humanistic approach, which rejects irrationality and discrimination against Jews. These positive examples will be discussed in chapter 11.

"WHAT PEOPLE SAY"

Participants referred to "what people say" as a source of their antisemitic beliefs. "What people say" can both be used as a reference if the exact source is unknown, and also as a justification and reinforcement for one's own thoughts. Therefore, rumors and stereotypes are often introduced by the phrase, "People say that. . . ." Participants have heard stereotypes such as Jews are greedy; and even if some think "*that's just being stereotypical,*" they rarely dismissed them as false: "*People say it. I don't know if it's true, but it's stereotyping them*" (Bankim, London). The knowledge of stereotypes about Jews often comes with the belief that they might be true in some way. "What people say" allows controversial statements to be voiced without claiming responsibility for them. Take the statement by a respondent in London on the terrorist attacks of 9/11:

> *I didn't know what happened, I won't blame Muslim because some people said: "Oh, most of Jewish people didn't work that day in the Twin Towers. All of them they chipped off" [. . .]. That's what people [were] saying. Some people they said: "Oh, it was the Muslim people in the plane when they blow up." How we gonna know?* (Nader, London)

He used "what people are saying" to introduce his conspiracy theory. By also portraying the fact that the terrorists were Muslims, as what "some people say," he suggests that both could equally be true.

"What people say" as a source of antisemitic beliefs can refer to common beliefs within the religious, ethnic, or local community. It is an expression of the assumption that many people think the same way and that there is something legitimate to what they think. A respondent of Pakistani origin in London referred to "what people say" in Pakistan about 9/11 and the Jews before admitting that he thinks the same:

> *Malik: Most of the people in Pakistan believe that Taliban wasn't behind the 9/11 attempts. It was actually the Yahudis who were behind, they say that.*
> *Interviewer: And what do you believe? What do you think?*
> *Malik: I think the same.*

But references to people in the neighborhood were more frequent than to the country of origin. Another interviewee in London knows some people in the neighborhood who do not like Jews and some older people who, he said, "*used to have fights [with them]*" (Agantuk, London). A French interviewee reports that in his neighborhood there are "*Blacks and Arabs who will tell you, 'yes, I don't like the Jews'*" (Haroun, Paris). Another acknowledged: "*There are some who don't like it. They don't like to hang out, to stay with Jews*" (Chafik, Paris), just like Ousmane, who declared that he knows people who do not like Jews.

Two French friends of Maghrebian origin stated that Arabs in particular say that they agree with Hitler: "*I think that the people say that they agree with Hitler [. . .] especially the Arabs,"* said one, whereupon the other confirmed this: "*Yes, the Arabs agree with Hitler*" (Azhar and Hafid, Paris). They then admitted, hesitantly, that they are also happy about what Hitler did, well knowing that this feeling is immoral.

A number of interviewees stated that "Jews" are a frequent theme in conversations about the Iraq war. A respondent from France noted: "*The people talk only about that [. . .], what's happening in Iraq; with the Jews and all that*" (Khalil, Paris). The knowledge that "*some Muslims, they hate America, hate Israel, hate the Jews [. . .]; some Muslims they told me Hitler was good, that he killed all the Jewish*" (Bashkar, London), contributes to a normalization and acceptance of anti-Jewish opinions, even if, as is the case for Bashkar, these extreme attitudes of hatred are not shared.

Antisemitism in jokes further adds to the perception that "people around" have negative views of Jews. A stronger reference to "what people say" is the allusion to the "common sense" behind stereotypes. This "common sense" claim gives the assumption more credibility. For an interviewee in Britain, it is "*a kind of common sense*" (Nirmal, London) that Jews are rich. He added that he knows this from friends, the internet, and leaflets distributed by groups attached to the local mosque. For another respondent, also from Britain, it is common sense to dislike Jews and, what is more, he believes that this attitude is shared by people he identifies with: "*Jewish people are Jewish, that's why we don't like them*" (Ganesh, London).

It is important to note that "what other people say" as a source of antisemitic views is not confined to Muslims, particularly in Germany. A man there is convinced: "*They try not to show it. But every German, inside, he hates the Jews*" (Mousa, Berlin). Salih said he had observed discrimination against Jews from native Germans and cited incidents of neo-Nazi prejudice. Tunay was even praised at a rally by a neo-Nazi for his hostile remarks against Jews. Another German interviewee believes that he has some common ground with neo-Nazis and said: "*If I happen to meet them, I just say 'Palestine!'*" (Naeem, Berlin). Çeto quoted a survey he likely read in school that shows that Germans wrongly believe that Jews constitute 5 percent of the population and are powerful in Germany. Such explicit references to anti-Jewish views among the native-born were made only in Germany. This might be explained by the general knowledge of antisemitism among German neo-Nazis and by the fact that antisemitism among the general population is more widely discussed in Germany than in France or Britain.

To conclude, interviewees know that negative views of Jews are common in their social circles and religious or ethnic communities and also partly in the wider society. Only rarely are these views dismissed as unacceptable or antisemitic. By these means, antisemitic attitudes become tenable.

SCHOOL

Interviewees know of anti-Jewish attitudes and behavior from fellow students in schools or universities. Naresh from London is convinced that a Jewish student in his school would be verbally and physically bullied just for being Jewish; Bilal from Paris reported that a fellow student hit a Jewish staff member; and many participants from Paris and Berlin are accustomed to antisemitic language from fellow students, such as the use of "Jew" as an insult. And, of course, the aforementioned incident of an antisemitic assault on a Holocaust survivor in school by Ismail's and Suleiman's fellow students adds to the normalization of antisemitism, though this kind of incident represents an exceptionally extreme case. But for Suleiman, the incident was a triumph against Jews: "*In school, there was a Jew. After that he really looked differently, because we threw him out from school [laughs] [. . .]. He came in, he was spat at by the Arab students, beaten, and then he ran away quickly*" (Suleiman, Berlin).

In some cases, interviewees quoted their teachers as a source of antisemitic stereotypes, such as that of undue "Jewish influence" in media, business, or political decision-making. Neoy, for example, insisted that it was his history teacher who told his class in a lesson about the Gulf War that Jews own the media and are very influential people. Others referred to their teachers as sources for biased views of the Israeli-Palestinian conflict. Hikmet recounted that he and his classmates were given a book by his teacher, from which he remembers that "the Jews" have thrown "the Arabs" out of Israel and have allegedly always killed them. A respondent in Germany quoted his schoolteacher as being on his side concerning the demonization of Ariel Sharon: *"My teacher said he [Sharon] will burn in hell"* (Kassim, Berlin). A respondent from France said that he has learned in school that after World War II and the persecution of the Jews by the Germans, *"The Europeans sent the Jews away [. . .], they put them on some land, and the English too, they put the Muslims on the same land as the Jews so they were fighting there to keep the country"* (Diaba, Paris). We cannot know what the teachers actually said in class. However, anti-Zionist and antisemitic attitudes are generally widespread in Europe and it would be surprising if teachers were exempt from having sentiments against Jews. Conspiracy theories and anti-Zionism are issues around which "honorable" antisemites[13] and youths who openly endorse hatred against Jews can meet.

Holocaust education in European schools is generally deficient,[14] not only in the sense that participants do not know enough about the Holocaust, but some also have wrong assumptions that need to be rectified. A British interviewee recounted learning in school that six million Jews were murdered, but he is not convinced by this vast number and asked, *"How do you still have so many Jews around?"* He believes it would have been impossible for Hitler to *"deal with six million Jews. And then the rest of the world. He can't"* (Aban, London). Both arguments point to serious deficits of knowledge that could have been dealt with more effectively in his school lessons about the Holocaust: Jewish communities in Europe today cannot be compared to the Jewish communities before the Holocaust, despite the presence of vibrant Jewish communities in some countries. His perception of the history of the Holocaust also seems to be wrong: it was neither Hitler alone who fought the Jews nor can the war against the Jews be compared to a war against an army. A French interviewee even declared that he had learned in school that Hitler was Jewish: *"He is Austrian and Jewish [. . .] and he wants to take revenge [. . .]. That's what they told us at school"* (Bilal, Paris). However, references to biased assumptions from teachers were exceptional, and other examples show the positive influence of teachers and their teaching methods. Moreover, some biased perceptions are explicitly opposed to teachings in school: the three friends Imran, Salim, and Manoj, for instance, are suspicious of Holocaust education in school, suspecting it of indirect support for the State of Israel.

THE MEDIA

European Muslims use the media of both their countries of origin and their country of residence, the latter being used more often by those born in the country.[15] It has been shown that the media exert influence on more than just the recipients' assessments of the specific issues being reported. Wilhelm Kempf found in his study on how people understand the Israeli-Palestinian conflict that "in addition, [reporting] also affects [the recipients'] assessments of issues related only via the structures of the mental models into which they integrate information."[16] It has been argued that biased coverage of the Israeli-Palestinian conflict in the mainstream media is related to anti-Israeli and antisemitic attitudes and also to antisemitic incidents.[17] How did interviewees relate their negative views of Jews to the media? Direct references of antisemitic assertions were made to television, the internet, books, and newspapers. Views of the Israeli-Palestinian conflict are often full of projection and hardly based on facts; and, as one interviewee rightly said: *"I'm not actually in Palestine, I haven't seen a Jewish soldier coming and fighting across [me], for me to have any problem with him or his people. But it's only media that is telling me"* (Hussein, London).

Television

Previous studies have analyzed the influence of television as a source of antisemitism.[18] Indeed, television is one of the most important sources cited for antisemitic beliefs about the Israeli-Palestinian conflict, as well as for stereotypes of rich Jews and Jewish control over large companies, and for conspiracy theories. In our interviews, both foreign and domestic TV were cited as sources of antisemitic beliefs. However, the influence of foreign TV channels on young European Muslims seems to be often indirect, via parents who regularly watch satellite channels emanating from their countries of origin. By contrast, the younger generation usually watches TV channels originating in their country of residence, in many cases because of linguistic barriers they face when watching TV from their parents' country of origin. Young Europeans of Arab background, for example, often have limited comprehension of the Standard

Arabic spoken on Arab news channels. Nevertheless, they may watch images on these channels at their parents' suggestion. Interviewees referenced foreign TV channels, and in particular Arab ones,[19] as inciting hatred against Jews. Bashir, for example, claimed that he learned from Arab news channels (namely, Al Manar and LBC) that all Jews, including those living in Berlin, are bad. He referred only to the images, however, admitting that he does not understand the Standard Arabic spoken on these channels.

Interviewees cited news channels from their countries of origin as their source for gruesome pictures of suffering Palestinians and Muslims, engendering their hostile attitudes to Israel and Jews, be it from Arab countries, Turkey, Pakistan, Bangladesh, or Guinea. Some accused the national or Western news media of not showing the "true picture." Interestingly, they often barely noted any difference between images of suffering Muslims in Palestinian territories and in war zones such as Iraq or Afghanistan; both were used as arguments against Israel.

Images and programs on German, French, and British television also were quoted as sources of antisemitic beliefs and conspiracy theories. The picture of the dying boy Muhammad al-Durah, whose death was wrongly attributed to Israeli soldiers, was shown worldwide in 2000 and referred to by a number of interviewees in France and Germany:[20]

> *I have looked at, I don't know if you've seen it, a picture in Palestine, the father who was killed with his son, they were shot at. They showed it on TV, it was going around for some while [. . .]. Frankly, you see a picture like that, what do you feel? Are you not angry against those guys? [. . .] Personally, I hate these guys.* (Jabar, Paris)

This statement shows not only the long-persisting impact of such images – in this case, a bogus image – but also the global impact of biased media. Some interviewees referred to TV as a source of antisemitic views without further specifying the source or distinguishing between foreign and domestic media. Rajsekar and also Hussein referred to TV and the news when they argued that Jews run most of the big companies, as did Bilal when he claimed that all the millionaires are Jews. Another said, "*Nowadays, everybody can see on TV for example all the actions by the Jews, by the Americans, by, I don't know what . . . whoever does something in the world*" (Ümit, Berlin). However, these general references to television might more likely be justifications for their views than sources behind them. Others point to television as an amplifying factor: "*For example on TV, what I see there, my hatred of this people becomes bigger and bigger*" (Suleiman, Berlin); or an interviewee in Paris who referred to French television and to the well-known image of stone-throwing Palestinians opposing an Israeli tank: "*What you see on TV can make you furious: [. . .] they are killing [. . .]. We, that's stones, you know it well, you've seen it on TV*" (Omar, Paris). Interviewees are aware of the fact that such images are shown worldwide, as with those of al-Durah: "*They showed it in the whole world*" (Jabar, Paris). Ramzi, of Lebanese background from Germany, even used the fact that the Israeli-Palestinian conflict is widely discussed in the news to accuse Jews in Berlin of rejoicing over Palestinian children who had been killed. Some remembered particular programs portraying Jews in a negative way, such as Labaan who saw vengeful Israeli schoolchildren on BBC allegedly calling for indiscriminate killing of Palestinians in a case of suspected terrorism. Channel 4 was mentioned as a source for interviewees' conspiracy theories about 9/11 and the Holocaust.

Images of suffering Palestinians as a cause of anger and even violence against Jews was a recurrent issue. Ismail recounted that news about the Israeli-Palestinian conflict generated anger, which could be directed against Jews in Berlin, even though they might have nothing to do with the conflict. He then referred to cruel images of injured Palestinians on Arab TV channels. Kassim referred to Al-Manar regarding pictures of children being killed, probably including al-Durah, which made him angry and gave him and others reason to insult Jews at a local synagogue. A French respondent, however, referred to French television when he said, "*It's because of the media, on TV, what happened [. . .] after the game PSG / Tel Aviv*" (Hamza, Paris), referring to antisemitic violence that followed a soccer match between the clubs Paris Saint-German (PSG) and Hapoel Tel Aviv that left one PSG fan dead, shot by the police.[21]

References to Films

A number of participants from all three countries referred to one of Michael Moore's films, most likely *Fahrenheit 9/11,* for their conspiracy theories on the involvement of the American president in the attacks of September 11, 2001, sometimes with added antisemitic allegations. Other films, such as *The Da Vinci Code,* also were sources for conspiracy theories. For Aban, the film *Schindler's List* supposedly indicates that many Jews were saved during the Holocaust and that not six million but "only" six hundred thousand Jews were killed. Thus, interviewees did not refer only to antisemitic films as sources of their opinions, and generally did not cite popular films and series with antisemitic themes, such as *Zarah's Blue Eyes*[22] or *Valley of the Wolves.*[23] However, most interviews took place before these films became popular. Another study, based on interviews with twenty-five young Muslim men and women in Berlin in 2009, found many indirect references to the film *Zeitgeist* from 2007 that features a number of conspiracy theories and has been popular on YouTube.[24]

The Internet

The 2014 ADL Global 100 survey identified the internet as a prime source of antisemitic attitudes among Muslims around the world: Muslims who get their information about Jews from the internet are much more likely to harbor antisemitic views than those who get their information from other sources. Which antisemitic tropes are adopted from internet sources?

The internet is used at home, in school, libraries, internet cafés, or on mobile phones, mostly in the language of the country of residence. The internet was referred to as a source of antisemitic views on the Israeli-Palestinian conflict, as well as of conspiracy theories, such as the rumor that Jews did not go to work in the Twin Towers on September 11, 2001. The internet adds to the myth that Jews are the power behind the American president and exaggerates "*the influence of Jewish people upon the world*" (Tarak, London). In addition, the internet was also cited as a reference for conspiracy theories about Freemasons and the alleged involvement of Israel in the war in Afghanistan. Hussein even claimed to have read *The Protocols of the Elders of Zion* on the internet,[25] a work that he does not see as a forgery. The internet was also cited as a source of distorted views of the Holocaust.

YouTube and search engines (even though they only list websites) are frequently used as references for antisemitic views and hatred against Israel. Participants use keywords such as "*American politics, signs, images, subliminal messages, stuff like that*" (Rahim, London) in their internet searches. Only a few interviewees remembered the names of particular websites, but some who did mentioned those that disseminate antisemitic material, such as the Al Jazeera website. Research on the internet can easily produce results of anti-Jewish tropes: "*Big companies, [. . .] you know Volvo? [. . .] is owned by Jewish [. . .]. We got that through the internet [. . .] We did some research*" (Debesh, London).

Many interviewees referred to pictures on the internet of suffering Palestinians or Muslims as a source of their hostile attitudes to Israel and Jews. Some said that the national news or CNN does not show the true picture, but "*when you go into the internet [. . .], you can see the real stuff*" (participant in group interview, London). "*It's on the internet where you really see what's going on*" (Omar, Paris). Khalil, who believes that what people say about Jews can be found on the internet, said that he was shocked by what he saw online in a video clip, shown to him by a colleague, which allegedly provides evidence of atrocities that "the Jews" did to Muslims, including rape and murder. Interestingly, there was often no differentiation between pictures of suffering Muslims in Palestinian territories and in war zones such as Iraq or Afghanistan; rather, such images were used indiscriminately as arguments for negative views of Israel.

One British interviewee had seen video clips "*made in Palestine*" (Bashkar, London) on the internet, and mentioned them to support his argument that the Israelis treat the Palestinians more cruelly than the Nazis treated the Jews. His description of the videos outlined British soldiers who tortured others and alleged footage of the war in Afghanistan in the 1980s. His claim that the videos were illegal, and his report that Muslims show each other such videos but might allegedly be imprisoned by British authorities if they are caught with them, enforces the perception of Muslims as a persecuted community. Communication with other peers via such forums as chat rooms were also quoted as a source of hatred against Jews.

Print Media

Antisemitic articles and cartoons have appeared in a number of mainstream newspapers in Germany, France, and Britain, mostly with comments on the Israeli-Palestinian conflict.[26] Blatant antisemitic tropes and imagery have been published in newspapers and books from the interviewees' countries of origin, particularly in Arab countries, but also in Turkey.[27] The Turkish newspaper *Vakit* was banned from being printed in Germany in 2005 for using antisemitic references.[28]

Participants read daily newspapers that are often distributed freely or found in cafés, but these are read irregularly. Some read newspapers bought by their parents and some read papers with higher journalistic standards, depending on their level of education.

In some cases, newspapers were presented as a source of conspiracy theories and antisemitic beliefs, or for biased information about the Israeli-Palestinian conflict. One German respondent, for instance, said that more than 5,000 Jews left the Twin Towers on September 11, 2001, before the attacks. "*More than 5,000, that's not a coincidence; after all. I've read it in the newspaper*" (Suleiman, Berlin). A French interviewee responded that he knows television is dominated by "the Jews" because "*we read journals and we know it, you can see it. We recognize [the Jews] by the face*" (Azhar, Paris). A British interviewee claimed that he had read in a magazine in his doctor's waiting room that George Bush and "*all the richest people, they are Jewish*" (Sabir, London). A respondent in Berlin referred to biased reports of the Israeli-Palestinian conflict in the Turkish newspaper *Hürriyet,* which was shown to him by his father, and concluded: "*The Jews are just starting it. They kill small Muslim children, they do everything, they rape small children, women, even grannies [. . .]. I always read it [. . .] in Turkish newspapers, in Persian, in German [newspapers]*" (Memduh, Berlin). Kashi has a similar perception based on his reading of a Pakistani magazine, which he looked at while visiting his country of origin.

However, some interviewees acknowledge that Arab and Turkish newspapers have disseminated antisemitic views and express their disapproval. Nabil, of Turkish origin, and Serkan, of Kurdish Turkish background, believe that antisemitic views can be found predominantly in Arab media, and Serkan reports that Turkish Islamic newspapers have also disseminated antisemitic views.

Books

Only a few interviewees seem influenced in their opinion of Jews by books, though books are generally seen as a very reliable source of knowledge, and biased information from them has a significant impact. A few interviewees, such as Neoy or Rahim from London or Hikmet from Berlin, cited books as a source of Holocaust denial, antisemitic theories about Freemasons, or biased information about the Israeli-Palestinian conflict. Interestingly, Neoy stated that he got these books from the public library, and Hikmet and his classmates were given an apparently biased book about the Middle East conflict by their teacher.

Music and Mobile Phones

Music, and rap music in particular, can transmit antisemitic messages.[29] Even some rappers' names contain antisemitic connotations. For Sabri, his first association with the word "Holocaust" is a rapper who calls himself "Holocaust." Another rapper, Sefyu,[30] is cited by a French participant, Kassi, as a source of the rumor that Jews dominate television.

Music is often distributed by mobile phones among youths. A German interviewee reported a song he and his friends had on their mobile phones in which, he said, Palestinians insulted Jews. Asked what he thinks about it, he responded: "*Nothing at all, I listened to it and that was all right, it sounded good but I don't know why they dislike Jews, there was war*" (Fatin, Berlin). He accepted anti-Jewish insults in songs even when he did not share the hatred, justifying this animosity as a result of war. Mobile phones can also be used for the dissemination of antisemitic propaganda in other forms. Another German interviewee, Ismail, carries excerpts of an infamous propaganda speech by Goebbels on his mobile phone. Hamudi showed his friends a burning Israeli flag being transformed into a Palestinian flag on his mobile phone.

THE INFLUENCE OF THE LEVEL OF FORMAL EDUCATION

The average level of formal education of respondents was lower than the general average in each respective country. Nevertheless, there was a wide variety of formal education, from early school dropouts to university graduates. The applied methods of non-standardized interviews and the different systems of education in each of the three countries make it difficult to analyze correlations between the level of formal education and antisemitic attitudes. However, it is clear that the form of expression of antisemitic attitudes changes with the level of education: those with a higher level of formal education tend to show antipathy toward Jews in more socially acceptable ways, such as insinuations and allegations about Jewish influence in the finance sector and media, conspiracy theories, or the demonization of Israel, instead of open approval of violence against Jews or expressions of hatred against Jews without rationales behind them. No one who classified into the two highest levels of education (those who have qualified for higher studies [category 4] and university students or graduates [category 5]) openly admitted to hatred against Jews. This matches the findings on antisemitic attitudes in the general society.[31] However, the methods of this study can only provide some clues to such correlations between the level of education and antisemitism, which should be investigated with quantitative methods.

RELIGIOUS IDENTITY

Muslim identity is salient for most participants, and many expressed a sense of belonging to the global Muslim community. Research on social identity has shown that "by identifying oneself as a group member, one effectively replaces aspects of individuality and unshared attitudes and behaviors with an 'ingroup prototype' that prescribes shared beliefs, attitudes, and behaviors appropriate to that particular categorization."[32] Therefore, widespread perception of Muslims and Jews as enemies influences young Muslims' own perceptions of Jews. This goes beyond the adoption of attitudes of friends and family members and can become part of the collective identity.

Interviewees used both this generalizing assumption of Muslims and Jews being enemies and specific arguments allegedly rooted in Islam and Islamic history as justification for their own negative attitudes toward Jews. In fact, these justifications form one of four main patterns of argumentation, described in detail in chapter 7. A few participants reject the assumption that Muslims and Jews are enemies, but many others use the Israel-Palestinian conflict to justify negative feelings toward Jews, from vague feelings of suspicion to open hatred. Some even believe that Muslims and Jews are at war with each other. The "enemies" claim is also used as a reassuring assumption that people of one's own community have similar antisemitic perceptions.

Some participants included allusions to the Israeli-Palestinian conflict, such as a French participant who generalized that "*all Muslims hate the Jews because the Jews have killed Muslims*" (Bilal, Paris). This claim was used as an argument to justify or explain violence against Jewish men in his neighborhood. Others, such as a respondent in Germany of Turkish origin, explicitly said that the animosity toward Jews is not rooted in the conflict: "*As a Muslim you of course have problems, not with Israelis, with Jews [. . .]. Because they were simply damned by God*" (Ümit, Berlin). A British respondent highlighted the "*religious issues we've got against Jewish people*" and explained, "*Jewish people, they're higher than us, they've got more money [. . .]. It is true, 'coz in the Qur'an it was written that God gave them everything*" (Baru, London).

Interestingly, the assumption that Muslims and Jews are enemies is not necessarily more common among people who practice Islam than among others. This discovery confirms the results of a study on Muslims in Germany by Brettfeld and Wetzels, who found that antisemitism is not only related to the level of religiosity but also to belief patterns. Those with "fundamentalist" beliefs are more likely to believe in antisemitic stereotypes than those with "orthodox-religious" beliefs.[33] Another study on prejudices against Muslims and Jews among Danes of Christian background shows similar results for Christians.[34] The content of religious perception is crucial, not the level of religiosity itself. However, certain perceptions of Islam and religious identity are only one factor among many that contribute to negative views of Jews.

ETHNIC IDENTITIES

Some scholars have pointed out that attitudes toward Jews are influenced by ethnic identities due to historical developments and narratives that are popular within a particular ethnic group.[35] The data does show some differences in such attitudes among people of different ethnic backgrounds, but for comparison of discourses among different ethnic communities, further investigations with a greater number of interviewees are needed. However, it can be said that among interviewees of Arab background, hostile attitudes are more frequent and intense than among other ethnic groups. However, the focus here is to show that in general, ethnic identities can be used as a source of hatred against Jews. Interviewees directly relate their perception of their ethnic identity to negative views of Jews, for example, by saying that their ethnic community and Jews are enemies or hate each other.

Bilal from France, who considers himself Arab, believes that "the Arabs" do not like "the Jews," but, as shown above, he argued similarly on the basis of his Muslim identity. Two other French interviewees, Azhar and Hafid, stated that many people, particularly Arabs, agree with Hitler and approve of the Holocaust. They know that this is morally wrong but offer it as a source of their own approval of the Holocaust.

Palestinian identity can also be strongly intertwined with hatred against Jews. When a respondent with German citizenship who considers himself Palestinian was asked about his definition of a Palestinian, he answered spontaneously: "*Yes, somebody who is against Jews.*" Even though he retracted the statement as a joke, it reveals how his animosity toward Jews is part of his Palestinian and also Arab identity: "*The Arabs, man, we all hate the Jews*" (Mousa, Berlin). Suleiman stated that all his Palestinian friends share his negative opinion of Jews. Another respondent in Germany with Turkish Kurdish background and Turkish citizenship even related his national identification to hostility against Jews. Consider his surprising answer to the question of ethnic identification:

> *Interviewer: Do you feel in some way like a German, or a Turk, or a Kurd, or . . . ?*
> *Beyar: Well, it doesn't matter actually, well, I am a Kurd. For me the main thing, is not to be a Jew or whatever. And no America.*

Beyar placed his ethnic identification against the Jews in the foreground, adding that he also identifies as anti-American – interestingly, in contrast to his wording of "Jews," he speaks of "America" instead of "Americans." In contrast to others who adopt antisemitic beliefs as part of their ethnic identification, he seems to make his choice of available ethnic identifications dependent on antisemitic views by asking a question: Which ethnic identity is most suitable to justify hatred against Jews?

For some, however, their ethnic identity drives them to distance themselves from antisemitic views. Serkan, for example, considers himself a Kurd and reported discrimination against him from Turks. He even sees analogies between his discrimination and contemporary antisemitism. He easily acknowledged and condemned antisemitism in Turkish and Arab media, possibly because he is not positively attached to either Turkish or Arab nationality.

ISLAMIST ORGANIZATIONS AND MOSQUES

A number of Islamist organizations that are active in Germany, France, and Britain purvey antisemitic themes and often use the Israeli-Palestinian conflict for the dissemination of hatred against Jews. Some of these organizations are influential in the participants' local mosques. However, only one interviewee, Tayfun, said that he is a member of an Islamic organization – in his case, a youth group at the local mosque affiliated to Milli Görüş.

Interviewees reported that the Israeli-Palestinian conflict is a constant theme of discourse in mosques and among Muslims gathering there, and that this discourse often contains strong anti-Israeli or anti-Jewish subject matter. Some Turkish interviewees in Germany believed that Jews are particularly cursed in Arab mosques. Whereas no interviewee directly cited a sermon from an imam as a source of anti-Jewish opinions, another study found that some young Muslims do. Anke Schu quotes one of her interviewees, a young Turkish men in Germany, as saying, "*The Jews shall all die.*" He was then asked why and responded: "*I remember, I was once in the mosque and [. . .] [the imam] recounted that Jews in earlier times and Turks and Arabs were always in conflict [. . .] and [. . .] fighting each other. And that's why.*"[36]

Teachings in *madrasas,* Islamic evening or weekend schools, were indirectly mentioned as sources of Jew hatred. The latter might be related to the fact that *madrasas* usually concentrate on reciting the Qur'an in Arabic, and that interviewees had visited *madrasas* years ago at a much younger age. Stories of Islamic history, however, which are often told in mosques and *madrasas,* can indirectly influence views of Jews. Omar and Housni, for instance, recalled a story in which Muhammad was saved from adversaries who wanted to kill him, and assumed that the detractors were Jews.[37] Some respondents were influenced by a Manichean perception of Islam, that is a split between "true Muslims" and non-Muslims, which facilitates anti-Jewish attitudes. Such views are taught in some European Islamic institutions.[38]

Participants are familiar with radical Islamist organizations, such as Hamas, Hezbollah, Muhajiroun, and YMO (Young Muslim Organization).[39] A few interviewees from London mentioned Hizb ut-Tahir as an influential Islamist organization and agree with some of its policies. "*They're saying they want an Islamic state in the Muslim world, which I also agree with,*" one said, adding, "*Hizb ut-Tahir is big in this country*" (Manoj, London). Another interviewee, who knows some of its members, confirmed the perception that Hizb ut-Tahir is very active: "*They put up stalls and stuff, in markets, and they distribute leaflets. They approach people and talk to them [. . .]. They're probably the most active out of all the groups within East London.*" He is aware of the organization's goal, too: "*Ultimately they wish to establish something called a khilāfah, it's like a Muslim state*" (Rahim, London). His friend Hussein referred directly to the organization's attitude on Zionism as a reflection of his own attitude: "*Perhaps you can have a link to Hizb ut-Tahrir [. . .]: they're kind of, the way like we're thinking about Zionists*" (Hussein, London). Interviewees from London also referred to leaflets from Muslim organizations that advocate the boycott of allegedly pro-Israeli companies as evidence for their belief that Jews are rich and run all the big companies. On top of that, these companies allegedly give financial support to the Israeli army.

Some respondents had participated in pro-Palestinian demonstrations organized mainly by Muslim organizations and remembered slogans such as "*Sha-ron-ist-ein-Mör-der-un-ter-Schutz*" (Sharon is a protected murderer) (Kassim, Berlin) or "*Bush, Sharon, a-ssas-sins!*" (Haroun,

Paris). Kassim reported that he and his cousin had participated in such a rally and that they threw stones at a group of people they considered Jews. Some interviewees even praised radical Islamist organizations, such as Hamas and Hezbollah, because they fight Israel and the Jews effectively: "*They [Hezbollah] revolted against them, that's good*" (Kamel's friend, Paris). Moreover, one German respondent stated, referring to Hamas: "*Finally a really good party, that is taking up something against the Jews. That is doing something for their country, not like the PLO*" (Suleiman, Berlin). Even though Hamas is active in Europe and disseminates propaganda material,[40] Hamas and Hezbollah are generally known in the mainstream media for their fight against Israel. These and other Islamist organizations also use the Israeli-Palestinian conflict for propaganda issues and often raise charity money for "the Palestinians." A French participant noted that these appeals for funds occur on a regular basis: "*Here in the area there are only Arab bakeries, that means, you go there and there is a little jar; where you can read 'for Palestine, help for Palestine'*" (Azhar, Paris).

The knowledge that there is an established antisemitic discourse within Muslim or Arab organizations or states lends anti-Jewish "opinions" more legitimacy and is used by some to justify their own bias. Kashi, for example, used the rejection and denial of the State of Israel by Saudi Arabia and other Arab countries, and the anti-Israeli discourse in Pakistani magazines, to undergird his anti-Israeli position and understanding for suicide bombers in Israel.

PROJECTION

Projection is a psychological defense mechanism whereby one projects one's own undesirable and suppressed thoughts, motivations, desires, and feelings onto someone else. Psychoanalytical theories on antisemitism have identified projection as the main mechanism of antisemitism.[41] Unfortunately, our interviews only give limited insights into the respondents' psychological motivations. Therefore, the hints of psychological motivations for antisemitic arguments presented below must be treated with caution. However, in some cases, participants directly linked their fantasies, which they know are immoral and thus have to be suppressed, to antisemitic assumptions. Hussein, for instance, explained the events of September 11, 2001, with his own wish to have more money and to do whatever it takes to obtain some. His friends in London agree that 9/11 probably was the result of a conspiracy. Consider the excerpt of the group interview with the three of them below:

> *Hussein: Who dunnit? Yeah, it's a mystery isn't it? [. . .] Money! [. . .] Money's a very powerful thing. Money, yeah. If all three of us had a million pound each, now yeah? We're trying to do something to obtain more money, 'coz we're losing our money if we don't sustain ourselves, so we want to take over more shops [. . .]. You know money makes people dream, so we might be thinking of somehow arranging robberies in other shops, premises, so people leave –*
> *Aban: Yeah, burn the whole premises down.*
> *Hussein: So we can buy this premises for ourselves now, and have no competition for ourselves, there's no competition to us. And we'll be making more money [. . .] now we're more greedy, we want more money . . . you know? I think that's the kind of thing that's taking place [. . .].*
> *Rahim: If you're planning to demolish that building before, and then, you know, why not implicate some terrorists while you're taking the building down? [. . .] They could do that [. . .]. And apparently no Jews were in the building.*

It can be argued that this is an expression of a link between the unfulfilled, suppressed wish to become rich at the expense of others, mixed with aggression, as manifested in statements like, "*Yeah, burn the whole premises down*" and antisemitic accusations against Jews for allegedly having done so.

Other examples in which Jews were blamed for terrorist attacks can also be interpreted as expressions of pathological projection. Many interviewees had difficulty in accepting that Muslims were the perpetrators of terrorist attacks and that they used their religious convictions to justify their deeds. The terrorist attacks are still seen as evil, but the responsibility of Muslim perpetrators is projected onto the Jews and the Jews are blamed for Islamist terrorism, a view facilitated by a supposed general hostility between Muslims and Jews. Consider this statement on 9/11:

> *I don't believe it was actually Muslim who done that [. . .]. None of the Jews were working that day [. . .]. It's all planned out [. . .]. Muslims are supposed to be the Jewish's worst enemies [. . .]. They will follow every opportunity.* (Sabir, London)

This rationale can also be applied to suicide bombings in general, even those perpetrated in Israel. Ümit from Berlin, for example, is convinced that people who believe in Islam cannot undertake suicide attacks. He feels that Muslims are unjustly accused of terrorism, and stated that Jews or Americans disguised as Muslims might have blown themselves up in Israel.

Another area of possible projection is the wish for solidarity or social stability. One interviewee seems to envy Jews for their alleged solidarity:

> *They help each other out. That means, like, they have lots of stores and if they see, like, a Jew begging, then they'll pick him up and put him in a store, you know what I mean [. . .]. But we, if we're doing well, we have a lot of stores, we see an Arab on the ground, we're gonna let him beg. We're gonna give him some bits and pieces maybe, something like that, but we're not, we don't help each other out.* (Azhar, Paris)

Azhar's wish to be supported in case he fails to find work is projected onto Jews, whom he accuses of being clannish. Another respondent's fears of becoming jobless lead to similar projections: "*The Jews are really smart [. . .]. They can get work really easily, not like us, they can do a lot of things that we can't do*" (Omar, Paris). The Jews allegedly always find work and possess skills he does not have; the Jews are clever and successful. This respondent also seems to project his wish to feel at home and to be respected where he lives on to Jews, thereby adopting the stereotype of the wandering Jew and contrasting this to his own community:

> *The Jews, they're everywhere [. . .], it's not like with us, we're in France, we're in Spain, but even though the Jews are everywhere [. . .]. They are more respected than [. . .] the Muslims [. . .]. If a Jew goes to the United States he feels at home. You know what I mean, but if a Muslim goes to the United States, he's not gonna feel at home. I don't know how to say it, we don't feel at home.* (Omar, Paris)

However, these and other comparisons of interviewees' own communities to that of the Jews, like the opposing images of the rich Jews and the Arab have-nots or contrasting portrayals of Jews and one's own community ("*we're weak Muslim, we're normal, we're not that rich [. . .]. But they've got everything [. . .] every big company Jewish people own it*" [Baru, London]), are only hints of possible projections.

Kristina Kraft, Manuela Freiheit, and Viktoria Spaiser have observed that some young Muslims in Berlin denounce Israelis as terrorists and interpret this as a "redirection of own experiences of discrimination" being labeled as terrorists.[42] I would argue rather that they wish to express their hatred against Israel and conveniently (as an argumentative strategy) use a term that is used to denounce members of their own community. Why should young Muslims in Germany label Israelis of all people with a term that is used against them? Antisemitic attitudes must have been predisposed. The "redirection of own experiences of discrimination" against Jews and Israel only makes sense in an antisemitic worldview and thus does not explain the genesis of antisemitic views. Given the (forbidden) admiration of terrorists among some young Muslims, projections against Jews might also be at play when Israelis are accused of terrorism.

The mechanisms and patterns of pathological projections should be investigated with interviews focusing more on psychological motivations and mechanisms. However, it becomes clear that the thesis suggested by Stender,[43] that youths of Muslim background project onto Jews their wish for social integration due to their racist exclusion, can only be an explanatory factor for a fraction of young European Muslims, if any. It is surely not the main psychological mechanism of antisemitism among young European Muslims. Antisemitic projections are far more complex and varied. Schu identified in her ongoing study on young Muslims in Germany a number of motivations for antisemitic projections, such as the wish for financial security and comfort, envy, feelings of powerlessness, suppressed rebellion against one's own community, and suppressed violent sentiments.[44]

INFLUENCES OF EXPERIENCES AND PERCEPTIONS OF DISCRIMINATION

What are the links between experiences or perceptions of discrimination and antisemitic attitudes? Esther Benbassa hypothesized for the French context that "an explanation for this anti-Semitism currently spreading among Arab-Moslem milieus could be found in the absence of a real integration policy and a social and professional mobility still in its embryonic stages."[45] A number of German authors have suggested that experiences of degradation result in the wish to valorize one's own community and "ethnocentrism," including degradation of others, such as Jews.[46] This, however, does not explain why non-Muslim migrants who also face discrimination show lower antisemitic attitudes. Moreover, it reduces antisemitism to a form of "ethnocentrism" and degradation that seems reductive in view of conspiracy theories and stereotypes such as the omnipotent and rich Jew.

Matti Bunzl and Paul A. Silverstein speculated that a crucial cause of antisemitism among European Muslims lies in their alleged perception of Jews as part of a European hegemony that is responsible for their marginalization.[47] However, if Bunzl and Silverstein are right, this would only confirm that an antisemitic interpretation of marginalization is related to antisemitism.

But one could also surmise the contrary: that suffering from discrimination and exclusion would lead to criticism of discrimination and prejudices against other minorities, including Jews.

An analysis of the interviews, with a focus on perceptions of discrimination and antisemitic attitudes, shows that there is no simple cause-and-effect relation.

Although the sample is not representative and questions were only semi-standardized, some basic observations and reflections on possible correlations are possible; a number of participants showed that, despite having suffered from discrimination, they do not believe in antisemitic stereotypes. Conversely, many who do not feel discriminated against showed very open forms of hatred against Jews. The same is true for those with a precarious residence status, in contrast to those who are citizens of their country of residence (among both groups there are those with and without antisemitic views). If there is a statistical correlation between discrimination and antisemitism, it is not striking within the sample. Focusing only on statistical correlations, however, may be misleading because the relation between discrimination and antisemitism is, as shown below, too complex to be described as a simple correlation and some perceptions of discrimination even incorporate antisemitic views. If the Muslim community is perceived as threatened and denigrated in the context of a war against Muslims, some participants believe that this war is led or supported by "the Jews." Jews can be imagined as the driving force behind U.S. military action in Afghanistan and Iraq, as fighting a war against "the Muslims" in Palestine, or as denigrating Muslims through their influence in the media. This very broad perception of discrimination and hostility against one's own community, which comprises negative views of that community as a whole rather than discrimination against individuals, is also related to hostility against Jews if discrimination is seen in the context of a global war between Muslims and non-Muslims.

In this Manichean worldview, the Jews are identified as enemies of "the Muslims" via the Israeli – Palestinian conflict, with accusations such as "*the Jews, what they do to the Muslims, they do barbaric things*" (Khalil, Paris), or the assumption that Jews conspire globally against Muslims. These general accusations and conspiracy theories, which are often antisemitic in themselves, relate to perceptions of Muslims as victims. A statistical correlation of these perceptions would therefore only confirm that antisemitic interpretations of discrimination or antisemitic and Manichean perceptions of wars between Muslims and non-Muslims are indeed related to antisemitic attitudes. It is thus helpful to distinguish between personal experiences of discrimination and perceptions of a general hostility against the Muslim community and Islam.

What other links did the participants make between discrimination against their community and their views of Jews?

Comparing Negative Attitudes toward Jews and toward One's Own Community

Participants compared negative views of Jews to negative views of Muslims or of people of their ethnic background, and drew different conclusions.

Serkan, from Germany, who had been discriminated against by peers of Turkish origin for his Kurdish identity, provides an example of someone who sees parallels between discrimination against his own community and discrimination against Jews. He compares prejudice against Kurds with present day anti-Jewish attitudes and rejects both. A British interviewee provides another example of someone who sees analogies between stereotyping one's own community and stereotyping Jews, and calls for less prejudice against both. The first part of his statement supports the thesis that experiences or perceptions of discrimination can insulate someone from antisemitic stereotyping:

> *If Jews have done something wrong in the past, it's not Jews who have done something wrong in the past . . . it's a Jew or a few Jews. Like I said, if a few Muslims blow up something then why does the whole of the Muslims have to be called terrorist, 'cause they're not Muslims then, innit. And any Jews who have done anything bad are not really Jews, because obviously I know that the Jewish religion don't teach bad things so I mean they have power according to money, because they've established themselves [. . .]. I mean companies like Coca Cola is very Jewish.* (Bahaar, London)

Even though Bahaar's definition of Jews and Muslims, which excludes anybody who does something bad from being Jewish or Muslim, is peculiar, he applies his call to stop generalizing and blaming all Muslims for the deeds of a few to the context of the Jews. Unfortunately, that does not hinder him from saying that Jews are rich and powerful and, a few lines before the quoted statement, that Jews therefore do not care much about being discriminated against. Thus experiences of discrimination against his community prevents Bahaar from stereotyping Jews only in specific instances, namely if antisemitism can be used as an argument against the discrimination of his own group or community.

The acknowledgment that similarities exist between endured discrimination or racism and negative attitudes toward Jews can also be used for downplaying both. A German respondent provided an example of how negative views of Jews can be diminished by normalizing them through their portrayal as part of daily racist stereotypes that everybody has: *"And I said, 'Look at the fucking Jew' [. . .]. Say something like that every now and then, everyone does it. But there's racism for sure [. . .]. 'Fucking Jew,' yeah, for example [. . .]. People also say, 'fucking Wog'"* (Tunay, Berlin). Similarly, a French interviewee admitted that there is hostility, or "racism," as he put it, against Jews, that there are antisemitic jokes and that the term "Jew" is used as an insult by Muslims. But he is eager to point out that this kind of racism also exists against other minorities and that it is nothing to worry about. He concluded: *"It's racist [. . .]. It's true that, personally, the Jews, they can feel a little bit of racism from the side of the Muslims. But not more. We, personally, after all, it's up to them to be like us"* (Haroun, Paris). In the end it is up to the Jews to change, he said, and he accepts hostility against Jews. These rationales might be interpreted as a result of discrimination in the sense that victims of discrimination can grow accustomed to it and then justify their own negative views of Jews as just another part of a racist society.

A third way of seeing similarities between discrimination or racism against one's own community and negative attitudes toward Jews is to view Muslims and Jews as rivals in the competition for victimhood.[48] A few participants argue in this way. One acknowledged that "Jew" is used as an insult but stressed: "*It didn't go at all as far as what is happening today with the Arabs. It's a lot less frequent*" (Massoud, Paris), thereby indicating that he thinks that discrimination against Arabs today is worse than the persecution of Jews in the past. A black respondent in London stated that "*black slavery is worse than the Holocaust*" (Aba, London), and deplored that there are no compensation claims for black people. Interestingly, only a handful of interviewees see Muslims as the new Jews.[49] Aba from London most explicitly used this absurd argument that Muslims are the new Jews. Although Aba personally considers himself to be Muslim, he does not feel affected by anti-Muslim discrimination because, he said, he primarily identified as black or as a "hoodie" rather than as Muslim. Therefore, Aba's feeling that Muslims are the new Jews and that Muslims are discriminated against today in similar ways as Jews were in Germany during World War II is not rooted in his own experiences of discrimination.[50]

Others compare discrimination against foreigners today to the situation of Jews in Germany in the past. Haroun, for instance, believes that, like the Jews in the past, all Arabs and blacks might be threatened with deportation one day. But there is no indication that this comparison leads to more or to less antisemitic attitudes. Hamza, for example, said jokingly that Hitler should have continued killing Jews and "Gypsies," but he also believes that today the Arabs and blacks have taken that stigmatized role and are targeted in France. The comparison between the persecution of the Jews by the Nazis with discrimination against the respondents' own community seems to be simply an expression of the wish to stress the victimization of that community, for which Jews' past suffering is used as a reference. Consequently, using the analogy of the Jews to stress discrimination today can easily diminish the sufferings of Jews during the Holocaust, particularly if the persecution of Jews during World War II and the situation of foreigners today are equated.

Some interviewees in France said that people in their community are regarded as less important than Jews when it comes to politicians' public condemnations of violence against members of both communities. These statements can also be interpreted as envy of Jews' social position and an expression of the competition resulting from comparative discourses of victimhood.[51] However, the following example illustrates that incidents are compared that are not comparable and rather reveal anti-Jewish prejudices:

> *As soon as they killed the Jew, there was a demonstration and everything. Sarkozy was with them and as soon as they killed those two boys there, an Arab and a Black guy, in '93, at Clichy, then, they didn't say anything, they didn't even talk [about it].* (Abed, Paris)

Abed referred to the antisemitic abduction, torture, and murder of Ilan Halimi,[52] which was condemned by Nicolas Sarkozy,[53] then the French interior minister, and to the death of Zyed Benna and Bouna Traoré in Clichy-sous-Bois, resulting from their electrocution in a power substation while they were hiding or running away from the police.[54] Abed compared the two incidents, which were both tragic, though quite different, to highlight the injustice of silence in the face of the "two guys'" deaths, and to portray Jews as privileged in French society. He used the comparison to stress his demand of recognition, and in his comparison he exposed the antisemitic stereotype of privileged Jews and Jewish influence in politics, in which he already believes.

Comparing Minorities

Others compare Muslims or people in their own ethnic community with Jews as minorities. Being a minority and thereby feeling excluded to some extent from mainstream society is reinforced by discrimination. However, comparing one's own ethnic group to Jews can result in a rationale that Jews are, in ways similar to people from their own community, attached to "their country" and have links to Israel. A respondent in Berlin, for example, believes that Jews in Germany "*naturally invest in their own [country], Israel. That's logical, isn't it? Just as our fathers did*" (Ümit, Berlin). Similarly, a French interviewee who is convinced that French Jews have to go to Israel, just as he regularly visits Algeria, said: "*it's in-*

evitable that they [the Jews] went there a least once, everybody has been to his country of origin" (Bilal, Paris). Likewise, Nader from London sees parallels between his connection to Morocco and that of Jews to Israel. These comparisons can include the antisemitic stereotype that Jews are not fully committed citizens, but that they feel Israeli, which can be seen as indirectly resulting from the perception that immigrants inevitably hold strong ties to their country of origin, which in turn can be enforced by a sense of exclusion from mainstream society. However, these possible links between discrimination and antisemitic stereotypes by no means form a direct line and are based on the antisemitic assumption that Jews are necessarily a migrant minority with Israel as their home country.

Jews as Perpetrators

A few participants see Jews as perpetrators of discrimination or, more commonly, believe that Jews are hostile to their community. Moukhtar gave an example of a Jewish employer who exploits Arab trainees for racist reasons. But accusations that Jews are racist were usually made in the context of alleged mutual hostility and as an explanation of why Muslims or people of their ethnic community do not like Jews: "*Jewish people [are] racist, Bengali people hate them. You know? This is how it goes*" (Sakti, London); "*They don't like us, bah, we don't like them, that's logical*" (Jabar's friend, Paris). While his perception that Jews are hostile to his ethnic or religious community serves to justify his own hatred against Jews, a French interviewee argued the opposite: "*I can't go and eat in a Jewish neighborhood and go into a restaurant alone and eat just like that. It's impossible! [. . .] They're going to say to themselves, that's an Arab, what's he doing here? I am going to feel bad [. . .]. But, [. . .] a Jew can come here and eat just like normal, that's normal for us [. . .]. Personally, I am open to everybody*" (Anis, Paris). He accused Jews indirectly of being racist, saying that they make him uncomfortable in their restaurants or areas. But instead of using this as an explanation for why he does not like Jews, he contrasted this (alleged) discriminatory attitude with his own openness toward Jews.

However, Jews are only seen in exceptional cases as being responsible for discrimination. Even those who see institutional racism in companies and who think that major firms are Jewish do not necessarily make the link. Imran and Salim, for instance, complained that in supermarket chains like Sainsbury's, only white people get up to the management level. Both also believe that Marks & Spencer, an upmarket major retailer, is a Jewish company that sends money to "Zionists."[55] But Salim reported that he has worked for Marks & Spencer and was treated very well. The accusations of Jews being racist, however, are often unsupported and are instead rooted in the wish to denounce Jews. A French man, for example, said: *"At school there are sometimes problems because the head teacher, she is Jewish, she is racist"* (Kamel's friend, Paris). The first problem seems to be that the headmaster is Jewish and therefore she is portrayed as racist. This serves as a justification for her fear of the district's young Arabs and blacks. Another friend of Kamel even sees the punishment he received for beating up a black girl in school as proof of racism from his headmaster. Ahlam, also from Paris, acknowledged that Jews are afraid of Muslims but justified it with the rationale that the Jews allegedly use anti-Arab slurs and portray all Arabs and Muslims as terrorists. His accusation appears to be a justification for hatred rather than an experience he has had with Jews he has met. Kassim from Berlin also accused Jews of being racist, but his example is questionable, too. He reported a pro-Palestinian demonstration in which he had participated and accused allegedly Jewish opponents, who participated in a counter-demonstration, of being racists. Ali also claimed that Jews are racist and reported that he was once beaten up by Jews. However, he insisted that he has always hated Jews, even prior to this incident. Perceived hostility by Jews against one's own community, based on some experiences that are sometimes completely imagined, is hardly a credible source of antisemitic attitudes.

Jews Made Responsible for An Alleged War against Muslims

The accusation that Jews are responsible for hostility against respondents' ethnic or religious community becomes even more questionable when Jews are made responsible for a global war against Muslims. Some put the perception of global hostility against Islam or against Arabs in the context of what Jochen Müller described as a discourse or myth of victimhood in which the community of Muslims is seen as a victim of a conspiracy.[56] The use of military force upon Muslims by non-Muslims in countries such as Iraq or the Palestinian territories can then be perceived as part of a global war against "the Muslims" that indirectly affects young European Muslims by impelling them to bond with the Islamic community as a whole. Sabir, for example, does not feel personally discriminated against, but believes there is a global conspiracy against Muslims in which America and a "Jewish plan" are the driving force. In his eyes, the fight against the regime of Saddam Hussein is part of a Jewish plan to weaken Muslims in anticipation of an apocalyptic war of religions.

The perception that Muslims are generally accused of terrorism is the most commonly quoted form of hostility against Islam. A few participants reported that they have experienced discrimination based on this stereotype. However, this perception can become distorted if it goes along with the assertion that terrorists cannot, by definition, be Muslims and others are blamed for terrorist attacks. In the resulting conspiracy theories, Western governments or "the Jews" are often seen as the real culprits. Therefore, there is a link between these perceptions and antisemitism: perceptions of global hostility against Muslims and Islam are often related to antisemitic conspiracies or apocalyptic views of an imminent war of religions.

Does the Sense of Exclusion Lead to an Emphasis on Religious Identity?

For some interviewees, Muslim identity includes, as shown above, hostility against Jews. Another thesis dealing with the relation between discrimination and antisemitic attitudes is that discrimination leads to the feeling of being excluded and thus makes a strong collective identity, such as being Muslim, appear more attractive.[57] If one assumes a general enmity between Muslims and Jews, then discrimination indirectly leads to the adoption of antisemitic beliefs. This might be a rationale for some individuals, but international comparison within the sample of interviews shows that this thesis cannot be generalized. The participants' identification as Muslim is strong in all three countries and the level of antisemitism is also similar, but the perception of exclusion from society is very different. Muslims in Germany identify less as German than their French counterparts identify as French, while British respondents identify the strongest with their national identity.[58] Therefore, exclusion from national identity does not seem to be a decisive factor for a stronger identification as Muslim. Representative surveys confirm strong levels of identification as a Muslim in all three countries among those with Muslim background, but identifications with the nationality of the country vary. From the three countries in question, identification with the country of residence and as Muslims are both strongest in Britain.[59]

Does Discrimination Lead to Projections of Suppressed Violent Sentiments onto Jews?

Undoubtedly, experiences of discrimination are frustrating and can lead to serious psychological implications. However, experiences of discrimination cannot explain why Jews are targeted and why the level of antisemitism is higher among Muslims compared to other, equally discriminated minorities. As outlined earlier for the scapegoat theory, frustrations alone do not result in the genesis of social prejudice and even less so specifically against Jews. Two of its basic hypotheses, the assumption that aggression is rooted in frustration and that aggression is then transferred onto Jews rather than targeting the origin of frustration, have been questioned and partly disproven in social psychological research.[60]

Does Discrimination Lead to Projections onto Jews Who Allegedly Feel at Home Everywhere?

Another related thesis is that a source of antisemitic attitudes lies in discrimination, which triggers psychological mechanisms of projection. Experiences of discrimination and the wish for belonging and acceptance in mainstream society might trigger antisemitic projections onto the Jews, who allegedly feel at home in many different countries and who are accepted and respected. Some of Didier Lapeyronnie's and Michel Wieviorka's observations can be interpreted in that way.[61] A few statements from interviewees in France also support this thesis, most clearly one respondent who used the stereotype of the wandering Jew to portray Jews as being respected and feeling at home and at ease anywhere, in contrast to his own community:

> *Jews, they're everywhere [. . .], it's not like with us, we're in France, we're in Spain, but even though the Jews are everywhere [. . .], they are more respected than [. . .] the Muslims [. . .]. If a Jew goes to the United States he feels at home. You know what I mean, but if a Muslim goes to the United States, he's not gonna feel at home. I don't know how to say it, we don't feel at home.* (Omar, Paris)

But this stereotype of the wandering Jew and of Jews feeling at home in many countries is used but rarely among interviewees. Slightly different is the perception of some interviewees, particularly in France, that Jews are a privileged minority. Jews allegedly have easier access to loans and are believed to get more public attention than Muslims or Arabs if they are attacked, and Jewish schools get better protection than others. This perception is related to stereotypes of Jews as being influential in politics and business. It is difficult to say if these observations or antisemitic stereotypes are cause or effect. In any case, the perception that Jews are a minority similar to the respondents' own community, but privileged and better off, is also not prevalent. Therefore, the thesis of projection motivated by racist exclusion cannot explain the genesis of antisemitic attitudes among a majority of interviewees. However, the applied methods of this study are very limited when it comes to conclusions about psychoanalytical projections. Racist exclusion might well be an additional psychological motivation for antisemitic projections onto Jews at large, something future studies might explore.

No (Clear) Linkage between Discrimination and Antisemitic Attitudes

To conclude, experiences of discrimination are not a decisive factor for or against the genesis of antisemitic attitudes. Rationales put forward by interviewees linking perceived discrimination and views of Jews show a variety of contradictory arguments. However, some perceptions of discrimination, such as a global war against Muslims, can contain antisemitic conspiracy theories in which hostility against Muslims and Islam is interpreted in an antisemitic way.

Focusing only on statistical correlations may be misleading for two reasons. First, possible correlations between discrimination and antisemitism are complex and not straightforward as cause and effect. Second, some perceptions of global discrimination against Muslims include antisemitic conspiracy theories. Similarly, the rhetoric of victimhood competition can contain antisemitic arguments.[62] Correlations between such attitudes would only confirm that antisemitic perceptions of discrimination and victimhood are linked to antisemitic worldviews. However, the formation of complex attitudes such as antisemitism are unlikely to be rooted in a single factor.

ELEVEN

Positive Examples: Rejecting Antisemitism

THROUGHOUT THIS BOOK, I HAVE HIGHLIGHTED ANTISEMITIC attitudes. Of course, not all interviewees displayed antisemitic stereotypes. A number did not have any opinion of Jews and some clearly reject hostility toward them, often in opposition to some of their friends or their parents. What is their motivation? Why do they stand up against hatred of Jews? Is theirs an advanced "emotional development," as Erich Fromm might have suggested?[1] Is it the positive influence of teachers, friends, or relatives? Is it a certain perception of Islam? Could it be attributed to a deep conviction that everybody is equal and to the belief in human rights? Portraits of five young Muslim men, all of whom value their religion, show very different rationales, but they all reject, and some actively fight, general hatred against Jews in their social circles.

JAMIL PLAYS WITH COLLECTIVE IDENTITIES: *"I'M COMPLETELY DIFFERENT FROM OTHER BOYS"*

Jamil from Berlin is an exception in many ways, starting with simple things. He is the only one who did not want to reveal his age to the interviewer, "*because I have never told anybody my age,*" probably out of pride. However, he indirectly gave it away, and at fourteen years old at the time of the interview he was one of the youngest participants. He has ambitions to take the *Abitur* (A-levels) and to go to university, eventually hoping to become an *Erzieher* (educator for children, usually in kindergarten). He certainly wants to stay in Germany and is confident about his future, counting on his achievements in school and particularly on the help of his teachers and his family. Nevertheless, Jamil is aware of his school's bad reputation and referred to a local newspaper report naming his school as one of the worst in Berlin.[2] Still, he praised the school for its multicultural character, and his "foreign" classmates, who come from Lebanon, Turkey, and Spain.

Jamil can be described as individualistic, gentle, a little narcissistic, soft-spoken, sensitive, and, above all, as he said on several occasions, different from other boys. When he was asked to describe himself, he answered: "*For me it is very important that I'm well-dressed, well, I'm completely different from other boys.... Yes, that's it.*" He seems to be popular, as he was elected student representative. He also sings in a school band – in Turkish, which he has learned from friends and his brother-in-law. His mother tongue, however, is Arabic, even though he is more fluent in German.

Jamil is the youngest of five children and came with his Kurdish family from Lebanon to Germany when he was three or four years old. But neither he nor his parents have ever gone back to Lebanon, "*because most of our friends are here,*" he said. The family seems to be patriarchal, and religion is valued. However, only one of his sisters wears a headscarf. His parents, both unemployed for a long time, live with three of their five children in a one-bedroom flat in Berlin-Kreuzberg. The two other children are married.

Jamil believes in God, but is "*not so devout as the others.*" However, he respects some Islamic laws and customs, such as abstaining from eating pork and drinking alcohol, fasting, and going to the mosque every day during Ramadan. He visits the local Mevlana mosque with his parents, which is run by Milli Görüş, an Islamist organization. But he generally does not pray and rarely reads the Qur'an, which seems to be an issue with his father, who would like him to study the Islamic holy book more.

Jamil only has Lebanese citizenship. He has experienced racism personally and recalled an incident in the neighboring district, Neukölln, where his school is situated: a woman with a stroller did not want to share the elevator and insulted him and his friends with the words "*Foreigners, piss off to your country.*" But he was quick to assure the interviewer that he does not see racism as a problem and believes most Germans respect "foreigners" like him. However, like most interviewees in Germany, he considers himself a foreigner and thus excluded in a way from German society, and does not see himself as German.

He watches Arab TV, mostly music channels. His parents often watch Arab news channels, including the Hezbollah-affiliated channel Al Manar, the Kurdish TV channel Roj, and Dubai TV. However, Jamil's understanding of Standard Arabic, used by TV announcers, is limited. He also watches German TV, but in general he likes to read rather than to watch TV.

A major influence on Jamil is his nineteen-year-old female cousin, who dropped out of school but loves reading and who has advised him on a few books that deal critically with women in Islam. He has read books such as "Wüstenblume" by Waris Dirie and "Bei lebendigem Leib" by Souad,[3] which he borrowed from the library. His cousin is also interested in other religions, such as Judaism, and Jamil believes that there are many similarities between "the four" religions (the three monotheistic ones and Buddhism).

Hearing negative views of Jews is nothing strange for Jamil: in his school the term "Jew" is used as an insult, he reported, and he knows people who hate Jews. It also is likely that he has been exposed to frequent antisemitic propaganda on Arab news channels. Moreover, Jamil has experienced hatred against Jews himself. He was threatened when he presented himself "for fun" to a Palestinian classmate as having a Jewish father. He believes that his father would have beaten him had he found out that he had invented the story because "*he doesn't like Jews. Yes. They are at war with the Muslims.*" Interestingly, when he described this rationale, he did not identify with "the Muslims." Pretending to have a Jewish identity, while knowing that such an identity is shunned by his father and peers, is a strong sign of both disagreement with anti-Jewish assumptions and of distancing from his religious collective identity, even if Jamil did it "just for fun." His individualism allows him to play with collective identities, as also reflected in his singing in Turkish.

Jamil argued that hatred against Jews comes from conflating politics with people. He agrees with others that "*Jewish politics*" is bad, referring particularly to the Lebanon war in 2006 and the Israeli-Palestinian conflict. But he believes that this political activity has to be separated from the Jewish people, who are not bad. Jamil did not show hatred against

Israel, either; he endorses a two-state-solution to the Israeli-Palestinian conflict.

It is also interesting to note why he condemns suicide bombers: Jamil argued that they have no feelings and do not care about suffering children, adding that suicide bombers are crazy and mostly devout and strict Muslims. He thereby demonstrated that, in contrast to many other participants, he is willing to criticize other Muslims and certain interpretations of Islam.

His views on Jews are astonishingly open. In passing, he mentioned that he had a Jewish female friend. He rejects stereotypes such as the belief that Jews have too much influence in society or equations of the sufferings of Palestinians today with the persecution of the Jews by the Nazis. However, Jamil did not recall having learned anything about the Holocaust and National Socialism in school, but knows that Jews were gassed and burned, recalling that his cousin read a book about it and that he watched a film on it.

Distinguishing between "Jewish" policies and Jews as individuals may help Jamil to reconcile himself to an environment in which negative views of Jews are common, but in which he lacks feelings of Jew hatred.[4] He can then dismiss antisemitism as a mistake arising from the conflation of politics with views of individual human beings (he stresses that he is not interested in politics or in what is going on in other countries).

Two major factors contribute to his resistance against anti-Jewish attitudes: first, his individualism and difference from others, and thus independence from other peers' and parents' views, including his distancing of himself from collective identification with "the Muslims." His perception that Jews and Muslims are at war does not imply for him that he should have negative views of Jews. Second, the positive influence of his elder cousin gave him some insights on issues that might have encouraged him to think independently from, and even be critical about, religious traditions and collective identities.

NABIL BELIEVES IN HUMAN RIGHTS

At the time of the interview, Nabil was seventeen years old and looking forward to his next birthday. He was born to Palestinian parents in

Beirut and came with them to Germany at the age of two. He attends a *gymnasium* in Berlin-Kreuzberg to do his *Abitur* and is well-spoken and self-confident. He has no particular hobbies, and only when he was younger did he regularly go to a local youth club where young people and educators sometimes held debates, including on issues discussed by the media, and debates about the conflicts between "*Jews or Arabs or [Arabs and] Germans.*" Nabil described himself as not very religious, particularly in comparison to his father, who taught in a mosque for a while and took Nabil with him when he did so. Now he prays at home, but from time to time he visits a local mosque, which he described as peaceful, without any kind of incitement to hatred. Nabil has experienced discrimination for his Arab background, but has said that it was meant as a joke and was an aberration. But, he added, he usually socializes with Arab friends anyway, though he does have some German friends, and so he does not expect to experience discrimination.

Nabil's family has roots and ties to the Palestinian territories. He said that his family fled from the Israeli-Palestinian conflict and that they still have relatives living there, whom they support. Sometimes, the relatives send letters and videos, which serve as a source of information about life in the Palestinian territories and the Israeli-Palestinian conflict, in addition to what he sees on television. He watches Arab news channels, including Al Jazeera, Dubai TV, Al Manar, and LBC, though his understanding of Standard Arabic is limited. But he is aware of the fact that Arab news channels usually take the point of view of "the Palestinians" and, as he said, influence people in their opinions. He contrasted this with German media, which he believes are neutral on the issue and which he prefers.

Nabil's parents' narrative of the Israeli-Palestinian conflict is one-sided and antisemitic. In their eyes, the Jews have settled in Palestinian land and evicted Palestinians from their houses. He quoted his mother saying, "*It was right, what Hitler did, he should have eradicated all Jews right away.*" However, he disagrees and argues with his mother, saying: "*For me, a human being is a human being.*" He tries to take a historical perspective that has room for the views both of Palestinians, who were evicted from their homes, leading to sufferings and eventually frustration and hatred, and the Jews, who survived the Holocaust and wanted to find a place where they were not chased and killed. This view allows him to find his mother's perspective acceptable, even if he does not see things in this way. "*I didn't experience that, all of this taking refuge in other countries [. . .]. People who experienced that, they have a whole other opinion [. . .], They have this hate toward them, that's why. They don't really say it because they mean it, but only out of hate, to let their frustration out on to people.*" His argument is that because he personally did not experience the suffering, he has no reason to develop indiscriminate hatred.

He has also argued with his father, who endorses suicide bombings and, in a moment of anger against Israel, told his son that he wished he would train to become a martyr. But Nabil opposed this wish: "*First of all, I'm not just going to kill myself for a meaningless thing, because that doesn't help anything. And secondly, people die then, because of the person who kills himself.*" Both his life and the life of others are precious to Nabil. Also, it is difficult for him to imagine becoming a suicide bomber. In the quote above, he immediately switches from the first to the third person. He is familiar with the concept of "*moral conception,*" as he puts it, that martyrs are believed to fight for freedom and to go to paradise, but he disagrees with this ideology, saying that it makes the conflict only worse. "*They should sit down and talk to each other and agree on something. Because, okay, they want their country back, the others don't want to give it back, but that's better than waging war for years and that people die during it, just agree on something already, that they share it or that each gets one piece, that's better, than when people are dying.*" Here again, he shows that, despite his Palestinian background, he does not strongly identify with "the Palestinians"; rather, he speaks of "them" (Palestinians and Israelis) needing to sit together and find a solution, and "them" (Palestinians) as the people who want "their" country back.

His parents' antisemitic attitudes are not restricted to the Israeli-Palestinian conflict. "*My mother tends to be against Jews, yeah, she also said that I shouldn't become friends with Jews.*" Nabil's argument against this view is, again: "*Mama, human beings are human beings,*" and he insists that he would not have any problems befriending a Jew. He has seen everyday anti-Jewish attitudes such as the use of the term "Jew" as an insult among his peers. However, he does not think of this insult as a serious problem, and instead believes that it is "just for fun." He observes anti-

Jewish attitudes mainly among "foreigners" and "Arabs," who are on the side of "the Palestinians." In his school, he suggested, these views come mainly from students he described as "*foreigners [. . .] and [. . .] Arabs. They are more for these suicide bombings and stuff. They represent more of the Palestinians' opinion.*"

Nabil reported that on the day of the terror attacks of September 11, 2001, Arab students celebrated by waiving flags and distributing sweets. Their rationale was: "*Yes, indeed, now we finally struck back, America deserves it.*" He fundamentally disagreed and challenged his classmates, pointing out the loss of life of a vast number of innocent people. He sees a connection between the endorsement of terrorist attacks, negative views of Jews, and a "Palestinian perspective," which he does not share despite his Palestinian identity. Why? The hints are few. Clearly, Nabil developed a strong personality by openly arguing against his parents' strong anti-Jewish views and by distancing himself from his father through his weaker religious feelings, as well as by challenging a significant number of his classmates who endorse terrorist attacks. Against all bigotry, he came up with his fundamental belief that "*a human being [is] a human being,*" a belief rooted in human rights and in the assumption that everybody is equal. He has a positive view of the German media, schools, and society. And as someone with a comparatively good education and a significant formal qualification in sight, the adoption of Article Three of the German Constitution (equality before the law)[5] can be seen as a form of integration into German society. Perhaps he was influenced by a good teacher or social worker and learned that people should be treated as individuals, for example when talking in his youth club about conflicts between "*Jews or Arabs or [Arabs and] Germans.*" Whatever further reasons he has, Nabil is an independent – and one could say enlightened – thinker who speaks out against hatred of Jews.

BOUALEM, ILLEGAL IN LONDON, LOVES A PEACEFUL LIFE

Boualem, twenty-four years old and of Algerian origin, leads a precarious life. He is an illegal resident of London, with no relatives or friends, and lives pretty much on his own. He does not interact with other Arabs and only occasionally does so with other Algerians. After leaving his home country about five years ago via a dangerous four-day boat trip in which he almost lost his life, he worked in vineyards and did other low-skill labor in Spain, France, and Belgium, which brought him to major European cities. He managed only recently to come to England, where, he said, there is a lot of work. He currently works as a dishwasher in restaurants.

Boualem stays in contact with his family by phone. He is the youngest of nine children, and has five sisters and three brothers. Boualem reported that he has always been a maverick, spending a lot of time on his own. He left school when he was thirteen or fourteen, but he values education and refinement and said that he has learned a lot on his own, mainly by observation. He can be characterized as friendly, modest, and optimistic about his future. However, his wishes are modest: he wants to have a family one day and does not even expect to eventually become legal in Britain.

Boualem is not a very religious person and rarely goes to mosque. But his religious perception serves him as a moral guide; or, rather, he adjusts his interpretation of Islam to his moral beliefs. For him, being Muslim means being in individual contact with God. He believes that religion should be a free choice and should be respected: *"I respect all religions [. . .] Jews, Christians, Buddhists, whatever the religion,"* he declared. He demands the same respect for his religion, giving the example that he would not force anybody to eat *halal* and he does not want to be forced to eat non-*halal* food.

"I like everybody," he said, *"a Jew or a Black, or . . . for me [we] are all the same."* He does not make any distinctions among people and, in contrast to many other interviewees, he would not have any problems marrying a Jewish woman. Boualem does not feel much affected by racism, not because he thinks that there is none, but because he tries to ignore people who dislike him, he explained. He wants to avoid conflict and argued that this is the teaching of Muhammad. His perception of religion, influenced mainly by his parents, includes tolerance for other religions and the principle of reciprocity: treating others the way you want to be treated yourself.

He reflected on his life: *"It's a life just like this, everybody goes his own way,"* which seems to be an expression of his view of society; all people live their lives individually and should not be bothered unnecessarily. Boualem is not interested in politics and he does not like wars: "*I don't like the wars. I don't like it, not even in books [. . .]. People are dying, that affects me.*" He is sensitive to other people's sufferings, and this is why he also does not like to watch the news and does not approve of terrorism. Consequently, he is not interested in the Israeli-Palestinian conflict or the war in Lebanon. Linking his views on wars with views on conflicts and his life, he explained: "*I'm not at all interested in the war; because I don't like wars. If I see someone fighting with somebody else, I don't like it. Why? I don't know why. I don't like it. Why don't they live like that: I smile, you smile, isn't that good? That's the real life, isn't it?*" He wants to live in peace. "*I don't like to hurt people and I don't like if somebody's hurting me.*" Terrorism and the civil war in Algeria were a reason for him to leave the country, he stated. His priorities are private matters: "*What is important? Living easy . . . to be alive and to be in love.*" This is what he wants: a quiet and private life, loving somebody. Politics, terrorism, hatred, and prejudice stand in opposition to this goal.

He also believes in equality – "*we are all human beings*" – and values rational thinking and love for each other: "*We have to live in peace [. . .] we are human beings [. . .] we have brains. We have to use it. We have to think, we have to understand, that's it. And we have to feel, because the heart and the head, these are the fundamental things of human beings. If there [. . .] is no love in the heart, the human being destroys himself. He doesn't think like the people, he thinks like an animal. And someone who doesn't use his brain, for me, that's not a human being. It's a madman.*"

Boualem is against prejudice. He suggests that Muslims who do not like Jews are "uncultivated" and do not know what they are talking about. At the end of the interview, I asked him directly why he thinks he has no prejudice against Jews. He responded: "*Those who haven't suffered in the world they cannot feel it; to walk in park like this; to see the people, the children. That is life. Life is not, it's not wars, hatred, racism. Why the racism? [. . .] I don't know, I don't understand that, either.*"

Why does Boualem resist any kind of resentment against Jews and prejudices in general? One can only make educated guesses. His hard and solitary life, including the fact that he lives clandestinely in Europe, has probably made him appreciate a simple and decent existence in private, a person whose opinions are independent of others'. Rational thinking has probably been necessary for Boualem's survival. He does not want to be bothered unnecessarily and wants to avoid any kind of trouble. Resentment would only be in his way in his (modest) pursuit of happiness.

RAHOUL BELIEVES THAT BLAMING THE JEWS IS OLD-FASHIONED

Rahoul, fifteen years old, was born in East London. He feels *"British-Bengali, because we are proud to be who we are!"* His parents both have a Muslim background, but his father is from Bangladesh and his mother is white. He has been to Bangladesh and described the area his father immigrated from as "back home," but he does not follow events there closely. He said that he is only interested in news of Bangladesh if there is major news, such as floods or "explosions," by which he probably meant terrorist bombings.

Rahoul likes soccer and boxing; he seems to be happy in his neighborhood, Bricklane, and states that it is never boring there. He said that the area is also called "Banglatown," but that there are more and more white people moving in, which he approves of because *"you get to learn lots of things."* He knows the people living in the area. However, he also sees downsides in his neighborhood, pointing to crime and violence on the street, even among boys of his age or younger. But, he said, that with Bricklane becoming more of a mixed society, things have calmed down and people have learned to live in peace.

Rahoul and his friends get stopped by the police regularly and perceive it as a form of racism; he said that they get stopped because they are (South) Asian. Rahoul experienced blatant discrimination when he went for an interview to do his internship and was told, *"'We don't hire Asian people' [. . .], straight into my face [. . .]. It was just a few months ago."* He was hurt and angry and wanted to beat "them" up with his friends.

Rahoul stated that there is racism from white people but acknowledged that there are prejudices among all groups, including his own. He admitted that he also stereotypes, not about race but about boys from different areas. Referring to "all races," he made the critical observation that *"they tend to think, just 'cause they're that color, they have to be like that.*

That's being prejudiced, discriminating them." He thereby criticized people who adopt prejudices and essentialize groups of people due to the color of their skin. However, he admitted that he also does this in a certain way: "*I don't do it toward races or culture [. . .]. I do it toward, like, different area-boys [. . .]. If they are from that area, they must be gay.*" Being gay is seen as very negative among his friends. Rahoul explained: "*Because, as Muslims we are not supposed to have homosexuals in our religion. That's why we're brought up to, you know, not like gay people.*"

Religion is important for Rahoul. He sees that it is useful for his mind: "*You feel safe, [. . .] you know there's something to look forward to after life.*" He has learned to read the Qur'an in Arabic in a *madrasa* and his parents encourage him to be more religious, in part to prevent him from turning to crime. "*But you know, with us kids it's like we want to explore life.*" He thinks that it is important to keep the faith strong but sees religion as a private matter: "*You should follow your own path, you know. Let people mind their own business.*" He does care, however, what is said publicly about Muhammad and condemns the Muhammad cartoons from Denmark.

He does not see much tension between followers of different religions in East London, and less tension between Muslims and Jews than between Muslims and Christians. He pointed to the East London mosque, which, he said, had been a church, then a synagogue, and has still a synagogue next to it, as an example of good relations among the neighborhood's three religions.

He has a differentiated opinion on the wars in Iraq and Afghanistan. While he understands the aim to catch Osama Bin Laden at the time, he disagrees with the war in Iraq. The issue of Palestinians, however, does not concern him. "*Fuck this bullshit man [. . .]. Let them get along with their business,*" said a friend of his, and Rahoul agreed. He reported that Muslim associations try to boycott companies such as Tesco because "*they give their money to the Jewish people [. . .]. But with Tesco, how can they give all the money to Jewish people, when they have shareholders?*" He also ridiculed the opinion that people like Rupert Murdoch are Jewish when in fact, he said, they are strict Catholics. He explained this prejudice as resulting from people's envy, and he is remarkably critical of his own community: "*With Bengali people, they tend to mix their culture with their religion [. . .]. Not tryin' to dismount culture, it's all about money, with*

Bengalis. And, if someone is rich, they say they are Jewish. You know, successful people like Bill Gates or [. . .] Rupert Murdoch." He believes that people should become successful themselves rather than being jealous of rich and successful people. Nevertheless, he thinks that "*the media is controlling everyone's head,*" and he gave the film *Spiderman 3* as an example of powerful and manipulative media, where someone was portrayed as bad but then it "*turned out it wasn't true, he is still good.*" Thus, he considers movies in part as examples of reality.

However, he believes that Muslims or Bengalis with biased views against Jews "*are more traditional and we are more modern [. . .]. They don't know how it's like for us kids to grow up; 'cause they grew up back in the days when it was more traditional. They had less facilities.*" It is not clear what he means by "facilities" and how they would work against antisemitic stereotypes and conspiracy theories. He may be alluding to the internet, which he knows how to use and which facilitates his own research. He mentioned how he got into trouble when he was caught hacking into his school's computer system.

Rahoul rejected the antisemitic views of what he described as "Muslim associations" and also "Bengalis" despite his identification both as a Muslim and as Bengali. Why? He is not very different from other participants who showed anti-Jewish attitudes, and he does express homophobic attitudes. However, he is critical of his own community. His distinction between traditional and modern members of his community helps him to reject some views while still feeling he is part of the group. He also is self-reflective about the relation between prejudice and collective identification and about the function of religion, which he sees as a private matter. Why does he not also reject homophobic attitudes? He accepts homophobia as part of his religion and, among his friends, homophobic and not antisemitic stereotypes are used in group dynamics for demarcation and exclusion; therefore, such stereotypes are very difficult to abandon.[6]

SAMED HAS JEWISH FRIENDS AND LOVES A JEWISH GIRL

Samed, eighteen years of age at the time of the interviews, was born in Paris. His parents came from Tunisia, where his entire family goes on holiday every year. He enjoys that country, particularly the weather, but he knows that he could not live there. He has an elder brother of twenty-four and a sister of twenty-one, and they all live with their parents.

Samed has a low level of education. He currently studies in a *collège* (vocational school) to take the "BEP électronique" qualifications, which, he said, is demanding. His parents both work a lot in their bakery and Samed sometimes helps out. They are not rich but Samed is content with the money he has. He likes his neighborhood, but he often spends time with friends in another, better-off district near his *collège* and enjoys a hookah in a café.

He speaks Arabic but does not understand the Standard Arabic spoken on Arab TV channels. Only his parents watch Arab TV, including Iraqi and Palestinian channels, but only a little because they work a lot, he said. Samed is interested in Islam, which he speaks about with his parents. He learned about the religion and the Qur'an in Arabic classes on Saturdays when he was younger, and now reads about Islam on the internet, using Google for questions such as, "How do I pray [according to the Muslim tradition]?" Samed has not experienced any anti-Muslim bigotry but he has heard about it. He thinks that terrorists give Islam a bad name by acting contrary to what God says in the Qur'an. Islam means "peace" in Arabic,[7] he said, and "*God never said 'kill the Jews.'*"

Samed is not free of antisemitic beliefs, however. He thinks that Jews are rich in general and that most of the big American companies "are Jewish." He also stated that some Jews in the United States financially support the Israeli army and the Israeli-Palestinian war to enrich themselves, despite the massacres. This is what he hears from acquaintances. He knows many people who do not like Jews and who use "Jew" as an insult. But he rejects hostility against Jews and some antisemitic beliefs, against which he counters with such statements as "*If I see in France, it's not the Jews who rule the society, its more . . . it's secular.*" He declares that he is against antisemitism, arguing that this is directed against Arabs and Jews, who are both "Semites."[8] Samed also rejects the generalization that all Jews are bad. He explained that he has learned to think differently from his parents and friends and to make up his own mind by spending time with both Jews and Muslims.

Samed has a Jewish friend, whom he knows from *collège*. His parents tell him to sever their friendship, but he rejects their advice: "*They told me, 'Stop it because one day he will cause you pain.' I just said, 'No, that's not true.' Because on the contrary [I think of] – all that he has done for me.*" Samed is fond of his friend and does not care if he is Jewish or not: "*I'm telling them, 'No, there is good and bad everywhere.' It's not because he is Jewish that he will do something bad and because if someone is Muslim he will do something good.*" He argues against an essentialist view of people based on their religious affiliation and against the attribution of character traits to all members of a religious community. This conviction is also revealed in his views on the Middle East conflict, for which he blames both sides. He is not very interested in this conflict but has gathered information about it from the internet, and his parents and friends keep him informed. He tries to keep a neutral position and argues for a two-state-solution: "*I'm not for any side [. . .]. [It] has to be shared. The earth is from God, it's not ours.*" He sees the conflict as a territorial conflict and disapproves of the view that the conflict is rooted in religion. He believes that God had created different religions and that they should accept each other and live together peacefully:

> *Knowing my religion [. . .]: the people who are saying this haven't understood anything of the religion. We have to live with the world, otherwise there will be only Jews, there will be only Muslims, there will be only Christians. We have to be open to everybody [. . .]. These are the people I don't like who say that [. . .] there will be Islam only [. . .]. God created different people, he created Jews, he created Muslims [. . .]. We have to live with the others.*

He showed empathy for both Jews and Muslims without giving up his identification as a Muslim: "*I saw for example the massacres they did in Lebanon and they did in Palestine, I see them, we hear them, it's crystal clear, it makes you sad all the time because we say, you say that there are Muslims, we say, for example the Jews, too, they say they're our brothers and sisters getting killed every day.*" He also said repeatedly that the younger generation understands this and wants the conflict to end, although his brother and sister also blame only "the Jews" for the Middle East conflict.

Samed has a very good reason for thinking the way he does: "*For love,*" he stated. He once had a Jewish girlfriend, and the relationship suffered because of his and her parents' views on the conflict, as well as his parents' rejection of Jews and her parents' of Muslims and Arabs. It is thus perfectly understandable why "*we young people, we are fed up with this conflict. Because that is the reason that everybody, we cannot live our live [. . .]. We cannot love somebody of another religion than our own [. . .]. But on the contrary, me personally, [I think that] God told us to be open to everybody.*" Their families would oppose a marriage between them, but he is convinced that their parents would not reject them completely. He predicted that if he and she had married, "*our parents they won't talk to us anymore. But this will calm down, I know it. Because father and mother – we can never disown our children.*"

Samed was obviously positively influenced by his Jewish friends and his girlfriend. When he was younger, he said, he had negative attitudes about Jews, like his parents. From his Jewish friends, he learned to see and accept their perspective both in everyday life and in the Middle East conflict. He has good reasons to reject negative views of Jews in general: he wants to keep his Jewish friend, and the common assumption of general hostility between Muslims and Jews made his relationship to a girl he still loves very difficult. This does not lead to a rejection of all antisemitic stereotypes, but it does lead to a general rejection of negative views of all Jews. He still believes that Jews are rich, but he thinks that the reason why people insult them is because they envy Jews and because, in the case of Muslims, they misunderstand Islam. Understanding Jewish perspectives on a number of issues, including the Middle East conflict, made him both reject hostility toward Jews based on perceptions of Islam and Muslim identity as well as hatred against Israel. He wants to find practical solutions and a way of living together in peace and acceptance between Muslims and Jews. But how did he become friends with a Jew and have a Jewish girlfriend in the first place? That is probably due to coincidence and to the fact that his parents show tolerance to some degree: they do not like the fact that he befriends Jews, but he can still speak to them about his unusual social connections. And as he claimed, even if he were to marry a Jewish woman they would still love him. For Samed, love leads to peace with Jews.

Conclusion

ANTISEMITISM FROM MUSLIMS HAS BECOME A SERIOUS ISSUE in Western Europe, although not often acknowledged as such. It adds to a general rise in antisemitism in twenty-first-century Europe. Many young male Muslims have been identified among the perpetrators of antisemitic violence and even terror attacks. Surveys show that antisemitic attitudes are significantly more widespread among Muslims than among non-Muslims. But why is that so?

This study provides detailed insights into the views and rationales of young male Muslims in the capitals of three Western European countries of various ethnic, cultural, religious, and educational backgrounds. It delineates the ways respondents think about Jews, how they express it, and what arguments they use to justify these negative views. Additionally, factors and sources of antisemitic attitudes as well as anti-antisemitic ones are discussed.

ANTISEMITIC VIEWS

The majority of interviewees displayed resentments against Jews in at least one way or another. Negative attitudes toward Jews were often openly exhibited, at times aggressively so, including calls for violence against Jews and intentions to carry out antisemitic actions. Some even reported that they were involved in antisemitic acts. Negative views of Jews have become the norm in some young Muslims' social circles. Some forms are specific to young European Muslims: anti-Jewish attitudes with direct reference to Islam, Muslim identity, or ethnic identity. In this sense, the use of the term "Muslim antisemitism" is apt. However, most antisemitic views embraced by young European Muslims are fragmented and multifaceted. They can neither be reduced solely to hatred of Israel nor solely to references to Islam or Muslim identity, and they are not a result of discrimination against Muslims. Jews are often thought of as a unitary category, generally as a malicious group of people, though partly admired by some. Individual Jews or different kinds of Jews are rarely differentiated, as linguistically manifested by the frequent use of the term "the Jews" when talking about them.

Four main categories of anti-Jewish hostility emerged: (1) the persistence of "classic" antisemitic attitudes, including stereotypes of Jews and conspiracy theories; (2) negative views of Jews with reference to Israel; (3) anti-Jewish attitudes with direct reference to Islam, Muslim identity, or ethnic identity; and (4) anti-Jewish hostility devoid of rationales. Most interviewees use a combination of these patterns to "argue" why they don't like Jews.

ATTITUDES OF "CLASSIC" MODERN ANTISEMITISM

A number of "classic" antisemitic tropes were voiced bluntly. The most prominent were conspiracy theories and stereotypes associating Jews with money, including characterizations of Jews as rich, stingy, treacherous, and clannish. The tropes characterize the Jews as one entity with common (sinister) "Jewish interests." The widely used terms "Jewish influence" and "Jewish companies" capture this notion. Jews are portrayed as being behind corporations, governments, or the media on a local, national, and, above all, global level, sometimes in association with the United States. Tropes of "classic" modern antisemitism enhance a negative and potentially threatening image of "the Jews."

"Classic" antisemitism is also widespread in mainstream society. In 2012, 22 percent in Germany, 35 percent in France, and 20 percent in the UK believed that it is "probably true" that Jews have too much power in the business world. Figures for 2008 and 2009 show similar results,[1] whereas they rose in 2014 in France and Germany and fell in the UK.[2] Classic antisemitic stereotypes and conspiracy theories among European Muslims connect to well-known negative tropes of Jews within mainstream society.

NEGATIVE VIEWS OF JEWS WITH REFERENCE TO ISRAEL

Antisemitic attitudes with reference to Israel are often based on a conflation of Jews with Israelis and on a Manichean view of the Middle East conflict. They can serve as justification for general hostility against Jews. These justifications of hostility can be limited to a brief reference to the Middle East conflict, such as "because of Palestine" or "because of the wars with Jews," but some lend more content by mentioning that Jews allegedly kill children or that "they" have taken away "Muslim," "Arab," or "Palestinian" land, ignoring the fact that Jews have an ancient connection to the land of Israel. Nevertheless, the latter is the main argument for delegitimization of the State of Israel.

One of the most common antisemitic tropes with reference to Israel is "Jews/Israelis kill children," including the allegation that "the Israelis" or "the Jews" (usually the latter) kill children on purpose, out of cruelty and evilness. It is part of a Manichean view of the Middle East conflict and vilifies Israel. It also relates to the old antisemitic trope of the blood libel.[3] If Israelis and Jews are conflated, this accusation is taken as evidence for the evilness of Jews and thus stirs up strong emotions against Jews.

The intensity of hostility against Jews as justified by the Middle East conflict seems to be related to an identification with "the Palestinians." Not all interviewees identify with Palestinians, but most of those of Arab background do. Therefore, Arab identity seems to be an important additional factor that can enhance hostility against European Jews through justifications related to the Israeli-Palestinian conflict.

Israel is rarely used as the "collective Jew,"[4] in the sense of replacing overtly negative attitudes toward Jews with such attitudes applied to the Jewish state. Rather, Israel and the Israeli government are all too often subordinated under the phrase "the Jews" as a common entity. However, negative perceptions of Israel serve as arguments for hostility against Jews and negative perceptions of Israel often are motivated by anti-Jewish attitudes. Negative views of Israel are frequently used as a rationale for antisemitism.

NEGATIVE VIEWS OF JEWS WITH REFERENCE TO ISLAM OR RELIGIOUS OR ETHNIC IDENTITY

The assumption of general animosity between Muslims and Jews or between a particular ethnic community and Jews is widespread, and is voiced in such assumptions as "Muslims and Jews are enemies" or "the Arabs dislike Jews." Participants often cannot explain this hostility properly but root it vaguely in Islamic history, the Qur'an, the Middle East conflict, or, strangely enough, in the wars in Afghanistan and Iraq. The majority do not distance themselves from a literal interpretation of the Qur'an, and they are thus likely to take hostile passages in Islamic scripture literally. Alternatively, some argue that there is mutual hatred, that Jews do not like Muslims or their ethnic community or that Jews are at war with Muslims or Arabs. Negative views of Jews are therefore in this case presented as a reaction to the Jews' alleged feelings toward them.

However, only certain perceptions of Islam and Muslim identity contribute to such forms of antisemitism. As in all purported rationales for Jew hatred, these notions are chimeric[5] and not the actual driving force behind antisemitic attitudes. Participants look for justifications of antisemitic views within what they perceive as Islam or part of their religious or ethnic identity, and they often find confirmation in Islamic sources and social circles, which both serve as strong, authoritative references.

NEGATIVE VIEWS OF JEWS WITHOUT RATIONALES

Antisemitic views of "the Jews" cannot be justified; they are always irrational. But some participants do not even attempt to offer arguments for their antisemitic hostility. They feel no need to justify or to explain negative views of Jews by holding Jews responsible for allegedly negative deeds or characteristics. Jewishness – being Jewish in and of itself – is considered reason enough to despise Jews. Many respondents "naturally" accept hatred of Jews and endorse its irrationality. They insist on it even if contradictions become obvious. Some openly hate Jews for being Jews or they adopt negative views of Jews and consider these views to be "common sense" and normal. Some respondents revealed that negative views of Jews are the norm within their social environment.

Expressions of such views defy rational argument more obviously than other patterns of argumentation. The pretense of putative rationality has fallen apart, indicating that expressions of antisemitism are rooted in chimeric assumptions and in the mindset and emotional dynamics of those who voice them. From this perspective, other patterns of justification of antisemitism are merely attempts to express antisemitic resentments in more plausible ways.

Negative views of Jews without rationalization can translate into language. The very term "Jew" is understood among many interviewees but also in general among many young people in Germany and France as bearing negative connotations.[6]

The negative use of the term can also lead to an endorsement of violence against Jews, in the neighborhood today or by justifying it during the Holocaust in the past. A small minority has the intention of spontaneously acting to harm or even kill Jews if they happen to meet them in their neighborhood, without offering any justification for their violent intentions.

FUNCTIONS OF DIFFERENT PATTERNS OF ARGUMENTATION FOR NEGATIVE VIEWS OF JEWS

The different patterns of argumentation for negative views of Jews work in distinctive ways, have different implications, and can serve different functions for young European Muslims. Justifications of hatred against Jews with reference to Israel are often emotional and include a perception of a demonized Jewish state and of "the Jews," as symbolized in the topos of Jews as murderers of innocent children. Such references thus have a radicalizing effect. This explains the peak of antisemitic violence during heightened tensions and extensive (often biased anti-Israel) media coverage of the Israeli-Palestinian conflict. Justifications for violence against Jews are often made with reference to Israel. On the other hand, references to the Muslim or ethnic collective identity are reinforcing: it is argued that the whole community dislikes Jews and it must therefore be right to do so. Religious references (to the Qur'an or Islamic history) even give such views God's alleged approval.

Negative views of Jews in the form of "classic" antisemitic stereotypes and conspiracy theories connect to well-known negative tropes of Jews within mainstream society. They are also expressions of psychological mechanisms in modern societies[7] or serve as simplistic explanations of the world's problems. The patterns of argumentation lacking any rationalized justification reveal that those who voice them do not feel the need for justification. They believe that their negative attitudes toward Jews are acceptable as such (or think that they should be accepted without justification). In effect, they enhance, more than other patterns, a normalization of open Jew hatred and violence even if these views contradict civil morality.[8]

DIFFERENCES IN NEGATIVE VIEWS OF JEWS BETWEEN BERLIN, PARIS, AND LONDON

Differences in antisemitic attitudes among people in the countries were surprisingly small. However, some antisemitic views were expressed differently among interviewees. Respondents in Germany, for example, voiced the antisemitic trope of Jews controlling the media in the context of coverage of the Middle East conflict, implying that Jews manipulate the media to conceal Israel's alleged atrocities. In France, respondents often said that Jews are dominant on French television, which highlights Jewish actors and television hosts. Respondents in Great Britain see Jewish influence in the media more in U.S. television channels such as Fox News, CNN, and the film industry. Surprisingly, despite the different national contexts and languages, there are only minor differences among the pejorative use of the term "Jew" in German and French, while the term is hardly known or used in this sense by interviewees from Britain.

A trope that was used almost exclusively by participants from France was the portrayal of Jews as exploitative. Some French respondents also see that country's Jewish communities as unjustly doing better than their own community. There is envy of the local Jewish community among participants from France, possibly related to the fact that the Jewish communities are more visible to them than to their counterparts in Germany and Britain.

Conspiracy theories of Freemasonry and the perception of a "war against Muslims" led by Jews were more frequent among participants in London than in Paris or Berlin. Quantitative conclusions of this study must be considered with caution, but it was striking that participants in Britain used religious arguments for negative views of Jews, and also assumed that most big companies are Jewish and support Israel in the war against "the Palestinians" more often than did interviewees from Paris or Berlin. The direct references to Islamist organizations were also more frequent among participants from Britain than from the other countries.

In Germany, some participants exhibited views of Jews that are often interpreted as secondary antisemitism – that is to say, motivated by a rejection of German guilt for the Holocaust. This is hardly a primary motive for young Muslims of migrant background. However, participants complained about allegedly high reparations payments to Israel, or used the argument that the Jews should be better people than others due to the Holocaust but that Israel had failed in this regard. These complaints indicate that specific antisemitic discourses from mainstream society can also be adopted by those who do not share the motives for these specific tropes. They are used as a more accepted way to voice antisemitic feelings.

DIFFERENCES AMONG ETHNIC BACKGROUNDS

Antisemitic attitudes can be enforced by certain ethnic collective identities. Arab identity in particular can be associated with negative views of Jews, such as "Arabs hate Jews," which are then adopted as part of a person's identity. What makes Arab identity more salient than other ethnic identities concerning negative views of Jews is their frequent identification with "the Palestinians" as fellow Arabs. Arab identity adds another dimension to the (often made) religious identification with "the Palestinians" as Muslims. However, this connection only becomes salient if "Israelis" and "Jews" are conflated and if the person believes in a Manichean view of the Middle East conflict – both of which, unfortunately, are often the case.

Participants of South Asian, Turkish, and black African backgrounds seem to be generally less interested in the Middle East conflict than those of Arab backgrounds. Statements such as "Turks dislike Jews" or "Bengalis and Jews hate each other" do occur but are relatively rare.

Some participants referred to discourses on Jews in their (or their parents') countries of origin and had adopted such views. Some respondents of Maghrebian background, for example, referred to the exodus of Jews from these countries and adopt the perception that Maghrebian Jews belong in Israel. Other tropes that are voiced in public discourses of the country of origin, such as the accusation in Turkey that some politicians are not truly Turkish but actually Dönme (crypto-Jews), were unknown to participants.

POSITIVE EXAMPLES

A few interviewees clearly rejected antisemitic attitudes, and at least some should be considered anti-antisemites.[9] The majority of those who were particularly outspoken in their rejection of antisemitism spoke out against the antisemitism expressed by their friends, parents, or their ethnic or religious community (or media). They prove that antisemitic attitudes are not necessarily absorbed from an environment in which negative attitudes toward Jews are the norm.

The motives for rejecting antisemitism are probably as diverse as its sources and tropes. Still, the in-depth analysis of interviews with participants who reject antisemitism hints at a number of motivations. At least for Nabil, who is of Palestinian origin, the conviction that everybody is equal and nobody should be discriminated against for his or her background seems to be a motive for speaking out against the antisemitism expressed by his parents and classmates.

Jamil's motivation to reject such assumptions as "Jews and Muslims are at war with each other" is rooted in his individualism, which prevents him from unquestionably adopting such views. He is also influenced by a close cousin's questioning of misogynistic aspects of Muslim societies.

Another motivation can be explained by Boualem's views. Living illegally in London, he longs for a simple and normal life and wishes the same for everybody. Ideologies of hatred are not helpful for him, but have only the potential to signify more trouble.

Raoul, also from London, believes negative views of Jews to be old-fashioned. He has observed that anti-Jewish assumptions are made too easily by some members of his (Bengali) community, which he perceives as having simplistic beliefs. Both his and Samed's notions of Islam allow them to openly criticize certain interpretations of their religion that endorse hatred against others. But Samed's motive to reject hostility against "the Jews," and to argue against assumptions of a general animosity between Muslims and Jews, lies in the fact that he is in love with a Jewish girl; negative perceptions about Jews by friends and family stand in the way of their relationship.

FACTORS THAT INFLUENCE ATTITUDES

Interviewees provide evidence of various factors that have contributed to their antisemitic views, and no single factor necessarily leads to antisemitic attitudes. Our study proves that the genesis of antisemitic attitudes among European Muslims cannot be reduced to religious beliefs or affiliation, to certain living conditions, or even to a family history of displacement in the Middle East conflict. Exposure to antisemitic remarks by friends and family members and antisemitism in the media or Islamist organizations certainly enhance negative views of Jews, but it also does not necessarily lead to antisemitic attitudes, as proven by interviewees who reject antisemitic views despite these factors. Ultimately, adopting antisemitic stereotypes and ways of thinking is a choice (within social restrictions) made by individuals.

Interviewees referred directly to some sources of their antisemitic beliefs: friends' and family members' anti-Jewish views; perceptions of their religious and ethnic identities; conversations in mosques; diverse media representations such as television, the internet, music, books, and newspapers; and schools.

Negative views of Jews among friends can have a particularly strong impact if holding such views is the norm or if social hierarchies are reinforced by antisemitic language, such as labeling someone "Jew" in a pejorative way. In particular, images of the Middle East conflict in the foreign and domestic media can incite strong feelings against "the Jews" when "Jews" and "Israelis" are conflated. In short, both religious and ethnic identities can be a source of anti-Jewish attitudes if these communities are essentialized and associated with animosity against Jews.

In some cases, respondents showed that Islamist propaganda has had an impact on their views of Jews. Individual level of education also seems to be a factor. Interviewees who obtained higher education in university or who were about to qualify for higher education voiced negative views of Jews less starkly than others. Experiences of discrimination and exclusion from mainstream society are not a decisive factor in the genesis of antisemitic attitudes. Rationales put forward by interviewees linking perceived discrimination and views of Jews show a variety of contradictory arguments. Experiences of discrimination are not a decisive factor for or against the genesis of antisemitic attitudes. However, some perceptions of discrimination, such as framing discrimination as part of a global war against Muslims, can contain antisemitic conspiracy theories in which hostility against Muslims and Islam is interpreted in an antisemitic way.

The adoption of "classic" antisemitic arguments and of country-specific rationales, such as tropes of secondary antisemitism in Germany, resulting in a rejection of guilt for the Holocaust, shows that antisemitism in particular European societies also influences how participants view Jews.

The findings prove that there are a large variety of sources, not a single predominant one, for antisemitic attitudes among European Muslims.

HOW TO COMBAT ANTISEMITISM AMONG EUROPEAN MUSLIMS?

Due to the large number of factors in the genesis of antisemitism, strategies to contain, reduce, and combat antisemitism must be numerous.

Open antisemitism can be reduced by a firm stance against antisemitism from the social environment and wider society: friends, family members, teachers, community and social workers, community leaders,

Imams, politicians, journalists, and so on. Antisemitism should not be excused, downplayed, tolerated, or ignored. Its consequences are all too often murderous. Anti-antisemites have to become active.

In education, two different approaches are promising: (1) Strengthening the individual and his or her personal responsibility in society in order to prevent unquestioned adoption of beliefs by proxy such as "Muslims and Jews are enemies"; and (2) promoting human rights education that emphasizes equal individual rights. The latter approach, however, should not be used to vilify Israel in a Manichean way and thereby shift antisemitic sentiments superficially (and temporarily) from Jews onto the Jewish state.

However, as Theodor W. Adorno outlined more than fifty years ago, in order to eradicate deeply rooted antisemitic sentiments and prevent another Holocaust,[10] we will also have to change our civilization in very profound ways so that such worldviews are not reproduced.[11]

APPENDIX A

Working Definition of Antisemitism

In 2004 the European Union Monitoring Centre on Racism and Xenophobia (EUMC) released its first comprehensive study of antisemitism in the EU. Although it relied heavily on its focal points in the then fifteen member countries for its information, a majority of those focal points had no working definition of antisemitism, and of those that did, no two were the same.

As a result the EUMC, in collaboration with key NGOs and representatives of the newly formed Tolerance and Non-Discrimination section of the Office of Democratic Institutions and Human Rights (ODIHR) drafted a single, comprehensive definition for use in the field. It employs plain language to enable the definition to be easily accessible to a wide range of law enforcement, justice, and government officials, as well as to NGOs and to experts who assist in the monitoring process.

The U.S. State Department's reports on contemporary global antisemitism make use of this definition for the purpose of their analysis.

The purpose of this document is to provide a practical guide for identifying incidents, collecting data, and supporting the implementation and enforcement of legislation dealing with antisemitism.

Working definition: "Antisemitism is a certain perception of Jews, which may be expressed as hatred toward Jews. Rhetorical and physical manifestations of antisemitism are directed toward Jewish or non-Jewish individuals and/or their property, toward Jewish community institutions and religious facilities."

In addition, such manifestations could also target the state of Israel, conceived as a Jewish collectivity. Antisemitism frequently charges Jews with conspiring to harm humanity, and it is often used to blame Jews for "why things go wrong." It is expressed in speech, writing, visual forms, and action, and employs sinister stereotypes and negative character traits.

Contemporary examples of antisemitism in public life, the media, schools, the workplace, and in the religious sphere could, taking into account the overall context, include but are not limited to:

- Calling for, aiding, or justifying the killing or harming of Jews in the name of a radical ideology or an extremist view of religion.
- Making mendacious, dehumanizing, demonizing, or stereotypical allegations about Jews as such or the power of Jews as a collective – such as, especially but not exclusively, the myth about a world Jewish conspiracy or of Jews controlling the media, economy, government or other societal institutions.
- Accusing Jews as a people of being responsible for real or imagined wrongdoing committed by a single Jewish person or group, or even for acts committed by non-Jews.
- Denying the fact, scope, mechanisms (e.g., gas chambers), or intentionality of the genocide of the Jewish people at the hands of National Socialist Germany and its supporters and accomplices during World War II (the Holocaust).
- Accusing the Jews as a people, or Israel as a state, of inventing or exaggerating the Holocaust.
- Accusing Jewish citizens of being more loyal to Israel, or to the alleged priorities of Jews worldwide, than to the interests of their own nations.

Examples of the ways in which antisemitism manifests itself with regard to the State of Israel, taking into account the overall context, could include:

- Denying the Jewish people their right to self-determination, e.g. by claiming that the existence of a State of Israel is a racist endeavor.
- Applying double standards by requiring of it a behavior not expected or demanded of any other democratic nation.
- Using the symbols and images associated with classic antisemitism (e.g., claims of Jews killing Jesus or blood libel) to characterize Israel or Israelis.

- Drawing comparisons of contemporary Israeli policy to that of the Nazis.
- Holding Jews collectively responsible for actions of the State of Israel.

However, criticism of Israel similar to that leveled against any other country cannot be regarded as antisemitic.

Antisemitic acts are criminal when they are so defined by law (for example, denial of the Holocaust or distribution of antisemitic materials in some countries).

Criminal acts are antisemitic when the targets of attacks, whether they are people or property – such as buildings, schools, places of worship and cemeteries – are selected because they are, or are perceived to be, Jewish or linked to Jews.

Antisemitic discrimination is the denial to Jews of opportunities or services available to others and is illegal in many countries.

APPENDIX B

List of Interviewees

All names are pseudonyms chosen from lists of popular boys' names from the respective ethnic community. Interviewees of Maghrebian background include respondents of Algerian, Moroccan, and Tunisian background. Interviewees of South Asian background include respondents of Bangladeshi and Pakistani background. The background of formal education has been classified in five categories for better comparison despite the difference in the educational systems in each of the three countries and the interviewees' different age groups (see chapter 4):

Category 1: Early school dropout or unemployed without any formal job qualification.

Category 2: Basic job qualification, either achieved or probably achieving in the future ("Lehre"; "CAP/PEB"; vocational/technical colleges)

Category 3: Students who intend to pass *Abitur, baccalaureat,* or A-levels.

Category 4: Participants who have passed *Abitur, baccalaureat.* or A-levels.

Category 5: University students and graduates.

LIST OF INTERVIEWEES IN ALPHABETICAL ORDER

Name	Age	Education Category	Ethnic Background	Country of Residence
Aba	20	2	Ghanian English	Great Britain
Aban	26	3	Asian	Great Britain
Abdullah	15	2	Lebanese	Germany
Abed	17	2	Maghrebian	France
Abhijt	25	2	Asian	Great Britain
Adnan	16	?	Palestinian	Germany
Agantuk	23	3	Asian	Great Britain
Ahlam	16	2	Maghrebian	France
Ahmed	20/21	1	Lebanese	Germany
Ajit	16	2	Asian	Great Britain
Ali	18	3	Maghrebian	France
Anis	24	1	Maghrebian	France
Assim	22	2	Maghrebian	France
Aswad	14	2/3	Egyptian Maghrebian	France
Azhar	17	2	Maghrebian	France
Bahaar	18	3/4	Asian	Great Britain
Bankim	17	3	Asian	Great Britain
Baru	20	2	Asian	Great Britain
Bashir	14	2	Lebanese	Germany
Bashkar	21	2	Asian	Great Britain
Beyar	16	2	Turkish (Kurdish)	Germany
Bilal	15	2	Maghrebian	France
Boualem	24	1	Maghrebian	Great Britain
Çeto	17	3	Turkish (Kurdish)	Germany
Chafik	15	2	Maghrebian	France
Cherif	15	3	Maghrebian	France
Debesh	15	2	Asian	Great Britain
Diaba	15	2	Guinean	France
Erdal	16	3	Turkish	Germany
Erdem	17	2/3	Turkish (Kurdish)	Germany
Erol	19	4	Turkish	Germany
Farid	16	2/3	Maghrebian	France
Farouk	18	3	Maghrebian	France
Fatin	17	2	Turkish	Germany
Ferhat	17	1	Turkish	Germany
Firat	17	4	Turkish (Kurdish)	Germany
Ganesh	16?	3	Asian	Great Britain
Gourab	18	1/2	Asian	Great Britain
Hachem	16	3	Maghrebian	France
Hafid	17	?	Maghrebian	France

Name	Age	Education Category	Ethnic Background	Country of Residence
Hakan	16	2	Turkish	Germany
Halil	17	2	Turkish	Germany
Hamid	16	2/3	Maghrebian	France
Hamudi	14	2	Palestinian	Germany
Hamza	17	2	Maghrebian	France
Haroun	20	3	Maghrebian	France
Hichem	?	?	Maghrebian	France
Hikmet	16	2	Turkish	Germany
Housni	19	2	Maghrebian	France
Hussein	27	2	Asian	Great Britain
Imran	23	5	Asian	Great Britain
Ismail	16	2	Palestinian	Germany
Ismet	17	1/2	Maghrebian Saudian	France
Jabar	26/25	2/3	Maghrebian	France
Jamil	14	3	Lebanese (Kurdish)	Germany
Kaba	20	1?	Guinean	France
Kajal	18	3	Asian	Great Britain
Kamel	14	3	Maghrebian	France
Kashi	?	2	Asian	Great Britain
Kassi	16	2	Ivorian	France
Kassim	18	1	Lebanese	Germany
Khalid	23	2	Egyptian	Great Britain
Khalil	20	2	Maghrebian Italian	France
Labaan	20	4	Somalian	Great Britain
Malik	24	5	Asian	Great Britain
Manoj	26	5	Asian	Great Britain
Masmud	26	2	Maghrebian (Berber*)	France
Massoud	19	2	Maghrebian	France
Mehmet	17	2	Turkish	Germany
Memduh	17?	3	Turkish	Germany
Mohamed	22	3	Maghrebian	France
Moukhtar	17?	2	Maghrebian	France
Mousa	15	2	Palestinian	Germany
Murat	13	2	Turkish (American**)	Germany
Nabil	17	3	Palestinian	Germany
Nadem	15	2/3	Maghrebian	France
Nader	27	2	Maghrebian	Great Britain
Nadim	18	2	Maghrebian	France
Naeem	15	2	Palestinian	Germany
Naresh	17	3	Asian	Great Britain
Necet	15	2	Turkish	Germany

Name	Age	Education Category	Ethnic Background	Country of Residence
Neoy	18	3	Asian	Great Britain
Nirmal	18	4	Asian	Great Britain
Omar	18	1	Maghrebian	France
Ömer	14	2/3	Turkish	Germany
Orhan	19	2	Turkish	Germany
Ousmane	19	3	Guinean	France
Rahim	25	2	Asian	Great Britain
Rahoul	15	2/3	Asian English	Great Britain
Rajsekar	23	1	Asian	Great Britain
Ramzi	20/21	1	Palestinian Lebanese	Germany
Ranjan	20	3	Asian	Great Britain
Sabir	30	1	Asian	Great Britain
Sabri	22	1	Maghrebian	France
Saibal	15	2	Asian	Great Britain
Saïdou	17	1/2	Guinean	France
Sakti	16	2/3	Asian	Great Britain
Salih	13	3	Turkish Egyptian	Germany
Salim	26	5	Asian	Great Britain
Samed	18	2	Maghrebian	France
Saroj	?	5	Asian	Great Britain
Serkan	16/17	3	Turkish (Kurdish)	Germany
Setu	17	3	Asian	Great Britain
Sharif	20	4	Palestinian	Germany
Siddhar	19	3	Asian	Great Britain
Sudhir	15	2	Asian	Great Britain
Suleiman	15	2	Palestinian	Germany
Sunay	16	3	Asian	Great Britain
Tarak	20	5	Asian	Great Britain
Tariq	20	5	Maghrebian	France
Tayfun	14	2	Turkish	Germany
Tunay	23	2	Turkish	Germany
Ümit	25	2	Turkish	Germany
Umur	18	2	Turkish	Germany
Utpal	18	2	Asian	Great Britain
Youssef	24	5	Maghrebian	France
Yusuf	22	5	Turkish	France

Notes:

* Masmud emphasized his Berber identity.

** Murat's father is an American soldier. However, Murat does not know him and identifies as Turkish.

Notes

Introduction

1. Bergmann and Wetzel, *Manifestations of Anti-Semitism in the European Union*, 25.

2. The self-described "gang des barbares" abducted Ilan Halimi because he was Jewish and then tortured and murdered him in a Parisian suburb. See article in *Le Monde*, from October 25, 2010, "Meurtre d'Ilan Halimi: le 'gang des barbares' jugé en appel, sans son leader."

3. Jikeli, "Der neue alte Antisemitismus."

4. Wiedeman, "Angriff auf Tanzgruppe."

5. Islamist movements strive for a society under Islamic law, the Shari'a, many with non-violent means, while others include the use of violence. For a distinction between Islam and Islamism see Tibi, *Islamism and Islam*.

6. Siddique, "BBC's Panorama Claims Islamic Schools Teach Antisemitism and Homophobia."

7. Amadeu Antonio Stiftung, *"Die Juden sind schuld" Antisemitismus in der Einwanderungsgesellschaft am Beispiel muslimisch sozialisierter Milieus.*

8. Brenner, *Les territoires perdus de la République : antisémitisme, racisme et sexisme en milieu scolaire.* For an English translation (available online) see Brenner, *The Lost Territories of the Republic.*

9. The Historical Association, *T.E.A.C.H. Teaching Emotive and Controversial History 3–19*, 2007, 15.

10. Jikeli and Allouche-Benayoun, *Perceptions of the Holocaust in Europe and Muslim Communities.* Some young Muslims openly voice hatred of Jews and approval of the Holocaust. An example was given in an interview aired on Dutch TV: "'Hitler Should Have Killed All Jews': Dutch TV Airs Shock Interview with Muslim Migrants," March 6, 2013.

11. On March 19, 2012, Mohamed Merah opened fire in front of the Ozar Hatorah school in Toulouse. The gunman chased people inside the building and shot at them. He grabbed a seven-year-old girl, Myriam Monsonégo, shooting her at close range. Gabriel (age four), Arieh (five), and Jonathan Sandler, their father and teacher at the school, were also killed. A seventeen-year-old student was gravely injured. He then retrieved his moped and drove off. The perpetrator, who also killed three unarmed French soldiers some days earlier, filmed his crimes, intending to publish them on the internet and on Al Jazeera.

12. After antisemitic incidents such as the Toulouse murders, Muslim lead-

ers in France, for example, have publicly condemned "anti-Semitism, racism and Islamophobia." Schneier, "Willingness of Muslim Leaders to Denounce Anti-Semitism." After the shooting at the Jewish Museum in Brussels on May 24, 2014, a number of imams, such as Drancy's Hassan Chalghoumi, condemned the antisemitic violence.

13. Some European Muslim have explicitly criticized Jew hatred among Muslims, such as Ahmad Mansour (Germany), Muhammad Sameer Murtaza (Germany), secular German politicians Cem Özdemir and Özcan Mutlu, British Muslim journalist Mehdi Hasan, French Muslim convert Didier Bourg, and the young Swedish activist Siavosh Derakhti.

14. Some populists essentialize Muslims in their criticism of Muslim antisemitism. See Widmann, "Der Feind Kommt Aus Dem Morgenland," 45–68.

15. In social psychology, attitudes are usually regarded as coherent. However, attitudes toward religious or ethnic groups are seen as general attitudes that can contain divergent specific attitudes. See Ajzen, *Attitudes, Personality and Behavior,* 34–36.

16. A conference in Weimar, Germany, in May 2010 was entitled "Everyday Antisemitisms – beyond Closed Worldviews" (author's translation). The title expresses the phenomenon that many people who voice antisemitic statements often do so as part of everyday life and not necessarily as part of coherent antisemitic worldviews.

17. Psychoanalytical theories on antisemitism have identified projection as the main mechanism of antisemitism. Beland, "Psychoanalytische Antisemitismustheorien im Vergleich," 187–218.

18. I would like to thank Jessica Ring for her help with the translation of ambiguous quotations.

1. European Muslims

1. Open Society Institute, *Muslims in Europe : A Report on 11 EU Cities,* 22; European Monitoring Centre on Racism and Xenophobia, *Muslims in the European Union,* 29.

2. Brettfeld and Wetzels, *Muslime in Deutschland,* 34; Haug, Müssig, and Stichs, *Muslimisches Leben in Deutschland,* 57–93.

3. Open Society Institute, *Muslims in the EU: Cities Report: Germany,* 14, http://www.opensocietyfoundations.org/sites/default/files/museucitiesger_20080101_0.pdf.

4. Brettfeld and Wetzels, *Muslime in Deutschland,* 34; Haug, Müssig, and Stichs, *Muslimisches Leben in Deutschland,* 57–93.

5. Open Society Institute, *Muslims in the EU: Cities Report: Germany,* 11.

6. Ibid.

7. Brettfeld and Wetzels, *Muslime in Deutschland,* 13.

8. Aydin, Halm, and Sen, *"Euro-Islam."*

9. Brettfeld and Wetzels, *Muslime in Deutschland,* 173–181.

10. The Islamrat has been excluded since 2010 due to preliminary investigations by public prosecution against leading members of the IGMG, the dominant organization within the Islamrat. The Zentralrat der Muslime boycotts the German Islam Conference.

11. Islamism is understood as a political ideology that aims to create a state and society in conformity with Islamic doctrine. Islamist movements strive for a society under Islamic law, the Shari'a. For a distinction between Islamism and Islam, the centrality of antisemitism in Islamist ideology, and Islamism's incompatibility with democracy, see Tibi, *Islamism and Islam.*

12. Bundesministerium des Inneren, *Verfassungsschutzbericht 2011,* 290–302.

13. Niewels, "Schwere Vorwürfe gegen Islam-Verein."

14. Dantschke, "Islam und Islamismus in Deutschland." On the extremist-nationalist "Grey Wolves" in Germany and their influence in youth culture, see Dantschke, "Graue Wölfe in Deutschland," 66–89.

15. Aydin, Halm, and Sen, "*Euro-Islam,*" 65.

16. Brettfeld and Wetzels, *Muslime in Deutschland,* 173–181.

17. The estimation based on a 2008/2009 representative survey of 18–60 years old individuals in France is 4–4.3 Muslims. Simon and Tiberj, *Sécularisation ou regain religieux,* 6; Open Society Institute, *Muslims in the EU: Cities Report,* 2007, 11–14; Laurence and Vaïsse, *Integrating Islam,* 15–48; Couvreur, *Musulmans de France,* 10–13; Vampouille, "France: comment est évalué le nombre de musulmans."

18. Laurence and Vaïsse, *Integrating Islam,* 21; Open Society Institute, *Muslims in the EU: Cities Report: France,* 11.

19. Open Society Institute, *Muslims in the EU: Cities Report: France,* 16–17.

20. For detailed statistics on asylum seekers in France, see Office français de protection des réfugiés et apatrides (OFPRA), *Rapport Annuel 2007.*

21. Laurence and Vaïsse, *Integrating Islam,* 83.

22. Caruso, *Au nom de l'islam,* 39–49.

23. Amghar, "Les mutations de l'islamisme en France."

24. Ternisien, *La France des mosquées;* Laurence and Vaïsse, *Integrating Islam,* 98–131.

25. Judge, "The Muslim Headscarf and French Schools," 8.

26. Çitak, "Between Turkish Islam and French Islam," 619–634.

27. Smith, "European Approaches to the Challenge of Radical Islam," 65–74.

28. Home Office, *The New and the Old,* 38–39; Office for National Statistics, *National Statistics – Focus on Religion;* "Born Abroad – Introduction and Figures for Britain."

29. Figures are for England and Wales.

30. Office for National Statistics, *Religion in England and Wales 2011.*

31. Ansari, *The Infidel Within,* 38–39.

32. Hansen, *Citizenship and Immigration in Post-War Britain.*

33. Philip Lewis, *Islamic Britain.*

34. Open Society Institute, *Muslims in the EU: Cities Report: United Kingdom,* 10.

35. Office for National Statistics, *Migration Statistics Quarterly Report, February 2013.*

36. This figure is usually offered by the Muslim Council of Britain (MCB). By the mid-1990s, over 800 mosques and some 950 Muslim organizations on various levels were established in Britain. Ansari, *Muslims in Britain.*

37. Mayor of London, *Muslims in London,* 45.

38. Whine, "The Advance of the Muslim Brotherhood in the UK," 30–40.

39. Mayor of London, *Muslims in London,* 82.

40. Bright, *When Progressives Treat with Reactionaries;* Ware, "MCB in the Dock."

41. Mirza, Ja'far, and Senthilkumaran, *Living Apart Together,* 27.

42. "Forked Tongues," *The Times (UK),* September 7, 2007.

43. Alexiev, "Tablighi Jamaat," 3–11; Norfolk, "Muslim Group Behind 'mega-mosque' Seeks to Convert All Britain."

44. Mirza, Ja'far, and Senthilkumaran, *Living Apart Together.*

45. The Muslim Brotherhood is the most influential Islamist organization in Europe, with ideological or direct links to many prominent Muslim organizations in

Europe. Maréchal, *The Muslim Brothers in Europe;* Rubin, *The Muslim Brotherhood.*

46. For Germany see Brettfeld and Wetzels, *Muslime in Deutschland,* 192–193; Open Society Institute, *Muslims in the EU: Cities Report: Germany,* 26–41. For France see Institut national de la statistique et des études économiques (Insee), *Immigrés et Descendants D'immigrés En France* (Paris, October 2012); Laurence and Vaïsse, *Integrating Islam,* 28–42; Brouard and Tiberj, *Français comme les autres?;* Open Society Institute, *Muslims in the EU: Cities Report: France,* 28–38. For the UK see Office for National Statistics (Great Britain), *Focus on Ethnicity and Religion.* Detailed socio-economic data on Muslims in London reflect these trends on unemployment, education, and housing. Mayor of London, *Muslims in London.*

47. Office for National Statistics (Great Britain), *Focus on Ethnicity and Religion,* 122.

48. The Open Society Foundations highlight a number of success stories of European Muslims in leading and prestigious positions: http://www.opensocietyfoundations.org/topics/muslims-europe.

49. Open Society Institute, *Muslims in the EU: Cities Report: United Kingdom,* 28–32.

50. Bundesamt für Migration und Flüchtlinge, *Migrationsbericht 2011.*

51. Jaxel-Truer and Vincent, "Voile intégral, polygamie: comment un fait divers devient une controverse politique."

52. Ramji, "Dynamics of Religion and Gender Amongst Young British Muslims," 1171–1189.

53. These figures have risen sharply since the economic crisis; see, for example, the annual CSA survey in France, http://www.csa-fr.com/multimedia/data/sondages/data2013/opi20130321-Barometre-CNCDH-pour-publication.pdf.

54. Zick, Hövermann, and Küpper, *Intolerance, Prejudice and Discrimination,* 54–61.

55. Decker, Kiess, and Brähler, *Die Mitte Im Umbruch;* INFO GmbH and Liljeberg Research International, *Wertewelten von Deutschen und Migrant/innen.* The study found "Ausländerfeindlichkeit" (hatred of foreigners) among 24.7 percent of the population.

56. Laurence and Vaïsse, *Integrating Islam,* 49–73.

57. Beaud and Masclet, "Un passage à l'acte improbable?," 159–170.

58. Ford, "Is Racial Prejudice Declining in Britain?," 609–636.

59. Surveys and reports also reveal growing hostility toward Roma (gypsies), arguably the most despised and discriminated minority group in many European countries and often forgotten in debates about discrimination against minorities. European Union Agency for Fundamental Rights (FRA), *European Union Minorities and Discrimination Survey,* 2009, http://fra.europa.eu/fraWebsite/attachments/eumidis_mainreport_conference-edition_en_.pdf.

60. Zick, Hövermann, and Küpper, *Intolerance, Prejudice and Discrimination,* 54–61.

61. Pew Global Attitudes Project, *Muslim-Western Tensions Persist.*

62. Pew Global Attitudes Project, *The Great Divide: How Westerners and Muslims View Each Other,* 6.

63. The same study revealed that only 64 to 83 percent of Muslims in various European countries confirmed that "violence against civilian targets in order to defend Islam" is never justified. The percentage was considerably lower in countries such as Egypt (45) or Jordan (43). While justifications for violence against civilians in the name of Islam is not shared by the

majority of Muslims, the item can indeed be taken as an indicator for fanatic views among significant parts of the Muslim population.

64. *Islamophobia: A Challenge for Us All.*

65. The Forum against Islamophobia & Racism has published a number of reports on Islamophobia on its website, http://www.fairuk.org/useful.htm, accessed May 9, 2010, including lists of incidents that have also been used in the report by the EUMC/FRA, European Monitoring Centre on Racism and Xenophobia, *Muslims in the European Union: Discrimination and Islamophobia.* For recent national surveys on attitudes toward Muslims, Islam, and immigrants see Heitmeyer, *Deutsche Zustände. Folge 10;* INFO GmbH and Liljeberg Research International, *Wertewelten von Deutschen und Migrant/innen – Migration zwischen Integration und Ausgrenzung;* IFOP for the Figaro, *L'image de l'Islam en France;* Park et al., *British Social Attitudes.*

66. The term Islamophobia is often used to describe anti-Muslim bias. However, due to the lack of a distinction between anti-Muslim bias and (legitimate) criticism of Islamic practice and doctrine, the term remains controversial and ill defined and is often used politically to silence criticism of Islamic practice. For a discussion see Bötticher, "Islamophobia? The German Discussion about Islamophobia," 210–229.

67. European Union Agency for Fundamental Rights (FRA), *Data in Focus Report | Muslims,* 5.

68. European Union Agency for Fundamental Rights, *EU-MIDIS: European Union Minorities and Discrimination Survey,* 36. See also European Monitoring Centre on Racism and Xenophobia, *Migrants' Experiences of Racism and Xenophobia in 12 EU Member States,* 61.

69. European Union Agency for Fundamental Rights (FRA), *Data in Focus Report | Muslims,* 5. In France, 35 percent of Muslims between ages 18–50 have experienced discrimination; 40 percent believe that this is due to racism and only 5 percent believe that the discrimination is based on their religion. Simon, "Muslims and Jews in France."

70. Commission nationale consultative des droits de l'homme (CNCDH), *La lutte contre le racisme, antisémitisme et la xénophobie,* 89. Figures are for a representative sample of individuals in France between ages 18–50 who experienced discrimination in the previous five years.

71. Simon, "Muslims and Jews in France."

72. European Monitoring Centre on Racism and Xenophobia, *Migrants' Experiences of Racism and Xenophobia in 12 EU Member States. Pilot Study,* 31–38.

73. Frindte et al., *Lebenswelten Junger Muslime in Deutschland,* 180–183.

74. European Monitoring Centre on Racism and Xenophobia, *Muslims in the European Union,* 86–87.

75. The interviewees' experiences of discrimination and self-identification are described in detail in Jikeli, "Discrimination of European Muslims," in *Minority Groups,* 77–96.

76. Police have been accused of ethnic and racial profiling. Racial minorities are far more likely to be stopped and searched by the police. For a discussion see Borooah, "Racial Disparity in Police Stop and Searches in England and Wales," 453–473.

77. Some districts are seen as bad neighborhoods, which can be used as a basis for discrimination against those who live there.

78. All names of interviewees are pseudonyms. The names are chosen from a list of common names among people of their particular ethnic background. The

interviews were conducted in the language of the country of residence. I translated the interview excerpts from German and French with the help of Jessica Ring, trying to stay true to the colloquial and at times incorrect usage of the language.

79. Pew Global Attitudes Project, *Unfavorable Views of Jews and Muslims on the Increase in Europe*; Pollack, *Wahrnehmung und Akzeptanz religiöser Vielfalt.*

80. Crown Prosecution Service, *Hate Crime and Crime against Older People Report 2011–2012*, 2012.

81. Commission nationale consultative des droits de l'homme (CNCDH), *La lutte contre le racisme, antisémitisme et la xénophobie. Année 2012.*

82. Bundesministerium des Inneren, *Verfassungsschutzbericht 2011.*

83. See the Federal Buereau of Investigation's annual reports, http://www.fbi.gov/about-us/cjis/ucr/hate-crime.

84. Gallup, *The Gallup Coexist Index 2009*, 19.

85. Jacobs, "Survey Findings of the EURISLAM Project," 41. Figures for France show that more than 75 percent of both Muslims and Jews between ages 18–50 give religion a strong or moderate importance in contrast to 24 percent among Catholics and 47 percent among Protestants. Beauchemin, Hamelle, and Simon, *Trajectories and Origins*, 126.

86. Pew Global Attitudes Project, *In Great Britain, Muslims Worry about Islamic Extremism.*

87. Gallup, *The Gallup Coexist Index 2009*, 19.

88. Brettfeld and Wetzels, *Muslime in Deutschland*, 92–93; Haug, Müssig, and Stichs, *Muslimisches Leben in Deutschland.*

89. CSA/Le monde des réligions, *Islam et citoyenneté.*

90. Nyiri and Mogahed, "Reinventing Integration," 14–21. Sixty-six percent of Muslims believed in 2006/2007 that religion is the most important thing in their lives and 49 percent pray five times a day. Mirza, Ja'far, and Senthilkumaran, *Living Apart Together*, 37. For more detailed figures differentiated by age and different faith groups on the importance of religion, see O'Beirne, *Religion in England and Wales*, 59. In 2009, 77 percent of British Muslims, 40 percent of German Muslims, and 52 percent of French Muslims "very or extremely strongly" identified with their country of residence. Gallup, *The Gallup Coexist Index 2009*, 19.

91. In 2005, 1.7 percent of Muslims in Germany felt exclusively German, 10.5 percent fairly German, 31.4 percent felt belonging equally to Germany and the country of origin, 28.1 percent felt more to the country of origin, and 28.3 percent felt exclusively to the country of origin. Brettfeld and Wetzels, *Muslime in Deutschland*, 92.

92. See also the excellent study by Voisin, *Ethnicity in Young People's Lives.*

93. Pew Global Attitudes Project, *The Great Divide*, 49. See also Frindte et al., *Lebenswelten Junger Muslime in Deutschland.*

94. Ruud Koopmans, "Religious Fundamentalism and Out-group Hostility among Muslims and Christians in Western Europe."

95. Jacobs, "Survey Findings of the EURISLAM Project," 42.

96. INFO GmbH and Liljeberg Research International, *Wertewelten von Deutschen und Migrant/innen – Migration zwischen Integration und Ausgrenzung*, 5–6.

97. Brettfeld and Wetzels, *Muslime in Deutschland*, 140–191.

98. Pew Global Attitudes Project, *The Great Divide*, 13.

99. CSA /Le monde des réligions, *Islam et citoyenneté*, 27, 9.

100. Brettfeld and Wetzels, *Muslime in Deutschland,* 141.

101. Four percent of British Muslims in July 2005 agreed that it is acceptable for religious or political groups to use violence for political ends. ICM Research, *Muslim Poll,* 19. In April 2006, however, 15 percent of British Muslims, 16 percent of French Muslims, and 7 percent of German Muslims thought that the use of violence against civilian targets in order to defend Islam can "often/sometimes" be justified. Pew Global Attitudes Project, *The Great Divide,* 4, 42.

102. Pew Global Attitudes Project, *In Great Britain, Muslims Worry about Islamic Extremism – Pew Research Center.*

103. Cf. Silverstein, "Comment on Bunzl," in *Anti-Semitism and Islamophobia;* Meer and Noorani, "A Sociological Comparison of Anti-Semitism and Anti-Muslim Sentiment in Britain," 195–219; Wetzel, "Parallelen zwischen Antisemitismus und Islamfeindschaft heute," 81–106.

104. Cesarani, "Why Muslims Are Not the New Jews"; Botsch et al., *Islamophobie und Antisemitismus ein umstrittener Vergleich;* Bruckner, "The Invention of Islamophobia."

105. Allouche-Benayoun and Jikeli, "Introduction," 1–12. See also Rosenfeld, *The End of the Holocaust.*

106. Cf. Schwarz-Friesel and Friesel, "Gestern die Juden, heute die Muslime," 43.

107. Kahlweiß and Salzborn, "Islamophobie," 248–263. Pascal Bruckner argued that "Islamophobia was invented to silence those Muslims who question the Koran and who demand equality of the sexes." Bruckner, "The Invention of Islamophobia." A distinction between (illegitimate) prejudice against Muslims and Islam and (legitimate) criticism of Islam can of course be made but is rarely put into practice. Imhoff and Recker, "Differentiating Islamophobia," 811–824.

108. Cesarani, "Why Muslims Are Not the New Jews."

109. Said, *Orientalism,* 286.

110. Akbari, "Placing the Jews in Late Medieval English Literature," 32. Akbari gave an example from the United States citing Hussein Ibish, communications director of the American-Arab Anti-Discrimination Committee in 2002, who said, in response to Pat Robertson's inciting description of Islam as being intrinsically violent: "We know the word for this. This is called anti-Semitism. . . . It's a resurgent anti-Semitism with the word 'Muslims' instead of the word 'Jews.'" "Pat Robertson Calls Islam Violent, Bent on Domination," *Washington Post,* February 22, 2002.

111. Said, *Orientalism.*

112. Wetzel, "Parallelen zwischen Antisemitismus und Islamfeindschaft heute."

113. Schiffer and Wagner, *Antisemitismus und Islamophobie – ein Vergleich* (Wassertrüdingen: HWK-Verl., 2009), 8.

114. Ibid., 84–85.

115. Ibid., 98–99.

116. Benz, *Handbuch des Antisemitismus,* 9.

117. Zumbini, *Die Wurzeln des Bösen;* Hoffmann, "Politische Kultur und Gewalt gegen Minderheiten," 93–120.

118. Mostly poor Orthodox Jews from Eastern European countries immigrated to Germany in the second half of the nineteenth century, amounting to approximately 10 percent of the Jewish population in Germany. This triggered a number of xenophobic antisemitic stereotypes that also targeted Judaism. Such stereotypes added to conspiracy theories about assimilated Jews, but it would be wrong not to mention the latter, dominating, conspiracy theories, when it comes to images and

stereotypes of Jews in the late nineteenth century Germany.

119. Meer and Noorani, "A Sociological Comparison of Anti-Semitism and Anti-Muslim Sentiment in Britain," 198.

120. Ibid., 206, 212.

121. Feldman, *Englishmen and Jews,* 143.

122. Bunzl, *Anti-Semitism and Islamophobia.*

123. Rinke, "Limpieza de sangre [Reinheit des Blutes]."

124. On a quantitative basis you only find more or less correlating group-focused enmity against out-groups, such as homosexuals, Jews, Muslims, ethnic minorities, and women. Zick, Hövermann, and Küpper, *Intolerance, Prejudice and Discrimination.*

125. Baer and López, "The Blind Spots of Secularization," 212–213. Images of Muslims and Arabs are often conflated.

126. The Living History Forum, *Antisemitism Och Islamofobi.*

127. Akbari, "Placing the Jews in Late Medieval English Literature."

2. Debates and Surveys on European Muslim Antisemitism

1. Schmidinger, "Zur Islamisierung des Antisemitismus," 103–139; Widmann, "Der Feind Kommt Aus Dem Morgenland."

2. The pervasiveness of antisemitism in general society is subject to debate and difficult to measure. Different surveys use different items for measurement. Also, the number and nature of antisemitic acts are difficult to compare either internationally or over longer periods of time because the methods and practices of registration are changing. The most detailed and annually updated database on antisemitic incidents in different European (and other) countries can be found at the Kantor Center for the Study of Contemporary European Jewry at Tel Aviv University, available at http://kantorcenter.tau.ac.il/.

3. Anti-Defamation League, *ADL Global 100.*

4. Zick, Küpper, and Wolf, *European Conditions.*

5. Bundesministerium des Inneren, *Antisemitismus in Deutschland,* 21.

6. Jikeli, Stoller, and Thoma, *Proceedings: Strategies and Effective Practices for Fighting Antisemitism among People with a Muslim or Arab Background in Europe.*

7. The report was not published by the EUMC, which sparked a public debate. However, the study has been made available online. Bergmann and Wetzel, *Manifestations of Anti-Semitism in the European Union.*

8. See the annual reports on antisemitic incidents by the CST and the CNCDH.

9. Annual reports from 2007 to 2010 by Commission nationale consultative des droits de l'homme (CNCDH), online at http://www.cncdh.fr. For 2011, see CNCDH, *La lutte contre le racisme, antisémitisme et la xénophobie. Année 2011,* 86, http://www.ladocumentationfrancaise.fr/var/storage/rapports-publics/124000269/0000.pdf.

10. At the time of writing, the two individuals who actually threw the hand grenade were still at large, but the Muslim convert and Jihadist Jérémie Louis-Sidney had handled the explosives.

11. Knobel, *Haine et violences antisémites.* See also the interview with Richard Prasquier, chairman of CRIF, the umbrella organization of French Jewry, at the time. Gerstenfeld, *Demonizing Israel and the Jews,* loc. 2507.

12. The Community Security Trust (CST) regularly publishes reports on antisemitic incidents. The reports are available

on the CST website, http://www.thecst.org.uk/.

13. In the 2001 census, 56 percent of Asians, 90 percent of Arabs, 11 percent of blacks, and 0.5 percent of whites identified as Muslim. Office for National Statistics (Great Britain), *Focus on Ethnicity and Religion.*

14. In the last decade, the German authorities each year registered between 1,200 and 1,600 antisemitic crimes they attribute to the extreme right, and between 30 and 60 cases of antisemitic violence each year. Between 90–95 percent of all registered antisemitic crimes were attributed to the extreme right, as were about 80 percent of the violent antisemitic acts. Bundesministerium des Inneren, *Antisemitismus in Deutschland,* 36. However, a detailed analysis of letters and emails sent to the Central Council of Jews in Germany and to the Israeli Embassy between 2002 and 2012 shows that the majority of antisemitic letters and emails come from mainstream society and only 11 percent from people of the extreme right. Schwarz-Friesel and Reinharz, *Die Sprache der Judenfeindschaft im 21. Jahrhundert.*

15. In an email sent on September 9, 2011, a representative of the Bundeskriminalamt informed the author that in 2009, nine of ten violent antisemitic acts by non-right-wing perpetrators were foreigners, as were six out of six in 2010. In 2009, 31 violent antisemitic acts were committed by right-wing perpetrators, as were 29 in 2010. Bundesministerium des Inneren, *Verfassungsschutzbericht 2010,* 37. For figures from 2001 to 2010 see Bundesministerium des Inneren, *Antisemitismus in Deutschland,* 80.

16. Senatsverwaltung (Berlin) für Inneres und Sport, Abteilung Verfassungsschutz, *Antisemitismus im extremistischen Spektrum Berlins,* 53.

17. The media have reported antisemitic incidents perpetrated by Muslims in a number of European cities, including Berlin, Paris, and London. See, for example, Schmitt, "Bei Gefahr 0800 880280"; "Un rabbin agressé à la gare du Nord"; Cohen, "Following Mosley's East End Footsteps"; Symons, "Teacher 'Sacked for Challenging Antisemitism'"; Khayata, "Battles of Paris." Examples from smaller cities in particular show that antisemitic attacks from Muslims have had a dramatic impact on the Jewish communities. Snyder, "For Jews, Swedish City Is a 'Place To Move Away From.'"

18. Bundesministerium des Inneren, *Antisemitismus in Deutschland,* 40.

19. The perpetrators of threats, including graffiti, often remain unknown, but according to figures from the French CNCDH for the year 2009, 13 percent of antisemitic threats in France were related to neo-Nazi ideology and 5 percent were committed by people of Arab or Muslim background. CNCDH, *La lutte contre le racisme, antisémitisme et la xénophobie. Année 2009,* 45. Bergmann and Wetzel observed already in 2003 that different forms of antisemitic actions can be assigned to different groups of perpetrators. Bergmann and Wetzel, *Manifestations of anti-Semitism in the European Union,* 25–26. The share of "Islamists" sending antisemitic letters and emails to the Israeli Embassy in Germany and to the Central Council of Jews in Germany in the last decade is only 3 percent. The vast majority comes from the center of society. Schwarz-Friesel and Reinharz, *Die Sprache der Judenfeindschaft im 21. Jahrhundert,* 21.

20. European Union Agency for Fundamental Rights (FRA), *Discrimination and Hate Crime against Jews in EU Member States.* Other citable victim testimonies are rare, but some of those that exist also point to the fact that perpetrators with

Muslim background are often responsible for harassment and even violence against Jews in public places. Gerstenfeld, "Nederlands: Harassment of Recognizable Jews."

21. Respondents could choose between a number of categories, including "someone with Muslim extremist view," "someone with an extremist Christian view," "teenagers," "someone with a left-wing political view," "someone with a right-wing political view," "a colleague or a supervisor at work," and "neighbour." There was no distinction between perpetrators "with Muslim extremist views" and people with Muslim background.

22. All-Party Parliamentary Group (United Kingdom) against Antisemitism, *Report of the All-Party Parliamentary Inquiry into Antisemitism,* September 2006, 11.

23. A study in Germany found that antisemitic attitudes are more widespread among male than female youths. Dirk Baier et al., *Jugendliche in Deutschland als Opfer und Täter von Gewalt,* 13. However, the study "Lebenswelten junger Muslime in Deutschland" found that there are no gender differences. Frindte et al., *Lebenswelten Junger Muslime in Deutschland,* 226.

24. Iganski, Kielinger, and Paterson, *Hate Crimes against London's Jews,* 29–33.

25. Wieviorka, *La tentation antisémite,* 24–25. (The book has been translated into English as *The Lure of Anti-Semitism.*)

26. Dencik, "The Dialectics of Diaspora." For the full report see European Union Agency for Fundamental Rights (FRA), *Discrimination and Hate Crime against Jews in EU Member States.* Obviously, Jews fear harassment and attacks from people with all backgrounds, not exclusively from Muslims. The fear of Muslim violence against Jews has been the focus of documentaries, such the fourth part of Zvi Yehezkeli's and David Deryi's 2012 documentary on Muslims in Europe ("Allah Islam"), http://www.youtube.com/watch?v=1Dwc40RtpDc.

27. For Germany see Amadeu Antonio Stiftung, *"Die Juden sind schuld" Antisemitismus in der Einwanderungsgesellschaft am Beispiel muslimisch sozialisierter Milieus.* For France see Brenner, *Les territoires perdus de la République.* A report for the French government for 2010 confirmed that antisemitic attitudes are often voiced by Muslim students, "can be manifested during lessons about the genocide of Jews," and are often related to anti-American attitudes. Haut Conseil à l'intégration, *Les Défis de L'intégration à L'école,* 2011, http://www.ladocumentationfrancaise.fr/var/storage/rapports-publics//114000053/0000.pdf.

28. Symons, "Teacher 'Sacked for Challenging Antisemitism'"; Sandelson, "Anti-Semitism Common in Norwegian Schools."

29. Ufuq.de noted that antisemitism is often manifested in pro-Palestinian demonstrations in Germany that involve Islamists, moderates, and secular Arab organisations. The themes and slogans of the manifestations are then taken up in internet fora and are sung about by rappers of Muslim background. "Proteste von Jugendlichen Gegen Den Krieg in Gaza."

30. Service de Protection de la Communauté Juive (SPCJ), *Rapport sur l'antisémitisme en France 2009.*

31. Whine, "The Advance of the Muslim Brotherhood in the UK."

32. Wistrich, *European Anti-Semitism Reinvents Itself,* 36; Snyder, "For Jews, Swedish City Is a 'Place To Move Away From.'"

33. Michaela Glaser came to similar conclusions in her review of surveys in Germany. Glaser, "Ethnozentrismus und Antisemitismus in Migrationskontexten," 10–25.

34. Pew Global Attitudes Project, *The Great Divide,* 42–43.

35. Koopmans, "Religious Fundamentalism and Out-Group Hostility among Muslims and Christians in Western Europe."

36. Brettfeld and Wetzels, *Muslime in Deutschland,* 274–275.

37. Frindte et al., *Lebenswelten Junger Muslime in Deutschland,* 227–247.

38. Heitmeyer, Müller, and Schröder, *Verlockender Fundamentalismus,* 181, 271.

39. Mansel and Spaiser, *Abschlussbericht Forschungsprojekt.*

40. These attitudes were measured with the following items: "Because of the Israeli policies, I increasingly dislike Jews"; "Regarding Israel's policy I do understand if one is against Jews"; "In my religion they warn us against trusting Jews"; "In my religion, it is the Jews who drive the world into disaster"; "Jews have too much influence in the world"; "What the State of Israel is doing with the Palestinians is principally nothing else than what the Nazis in the Third Reich did with the Jews"; "The Jews in all the world feel more strongly attached to Israel than to the country where they live."

41. Decker, Kiess, and Brähler, *Die Mitte Im Umbruch. Rechtsextreme Einstellungen in Deutschland 2012,* 79. The study found "primary" antisemitism among 11.5 percent of the overall population and 16.7 percent among Muslims, but 23.8 percent of "secondary" antisemitism among the overall population and 20.8 percent among Muslims. However, the poll included only 86 Muslims out of a sample of 2,510 people.

42. Nannestad, "Frø af ugræs? Antijødiske holdninger i fem ikke-vestlige indvandrergrupper i Danmark," 43–62; Andersen et al., *Danmark og de fremmede: om mødet med den arabisk-muslimske verden.*

43. Elchardus, "Antisemitisme in de Brusselse Scholen," 265–296.

44. Antisemitic attitudes were somewhat stronger among "conservative Muslims" than among "progressive Muslims." Vettenburg, Elchardus, and Pleysier, *Jong in Antwerpen En Gent,* 187–222.

45. Wolf, Berger, and Ruig, *Antisemitisme in het voortgezet onderwijs,* 16, 21, 31.

46. Populus/Times, *Muslim Poll,* December 2005, http://www.populus.co.uk/uploads/Muslim_Poll-Times.pdf.

47. The Living History Forum, *Intolerance,* 59 and 152–153.

48. Frindte et al., *Lebenswelten Junger Muslime in Deutschland,* 222.

49. People of Turkish origin make up to three-quarters of Muslims in Germany (Brettfeld and Wetzels, *Muslime in Deutschland,* 86), and about 90 percent of people with Turkish origin in Germany consider themselves to be Muslim. Cf. Konrad-Adenauer-Stiftung, *Türken in Deutschland,* 4; Penn and Lambert, *Children of International Migrants in Europe,* 107.

50. INFO GmbH and Liljeberg Research International Ltd. Sti., "Erste internationale Studie zur Wertewelt der Deutschen, Deutsch-Türken und Türken (Pressemitteilung)," 10.

51. Wistrich, *European Anti-Semitism Reinvents Itself,* 8. On the theological difficulties of Muslims living in non-Muslim majority countries and perceptions of Islamists of those countries, see Wiedl, "Dawa and the Islamist Revival in the West."

52. Holz, *Die Gegenwart des Antisemitismus,* 9.

53. Ibid.

54. Klug, "Anti-Semitism – New or Old?" John Bunzl cites this quote approvingly in "Spiegelbilder – Wahrnehmung und Interesse im Israel-Palästina-Konflikt," 141.

55. Wieviorka, *La tentation antisémite,* 143–158.

56. Klug, "The Myth of the New Anti-Semitism."

57. Taguieff, *Prêcheurs de haine,* 185.

58. Iganski, "Eine Frage der Definition?," 455–472.

59. Silverstein, "The Context of Antisemitism and Islamophobia in France," 1.

60. Silverstein, "Comment on Bunzl," 64–65.

61. Bunzl, *Anti-Semitism and Islamophobia,* 26–27.

62. Nordbruch, *Dreaming of a "Free Palestine,"* 11.

63. Holz and Kiefer mention Milli Görüş, the outlawed Hilafet Devleti, the Verband islamischer Kulturzentren and organisations close to the Muslim Brotherhood, Hamas and Hezbollah. Holz and Kiefer, "Islamistischer Antisemititsmus," 109–137.

64. Ibid., 136–137.

65. Wieviorka, *The Lure of Anti-Semitism.*

66. Ibid., 99–100.

67. Lapeyronnie, "La Demande D'Antisémitisme."

68. Jikeli, "Anti-Semitism in Youth Language," 1–13. See also Schäuble and Scherr, *"Ich habe nichts gegen Juden, aber. . . ."*

69. Wolf, Berger, and Ruig, *Antisemitisme in het voortgezet onderwijs,* 21.

70. Laurence and Vaïsse, *Integrating Islam,* 222–243. For an overview and numerous examples of Muslim antisemitism in France see also Wistrich, *A Lethal Obsession,* 288–317.

71. Kraft, Freiheit, and Spaiser, "Junge Muslime in Deutschland und der Nahost-Konflikt," 227–254. The interviews are part of the research project led by Wilhelm Heitmeyer, Jürgen Mansel, and Viktoria Spaiser. See Mansel and Spaiser, *Abschlussbericht Forschungsprojekt (Final Research Project Report).* The study provides the most interesting qualitative and quantitative data on antisemitism among young Muslims in Germany. Unfortunately, the authors seem to look for confirmation of specific theories on antisemitism (using predominantly Klaus Holz's somewhat simplistic theory of the "figure of the third") instead of developing their own interpretation or theory based on their rich empirical data. Simona Pagona also frames antisemitism among young Muslims in the context of racism. She suggests that identifying antisemitism among Muslims in Germany might whitewash antisemitism in mainstream society. However, her study based on interviews with four Turkish and Muslim youths in Berlin reveals interesting aspects of the relation between masculinity and antisemitism. Pagano, *"Also der Körper is da, die Seele nich."* Anke Shu, who interviewed sixteen young male Muslim men in Germany, takes a somewhat different approach. She interprets antisemitic views in her preliminary results mainly as projections, often indirectly related to discrimination. Schu, "Biografie und Antisemitismusn," 26–53.

72. Wieviorka, *La tentation antisémite,* 196–197.

73. Frindte et al., *Lebenswelten Junger Muslime in Deutschland;* Brouard and Tiberj, *Français comme les autres.* For an English translation see Brouard and Tiberj, *As French as Everyone Else.*

74. Elchardus, "Antisemitisme in de Brusselse Scholen."

75. Among Frenchmen of African or Turkish origin, antisemitism reaches 46 percent among practising Muslims, 40 percent among "infrequently" observant Muslims, 30 percent among nonpracticing Muslims, and 23 percent among those who have no religion. Brouard and Tiberj, *Français comme les autres,* 104.

76. Tiberj, "Anti-Semitism in an Ethnically Diverse France"; Brouard and Tiberj, *As French as Everyone Else?*

77. Frindte et al., *Lebenswelten Junger Muslime in Deutschland,* 218, 230, 240, 245, 276, 298, 302.

78. Schmidinger, "Zur Islamisierung des Antisemitismus."

79. Wistrich, *A Lethal Obsession;* Kepel, Milelli, and Ghazaleh, *Al Qaeda in Its Own Words;* Mallmann and Cüppers, *Nazi Palestine;* Kiefer, *Antisemitismus in den islamischen Gesellschaften;* Müller, "Von Antizionismus und Antisemitismus," 163–182.

80. See also Fatah, *The Jew Is Not My Enemy.*

81. Pew Global Attitudes Project, *Muslim-Western Tensions Persist.*

82. http://global100.adl.org/#map.

83. Friedman, "America vs. the Narrative."

84. Webman, "The Global Impact of the 'Protocols of the Elders of Zion'"; Litvak and Webman, *From Empathy to Denial;* Wistrich, *Muslim Anti-Semitism;* Kotek, *Cartoons and Extremism.* For frequently updated reports see http://www.adl.org/anti-semitism/muslim-arab-world/.

85. MEMRI – Middle East Media Research Institute and Lantos Foundation, "The Tom Lantos Archives on Anti-Semitism and Holocaust Denial."

86. Litvak and Webman, *From Empathy to Denial;* Litvak, "The Islamic Republic of Iran and the Holocaust," 245–266; Bali, *Antisemitism and Conspiracy Theories in Turkey;* Bali, "Present-Day Anti-Semitism in Turkey."

87. Bundesministerium des Inneren, *Verfassungsschutzbericht 2011,* 290–304; Jikeli, Stoller, and Thoma, *Proceedings: Strategies and Effective Practices for Fighting Antisemitism,* 57–65.

88. Amghar, "Les mutations de l'islamisme en France."

89. Bright, *When Progressives Treat with Reactionaries;* Ware, "MCB in the Dock."

90. Am Orde et al., "Islamismus in Deutschland."

91. Demirel, "Kreuzberger Initiative Gegen Antisemitismus."

92. Stephen Roth Institute, "Country Report: France 2007."

93. Ul Haq, "Riyadh Ul Haq Sermon on 'Jewish Fundamentalism' in Full."

94. Whine, "The Advance of the Muslim Brotherhood in the UK."

95. All-Party Parliamentary Group (United Kingdom) against Antisemitism, *Report of the All-Party Parliamentary Inquiry into Antisemitism,* 27–29. See also Wistrich, *A Lethal Obsession,* 397–398.

96. MacEoin, *The Hijacking of British Islam.*

97. Brandon and Murray, *Hate on the State : How British Libraries Encourage Islamic Extremism.*

98. In particular, textbooks of the twenty-four Saudi schools in the UK have been criticized in the past for their messages of hate and antisemitism. See Shea, "This Is a Saudi Textbook"; MacEoin, *Music, Chess and Other Sins.*

99. Hans-Peter Raddatz, for example, generalizes about Muslims in an essentialist way. Raddatz, *Allah Und Die Juden.*

100. Vajda, "Jews and Muslims according to the Hadith," 235–260.

101. Bostom, *The Legacy of Islamic Antisemitism;* Kressel, *The Sons of Pigs and Apes.*

102. For a debate on the role of Arab Muslims during the Holocaust see Nordbruch, *Nazism in Syria and Lebanon;* Satloff, *Among the Righteous;* Küntzel, *Jihad and Jew-hatred;* Mallmann and Cüppers, *Nazi Palestine.* But there are also examples of Muslims who rescued Jews during the Holocaust. See Mughal and Rosen, *The Role of Righteous Muslims.*

103. Bergmann, "Vergleichende Meinungsforschung zum Antisemitismus in Europa," 473–507.

104. Diner, "Negative Symbiose," 185–197.

105. Laurence and Vaïsse, *Integrating Islam,* 234–235.

106. Jikeli, "Überlegungen Zur Bewertung von Antisemitismus Unter Muslimen in Deutschland," 15–28. Jikeli, "Überlegungen Zur Bewertung von Antisemitismus Unter Muslimen in Deutschland," 15–28.

3. Interviews with Young Muslim Men in Europe

The chapter epigraph comes from Michèle Lamont, "A Life of Sad, But Justified, Choices: Interviewing Across (Too) Many Divides," in *Researching Race and Racism,* ed. Martin Bulmer and John Solomos (New York: Routledge, 2004), 163.

1. For a discussion of difficulties and strategies of cross-national comparison studies, see Van de Vijver, "Towards a Theory of Bias and Equivalence," 41–65; Hoffmeyer-Zlotnik and Harkness, *Methodological Aspects in Cross National Research.*

2. Ines Steinke has produced a useful catalogue of core qualitative criteria to produce intersubjective comprehensibility, putting the documentation of the research process in its center and thus allowing readers to evaluate using their own criteria. I use this catalogue as a guideline. Steinke, "Quality Criteria in Qualitative Research," 184–190.

3. Jikeli, "The Kreuzberg Initiative against Antisemitism," 198–211; Jikeli, "Pädagogische Arbeit gegen Antisemitismus," 201–214.

4. The Dönmes (converts) descended from the disciples and adherents of Sabbatai Tsevi, who claimed to be the new messiah in the late seventeenth century in the Ottoman Empire and was then forced to abandon Judaism and to adopt Islam. "Dönme" today can be used as an antisemitic accusation in Turkey. Landau, "The Dönmes: Crypto-Jews under Turkish Rule."

5. Jikeli, "Pädagogische Arbeit gegen Antisemitismus."

6. Brenner, *Les territoires perdus de la République;* Lapeyronnie, "La Demande D'Antisémitisme. Antisémitisme, racisme et exclusion sociale."

7. The European edition of Vakit (in Turkish) had been published and printed in Germany since 2001. It was banned in Germany in 2005 for its antisemitic propaganda. For a documentation of some of their antisemitic caricatures and articles, see Kreuzberger Initiative gegen Antisemitismus.

8. Al-Manar is banned in France, the Netherlands, Spain, and Germany. However, it can still be watched in these countries via satellite TV. Authorities have begun taking a firmer stance against Arab TV channels that propagate hatred. In 2010, the French government outlawed Hamas Al-Aqsa broadcasts because the channel repeatedly incited hatred, mostly against Jews and Zionism. In 2009, a similar decision was taken against the Egyptian channel Al-Rahma.

9. Hiz-but Tahir regularly distributed its antisemitic magazine *Explizit* in its German edition at public places such as the popular weekly market in Berlin-Kreuzberg, until the organization was banned in Germany in 2003.

10. Eight out of 117 interviewees were interviewed individually in a youth club. All other interviews took place outdoors in public places.

11. Iganski, Kielinger, and Paterson, *Hate Crimes against London's Jews.*

12. We also interviewed a small number of female interviewees, but the analysis

is restricted to male interviewees for methodological reasons. The role of gender in attitudes toward Jews is unclear. Different surveys show contradictory results. The study by Frindte et al. on young Muslims in Germany found no gender differences, whereas the study by the Living History Forum found significant gender differences among young Muslims in Sweden. Cf. Frindte et al., *Lebenswelten Junger Muslime in Deutschland,* 226; Living History Forum, *Intolerance,* 59 and 152–153.

13. Many respondents talked about Jews before the interviewer raised questions on Jews.

14. This approach has been used successfully in research on racism. Young, "Experiences in Ethnographic Interviewing about Race," 187–202.

15. One interviewee in London was interviewed in French.

16. Respondents were asked about their age and religious affiliation in the course of the interview and not necessarily in the beginning. Therefore, some interviews were conducted with people of other ages and other religious affiliation. Two are included in the analysis with respondents who were thirteen years old and one with a respondent of thirty years at the time of the interview. Their views do not stand out from the rest of the participants.

17. Heiner Legewie and Elke Partzold-Teske, "Transkriptionsempfehlungen und Formatierungsangaben," TU Berlin, FB 07, Institut für Psychologie 1996. Online at siemer.npage.de/get_file.php?id=7033589&vnr=886937, accessed May 10, 2013.

18. Anke Schu observed in her interviews with sixteen young male Muslims in Germany that interviewees often try to avoid open antisemitic statements because they feel that such statements would be socially unacceptable to a German interviewer and in Germany in general. Schu, "Biografie und Antisemitismus."

19. This approach is used in Grounded Theory ("saturation" of arguments). However, the analytical strategy might be considered too focused for an orthodox method of Grounded Theory. See Hood, "Orthodoxy vs. Power," 151–164.

20. Other studies might look for "types of discourse." A qualitative study on antisemitism in Spain found three types of discourse where antisemitism is expressed: religious, economic, and political, while the religious element acts as a matrix for all the other. Baer and López, "The Blind Spots of Secularization."

21. Schmidt, "The Analysis of Semistructured Interviews," 253–258. The analytical strategy proposed by Schmidt was adopted to this study. It was successfully applied by Walter R. Heinz et al. on semistructured interviews with young people on work-related issues. Heinz et al., "Vocational Training and Career Development in Germany," 77–101.

22. Mayring, "Qualitative Content Analysis," 266–269.

23. This software was chosen for its capability to cope with a large quantity of data and for its ability to code and relate analytical categories visually. The interviews were coded only by me, with the exception of two interviews that were coded also by another researcher. The differences in coding were discussed, which improved the quality of the analytical and coding guide.

24. The Working Definition of Antisemitism was adopted in 2005 by the EUMC, now called the European Union Agency for Fundamental Rights (FRA). Although it has never been officially adopted by the European Union, it is used by a number of international organizations such as the OSCE. Its translation into

more than thirty languages is available online at http://www.european-forum-on-antisemitism.org/working-definition-of-antisemitism/. The full text in English can be found in Appendix A.

25. Fein, "Dimensions of Antisemitism: Attitudes, Collective Accusations, and Actions," 67 (emphasis in the original).

26. I examined the practicability of this definition with regard to specific forms of criticism of the State of Israel that may have originated in personal experiences, experiences of the interviewee's social circle, or knowledge related to the family or culture. Three interviewees reported direct suffering of family members from the wars between Israel and the Palestinians, Hezbollah, or Egypt. Their accounts did not pose any problems regarding this definition's clarity on the distinction between criticism of Israel and antisemitic manifestations with reference to Israel.

27. Silverman, *Doing Qualitative Research*, 287.

28. Students of vocational/technical colleges are usually between sixteen and nineteen years old. A diploma does not qualify students for studies at university.

29. This is the result of a comparison to data provided by the ministries of education in each country. (Unfortunately, the available data on the level of education among Muslims is not detailed enough for such comparisons.) Bundesministerium für Bildung und Forschung, *Grund- Und Strukturdaten 2007/2008*; Le ministère de l'Éducation nationale, *Repères et références statistiques sur les enseignements, la formation et la recherche – édition 2010*; Department for Education, Ethnicity and Education (UK), *The Evidence on Minority Ethnic Pupils*.

30. The categories are adapted from United Nations Educational, Scientific, and Cultural Organiszation (UNESCO), *International Standard Classification of Education 1997 (Re-edition)*, 19. For a discussion of cross-national comparisons of educational levels, see Hoffmeyer-Zlotnik and Warner, "How to Survey Education for Cross-national Comparisons," 117–148.

31. I chose to ascribe interviewees with the French "Baccalaureat professionel" (Bac pro) to category 3 as well, because it is a higher qualification than the BEP and can be used as a qualification for further studies in university. However, it is not necessarily used for entry into higher education at a university and it is part of the vocational stream of the French educational system.

32. One interviewee stays some of the time with his father.

33. For more details see Organisation for Economic Co-operation and Development (OECD), *Equal Opportunities?*

34. All names of interviewees are pseudonyms. The names are chosen from a list of common names among people of their particular ethnic background.

35. The experiences of discrimination, exclusion, and self-identifications are described in detail in Jikeli, "Discrimination of European Muslims."

36. Some districts are seen as bad neighborhoods, which can be used as a basis for discrimination against those who live there.

37. In Britain, "Asian" is understood as South Asian, that is, of Indian, Pakistani, or Bangladeshi origin.

4. Patterns of Antisemitism among Interviewees and Beyond

1. See Schäuble and Scherr, "'Ich habe nichts gegen Juden, aber . . .'"; Wieviorka, *The Lure of Anti-Semitism*.

2. Glynis Cousin uses the term "unitary otherized category" to describe a

process of racialization by racists. Cousin, "Positioning Positionality," 9–18.

3. Fein, "Dimensions of Antisemitism," 67. The definition is discussed in chapter 3. The Working Definition of Antisemitism can be found in Appendix A.

4. See discussion on differences between Muslim men's and women's attitudes toward Jews in chapter 2 of the present volume.

5. "Classic" Modern Antisemitism

1. Theodor W. Adorno described antisemitism as "the rumour about Jews."

2. Kraft, Freiheit, and Spaiser, "Junge Muslime in Deutschland und der Nahost-Konflikt. Eine wissenssoziologische Analyse antisemitischer Deutungsmuster." The study also found a conspiracy theory among Arab interviewees that "the Jews" allegedly try to make people forget about those of their religion in the entertainment industry.

3. Wolfgang Benz, *Was Ist Antisemitismus?*, 192.

4. Iceland is the name of a British retailer specialized in frozen food.

5. It is worth noting that almost all interviewees who believe that Israel or Israelis pull the strings behind conspiracies conflated Israelis with "the Jews" at some point.

6. Conspiracy theories about the terrorist attacks of September 11, 2001, are widespread worldwide, particularly in Muslim countries. See Anti-Defamation League, *Unraveling Anti-Semitic 9/11 Conspiracy Theories;* Middle East Media Research Institute, *A New Antisemitic Myth in the Middle East.* In 2006, 45 percent of the Muslim population in Britain believed that the attacks were a conspiracy by the United States and Israel. GfK NOP, "Attitudes to Living in Britain – A Survey of Muslim Opinion."

7. Benz, *Was Ist Antisemitismus?*, 192.

8. Çeto also gave a presentation on the Holocaust in school.

9. Léon Poliakov, *The History of Anti-Semitism, vol. 1,* 101–122.

10. Bill Gates has never considered himself Jewish and has no Jewish ancestry.

11. Pier Cesare Bori, *The Golden Calf.*

12. "Feuj" means Jew or Jewish in French slang. It is not necessarily pejorative.

13. Michael Marks, joined by Thomas Spencer, founded the company in 1894. Michael Marks had Jewish Lithuanian ancestry. There is currently a boycott held by Muslim and non-Muslim groups against Marks & Spencer for allegations such as those voiced by Salim. See http://www.somethingjewish.co.uk/articles/186_palestinian_harassme.htm and http://www.ummah.com/forum/showthread.php?t=123583, accessed March 13, 2013.

14. "Meurtre d'Ilan Halimi."

15. Bremner, "Youssouf Fofana Jailed for the Torture and Murder of Ilan Halimi."

16. Jikeli, "'Jew' as a Slur in German and French Today," 209–232.

17. Bankim from London also claimed that he recognizes Jews because "*they got one hand covered all the time*" (Bankim, London), which is curious and which was not repeated in any other interview.

18. Léon Poliakov interpreted new forms of antisemitism during the Emancipation as a racist reaction in the age of science, with the aim of conceptualizing the nation in distinction from the Jews. Poliakov, *The History of Anti-Semitism, vol. 3.* "Accusing Jewish citizens of being more loyal to Israel, or to the alleged priorities of Jews worldwide, than to the interests of their own nations" is mentioned in the Working Definition of Antisemitism as an example of contemporary antisemitism (see Appendix A).

6. Antisemitism Related to Israel

1. Yakira, *Post-Zionism, Post-Holocaust;* Zuckermann, *Antisemitismus Antizionismus Israelkritik;* Hirsh, *Anti-Zionism and Antisemitism.*

2. The Working Definition of Antisemitism can be found in Appendix A.

3. Fein, "Dimensions of Antisemitism: Attitudes, Collective Accusations, and Actions."

4. Bergmann, *Geschichte Des Antisemitismus,* 3., 138.

5. No distinctions were made between the Israeli government and different fractions within Israel. But one interviewee, Jamil, who is portrayed in more detail as one of the positive examples at the end of the book, distinguished between the Jewish population and "Jewish" politics.

6. Klug, "The Myth of the New Anti-Semitism."

7. Lakoff and Johnson, *Metaphors We Live By.* See also Adorno's work on the complex relationship between terms and things, *Philosophische Terminologie. Band I.*

8. The Israeli and U.S. governments declared that Hezbollah lost the conflict, while Hezbollah, Syria, and Iran proclaimed a victory for Hezbollah. "Hezbollah Leader: Militants 'Won't Surrender Arms'"; Blair, "Syria and Iran Claim Victory over West."

9. Figures released from the Israeli Central Bureau of Statistics in 2010. See http://www1.cbs.gov.il/www/statistical/isr_pop_heb.pdf, accessed March 15, 2013.

10. Endelman, *The Jews of Modern Britain, 1656–2000.*

11. A minority of ultra-Orthodox congregations or movements, such as Neturei Karta, are indeed opposed to a Jewish state. Members of the Neturei Karta often participate in pro-Palestinian rallies. This might be a reason why their positions are perceived as representative of Orthodox Jews.

12. The Middle Eastern conflict is also described as the "Israeli-Palestinian" or "Israeli-Arab conflict," emphasizing different aspects of the conflict.

13. No interviewee identified Israel as "good" and the Palestinians as "bad" in a Manichean way.

14. Sharansky, "3D Test of Anti-Semitism."

15. People in the Palestinian territories do not suffer from famine. The Human Development Report of the UN shows that the human development index in the Palestinian territories is slightly higher than the average of Arab countries. United Nations Development Programme, "Explanatory Note on 2011 HDR Composite Indices."

16. Rensmann, *Demokratie und Judenbild,* 90–91.

17. Poliakov, *The History of Anti-Semitism, vol. 1.* The image is also mentioned in the Working Definition of Antisemitism; see Appendix A.

18. Schapira, "Propaganda against Israel"; CAMERA, "Timeline of the Al Dura Affair."

19. The Working Definition of Antisemitism (see Appendix A) includes "Denying the Jewish people their right to self-determination" as an example of the ways in which antisemitism manifests itself with regard to the State of Israel. The term "delegitimization" is used in Sharansky, "3D Test of Anti-Semitism."

20. For an introduction into the history of the State of Israel and the fights and wars for its territory with its Arab neighbors, see Morris, *1948: A History of the First Arab-Israeli War;* Segev, *One Palestine, Complete.*

21. For a more detailed analysis of the interviews with twelve of the fourteen par-

ticipants of Palestinian or Lebanese background, see Arnold and Jikeli, "Judenhass Und Gruppendruck," 105–130.

22. Bergmann, "Judenfeindliche Haltungen nehmen kaum zu, wohl aber Straftaten."

23. The Nazis proclaimed the Jews as the "Gegenrasse" (anti-race), a term coined by the Nazi ideologue Arno Schickedanz, who compared the Jews to parasitic ants that undermine other ant colonies.

24. There is an irony here: Sharif has German nationality and he sees his future in Germany. He endorses the relocation of Israel to a part of Germany but rejects Israel in "Palestine" because he is opposed to a Jewish state "bei uns" (at our home). This is part of his contradictory national identification.

25. I only deal with the participants' justifications for suicide attacks and not with rationales of suicide bombers. The rationales of suicide bombers are diverse and focus of extensive research. Alan B. Krueger, for example, shows interesting data on the economic and educational background of supporters of terrorism and suicide bombers including data on Palestinian suicide bombers. Krueger, *What Makes a Terrorist.*

7. Antisemitism Related to Islam or Religious or Ethnic Identity

1. Kraft, Freiheit, and Spaiser, "Junge Muslime in Deutschland und der Nahost-Konflikt."

2. Tarek Fatah is probably the most prominent contemporary scholar who writes from a Muslim perspective against the assumption that Muslims and Jews are enemies. Fatah, *The Jew Is Not My Enemy.*

3. Bhat, "Muslim Policeman in Israeli Row Was 'Worried for Family.'"

4. This Arabic formula meaning, "May the peace and blessings of Allah be upon him" is used as a sign of devoutness and to honor the prophet Muhammad whenever his name is mentioned. It was used only by a few interviewees.

5. A popular story, based on a Hadith about Muhammad's flight to Medinah in 622, known as the Hijrah, imparts that Muhammad hid in a cave and a spider's freshly woven web misled his detractors – usually described as unbelievers or polytheists, not Jews. However, Omar and Housni may have mixed that up with descriptions of fights between Muhammad and Jews or with another popular story in which a Jewish woman tried to poison Muhammad, described in the Sira of Ibn Sa'd. For an English translation of relevant parts of the Sira, see Bostom, *The Legacy of Islamic Antisemitism,* 294.

6. In Christian doctrine, the analogous contradiction is solved by introducing the New Testament as fulfilling or replacing the Old Testament. Almost all Christian churches, for example, include formulas such as "This is the cup of my blood, the blood of the new and everlasting covenant" in their Words of Consecration. The accusation that Jews (and Christians) had altered their sacred books to efface from them the name and description of Muhammad is commonplace in a number of Hadiths. Vajda, "The Legacy of Islamic Antisemitism," 242.

7. However, Diaba subsequently portrayed the Israeli–Palestinian conflict as a war about territory, referring to what he has learned in school. This is another example of the fact that the participants' views are often not cast in stone but are ambivalent. It also shows that to some extent education can have a positive impact on bias.

8. Shavit, *The New Imagined Community.*

9. Shavit, *Islamism and the West.*

10. Koopmans, "Religious Fundamentalism and Out-Group Hostility among Muslims and Christians in Western Europe."

11. In August 1969, Michael Dennis Rohan, a deranged Christian Australian, set fire to the Al Aqsa Mosque; it was extinguished by Israeli and Palestinian firefighters. However, conspiracy theories about "Zionists" planning to destroy the Al Aqsa Mosque by fire have been repeated until today. The Iranian news agency IRIB, for example, published an article as recent as February 27, 2013, in which Rohan was portrayed as an "extremist Australian Zionist" who acted "with the full complicity of the Zionist officials." See english.irib.ir/analysis/articles2/item/107539-zionists-dream-of-destroying-al-aqsa-mosque-2. One of the consequences of the fire in 1969 was the creation of the Organization of the Islamic Conference.

12. Justifications for suicide attacks in Israel for non-religious reasons are discussed in detail in the previous chapter on anti-Jewish attitudes with reference to Israel.

13. Interestingly, these kind of positive references to the Ottoman Empire were made not only by participants of Turkish origin, but also by others, such as Labaan from London, who is of Somali origin.

14. Islam is usually translated as "submission to God."

15. Samed's rationales are discussed in more detail in one of the positive examples in chapter 11.

16. Pan-Arabist leaders, since the beginnings of the movement in the early twentieth century, frequently turned against Jews and – after 1948 – also against Israel, both in words and deeds. One of the main protagonists, Egypt's president Gamal Abdel Nasser, was responsible for a number of antisemitic and anti-Zionist actions, including measures against Egyptian Jews and a war against Israel. He also endorsed *The Protocols of the Elders of Zion* and employed Nazi propagandist Johann von Leers in the Egyptian information agencies. Herf, *Nazi Propaganda for the Arab World,* 265; Laskier, "Egyptian Jewry under the Nasser Regime, 1956–70," 573–619. Founding and leading members of the Arab nationalist Ba'ath party in a number of Arab countries also endorsed antisemitism. See Nordbruch, *Nazism in Syria and Lebanon.*

17. Algerian Nationality Code, Law no. 63–69, March 27, 1963, section 34.

18. Boualem Sansal is one of the few Algerian intellectuals who have discussed the impact of the Holocaust in Algeria. See Sansal, *The German Mujahid.*

19. Langmuir, "Towards a Definition of Antisemitism," 86–127. See also Sartre, *Anti-Semite and Jew.*

8. Antisemitism without Rationalization

1. Harrison, "Anti-Zionism, Antisemitism, and the Rhetorical Manipulation of Reality," 16.

2. The German term "Rasse" is not used today to describe ethnic backgrounds. In German, it has clear racist connotations and thus differs from the English term "race."

3. However, the racist connotations would also justify the classification of his rationale in the category of "classic" antisemitism. It is another example of the fact that categories of antisemitic arguments overlap.

4. Sartre, *Anti-Semite and Jew,* 49 (emphasis in original).

5. For a more extensive analysis of this phenomenon, see Jikeli, "'Jew' as a Slur in German and French Today."

6. The interviews in London indicate that this usage of the word "Jew" in Britain is not as common as in France and Germany

among youths. Anna-Brita Stenström et al. did research on common insults among youths in London and did not report the use of "Jew" as an insult. Stenström, Andersen, and Hasund, *Trends in Teenage Talk*. However, there were reports of such usage in the UK in the late 1990s. Margolis, "Anti-Semitism in the Playground."

7. Lapeyronnie, "La Demande D'Antisémitisme." See also Lapeyronnie, *Ghetto urbain: ségrégation, violence, pauvreté en France aujourd'hui.*

8. This confirms results of a study in France by Lapeyronnie, "La Demande D'Antisémitisme."

9. Most interviewees of Arab background expressed the belief that an Arab and Jewish identity are exclusive, although many French interviewees are aware that Arab Jews exist.

10. Lakoff and Johnson, *Metaphors We Live By.*

11. Schwarz-Friesel and Braune, "Textwelten," 1–29.

12. Schwarz-Friesel, "Judenfeindliche Einstellungen."

13. The three relevant studies and reports from France by Lapeyronnie, Wieviorka, and Brenner and the study from Germany by Schäuble and Scherr come to similar results and are presented in chapter 2 on the current state of research. Reichelt's conclusions of his analysis of the pejorative use of "Jew" among soccer fans and players in Germany differ in view of the fact that he distinguishes between antisemitic and non-antisemitic usage of the word "Jude" as insult. He neglects the antisemitic impact of the pejorative use of "Jew" and his focus on the alleged intentions is methodologically questionable. Reichelt, "Das Lexem 'Jude' im jugendlichen Sprachgebrauch," 17–42.

14. The school is Ferdinand-Freiligrath-Oberschule in Berlin.

15. Translation from the French by the author. "Un rabbin agressé à la gare du Nord."

16. Propaganda of the National Socialists portrayed Jews spreading typhus. Vidal-Naquet, *Les Assassins de La Mémoire;* Lipstadt, *Denying the Holocaust;* Schmid, "Frankreich und Auschwitz-Leugner."

17. The strength of an attitude is regarded as its accessibility, which can be measured in the time of latency of responses to attitudinal questions: the faster the response, the more accessible the attitude is assumed to be. Ajzen, *Attitudes, Personality and Behavior,* 185.

18. Kressel, *The Sons of Pigs and Apes.*

19. This rationale exists nevertheless in the mind of some (deranged) Muslim youths. Adel Amastaibou from Paris made this connection. After killing his Jewish neighbour Sébastien Selam in 2003, he was quoted as saying: "J'ai tué un Juif ! J'irai au paradis!" (I have killed a Jew! I will go to paradise). Conseil Représentatif des Institutions juives de France, "Le Meurtrier Antisémite de Sébastien Selam Va Enfin Être Jugé." In a trial on January 5, 2010, he was declared not responsible for his actions on account of insanity. "Meurtre D'un Disc-jockey Juif."

20. Gessler, "Attacken auf den Davidstern."

21. Rada, "Nahost-Demos weitgehend friedlich."

22. After the match, a French fan of Hapoel Tel Aviv was chased and threatened. A lone black police officer came to his rescue, with the crowd reportedly shouting racial abuse at both the policeman and the fan. After firing warning tear gas shells, the police officer fired his gun twice, killing one perpetrator and wounding another. "Chirac Condemns Football Violence."

9. Perceptions of the Holocaust

Another version of this chapter was published in Günther Jikeli, "Perceptions of the Holocaust among Young Muslims in Berlin, Paris, and London," in *Perceptions of the Holocaust in Europe and Muslim Communities: Sources, Comparisons and Educational Challenges,* ed. Günther Jikeli and Joëlle Allouche-Benayoun (New York: Springer, 2013), 105–132. Reprinted with kind permission from Springer Science+Business Media B.V.

1. Rosenfeld, *The End of the Holocaust.*

2. Jikeli and Allouche-Benayoun, *Perceptions of the Holocaust in Europe and Muslim Communities Sources.*

3. Bosnia is the exception to the rule. The history of Albania shows that some Muslims played an extraordinary role in saving Jews from deportation despite German occupation from 1943–44 while others collaborated with the National Socialists in the persecution of Jews. For a debate on the role of Arab Muslims during the Holocaust, see Satloff, *Among the Righteous;* Nordbruch, *Nazism in Syria and Lebanon;* Mallmann and Cüppers, *Nazi Palestine.* For the role of Turkey see Guttstadt, *Turkey, the Jews, and the Holocaust.*

4. See Litvak and Webman, *From Empathy to Denial.* In a number of Turkish newspapers Israel is frequently equated with the Nazis and it is claimed that the Holocaust is turned into an industry to act as a cover for all of Israel's atrocities, to a level uncommon in German, French, and British newspapers (Bali, *Antisemitism and Conspiracy Theories in Turkey;* Bali, "Present-Day Anti-Semitism in Turkey"). To the best of my knowledge, no studies have examined the discourses about the Holocaust in South Asian countries, the countries of origin of most Muslims in Britain. However, the 2014 ADL Global 100 survey provides some interesting information, including attitudes in Bangladesh and India. In Bangladesh, only 14 percent had heard about the term Holocaust, of which 51 percent believed that the number of Jews who died in it has been greatly exaggerated and 16 percent thought of it as a myth altogether. The numbers are only slightly better for India. There is an encouraging development in Morocco today. The Moroccan king publicly spoke of the importance of Holocaust commemoration for the first time in March 2009: Mohammed VI, Roi du Maroc, "Official Message to Aladdin Projet." Independent from the Monarchy, a group of Moroccan educators and activists visited Yad Vashem in Israel for the first time in 2009. Maddy-Weitzman, "Sounds from North Africa." The Aladdin Project launched a first-time series of public lectures on the Holocaust in Muslim countries in 2010 known in French as Projet Aladin; see http://www.projetaladin.org/.

5. Kreuzberger Initiative gegen Antisemitismus, *Sonderbeilage Zu Vakit.*

6. Stremmelaar, "Dutch and Turkish Memories of Genocide."

7. The Muslim Council of Britain has repeatedly and explicitly boycotted the national Holocaust Memorial Day commemoration in the UK. Whine, "Participation of European Muslim Organisations in Holocaust Commemorations," 29–40; Spencer and Di Palma, "Antisemitism and the Politics of Holocaust Memorial Day in the UK and Italy," 71–84.

8. Brenner, *The Lost Territories of the Republic.*

9. Wolf, Berger, and Ruig, *Antisemitisme in het voortgezet onderwijs,* 16, 32, 45.

10. "Deutschtürken und der Holocaust: Geteilte Erinnerung."

11. GfK NOP, "Attitudes to Living in Britain – A Survey of Muslim Opinion."

12. A few interviewees in France associated the term Holocaust with a group of French rappers who call themselves "Holocauste," such as Sabri from Paris who was asked: *"Have you heard already of the word Holocaust?"* To which he answered: *"This a rapper among us [. . .]. But I don't know what it means. What does it mean?"*

13. Interviewees are generally not aware of the fact that most Jews were actually killed outside Germany.

14. This is also the case for many non-Muslim Europeans. The authors of a report on Holocaust Education in OSCE countries noted a "Holocaust fatigue" among some students. OSCE/ODIHR, *Education on the Holocaust and on Anti-Semitism.*

15. Less accessible attitudes are regarded as weak attitudes with a lower impact on perceptions and judgments. Ajzen and Fishbein, "The Influence of Attitude on Behavior."

16. Some gave examples of how they have dealt with the Holocaust in school. Çeto from Berlin reported that he had given a presentation in school about the Holocaust. Mousa, Ismail, and Suleiman, also from Berlin, met a Holocaust survivor in school. Diaba from Paris mentioned a project with his school remembering Jewish students of his college who had been deported to concentration camps by putting up a plaque of remembrance at his school. Masmud from Paris visited the memorial sites in Drancy with school. Neoy from London said that he saw a video about Anne Frank in school. Many of those interviewees still hold deeply antisemitic views.

17. See Harrison, "Anti-Zionism, Antisemitism, and the Rhetorical Manipulation of Reality" and Salzborn, *Antisemitismus als negative Leitidee der Moderne.*

18. See, for example, *Hitler's Holocaust.*

19. More than 60 percent of the Jews in Europe were killed. See Gribetz, *The Timetables of Jewish History.*

20. One of Claude Lanzmann's objections to *Schindler's List* was that the history of the Shoah must get distorted when the focus of the film is on the salvation of 1,300 Jews while the overwhelming majority of Jews were not saved. Lanzmann, "Holocauste, La Représentation Impossible"; Walter, "La Liste de Schindler Au Miroir de La Presse," 69–89.

21. Unfortunately, he did not provide more details about this source.

22. Lipstadt, *Denying the Holocaust.*

23. Since the mid-1920 there have been rumors that Hitler had Jewish ancestry. This has been proved false. See Kershaw, *Hitler: 1889–1936.*

24. EUMC/FRA, "Working Definition of Antisemitism,"

25. In 2004 about half of the German population thought that Israel's treatment of the Palestinians is basically the same as the treatment of Jews by the Nazis in the Third Reich. Heitmeyer, *Deutsche Zustände. Folge* 3. The number dropped to 30 percent in another survey. Bertelsmann Stiftung, *Deutsche Und Juden.*

26. Quoted by Paul, "Holocaust Scholar Warns of New 'Soft-Core' Denial."

27. Rensmann, *Demokratie und Judenbild.*

28. Ibid.

29. Hasan-Rokem and Dundes, *The Wandering Jew.*

30. Bergmann, *Antisemitismus in Offentlichen Konflikten,* 316; Gerlich, "Sekundärer Antisemitismus in Deutschland Nach 1989."

31. Benz, "Antisemiten Und Islamfeinde"; Cesarani, "Why Muslims Are Not the New Jews."

32. Naulleau, "L'objet Du Scandale"; Lau, "Zu Faruk Sens Vergleich

Der Türken Mit Den Juden Im Dritten Reich."

33. Billig, *Social Psychology and Intergroup Relations;* Allport, *The Nature of Prejudice;* Glick, "Sacrificial Lambs Dressed in Wolves' Clothing," 113–142.

34. Hasan-Rokem and Dundes, *The Wandering Jew.*

35. Rensmann, *Demokratie und Judenbild,* 90–91; Gerlich, "Sekundärer Antisemitismus in Deutschland Nach 1989."

36. Young Muslims (and people of migrant background for that matter) rarely identify as German. Jikeli, "Discrimination of European Muslims."

37. Ramzi has a Palestinian background and Lebanese nationality; Ahmed is of Lebanese origin and a German citizen.

38. This perception is generally widespread and was discussed extensively in Germany after Martin Walser said that the Holocaust is a moral club [Moralkeule]. Kovach and Walser, *The Burden of the Past.*

39. Hirsh, "Accusations of Malicious Intent in Debates about the Palestine-Israel Conflict and about Antisemitism," 47–77.

40. Benz, *Was Ist Antisemitismus?,* 146–154.

41. The latter confirms experiences of Holocaust Education in OSCE countries. OSCE/ODIHR, *Education on the Holocaust and on Anti-Semitism.*

42. Forty percent of the population of Turkish background in Germany stated in 2010 that people of Turkish background should not be bothered to learn more about the persecution of Jews in Germany; 46 percent stated that they should. "Deutschtürken und der Holocaust."

43. Some Muslim organizations oppose current forms of Holocaust remembrance. For example, the Muslim Council of Britain has repeatedly and explicitly boycotted the national Holocaust Memorial Day commemoration in the UK.

44. Alexander, *Remembering the Holocaust.*

45. In a survey conducted in eight European countries in 2009, 41.2 percent supposed that "Jews try to take advantage of having been victims during the Nazi era." Zick, Küpper, and Wolf, *European Conditions.* See also Zick, Hövermann, and Küpper, *Intolerance, Prejudice and Discrimination.*

46. Imran and Manoj from London with South Asian backgrounds, for example, praised the family values of the Nazis. They both show antisemitic attitudes elsewhere, and Manoj has serious doubts about the Holocaust as historical fact.

47. Hale, "Explaining Ethnicity," 470. See also Abrams and Hogg, *Social Identity and Social Cognition.*

10. Sources of Antisemitic Attitudes

1. Crano and Prislin, *Attitudes and Attitude Change.*

2. Cf. Sartre, *Réflexions sur la question juive.* However, the notion of free choice is disputed. For a critical debate on free choice and antisemitism see Maul, "Dialektik und Determinismus," 46–52.

3. Scholars have discussed a number of reasons for the development of antisemitic attitudes, such as transmission of stereotypes and beliefs, and psychological mechanisms of group dynamics or unreflected projections. For a discussion of different theories, see Salzborn, *Antisemitismus als negative Leitidee der Moderne.*

4. Fréville, Harms, and Karakayali, "'Antisemitismus – ein Problem unter vielen'," 185–198.

5. Kraft, Freiheit, and Spaiser, "Junge Muslime in Deutschland und der Nahost-Konflikt," 250. Interestingly, they found

that those between thirteen and eighteen years of age have rather fragmented antisemitic views, whereas those between eighteen and twenty-four have consistent antisemitic worldviews. Antisemitic attitudes are more than reproduced stereotypes. They are part of an antisemitic interpretation of the world and provide explanations for their own situation. Kraft, Freiheit, and Spaiser, "Junge Muslime in Deutschland," 251.

6. Prinstein and Dodge, *Understanding Peer Influence in Children and Adolescents.*

7. Jikeli, "Anti-Semitism in Youth Language."

8. Agantuk's friend is Christian but wants to convert to Islam, he said.

9. "Meurtre d'Ilan Halimi."

10. Jamil's rationales are analyzed in detail in chapter 11 on positive examples rejecting antisemitic attitudes.

11. Wolfram Stender observed the same reluctance to contradict antisemitic statements in six group interviews with youths of different ethnic backgrounds in Germany. Wolfram Stender, "Konstellationen des Antisemitismus. Zur Einleitung," 20.

12. Jikeli, "Anti-Semitism in Youth Language."

13. Jean Améry coined the term "honorable antisemitism" in 1969 in reference to anti-Zionism. Améry, "Der ehrbare Antisemitismus."

14. OSCE/ODIHR, *Education on the Holocaust and on Anti-Semitism.*

15. Cf. Simon and Kloppenburg, "Das Fernsehpublikum türkischer Herkunft," 142–152; Brettfeld and Wetzels, *Muslime in Deutschland,* 95–98.

16. Kempf, "The Impact of Political News on German Students' Assessments of the Israeli-Palestinian Conflict," 1–19.

17. Julian, "Dutch Media Influencing Rise in Anti-Semitism?"

18. Institute for Strategic Dialogue, *Muslims in the European "Mediascape";* Ritzmann, "Fernsehsender verbreiten Antisemitismus."

19. Interviewees referred to Al Manar, LBC (Lebanese Broadcasting Corporation), Al Jazeera, and others. Arab news channels are notorious for their antisemitic programs. For examples and reports, see MEMRI – Middle East Media Research Institute and Lantos Foundation, "The Tom Lantos Archives on Anti-Semitism and Holocaust Denial."

20. Taguieff, "L'affaire al-Dura ou le renforcement des stéréotypes antijuifs."

21. "Un supporter du PSG tué par un policier."

22. MEMRI TV Project Special Report, "Iranian TV Drama Series about Israeli Government Stealing Palestinian Children's Eyes."

23. Küper-Büsch, "Antisemitismus und Multikulturalismus in der Türkei."

24. Kraft, Freiheit, and Spaiser, "Junge Muslime in Deutschland."

25. Webman, "The Global Impact of the 'Protocols of the Elders of Zion.'"

26. Jäger and Jäger, *Medienbild Israel;* Koren, "Antisémitisme et antisionisme"; "6 Month Analysis of the BBC."

27. "Hate Speech and Hate Crimes: Wounding Words and Acts."

28. "Nach systematischer Volksverhetzung: Yeni Akit verboten."

29. "Proteste von Jugendlichen Gegen Den Krieg in Gaza"; "Proteste von Jugendlichen Gegen Den Krieg in Gaza."

30. The rapper Sefyu criticizes stereotypes in his song "La Legende," which came out in April 2006. However, his text about Jews can be misunderstood: "Juifs dans les medias la télé etc. . . . Ils sont devant et même par derrière la caméra. Doués dans les finances ils touchent en économie bon. La légende les appelle les

caméléons. . . . Bon." Rap2france.com, "Paroles La Légende Sefyu Parole La Légende."

31. Baier et al., *Jugendliche in Deutschland als Opfer und Täter von Gewalt,* 116; Bergmann and Erb, "Antisemitismus in der Bundesrepublik Deutschland 1996," 414; Mayer, "Transformations in French Anti-Semitism," 57.

32. Hale, "Explaining Ethnicity"; see also Abrams and Hogg, *Social Identity and Social Cognition.*

33. Brettfeld and Wetzels, *Muslime in Deutschland,* describe orthodox religious Muslims: "This group is characterized by a rigid individual orientation toward religious dos and don'ts, as well as a strong faith in principles and rules of the holy Islamic scriptures of Islam" (263). "Fundamentalist orientations that combine a close religious attachment, a high relevance of religion in daily life, and a strong orientation on religious rules and rituals with a tendency to exclude Muslims who do not observe these, as well as with the tendency generally to heighten the value of Islam and to derogate Western, Christian-influenced cultures, show an enormous dissemination. In the general population, about 40 percent are to be assigned to such a pattern of orientation" (493); see also 279–280.

34. van der Slik and Konig, "Orthodox, Humanitarian, and Science-Inspired Belief in Relation to Prejudice against Jews, Muslims, and Ethnic Minorities," 113–126.

35. See chapter 2 in the present volume, as well as Frindte et al., *Lebenswelten Junger Muslime in Deutschland,* 218, 230, 240, 245, 276, 298, 302; Fréville, Harms, and Karakayali, "'Antisemitismus – ein Problem unter vielen.'"

36. Schu, "Biografie und Antisemitismus," 41. The young man continued identifying himself as "Bozkurt" (an extreme right Turkish-nationalist organization) and as "a Turkish Nazi."

37. A popular story, based on a Hadith about Muhammad's flight to Medinah in 622, known as the Hijrah, relates that Muhammad hid in a cave and a spider's freshly woven web misled his detractors, usually described as unbelievers or polytheists and not Jews. However, Omar and Housni may have mixed that up with descriptions of fights between Muhammad and Jews or with another popular story in which a Jewish woman tried to poison Muhammad, described in the Sira of Ibn Sa'd. See Vajda, "The Legacy of Islamic Antisemitism."

38. MacEoin, *Music, Chess and Other Sins.*

39. These organizations strive for a society under Islamic law, the Shari'a, some with non-violent means, others through violence. For more details see chapter 1 in the present volume.

40. Intelligence and Terrorism Information Center, "Britain as a Focus for Hamas' Political, Propaganda and Legal Activities in Europe."

41. Beland, "Psychoanalytische Antisemitismustheorien im Vergleich."

42. Kraft, Freiheit, and Spaiser, "Junge Muslime in Deutschland," 248.

43. Stender, "Konstellationen des Antisemitismus. Zur Einleitung," 27.

44. Schu, "Biografie und Antisemitismus."

45. Benbassa, "Jewish-Moslem Relations in Contemporary France," 189–194. Klaus Holz adopted a similar argument and mentioned the social, racist, and religious exclusion of Muslims as indirect reasons for the manifestation of antisemitism. Holz, *Die Gegenwart des Antisemitismus,* 9.

46. Glaser, "Ethnozentrismus und Antisemitismus in Migrationskontexten."

47. Bunzl, *Anti-Semitism and Islamophobia,* 26–27. Paul A. Silverstein wrote a "Comment on Bunzl" in the same volume.

48. Lévy, *Ce grand cadavre à la renverse.*

49. Since about 2005, a number of journalists, politicians, scholars and Muslim representatives in the UK, France, and Germany have argued that Muslims are the new Jews in Europe today. The flaws of such allegations are discussed in the excursus on differences between discrimination against Muslims and antisemitism in chapter 2.

50. However, he adopts stereotypes, such as rich and powerful Jews and black people allegedly running the crime world. This might explain why he does not see hatred against Jews as a serious problem.

51. Müller, "Auf den Spuren von Nasser. Nationalismus und Antisemitismus im radikalen Islamismus," 85–101.

52. Smith, "Torture and Death of Jew Deepen Fears in France."

53. Willsher, "Brutal Murder Was Anti-Semitic Crime, Says Sarkozy."

54. Crampton, "Behind the Furor, the Last Moments of Two Youths

55. Michael Marks, joined by Thomas Spencer, founded the company in 1894. Michael Marks had Jewish Lithuanian ancestry. This does not make the company Jewish and it certainly has not convinced its shareholders that financial support for Zionism suits their interests, to use a British interviewee's argument (Raoul).

56. Müller, "Auf den Spuren von Nasser."

57. Schu, "Biografie und Antisemitismus."

58. The perceptions of discrimination and exclusion and the different degrees and ways of identification with the national identity are discussed in detail in Jikeli, "Discrimination of European Muslims."

59. Gallup, *The Gallup Coexist Index 2009: A Global Study of Interfaith Relations,* 19.

60. Billig, *Social Psychology and Intergroup Relations;* Allport, *The Nature of Prejudice;* Glick, "Sacrificial Lambs Dressed in Wolves' Clothing," 113–142.

61. Stender, "Konstellationen des Antisemitismus," 27.

62. Lévy, *Ce grand cadavre à la renverse.* See also Müller, "Auf den Spuren von Nasser."

11. Positive Examples

1. Fromm, *For the Love of Life.*

2. "Die Liste Der Schlimmsten Schulen."

3. The book was first published in French with the title *Brûlée vive.* It was also published in English by Bantam as *Burned Alive.*

4. Jamil makes a similar distinction between American policies, which he does not like, and America, which he loves and would like to visit.

5. Constitution of Germany, Article 3, paragraph (3): "No person shall be favored or disfavored because of sex, parentage, race, language, homeland and origin, faith, or religious or political opinions. No person shall be disfavored because of disability."

6. Lapeyronnie observed such mechanisms through antisemitic stereotypes. Lapeyronnie, "La Demande D'Antisémitisme."

7. Islam is usually translated as "submission to God."

8. Though Arabic and Hebrew are both Semitic languages, there is no ethnic group of "Semites." The term antisemitism

was coined in the end of the nineteenth century and has never been used to describe hostility against Arabs. However, it is a popular argument that Arabs cannot be antisemites because they are "Semites" themselves. Samed uses it differently, as an argument that Arabs should not be antisemitic because it would include hatred against themselves.

Conclusion

1. Anti-Defamation League, *Attitudes toward Jews in Seven European Countries;* Anti-Defamation League, *Attitudes toward Jews in Ten European Countries.*

2. See http://global100.adl.org.

3. Poliakov, *The History of Anti-Semitism, vol. 1.*

4. Klug, "The Collective Jew," 117–138.

5. Langmuir, "Towards a Definition of Antisemitism."

6. Jikeli, "Anti-Semitism in Youth Language"; Jikeli, "'Jew' as a Slur in German and French Today."

7. Adorno and Horkheimer, *Dialectic of Enlightenment.*

8. Offending civil morality and violent harassment, including the killing of Jews, can even become an important marker and the norm of an in-group, as Thomas Kühne has shown not only for Nazi comrades and German soldiers in the East but, eventually, for the entire German "people's community" (Volksgemeinschaft). Kühne, *Belonging and Genocide.*

9. Fein, "Dimensions of Antisemitism."

10. Rosenfeld, "The End of the Holocaust and the Beginnings of a New Antisemitism."

11. Adorno, "Education after Auschwitz," 191–204.

References

Abrams, Dominic, and Michael A. Hogg. *Social Identity and Social Cognition*. Malden, Mass.: Blackwell, 1999.

Adorno, Theodor W. "Education after Auschwitz." In *Critical Models: Interventions and Catchwords*, 191–204. New York: Columbia University Press, 2012.

——. *Minima Moralia: Reflections from Damaged Life*. London: New Left Books, 1974.

——. *Philosophische Terminologie. Band I*. Frankfurt a. M.: Suhrkamp, 1973.

Adorno, Theodor W., and Max Horkheimer. *Dialectic of Enlightenment*. London: Verso, 1972.

Ajzen, Icek. *Attitudes, Personality and Behavior*. Maidenhead: Open University Press, 2005.

Ajzen, Icek, and Martin Fishbein. "The Influence of Attitude on Behavior." In *The Handbook of Attitudes*, edited by Dolores Albarraci, Blair T. Johnson, and Mark P. Zanna, 173–221. Mahwah, N.J.: Lawrence Erlbaum, 2005.

Akbari, Suzanne Conklin. "Placing the Jews in Late Medieval English Literature." In *Orientalism and the Jews*, edited by Ivan D. Kalmár and Derek J. Penslar, 32–50. Hanover, N.H.: Brandeis University Press, 2005.

Alexander, Jeffrey. *Remembering the Holocaust: A Debate*. Oxford: Oxford University Press, 2009.

Alexiev, Alex. "Tablighi Jamaat: Jihad's Stealthy Legions." *Middle East Quarterly* 12, no. 1 (2005): 3–11.

Allouche-Benayoun, Joëlle, and Günther Jikeli. "Introduction." In *Perceptions of the Holocaust in Europe and Muslim Communities: Sources, Comparisons and Educational Challenges*, edited by Günther Jikeli and Joëlle Allouche-Benayoun, 1–12. New York: Springer, 2013.

All-Party Parliamentary Group (United Kingdom) against Antisemitism. *Report of the All-Party Parliamentary Inquiry into Antisemitism*, September 2006. http://www.antisemitism.org.uk/wp-content/uploads/All-Party-Parliamentary-Inquiry-into-Anti semitism-REPORT.pd6.

Allport, Gordon W. *The Nature of Prejudice*. Cambridge, Mass.: Addison-Wesley, 1954.

Am Orde, Sabine, Pascal Beucker, Wolf Schmidt, and Daniel Wiese. "Islamismus in Deutschland: Die netten Herren von Milli Görüs." *Die tageszeitung*, July 18, 2010.

Amadeu Antonio Stiftung. *"Die Juden sind schuld" Antisemitismus in der Einwande-*

rungsgesellschaft am Beispiel muslimisch sozialisierter Milieus. Beispiele, Erfahrungen und Handlungsoptionen aus der pädagogischen und kommunalen Arbeit. Berlin: Amadeu Antonio Stiftung, 2009. http://www.amadeu-antonio-stiftung.de/w/files/pdfs/diejuden.pdf.

Améry, Jean. "Der ehrbare Antisemitismus." *Die Zeit*, July 25, 1969.

Amghar, Samir. "Les mutations de l'islam-isme en France. Portrait de l'UOIF, porte-parole de l' 'islamisme de minorité .'" *La Vie des idées* (October 1, 2007). http://www.laviedesidees.fr/Les-mutations-de-l-islamisme-en.html.

Andersen, Svend, Tonny Brems Knudsen, Jørgen Dige Pedersen, and Georg Sørensen. *Danmark og de fremmede: Om mødet med den arabisk-muslimske verden.* Århus: Academica, 2009.

Ansari, Humayun. *The Infidel Within: The History of Muslims in Britain, 1800 to the Present.* London: C. Hurst & Co., 2004.

——. *Muslims in Britain.* London: Minority Rights Group, 2002. http://www.wnss.agh.edu.pl/other/materialy/90_2011_03_31_10_03_41_MRG%20muslimsinbritain.pdf.

Anti-Defamation League. *Attitudes toward Jews in Seven European Countries.* New York, February 2009. http://www.adl.org/Public%20ADL%20Anti-Semitism%20Presentation%20February%202009%20_3_.pdf.

——. *Attitudes toward Jews in Ten European Countries.* New York, March 2012. http://www.adl.org/assets/pdf/israel-international/adl_anti-semitism_presentation_february_2012.pdf.

——. *ADL Global 100. A Survey of Attitudes toward Jews in over 100 Countries around the World.* New York, 2014. http://global100.adl.org/public/ADL-Global-100-Executive-Summary.pdf.

——. *Unraveling Anti-Semitic 9/11 Conspiracy Theories.* New York, 2003. http://archive.adl.org/anti_semitism/9-11conspiracytheories.pdf.

Arnold, Sina, and Günther Jikeli. "Judenhass und Gruppendruck – Zwölf Gespräche Mit Jungen Berlinern Palästinensischen Und Libanesischen Hintergrunds." In *Jahrbuch Für Antisemitismusforschung 17,* edited by Wolfgang Benz, 105–130. Berlin, 2008. http://iibsa.org/cms/fileadmin/downloads/Arnold_Jikeli_2008_Judenhass_und_Gruppendruck_Jahrbuch_17.pdf.

Aydin, Hayrettin, Dirk Halm, and Faruk Sen. *"Euro-Islam." Das neue Islamverständnis der Muslime in der Migration.* Essen: Zentrum für Türkeistudien, 2003.

Baer, Alejandro, and Paula López. "The Blind Spots of Secularization: A Qualitative Approach to the Study of Antisemitism in Spain." *European Societies* 14, no. 2 (May 2012): 203–221.

Baier, Dirk, Christian Pfeiffer, Julia Simonson, and Susann Rabold. *Jugendliche in Deutschland als Opfer und Täter von Gewalt.* Forschungsbericht Nr. 107. Hannover: Kriminologisches Forschungsinstitut Niedersachsen, 2009. http://www.kfn.de/versions/kfn/assets/fb107.pdf.

Bali, Rıfat N. *Antisemitism and Conspiracy Theories in Turkey.* Istanbul: Libra Kitap, 2013.

——. "Present-Day Anti-Semitism in Turkey." *Post-Holocaust and Anti-Semitism (Institute for Global Jewish Affairs)* no. 84 (August 16, 2009). http://jcpa.org/article/present-day-anti-semitism-in-turkey/.

Beauchemin, Cris, Christelle Hamelle, and Patrick Simon. *Trajectories and Origins: Survey on Population Diversity* in France. Initial Findings. Documents de Travail 168. Paris: Institut national d'études démographique, 2010.

Beaud, Stéphane, and Olivier Masclet. "Un passage à l'acte improbable? Notes de recherche sur la trajectoire sociale de Zacarias Moussaoui." *French Politics, Culture and Society* 20, no. 2 (2002): 159–170.

Beland, Hermann. "Psychoanalytische Antisemitismustheorien im Vergleich." In *Antisemitismusforschung in den Wissenschaften,* edited by Werner Bergmann and Monika Körte, 187–218. Berlin: Metropol, 2004.

Benbassa, Esther. "Jewish-Moslem Relations in Contemporary France." *Contemporary French and Francophone Studies* 11, no. 2 (2007): 189–194.

Benz, Wolfgang. "Antisemiten Und Islamfeinde – Hetzer Mit Parallelen." *Sueddeutsche Zeitung,* January 4, 2010.

——, ed. *Handbuch des Antisemitismus Bd. 4. Ereignisse, Dekrete, Kontroversen.* Berlin: De Gruyter Saur, 2011.

——. *Was Ist Antisemitismus?* Bonn: Bundeszentrale für politische Bildung, 2004.

Bergmann, Werner. *Antisemitismus in Offentlichen Konflikten: Kollektives Lernen in Der Politischen Kultur Der Bundesrepublik 1949–1989.* New York: Campus, 1997.

——. *Geschichte Des Antisemitismus.* 3. durchges. Aufl. München: C. H. Beck, 2006.

——. "Judenfeindliche Haltungen nehmen kaum zu, wohl aber Straftaten." *Neue Zürcher Zeitung Online,* February 9, 2009.

——. "Vergleichende Meinungsforschung zum Antisemitismus in Europa und die Frage nach einem 'neuen europäischen Antisemitismus.'" In *Feindbild Judentum: Antisemitismus in Europa,* edited by Lars Rensmann and Julius H. Schoeps, 473–507. Berlin: VBB Verlag für Berlin-Brandenburg, 2008.

Bergmann, Werner, and Rainer Erb. "Antisemitismus in der Bundesrepublik Deutschland 1996." In *Deutsche und Ausländer: Freunde, Fremde oder Feinde?: Empirische Befunde und theoretische Erklärungen,* edited by Richard D. Alba, Peter Schmidt, and Martina Wasmer, 401–438. Wiesbaden: Westdeutscher Verlag, 2000. http://www.gesis.org/fileadmin/upload/forschung/publikationen/gesis_reihen/Blickpunkt/5/bergerb.pdf.

Bergmann, Werner, and Juliane Wetzel. *Manifestations of Anti-Semitism in the European Union. First Semester 2002. Synthesis Report on Behalf of the EUMC,* 2003. http://www.erinnern.at/bundeslaender/oesterreich/e_bibliothek/antisemitismus-1/431_anti-semitism_in_the_european_union.pdf.

Bertelsmann Stiftung. *Deutsche und Juden – Verbindende Vergangenheit, Trennende Gegenwart?* Gütersloh, Berlin, February 2007.

Bhat, Devika. "Muslim Policeman in Israeli Row Was 'Worried for Family.'" *Times Online,* October 5, 2006.

Billig, Michael. *Social Psychology and Intergroup Relations.* New York: Academic Press, 1976.

Blair, David. "Syria and Iran Claim Victory over West." Telegraph.co.uk, August 16, 2006. http://www.telegraph.co.uk/news/1526476/Syria-and-Iran-claim-victory-over-West.html.

Bori, Pier Cesare. *The Golden Calf and the Origins of the Anti-Jewish Controversy.* Atlanta: Scholars Press, 1990.

"Born Abroad – Introduction and Figures for Britain." *BBC,* September 7, 2005.

http://news.bbc.co.uk/1/shared/spl/hi/uk/05/born_abroad/html/overview.stm.

Borooah, Vani. "Racial Disparity in Police Stop and Searches in England and Wales." *Journal of Quantitative Criminology* 27, no. 4 (2011): 453–473.

Bostom, Andrew G., ed. *The Legacy of Islamic Antisemitism: From Sacred Texts to Solemn History.* Amherst, N.Y.: Prometheus Books, 2008.

Botsch, Gideon, Olaf Glöckner, Christoph Kopke, and Michael Spieker, eds. *Islamophobie und Antisemitismus ein umstrittener Vergleich.* Berlin: De Gruyter, 2012.

Bötticher, Astrid. "Islamophobia? The German Discussion about Islamophobia." *Central European Political Studies Review* 11, no. 2–3 (2009): 210–229.

Brandon, James, and Douglas Murray. *Hate on the State: How British Libraries Encourage Islamic Extremism.* London: Centre for Social Cohesion, 2007.

Bremner, Charles. "Youssouf Fofana Jailed for the Torture and Murder of Ilan Halimi." *Times Online,* July 11, 2009.

Brenner, Emmanuel. *Les territoires perdus de la République: Antisémitisme, racisme et sexisme en milieu scolaire.* Paris: Mille et une nuits, 2004.

——. *The Lost Territories of the Republic.* Translated by Bob Chodos and Susan Joanis. New York: American Jewish Committee, 2006. http://www.ajc.org/atf/cf/%7B42d75369-d582-4380-8395-d25925b85eaf%7D/LOST%20TERRITORIES.PDF.

Brettfeld, Katrin, and Peter Wetzels. *Muslime in Deutschland.* Berlin: Bundesministerium des Inneren, 2007.

Bright, Martin. *When Progressives Treat with Reactionaries: The British State's Flirtation with Radical Islamism.* London: Policy Exchange, 2006.

Brouard, Sylvain, and Vincent Tiberj. *As French as Everyone Else? A Survey of French Citizens of Maghrebin, African, and Turkish Origin.* Philadelphia: Temple University Press, 2011.

——. *Français comme les autres? Enquête sur les citoyens d'origine maghrébine, africaine et turque.* Paris: Presses de la fondation nationale des sciences politiques, 2005.

Bruckner, Pascal. "The Invention of Islamophobia." *Signandsight,* January 3, 2011. http://www.signandsight.com/features/2123.html.

Bundesamt für Migration und Flüchtlinge. *Migrationsbericht 2011.* Nürnberg: Bundesministerium des Inneren, 2013.

Bundesministerium des Inneren. *Antisemitismus in Deutschland. Erscheinungsformen, Bedingungen, Präventionsansätze. Bericht des unabhängigen Expertenkreises Antisemitismus.* Berlin, 2011.

——. *Verfassungsschutzbericht 2010.* Berlin, 2011.

——. *Verfassungsschutzbericht 2011.* Berlin, 2012.

Bundesministerium für Bildung und Forschung (BMBF). *Grund- Und Strukturdaten 2007/2008. Daten Zur Bildung in Deutschland.* Berlin, 2008.

Bunzl, John. "Spiegelbilder – Wahrnehmung und Interesse im Israel-Palästina-Konflikt." In *Zwischen Antisemitismus und Islamophobie: Vorurteile und Projektionen in Europa und Nahost,* edited by John Bunzl and Alexandra Senfft, 127–144. Hamburg: VSA-Verlag, 2008.

Bunzl, Matti. *Anti-Semitism and Islamophobia: Hatreds Old and New in Europe.* Chicago: Prickly Paradigm Press, 2007.

Caruso, Antonella. *Au nom de l'islam: Quel dialogue avec les minorités musulmanes en Europe?* Paris: Institut Montaigne, 2007.

Cesarani, David. "Why Muslims Are Not the New Jews." *Jewish Chronicle Online,*

October 22, 2009. http://www.thejc.com/comment/comment/21173/why-muslims-are-not-new-jews.

"Chirac Condemns Football Violence." BBC, November 25, 2006. http://news.bbc.co.uk/2/hi/europe/6182414.stm.

Çitak, Zana. "Between Turkish Islam and French Islam: The Role of the Diyanet in the Conseil Français Du Culte Musulman." *Journal of Ethnic and Migration Studies* 36, no. 4 (2010): 619–634.

Cohen, Nick. "Following Mosley's East End Footsteps." *The Observer,* April 17, 2005.

Commission nationale consultative des droits de l'homme (CNCDH). *La lutte contre le racisme, antisémitisme et la xénophobie. Année 2009.* Paris: La Documentation Française, 2010. http://lesrapports.ladocumentationfrancaise.fr/BRP/104000267/0000.pdf.

———. *La lutte contre le racisme, antisémitisme et la xénophobie. Année 2010.* Paris: La Documentation Française, 2011. http://www.ladocumentationfrancaise.fr/rapports-publics/114000197/.

———. *La lutte contre le racisme, antisémitisme et la xénophobie. Année 2011.* Paris: La Documentation Française, 2012. http://www.ladocumentationfrancaise.fr/var/storage/rapports-publics/124000269/0000.pdf.

———. *La lutte contre le racisme, antisémitisme et la xénophobie. Année 2012.* Paris: La Documentation Française, 2013. http://www.ladocumentationfrancaise.fr/ouvrages/9782110092359-la-lutte-contre-le-racisme-l-antisemitisme-et-la-xenophobie-annee-2012.

Committee for Accuracy in Middle East Reporting in America (CAMERA). "Timeline of the Al Dura Affair: A French Media Scandal." June 15, 2010. http://www.camera.org/index.asp?x_context=3&x_outlet=167&x_article=1401.

Conseil Représentatif des Institutions juives de France. "Le Meurtrier Antisémite de Sébastien Selam Va Enfin Être Jugé." *Newsletter Du CRIF,* November 17, 2009.

Conseil, sondage et analyse (CSA) / Le monde des réligions. *Islam et citoyenneté,* 2008. http://www.csa-fr.com/dataset/data2008/opi20080730-islam-et-citoyennete.pdf.

Cousin, Glynis. "Positioning Positionality: The Reflexive Turn." In *New Approaches to Qualitative Research: Wisdom and Uncertainty,* edited by Maggi Savin-Baden and Claire Howell Major, 9–18. New York: Routledge, 2010.

Couvreur, Gilles. *Musulmans de France: Diversité, mutations et perspectives de l'islam français.* Paris: Editions de l'Atelier/Editions Ouvrières, 1998.

Crampton, Thomas. "Behind the Furor, the Last Moments of Two Youths." *New York Times,* November 7, 2005.

Crano, William D., and Radmila Prislin. *Attitudes and Attitude Change.* London: Psychology Press, 2008.

Crown Prosecution Service. *Hate Crime and Crime against Older People Report 2011–2012,* 2012. http://www.cps.gov.uk/publications/docs/cps_hate_crime_report_2012.pdf.

Dantschke, Claudia. "'Graue Wölfe' in Deutschland. Türkischer Ultranationalismus und Rechtsextremismus." In *Ethnozentrismus und Antisemitismus bei Jugendlichen mit Migrationshintergrund: Erscheinungsformen und pädagogische Praxis in der Einwanderungsgesellschaft,* edited by Frank Greuel and Michaela Glaser, 66–89. Halle: Deutsches Jugendinstitut, 2012.

———. "Islam und Islamismus in Deutschland." ZDK Gesellschaft Demokratische Kultur, 2006. http://www.zentrum-demokratische-kultur.de/Startseite/ZDK/Islamismus/K259.htm.

Decker, Oliver, Johannes Kiess, and Elmar Brähler. *Die Mitte Im Umbruch. Rechtsextreme Einstellungen in Deutschland 2012.* Edited by Ralf Melzer. Bonn: Dietz, 2012.

Demirel, Aycan. "Kreuzberger Initiative Gegen Antisemitismus." *DAVID – Jüdische Kulturzeitschrift,* June 2006. http://www.david.juden.at/kulturzeitschrift/66-70/69-demirel.htm.

Dencik, Lars. "The Dialectics of Diaspora: The Art of Being Jewish in Contemporary Modernity." Paper presented at the Seventh International Symposium of The Klal Yisrael Project, "Reconsidering Israel-Diaspora Relations," Tel Aviv University, January 7, 2013.

Department for Education, Ethnicity, and Education (UK). *The Evidence on Minority Ethnic Pupils.* Research Topic Paper: RTP01–05. London, 2005. http://www.acert.org.uk/?wpdmact=process&did=MTE1LmhvdGxpbms=.

"Deutschtürken und Der Holocaust: Geteilte Erinnerung." *Die Zeit,* January 21, 2010. http://www.zeit.de/2010/04/Editorial-Umfrage.

Diner, Dan. "Negative Symbiose. Deutsche und Juden nach Auschwitz." In *Ist der Nationalsozialismus Geschichte? Zu Historisierung und Historikerstreit,* edited by Dan Diner, 185–197. Frankfurt a. M.: Fischer, 1987.

Elchardus, Mark. "Antisemitisme in de Brusselse Scholen." In *Jong in Brussel. Bevindingen Uit de Jop-monitor Brussel,* edited by Nicole Vettenburg, Mark Elchardus, and Johan Put, 265–296. Leuven: Acco, 2011.

Endelman, Todd M. *The Jews of Modern Britain, 1656–2000.* Berkeley: University of California Press, 2002.

European Monitoring Centre on Racism and Xenophobia. *Migrants' Experiences of Racism and Xenophobia in 12 EU Member States. Pilot Study.* Vienna, 2006. http://www.libertysecurity.org/IMG/pdf_Migrants-Experiences-web.pdf.

———. *Muslims in the European Union. Discrimination and Islamophobia,* 2006. http://fra.europa.eu/fraWebsite/attachments/Manifestations_EN.pdf.

European Union Agency for Fundamental Rights. *EU-MIDIS: European Union Minorities and Discrimination Survey: Main Results Report.* Luxembourg: Publications Office of the European Union, 2009.

European Union Agency for Fundamental Rights. *Data in Focus Report: Muslims.* European Union Minorities and Discrimination Survey, 2009. http://fra.europa.eu/fraWebsite/attachments/EU-MIDIS_MUSLIMS_EN.pdf.

———. *European Union Minorities and Discrimination Survey.* 2009. http://fra.europa.eu/fraWebsite/attachments/eumidis_mainreport_conference-edition_en_.pdf.

Fatah, Tarek. *The Jew Is Not My Enemy: Unveiling the Myths That Fuel Muslim Anti-Semitism.* Toronto: McClelland & Stewart, 2010.

Fein, Helen. "Dimensions of Antisemitism: Attitudes, Collective Accusations, and Actions." In *The Persisting Question: Sociological Perspectives and Social Contexts of Modern Antisemitism,* edited by Helen Fein, 67–85. New York: De Gruyter, 1987.

Feldman, David. *Englishmen and Jews: Social Relations and Political Culture, 1840–1914.* New Haven, Conn.: Yale University Press, 1994.

Ford, Robert. "Is Racial Prejudice Declining in Britain?" *British Journal of Sociology* 59, no. 4 (December 2008): 609–636.

"Forked Tongues." *The Times (UK),* September 7, 2007.

Fréville, Gabriel, Susanna Harms, and Serhat Karakayali. "'Antisemitismus – ein Problem unter vielen.' Ergebnisse einer Befragung in Jugendclubs und Migrant/innen-Organisationen." In *Konstellationen des Antisemitismus Antisemitismusforschung und sozialpädagogische Praxis,* edited by Wolfram Stender, Guido Follert, and Mihri Özdogan, 185–198. Wiesbaden: VS Verlag für Sozialwissenschaften, 2010.

Friedman, Thomas L. "America vs. the Narrative." *New York Times,* November 29, 2009.

Frindte, Wolfgang, Klaus Boehnke, Henry Kreikenbom, and Wolfgang Wagner. *Lebenswelten Junger Muslime in Deutschland.* Berlin: Bundesministerium des Inneren, 2012.

Fromm, Erich. *For the Love of Life.* Edited by Hans Jürgen Schultz. New York: Free Press, 1986.

The Gallup Coexist Index 2009: A Global Study of Interfaith Relations. With an In-depth Analysis of Muslim Integration in France, Germany, and the United Kingdom. Gallup, Inc., 2009. http://www.gallup.com/strategicconsulting/153578/REPORT-Gallup-Coexist-Index-2009.aspx.

Gerlich, Horst Peter. "Sekundärer Antisemitismus in Deutschland Nach 1989." 2001. http://www.fasena.de/download/forschung/Gerlich.pdf.

Gerstenfeld, Manfred. *Demonizing Israel and the Jews.* Kindle edition. RVP Publishers, 2013.

——. "Nederlands: Harassment of Recognizable Jews." *Arutz Sheva 7 Israel National News,* April 8, 2013. http://www.israelnationalnews.com/Articles/Article.aspx/13113#.UWrI4df7s5Y.

Gessler, Philipp. "Attacken auf den Davidstern." *Tageszeitung (taz),* October 6, 2004.

GfK NOP. "Attitudes to Living in Britain – A Survey of Muslim Opinion." April 27, 2006. http://www.slideshare.net/brighteyes/attitudes-to-living-in-britain.

Glaser, Michaela. "Ethnozentrismus und Antisemitismus in Migrationskontexten – ein Überblick über den Forschungsstand." In *Ethnozentrismus und Antisemitismus bei Jugendlichen mit Migrationshintergrund: Erscheinungsformen und pädagogische Praxis in der Einwanderungsgesellschaft,* edited by Frank Greuel and Michaela Glaser, 10–25. Halle: Deutsches Jugendinstitut, 2012.

Glick, Peter. "Sacrificial Lambs Dressed in Wolves' Clothing: Envious Prejudice, Ideology, and the Scapegoating of Jews." In *Understanding Genocide: The Social Psychology of the Holocaust,* edited by Leonard S. Newman and Ralph Erber, 113–142. New York: Oxford University Press, 2002.

Gribetz, Judah. *The Timetables of Jewish History: A Chronology of the Most Important People and Events in Jewish History.* New York: Simon & Schuster, 1994.

Guttstadt, Corry. *Turkey, the Jews, and the Holocaust.* Cambridge: Cambridge University Press, 2013.

Hale, Henry E. "Explaining Ethnicity." *Comparative Political Studies* 37, no. 4 (May 1, 2004): 458–485.

Hansen, Randall. *Citizenship and Immigration in Post-War Britain: The Institutional Origins of a Multicultural Nation.* Oxford: Oxford University Press, 2000.

Harrison, Bernard. "Anti-Zionism, Antisemitism, and the Rhetorical Manipulation of Reality." In *Resurgent Antisemitism: Global Perspectives,* edited by Alvin H. Rosenfeld, 8–41. Bloomington: Indiana University Press, 2013.

Hasan-Rokem, Galit, and Alan Dundes. *The Wandering Jew : Essays in the Inter-*

pretation of a Christian Legend. Bloomington: Indiana University Press, 1986.

"Hate Speech and Hate Crimes: Wounding Words and Acts." *Today's Zaman*. April 25, 2010.

Haug, Sonja, Stephanie Müssig, and Anja Stichs. *Muslimisches Leben in Deutschland*. Nürnberg: Bundesamt für Migration und Flüchtlinge, 2009.

Haut Conseil à l'intégration. *Les Défis de L'intégration à L'école*, 2011. http://www.ladocumentationfrancaise.fr/var/storage/rapports-publics//114000053/0000.pdf.

Heinz, Walter R., Udo Kelle, Andreas Witzel, and Jens Zinn. "Vocational Training and Career Development in Germany: Results from a Longitudinal Study." *International Journal of Behavioral Development* 22, no. 1 (March 1, 1998): 77–101.

Heitmeyer, Wilhelm. *Deutsche Zustände. Folge 10*. Frankfurt a. M.: Suhrkamp, 2011.

———. *Deutsche Zustände. Folge 3*. Frankfurt a. M.: Suhrkamp, 2005.

Heitmeyer, Wilhelm, Joachim Müller, and Helmut Schröder. *Verlockender Fundamentalismus: Türkische Jugendliche in Deutschland*. Frankfurt a. M.: Suhrkamp, 1997.

Herf, Jeffrey. *Nazi Propaganda for the Arab World*. New Haven, Conn.: Yale University Press, 2010.

"Hezbollah Leader: Militants 'Won't Surrender Arms.'" CNN. September 22, 2006. http://edition.cnn.com/2006/WORLD/meast/09/22/lebanon.rally/.

Hirsh, David. "Accusations of Malicious Intent in Debates about the Palestine-Israel Conflict and about Antisemitism. The Livingstone Formulation, 'Playing the Antisemitism Card' and Contesting the Boundaries of Antiracist Discourse." *Transversal – Zeitschrift Für Jüdische Studien* no. 1 (2010): 47–77.

———. *Anti-Zionism and Antisemitism: Cosmopolitan Reflections*. Working Paper Series. The Yale Initiative for the Interdisciplinary Study of Antisemitism, 2007. http://www.yale.edu/yiisa/workingpaper/hirsh/David%20Hirsh%20YIISA%20Working%20Paper1.pdf.

The Historical Association. *T.E.A.C.H. Teaching Emotive and Controversial History 3–19*. London, 2007. https://www.education.gov.uk/publications/eOrderingDownload/RW100.pdf.

"'Hitler Should Have Killed All Jews': Dutch TV Airs Shock Interview with Muslim Migrants." *TheBlaze*, March 6, 2013. http://www.theblaze.com/stories/2013/03/06/hitler-should-have-killed-all-jews-dutch-tv-airs-shock-interview-with-muslim-immigrants/.

Hoffmann, Christhard. "Politische Kultur und Gewalt gegen Minderheiten. Die antisemitischen Ausschreitungen in Pommern und Westpreußen 1881." In *Jahrbuch für Antisemitismusforschung 3*, edited by Wolfgang Benz, 93–120. Frankfurt a. M.: New York: Campus Verlag, 1994.

Hoffmeyer-Zlotnik, Jürgen, and Janet A. Harkness, eds. *Methodological Aspects in Cross National Research*. ZUMA-Nachrichten Spezial 11. Mannheim: ZUMA, 2005.

Hoffmeyer-Zlotnik, Jürgen H.P., and Uwe Warner. "How to Survey Education for Cross-National Comparisons: The Hoffmeyer-Zlotnik/Warner-Matrix of Education." *Metodoloski Zvezki* 4, no. 2 (2007): 117–148.

Holz, Klaus. *Die Gegenwart des Antisemitismus: Islamistische, demokratische und antizionistische Judenfeindschaft*. Hamburg: Hamburger Edition, 2005.

Holz, Klaus, and Michael Kiefer. "Islamistischer Antisemititsmus – Phänomen und Forschungsstand." In *Konstel-*

lationen des Antisemitismus Antisemitismusforschung und sozialpädagogische Praxis, edited by Wolfram Stender, Guido Follert, and Mihri Özdogan, 109–137. Wiesbaden: VS Verlag für Sozialwissenschaften / GWV Fachverlage GmbH, Wiesbaden, 2010.

Home Office. *The New and the Old: The Report of the "Life in the United Kingdom" Advisory Group.* Croydon, 2003. http://ec.europa.eu/ewsi/UDRW/images/items/docl_19546_997974966.pdf.

Hood, Jane C. "Orthodoxy vs. Power: The Defining Traits of Grounded Theory." In *The SAGE Handbook of Grounded Theory,* edited by Antony Bryant and Kathy Charmaz, 151–164. Thousand Oaks, Calif.: Sage Publications, 2010.

ICM Research. *Muslim Poll,* July 20, 2005. http://image.guardian.co.uk/sys-files/Politics/documents/2005/07/26/Muslim-Poll.pdf.

Iganski, Paul. "Eine Frage der Definition? Judenfeindschaft in Europa, der Nahost-Konflikt und die Ursachen antisemitischer Gewalt 'auf der Straße.'" In *Feindbild Judentum: Antisemitismus in Europa,* edited by Lars Rensmann and Julius H. Schoeps, 455–472. Berlin: VBB Verlag für Berlin-Brandenburg, 2008.

Iganski, Paul, Vicky Kielinger, and Susan Paterson. *Hate Crimes against London's Jews: An Analysis of Incidents Recorded by the Metropolitan Police Service 2001–2004.* London: Institute for Jewish Policy Research, 2005.

Imhoff, Roland, and Julia Recker. "Differentiating Islamophobia: Introducing a New Scale to Measure Islamoprejudice and Secular Islam Critique." *Political Psychology* 33, no. 6 (2012): 811–824.

INFO GmbH, and iljeberg Research InLternational. *Wertewelten von Deutschen und Migrant/innen – Migration zwischen Integration und Ausgrenzung.* Berlin, May 11, 2010. http://www.liljeberg.net/aktuell/Wertewelten-summary_07.pdf.

INFO GmbH, and Liljeberg Research International Ltd. Sti. "Erste internationale Studie zur Wertewelt der Deutschen, Deutsch-Türken und Türken (Pressemitteilung)." November 19, 2009. http://www.liljeberg.net/aktuell/Pressemitteilung-fuer-pressekonferenz4.pdf.

Institut français d'opinion publique (IFOP). *L'image de l'Islam en France.* Paris, 2012. http://www.lefigaro.fr/assets/pdf/sondage-ipsos-islam-france.pdf.

Institut national de la statistique et des études économiques (Insee). *Immigrés et Descendants D'immigrés en France.* Paris, October 2012.

Institute for Strategic Dialogue. *Muslims in the European "Mediascape": Integration and Social Cohesion Dynamics,* 2009. http://www.strategicdialogue.org/documents/isd_intranet/ISD%20muslims%20media%20WEB.pdf.

Intelligence and Terrorism Information Center. "Britain as a Focus for Hamas' Political, Propaganda and Legal Activities in Europe." February 21, 2010. http://www.terrorism-info.org.il/malam_multimedia/English/eng_n/html/hamas_e097.htm.

Islamophobia: A Challenge for Us All. London: Runnymede Trust, 1997.

Jacobs, Dirk. "Survey Findings of the EURISLAM Project." Paper presented at the "The Sociocultural Integration of Muslim Minorities in Europe EURISLAM project" final conference, Brussels, June 20, 2012. http://www.eurislam.eu/var/WP4_Survey_data.pdf.

Jäger, Siegfried, and Margarete Jäger. *Medienbild Israel: Zwischen Solidarität und Antisemitismus.* Münster: Lit, 2003.

Jaxel-Truer, Pierre, and Elise Vincent. "Voile intégral, polygamie: comment un fait divers devient une controverse politique." *Le Monde,* April 26, 2010.

Jikeli, Günther. "Anti-Semitism in Youth Language: The Pejorative Use of the Terms for 'Jew' in German and French Today." *Conflict & Communication Online* 9, no. 1 (2010): 1–13.

——. "Der neue alte Antisemitismus Müssen Juden sich wieder verstecken?" *Stern,* September 14, 2012.

——. "Discrimination of European Muslims: Self-Perceptions, Experiences and Discourses of Victimhood." In *Minority Groups: Coercion, Discrimination, Exclusion, Deviance and the Quest for Equality,* edited by Dan Soen, Mally Shechory, and Sarah Ben-David, 77–96. New York: Nova Science, 2012.

——. "'Jew' as a Slur in German and French Today." *Journal for the Study of Antisemitism* 1, no. 2 (2009): 209–232.

——. "The Kreuzberg Initiative against Antisemitism among Youth from Muslim and Non-Muslim Backgrounds in Berlin." In *Antisemitism: The Generic Hatred: Essays in Memory of Simon Wiesenthal,* edited by Michael Fineberg, Shimon Samuels, and Mark Weitzman, 198–211. Portland, Ore.: Vallentine Mitchell, 2007.

——. "Pädagogische Arbeit gegen Antisemitismus mit Jugendlichen mit arabischem/muslimischem Familienhintergrund." In *Antisemitismus und radikaler Islamismus,* edited by Wolfgang Benz and Juliane Wetzel, 201–214. Essen, 2007.

——. "Überlegungen Zur Bewertung von Antisemitismus Unter Muslimen in Deutschland." *Transversal – Zeitschrift Für Jüdische Studien* 1 (2010): 15–28.

Jikeli, Günther, and Joëlle Allouche-Benayoun, eds. *Perceptions of the Holocaust in Europe and Muslim Communities: Sources, Comparisons and Educational Challenges.* New York: Springer, 2013.

Jikeli, Günther, Robin Stoller, and Hanne Thoma. *Proceedings: Strategies and Effective Practices for Fighting Antisemitism among People with a Muslim or Arab Background in Europe.* Berlin: IIBSA, 2007. http://iibsa.org/cms/wp-content/uploads/2012/08/proceedings_summer_school.pdf.

Judge, Harry. "The Muslim Headscarf and French Schools." *American Journal of Education* 111, no. 1 (2004): 1–24.

Julian, Hana Levi. "Dutch Media Influencing Rise in Anti-Semitism?" *Arutz Sheva 7 Israel National News,* March 25, 2010.

Kahlweiß, Luzie H., and Samuel Salzborn. "'Islamophobie" als politischer Kampfbegriff. Zur konzeptionellen und empirischen Kritik des Islamophobiebegriffs." In *Islamophobie und Antisemitismus ein umstrittener Vergleich,* edited by Armin Pfahl-Traughber, 248–263. Brühl: Statistisches Bundesamt, 2012.

Kempf, Wilhelm. "The Impact of Political News on German Students' Assessments of the Israeli-Palestinian Conflict." *Conflict & Communication Online* 7, no. 2 (2008): 1–19.

Kepel, Gilles, Jean-Pierre Milelli, and Pascale Ghazaleh. *Al Qaeda in Its Own Words.* Cambridge, Mass.: Belknap Press of Harvard University Press, 2008.

Kershaw, Ian. *Hitler: 1889–1936. Hubris.* W. W. Norton & Company, 1999.

Khayata, Léa. "Battles of Paris. Anti-Semitism in the 19th Arrondissement, a Neighborhood with a Recent History of Violence." *Tablet,* February 11, 2010. http://www.tabletmag.com/jewish-news-and-politics/25494/battles-of-paris.

Kiefer, Michael. *Antisemitismus in den islamischen Gesellschaften: der Palästina-Konflikt und der Transfer eines Feindbildes.* Düsseldorf: Verein zur Förderung Gleichberechtigter Kommunikation, 2002.

Klug, Brian. "Anti-Semitism – New or Old?" *The Nation,* April 12, 2004. http://www.thenation.com/article/anti-semitism-new-or-old#.

———. "The Collective Jew: Israel and the New Antisemitism." *Patterns of Prejudice* 37, no. 2 (2003): 117–138.

———. "The Myth of the New Anti-Semitism." *The Nation,* February 2, 2004. http://www.thenation.com/article/myth-new-anti-semitism.

Knobel, Marc. *Haine et violences antisémites. Une rétrospective: 2000–2013.* Paris: Berg International, 2013.

Knopp, Guido. *Hitler's Holocaust.* Stroud: Sutton, 2004.

Konrad-Adenauer-Stiftung. *Türken in Deutschland – Einstellungen zu Staat und Gesellschaft.* Sankt Augustin, 2001. http://www.kas.de/db_files/dokumente/arbeitspapiere/7_dokument_dok_pdf_12_1.pdf.

Koren, Roseline. "Antisémitisme et antisionisme: Les dérives de la presse française." Tel Aviv: Akadem, 2006. http://www.akadem.org/sommaire/themes/politique/1/2/module_971.php.

Kotek, Joël. *Cartoons and Extremism: Israel and the Jews in Arab and Western Media.* Edgware: Vallentine Mitchell, 2009.

Kovach, Thomas A., and Martin Walser. *The Burden of the Past: Martin Walser on Modern German Identity: Texts, Contexts, Commentary.* Rochester: Camden House, 2008.

Kraft, Kristina, Manuela Freiheit, and Victoria Spaiser. "Junge Muslime in Deutschland und der Nahost-Konflikt. Eine wissenssoziologische Analyse antisemitischer Deutungsmuster." In *Islamophobie und Antisemitismus ein umstrittener Vergleich,* edited by Gideon Botsch, Olaf Glöckner, Christoph Kopke, and Michael Spieker, 227–254. Berlin: De Gruyter, 2012.

Kressel, Neil J. *The Sons of Pigs and Apes: Muslim Antisemitism and the Conspiracy of Silence.* Washington, D.C.: Potomac Books, 2012.

Kreuzberger Initiative gegen Antisemitismus. *Sonderbeilage Zu Vakit,* 2004. http://www.kiga-berlin.org/uploads/Material/Kiga%20Sonderbeilage%20Vakit.pdf.

Krueger, Alan B. *What Makes a Terrorist: Economics and the Roots of Terrorism.* Princeton, N.J.: Princeton University Press, 2008.

Kühne, Thomas. *Belonging and Genocide: Hitler's Community, 1918–1945.* New Haven, Conn.: Yale University Press, 2010.

Küntzel, Matthias. *Jihad and Jew-Hatred: Islamism, Nazism and the Roots of 9/11.* New York: Telos Press, 2007.

Küper-Büsch, Sabine. "Antisemitismus und Multikulturalismus in der Türkei." *Jungle World* no. 45 (November 6, 2008).

Lakoff, George, and Mark Johnson. *Metaphors We Live By.* Chicago: University of Chicago Press, 1980.

Lamont, Michèle. "A Life of Sad, But Justified, Choices: Interviewing Across (Too) Many Divides." In *Researching Race and Racism,* edited by Martin Bulmer and John Solomos, 163–171. New York: Routledge, 2004.

Landau, Jacob M. "The Dönmes: Crypto-Jews Under Turkish Rule." *Jewish Political Studies Review* 19, no. 1–2 (March 2007).

Langmuir, Gavin I. "Towards a Definition of Antisemitism." In *The Persisting Ques-*

tion: Sociological Perspectives and Social Contexts of Modern Antisemitism, edited by Helen Fein, 86–127. New York: De Gruyter, 1987.

Lanzmann, Claude. "Holocauste, La Représentation Impossible." *Le Monde,* March 3, 1994.

Lapeyronnie, Didier. "La Demande D'Antisémitisme. Antisémitisme, racisme et exclusion sociale." *Les Études du CRIF* n°9 (September 2005).

———. *Ghetto urbain: Ségrégation, violence, pauvreté en France aujourd'hui.* Paris: Laffont, 2008.

Laskier, Michael M. "Egyptian Jewry under the Nasser Regime, 1956–70." *Middle Eastern Studies* 31, no. 3 (1995): 573–619.

Lau, Jörg. "Zu Faruk Sens Vergleich Der Türken Mit Den Juden Im Dritten Reich." *Zeit Online,* June 30, 2008. http://blog.zeit.de/joerglau/2008/06/30/zu-faruk-sens-vergleich-der-turken-mit-den-juden-im-dritten-reich_1244.

Laurence, Jonathan, and Justin Vaïsse. *Integrating Islam: Political and Religious Challenges in Contemporary France.* Washington, D.C.: Brookings Institution Press, 2006.

Lévy, Bernard Henri. *Ce grand cadavre à la renverse.* Paris: Grasset, 2007.

Lewis, Philip. *Islamic Britain: Religion, Politics and Identity among British Muslims.* London: I. B. Tauris, 2002.

The Living History Forum. *Antisemitism Och Islamofobi – Utbredning, Orsaker Och Preventivt Arbete.* Stockholm: Ministry of Employment, 2011. http://www.levandehistoria.se/files/Antisemitism%20och%20islamofobi.pdf.

———. *Intolerance: Anti-Semitic, Homophobic, Islamophobic and Xenophobic Tendencies among the Young.* Stockholm: Brottsförebyggande rådet (BRÅ), 2005. http://www.levandehistoria.se/files/INTOLERANCEENG_0.pdf.

Lipstadt, Deborah E. *Denying the Holocaust: The Growing Assault on Truth and Memory.* New York: Plume, 1993.

"Die Liste Der Schlimmsten Schulen." *BZ Berlin,* November 24, 2004.

Litvak, Meir. "The Islamic Republic of Iran and the Holocaust: Anti-Zionism and Anti-Semitism." *Journal of Israeli History* 25 (2006): 245–266.

Litvak, Meir, and Esther Webman. *From Empathy to Denial: Arab Responses to the Holocaust.* New York: Columbia University Press, 2009.

MacEoin, Denis. *The Hijacking of British Islam: How Extremist Literature Is Subverting Mosques in the UK.* London: Policy Exchange, 2007.

———. *Music, Chess and Other Sins: Segregation, Integration, and Muslim Schools in Britain.* London: Civitas: Institute for the Study of Civil Society, 2009. http://www.civitas.org.uk/pdf/MusicChessAndOtherSins.pdf.

Maddy-Weitzman, Bruce. "Sounds from North Africa." *Jerusalem Report,* January 18, 2010.

Mallmann, Klaus-Michael, and Martin Cüppers. *Nazi Palestine: The Plans for the Extermination of the Jews in Palestine.* Translated by Krista Smith. New York: Enigma Books, 2010.

Mansel, Jürgen, and Victoria Spaiser. *Abschlussbericht Forschungsprojekt (Final Research Project Report) "Soziale Beziehungen, Konfliktpotentiale und Vorurteile im Kontext von Erfahrungen verweigerter Teilhabe und Anerkennung bei Jugendlichen mit und ohne Migrationshintergrund."* Bielefeld, 2010. http://www.vielfalt-tut-gut.de/content/e4458/e8260/Uni_Bielefeld_Abschlussbericht_Forschungsprojekt.pdf and http://www.vielfalt-tut-gut.de/content/e4458/e8277/Uni_Bielefeld_Tabellenanhang.pdf.

Maréchal, Brigitte. *The Muslim Brothers in Europe: Roots and Discourse*. Leiden: Brill, 2008.

Margolis, David. "Anti-Semitism in the Playground." *The Independent*, February 1, 1999.

Maul, Thomas. "Dialektik und Determinismus. Zum Verhältnis von Adorno, Sartre und Améry." *Bahamas* 64 (2012): 46–52.

Mayer, Nonna. "Transformations in French Anti-Semitism." *International Journal of Conflict and Violence* 1, no. 1 (2007): 51–60.

Mayor of London. *Muslims in London*. London: Greater London Authority, October 2006. http://legacy.london.gov.uk/gla/publications/equalities/muslims-in-london.pdf.

Mayring, Philipp. "Qualitative Content Analysis." In *A Companion to Qualitative Research*, edited by Uwe Flick, Ernst von Kardoff, and Ines Steinke, 266–269. Thousand Oaks, Calif.: Sage Publications, 2004.

Meer, Nasar, and Tehseen Noorani. "A Sociological Comparison of Anti-Semitism and Anti-Muslim Sentiment in Britain." *Sociological Review* 56, no. 2 (2008): 195–219.

"Meurtre d'Ilan Halimi: Le 'gang des barbares' jugé en appel, sans son leader." *Le Monde*, October 25, 2010.

"Meurtre d'un Disc-jockey Juif: Le Meurtrier Jugé Irresponsable Pénalement." *Le Point*, January 5, 2010.

Middle East Media Research Institute (MEMRI). *A New Antisemitic Myth in the Middle East: The September 11 Attacks Were Perpetrated by the Jews*. Washington, D.C., 2002.

Middle East Media Research Institute TV Project Special Report. "Iranian TV Drama Series about Israeli Government Stealing Palestinian Children's Eyes." December 22, 2004. http://www.memri.org/report/en/0/0/0/0/0/0/1282.htm.

Middle East Media Research Institute (MEMRI) and Lantos Foundation. "The Tom Lantos Archives on Anti-Semitism and Holocaust Denial," n.d. http://www.memri.org/antisemitism.html.

Le ministère de l'Éducation nationale. *Repères et références statistiques sur les enseignements, la formation et la recherche – édition 2010*. Paris, 2010.

Mirza, Munira, Zain Ja'far, and Abi Senthilkumaran. *Living Apart Together: British Muslims and the Paradox of Multiculturalism*. London: Policy Exchange, 2007.

Mohammed VI, Roi du Maroc. "Official Message to Aladdin Projet." March 18, 2009. http://www.fondationshoah.info/FMS/IMG/pdf/Message_-_Roi_Maroc_fr.pdf.

Morris, Benny. *1948: A History of the First Arab-Israeli War*. New Haven, Conn.: Yale University Press, 2008.

Mughal, Fiyaz, and Esmond Rosen. *The Role of Righteous Muslims*. London: Faith Matters, 2010.

Müller, Jochen. "Auf den Spuren von Nasser. Nationalismus und Antisemitismus im radikalen Islamismus." In *Antisemitismus und radikaler Islamismus*, edited by Wolfgang Benz and Juliane Wetzel, 85–101. Essen: Klartext, 2007.

———. "Von Antizionismus und Antisemitismus. Stereotypenbildung in der arabischen Öffentlichkeit." In *Anitsemitismus in Europa und in der arabischen Welt. Ursachen und Wechselbeziehungen eines komplexen Phänomens*, edited by Wolfgang Ansorge, 163–182. Paderborn: Bonifatius, 2006.

"Nach systematischer Volksverhetzung: Yeni Akit verboten." Hagalil.com. February 18, 2005. http://www.hagalil.com/archiv/2005/02/yeni-akit.htm.

Nannestad, Peter. "Frø af ugræs? Antijødiske holdninger i fem ikke-vestlige indvandrergrupper i Danmark." In *Danmark og de fremmede: om mødet med den arabisk-muslimske verden,* edited by Tonny Brems Knudsen, Jørgen Dige Pedersen, and Georg Sørensen, 43–62. Århus: Academica, 2009.

Naulleau, Eric. "L'objet Du Scandale." France 2, January 12, 2010.

Niewels, Matthias. "Schwere Vorwürfe gegen Islam-Verein." *Kölner Stadtanzeiger,* April 10, 2008.

Nordbruch, Götz. *Dreaming of a "Free Palestine": Muslim Youth in Germany and the Israel-Palestine Conflict.* Center for Mellemoeststudier, May 2009. http://www.sdu.dk/~/media/Files/Om_SDU/Centre/C_Mellemoest/Videncenter/Nyheder/2009/090505GN.ashx.

——. *Nazism in Syria and Lebanon: The Ambivalence of the German Option, 1933–1945.* New York: Routledge, 2009.

Norfolk, Andrew. "Muslim Group behind 'Mega-mosque' Seeks to Convert All Britain." *The Times (UK),* September 10, 2007.

Nyiri, Zsolt, and Dalia Mogahed. "Reinventing Integration." *Harvard International Review* 29, no. 2 (2007): 14–21.

O'Beirne, Maria. *Religion in England and Wales: Findings from the 2001 Home Office Citizenship Survey.* Home Office Research Study 274. Home Office Research, Development and Statistics Directorate, March 2004.

Office for National Statistics. *Migration Statistics Quarterly Report, February 2013.* Statistical Bulletin, 2013. http://www.ons.gov.uk/ons/dcp171778_300382.pdf.

——. *National Statistics – Focus on Religion,* October 2004. http://www.ons.gov.uk/ons/rel/ethnicity/focus-on-religion/2004-edition/focus-on-religion-summary-report.pdf.

——. *Religion in England and Wales 2011,* December 2012. http://www.ons.gov.uk/ons/dcp171776_290510.pdf.

Office for National Statistics (Great Britain). *Focus on Ethnicity and Religion.* Edited by Joy Dobbs, Hazel Green, and Linda Zealey. Basingstoke: Palgrave Macmillan, 2006.

Office français de protection des réfugiés et apatrides (OFPRA). *Rapport Annuel 2007,* 2008. http://lesrapports.ladocumentationfrancaise.fr/BRP/084000198/0000.pdf.

Open Society Institute. *Muslims in Europe: A Report on 11 EU Cities.* 2nd ed. New York: Open Society Institute, 2010.

——. *Muslims in the EU: Cities Report: France. Preliminary Research Report and Literature Survey,* 2007. http://www.opensocietyfoundations.org/sites/default/files/museucitiesfra_20080101_0.pdf.

——. *Muslims in the EU: Cities Report: Germany. Preliminary Research Report and Literature Survey,* 2007. http://www.opensocietyfoundations.org/sites/default/files/museucitiesger_20080101_0.pdf.

——. *Muslims in the EU: Cities Report: United Kingdom. Preliminary Research Report and Literature Survey,* 2007. http://www.opensocietyfoundations.org/sites/default/files/museucitiesuk_20080101_0.pdf.

Organisation for Economic Co-operation and Development (OECD). *Equal Opportunities? The Labour Market Integration of the Children of Immigrants.* Paris: OECD, 2010. http://dx.doi.org/10.1787/9789264086395-en.

OSCE/ODIHR, ed. *Education on the Holocaust and on Anti-Semitism: An*

Overview and Analysis of Educational Approaches. Warsaw: OSCE Office for Democratic Institutions and Human Rights, 2006.

Pagano, Simona. *"Also der Körper is da, die Seele nich": Zur Funktion antisemitischer Äußerungen in Männlichkeitskonstruktionen vier Berliner Jugendlicher mit türkischem und arabischem Migrationshintergrund.* Münster: LIT Verlar, 2011.

Park, Alison, Elizabeth Clery, John Curtice, Miranda Philips, and David Utting, eds. *British Social Attitudes: The 29th Report.* London: SAGE in association with the National Centre for Social Research, 2012.

"Pat Robertson Calls Islam Violent, Bent on Domination." *Washington Post,* February 22, 2002.

Paul, Jonny. "Holocaust Scholar Warns of New 'Soft-core' Denial." *Jerusalem Post,* February 6, 2007.

Penn, Roger D., and Paul S. Lambert. *Children of International Migrants in Europe: Comparative Perspectives.* Basingstoke: Palgrave Macmillan, 2009.

Pew Global Attitudes Project. *The Great Divide: How Westerners and Muslims View Each Other.* 2006. http://pewglobal.org/reports/pdf/253.pdf.

——. *In Great Britain, Muslims Worry about Islamic Extremism – Pew Research Center.* August 10, 2006. http://pewresearch.org/pubs/48/in-great-britain-muslims-worry-about-islamic-extremism.

——. *Muslim-Western Tensions Persist.* 2011. http://www.ab.gov.tr/files/ardb/evt/1_avrupa_birligi/1_6_raporlar/1_3_diger/Pew-Global-Attitudes-Muslim-Western-Relations-FINAL-FOR-PRINT-July-21-2011.pdf.

——. *Unfavorable Views of Jews and Muslims on the Increase in Europe.* 2008. http://pewglobal.org/2008/09/17/unfavorable-views-of-jews-and-muslims-on-the-increase-in-europe/.

Poliakov, Léon. *The History of Anti-Semitism. Volume 1: From the Time of Christ to the Court Jews.* Philadelphia: University of Pennsylvania Press, 2003.

——. *The History of Anti-Semitism. Volume 3: From Voltaire to Wagner.* Philadelphia: University of Pennsylvania Press, 2003.

Pollack, Detlef. *Wahrnehmung und Akzeptanz religiöser Vielfalt,* December 2010. http://www.uni-muenster.de/imperia/md/content/religion_und_politik/aktuelles/2010/ 12_2010/studie_wahrnehmung_und_akzeptanz_religioeser_vielfalt.pdf.

Populus/Times. *Muslim Poll.* December 2005. http://www.populus.co.uk/wp-content/uploads/Muslim_Poll-Times.pdf.

Prinstein, Mitchell J., and Kenneth A. Dodge. *Understanding Peer Influence in Children and Adolescents.* New York: Guilford Press, 2008.

"Proteste von Jugendlichen Gegen Den Krieg in Gaza." *Ufuq.de,* January 8, 2009. http://www.ufuq.de/newsblog/277-proteste-von-jugendlichen-gegen-den-krieg-in-gaza.

"Un rabbin agressé à la gare du Nord." *Le Monde,* April 21, 2007.

Rada, Uwe. "Nahost-Demos weitgehend friedlich." *Tageszeitung (taz),* April 15, 2002.

Raddatz, Hans-Peter. *Allah Und Die Juden. Die Islamische Renaissance Des Antisemitismus.* Berlin: Wolf Jobst Siedler, 2007.

Ramji, Hasmita. "Dynamics of Religion and Gender amongst Young British Muslims." *Sociology* 41, no. 6 (December 1, 2007): 1171–1189.

Rap2france.com. "Paroles La Légende Sefyu Parole La Légende." May 12, 2013.

http://www.rap2france.com/paroles-sefyu-la-legende.php.

Reichelt, Michael. "Das Lexem 'Jude' im jugendlichen Sprachgebrauch." In *Jahrbuch für Antisemitismusforschung 18*, edited by Wolfgang Benz, 17–42. Berlin: Metropol, 2009.

Rensmann, Lars. *Demokratie und Judenbild. Antisemitismus in der politischen Kultur der Bundesrepublik Deutschland.* Wiesbaden, 2005.

Rinke, Stefan. "Limpieza de sangre [Reinheit des Blutes]." In *Handbuch des Antisemitismus. Judenfeindschaft in Geschichte und Gegenwart, Bd. 3: Begriffe, Theorien, Ideologien,* edited by Wolfgang Benz. Berlin: De Gruyter, 2010.

Ritzmann, Alexander. "Fernsehsender verbreiten Antisemitismus." *Der Tagesspiegel,* July 7, 2010.

Rosenfeld, Alvin. *The End of the Holocaust.* Bloomington: Indiana University Press, 2011.

——. "The End of the Holocaust and the Beginnings of a New Antisemitism." In *Resurgent Antisemitism: Global Perspectives,* edited by Alvin H. Rosenfeld, 521–533. Bloomington: Indiana University Press, 2013.

Rubin, Barry. *The Muslim Brotherhood: The Organization and Policies of a Global Islamist Movement.* New York: Palgrave Macmillan, 2010.

Said, Edward W. *Orientalism.* 1978. Reprint, London: Penguin, 2003.

Salzborn, Samuel. *Antisemitismus als negative Leitidee der Moderne: Sozialwissenschaftliche Theorien im Vergleich.* Frankfurt: Campus, 2010.

Sandelson, Michael. "Anti-Semitism Common in Norwegian Schools." *The Foreigner,* March 15, 2010. http://theforeigner.no/pages/news/anti-semitism-common-in-norwegian-schools/.

Sansal, Boualem. *The German Mujahid.* New York: Europa Editions, 2009.

Sartre, Jean-Paul. *Anti-Semite and Jew.* 1946. Reprint, New York: Schocken Books, 1995.

——. *Réflexions sur la question juive.* Paris: Gallimard, 1954.

Satloff, Robert. *Among the Righteous: Lost Stories from the Holocaust's Long Reach into Arab Lands.* New York: Public Affairs, 2006.

Schapira, Esther. "Propaganda against Israel: The Mohammed Al Durah Case and Staging Reality in the Media." June 18, 2008. http://www.european-forum-on-antisemitism.org/berlin-alert/view/article/propaganda-against-israel-the-mohammed-al-durah-case-and-staging-reality-in-the-media/.

Schäuble, Barbara, and Albert Scherr. *"Ich habe nichts gegen Juden, aber . . ." Ausgangsbedingungen und Perspektiven gesellschaftspolitischer Bildungsarbeit gegen Antisemitismus.* Amadeu Antonio Stiftung, 2007. http://www.amadeu-antonio-stiftung.de/w/files/pdfs/ich_habe_nichts_2.pdf.

Schiffer, Sabine, and Constantin Wagner. *Antisemitismus und Islamophobie – ein Vergleich.* Wassertrüdingen: HWK-Verl., 2009.

Schmid, Bernhard. "Frankreich und Auschwitz-Leugner." *Jungle World,* February 11, 2004.

Schmidinger, Thomas. "Zur Islamisierung des Antisemitismus." In *Jahrbuch 2008,* 103–139. Dokumentationsarchiv des österreichischen Widerstandes. Wien: Lit Verlag, 2008.

Schmidt, Christiane. "The Analysis of Semi-structured Interviews." In *A Companion to Qualitative Research,* edited by Uwe Flick, Ernst von Kardoff, and Ines Steinke, 253–258. Thousand Oaks, Calif.: Sage Publications, 2004.

Schmitt, Christine. "Bei Gefahr 0800 880280." *Jüdische Allgemeine,* February 25, 2010.

Schneier, Marc. "Willingness of Muslim Leaders to Denounce Anti-Semitism." *Jerusalem Post,* February 4, 2013.

Schu, Anke. "Biografie und Antisemitismus. Zum Zusammenhang von biografischer Erfahrung und dem Gebrauch antisemitischer Konstruktionen." In *Ethnozentrismus und Antisemitismus bei Jugendlichen mit Migrationshintergrund: Erscheinungsformen und pädagogische Praxis in der Einwanderungsgesellschaft,* edited by Frank Greuel and Michaela Glaser, 26–53. Halle: Deutsches Jugendinstitut, 2012.

Schwarz-Friesel, Monika. *Judenfeindliche Einstellungen: Antisemitismus erreicht die bürgerliche Mitte. Die Welt* Online, April 23, 2009. http://www.welt.de/politik/article3608092/Antisemitismus-erreicht-die-buergerliche-Mitte.html.

Schwarz-Friesel, Monika, and Holger Braune. "Textwelten: Geschlossene Konzeptualisierungsmuster in Aktuellen Antisemitischen Texten." *Sprachtheorie Und Germanistische Linguistik* 17, no. 1 (2007): 1–29.

Schwarz-Friesel, Monika, and Evyatar Friesel. "'Gestern die Juden, heute die Muslime . . .'? – Von den Gefahren falscher Analogien." In *Islamophobie und Antisemitismus ein umstrittener Vergleich,* edited by Gideon Botsch, Olaf Glöckner, Christoph Kopke, and Michael Spieker, 29–50. Berlin: De Gruyter, 2012.

Schwarz-Friesel, Monika, and Jehuda Reinharz. *Die Sprache der Judenfeindschaft im 21. Jahrhundert.* Berlin: De Gruyter, 2013.

Segev, Tom. *One Palestine, Complete: Jews and Arabs under the British Mandate.* New York: Owl Books, 2001.

Senatsverwaltung (Berlin) für Inneres und Sport, Abteilung Verfassungsschutz. *Antisemitismus im extremistischen Spektrum Berlins.* Berlin, 2006. http://www.berlin.de/imperia/md/content/seninn/verfassungsschutz/fokus_antisemitismus_2._aufl..pdf?start&ts=1234285743&file=fokus_antisemitismus_2._aufl.pdf.

Service de Protection de la Communauté Juive (SPCJ). *Rapport sur l'antisémitisme en France 2009.* January 27, 2010. http://www.spcj.org/rapport2009.pdf.

Sharansky, Natan. "3D Test of Anti-Semitism: Demonization, Double Standards, Delegitimization." *Jewish Political Studies Review* 16, no. 3–4 (October 2004). http://jcpa.org/phas/phas-sharansky-f04.htm.

Shavit, Uriya. *Islamism and the West: From "Cultural Attack" to "Missionary Migrant."* Routledge Studies in Political Islam. London: Routledge, 2014.

———. *The New Imagined Community: Global Media and the Construction of National and Muslim Identities of Migrants.* Portland, Ore.: Sussex Academic Press, 2009.

Shea, Nina. "This Is a Saudi Textbook. (After the Intolerance Was Removed.)" *Washington Post,* May 21, 2006.

Siddique, Haroon. "BBC's Panorama Claims Islamic Schools Teach Antisemitism and Homophobia." *The Guardian,* November 22, 2010.

Silverman, David. *Doing Qualitative Research: A Practical Handbook.* 3rd ed. Los Angeles: Sage, 2010.

Silverstein, Paul A. "Comment on Bunzl." In *Anti-Semitism and Islamophobia: Hatreds Old and New in Europe,* edited by Matti Bunzl. Chicago: Prickly Paradigm Press, 2007.

———. "The Context of Antisemitism and Islamophobia in France." *Patterns of Prejudice* 42, no. 1 (2008): 1.

Simon, Erk, and Gerhard Kloppenburg. "Das Fernsehpublikum türkischer Herkunft – Fernsehnutzung, Einstellungen und Programmerwartungen." *Media Perspektiven* no. 3 (2007): 142–152.

Simon, Patrick. "Muslims and Jews in France: Profiles and Experiences of Discrimination and Racism according to the TeO Survey." Paper presented at the Symposium "Attitudinal Change towards Jews and Muslims in France in a Comparative Perspective," Institut d'études politiques de Paris, Paris, April 18, 2013.

Simon, Patrick, and Vincent Tiberj. *Sécularisation ou regain religieux: la religiosité des immigrés et de leurs descendants.* Documents de Travail 196. Paris: Institut national d'études démographique, 2013.

"6 Month Analysis of the BBC: The Subtle Bias." HonestReporting.com. July 19, 2007. http://www.honestreporting.com/articles/45884734/critiques/6_Month_Analysis_of_the_BBC_The_Subtle_Bias.asp.

Smith, Craig S. "Torture and Death of Jew Deepen Fears in France." *New York Times,* March 5, 2006.

Smith, Julianne. "European Approaches to the Challenge of Radical Islam." In *Muslim Integration Challenging Conventional Wisdom in Europe and the United States,* 65–74. Washington, D.C.: Center for Strategic and International Studies, 2007. http://www.csis.org/media/csis/pubs/070920_muslimintegration.pdf.

Snyder, Donald. "For Jews, Swedish City Is a 'Place to Move Away From.'" *Jewish Daily Forward,* July 7, 2010.

Spencer, Philip, and Sara Valentina Di Palma. "Antisemitism and the Politics of Holocaust Memorial Day in the UK and Italy." In *Perceptions of the Holocaust in Europe and Muslim Communities: Sources, Comparisons and Educational Challenges,* edited by Günther Jikeli and Joëlle Allouche-Benayoun, 71–84. New York: Springer, 2013.

Steinke, Ines. "Quality Criteria in Qualitative Research." In *A Companion to Qualitative Research,* edited by Uwe Flick, Ernst von Kardoff, and Ines Steinke, 184–190. Thousand Oaks, Calif.: Sage Publications, 2004.

Stender, Wolfram. "Konstellationen des Antisemitismus. Zur Einleitung." In *Konstellationen des Antisemitismus Antisemitismusforschung und sozialpädagogische Praxis,* edited by Wolfram Stender, Guido Follert, and Mihri Özdogan, 7–39. Wiesbaden: VS Verlag für Sozialwissenschaften, 2010.

Stenström, Anna-Brita, Gisle Andersen, and Ingrid Kristine Hasund. *Trends in Teenage Talk.* Amsterdam: Benjamins, 2002.

Stephen Roth Institute. "Country Report: France 2007." 2008. http://www.tau.ac.il/Anti-Semitism/asw2007/france.html.

Stremmelaar, Annemarike. "Dutch and Turkish Memories of Genocide: Contact or Competition?" Expert-Meeting presented at the conference "Changing Perceptions of the Holocaust: Competing Histories and Collective Memory," Amsterdam, June 5, 2013.

"Un supporter du PSG tué par un policier." TF1 News, November 24, 2006.

Symons, Leon. "Teacher 'Sacked for Challenging Antisemitism.'" *Jewish Chronicle,* February 9, 2010.

Taguieff, Pierre-André. "L'affaire al-Dura ou le renforcement des stéréotypes antijuifs . . ." *Le meilleur des mondes,* September 2008. http://www.lemeilleurdesmondes.org/A_chaud

_Pierre-Andre-Taguieff-affaire-al-Dura-ou-le-renforcement-des-stereotypes-an.htm.

——. *Prêcheurs de haine: Traversée de la judéophobie planétaire*. Paris: Mille et une nuits, 2004.

Ternisien, Xavier. *La France des mosquées*. Paris: Albin Michel, 2002.

Tiberj, Vincent. "Anti-Semitism in an Ethnically Diverse France: Questioning and Explaining the Specificities of African-, Turkish-, and Maghrebian-French." 2006. http://www.aup.fr/pdf/WPSeries/AUP_wp33-Tiberj.pdf.

Tibi, Bassam. *Islamism and Islam*. New Haven, Conn.: Yale University Press, 2012.

Ul Haq, Riyadh. "Riyadh Ul Haq Sermon on 'Jewish Fundamentalism' in Full." *The Times (UK)*, September 6, 2007.

United Nations Development Programme. *Explanatory Note on 2011 HDR Composite Indices: Occupied Palestinian Territory*. Human Development Report, 2011. http://hdrstats.undp.org/images/explanations/PSE.pdf.

United Nations Educational, Scientific, and Cultural Organiszation (UNESCO). *International Standard Classification of Education 1997 (Re-edition)*. UNESCO-UIS, 2006.

Vajda, Georges. "Jews and Muslims according to the Hadith." In *The Legacy of Islamic Antisemitism*, edited by Andrew Bostom, 235–260. Amherst, N.Y.: Prometheus Books, 2008.

Vampouille, Thomas. "France: Comment est évalué le nombre de musulmans." *Le Figaro*, April 5, 2011.

Van de Vijver, Fons J. R. "Towards a Theory of Bias and Equivalence." *ZUMA-Nachrichten Spezial* (January 1998): 41–65.

Van der Slik, Frans W. P., and Ruben P. Konig. "Orthodox, Humanitarian, and Science-Inspired Belief in Relation to Prejudice against Jews, Muslims, and Ethnic Minorities: The Content of One's Belief Does Matter." *International Journal for the Psychology of Religion* 16, no. 2 (2006): 113–126.

Vettenburg, Nicole, Mark Elchardus, and Stefaan Pleysier, eds. *Jong in Antwerpen En Gent*. Leuven: Acco, 2013.

Vidal-Naquet, Pierre. *Les Assassins de La Mémoire*. Paris: Seuil, 1995.

Voisin, Agathe. *Ethnicity in Young People's Lives: From Discrimination to New Individuations in French and British Societies*. Working Papers Du Programme Villes & Territoires, 2012–02. Paris: Sciences PO, 2012. http://blogs.sciences-po.fr/recherche-villes/files/2012/05/WP-Voisin-2012-2.pdf.

Walter, Jacques. "La Liste de Schindler Au Miroir de La Presse." *Mots* 56, no. 1 (1998): 69–89. doi:10.3406/mots.1998.2366.

Ware, John. "MCB in the Dock." *Prospect Magazine* no. 129 (December 2006).

Webman, Esther. "The Global Impact of the 'Protocols of the Elders of Zion': A Century-Old Myth." London: Routledge, 2011.

Wetzel, Juliane. "Parallelen zwischen Antisemitismus und Islamfeindschaft heute." In *Islamophobie und Antisemitismus ein umstrittener Vergleich*, edited by Gideon Botsch, Olaf Glöckner, Christoph Kopke, and Michael Spieker, 81–106. Berlin: De Gruyter, 2012.

Whine, Michael. "The Advance of the Muslim Brotherhood in the UK." *Current Trends in Islamist Ideology* no. 2 (2005): 30–40.

——. "Participation of European Muslim Organisations in Holocaust Commemorations." In *Perceptions of the Holocaust in Europe and Muslim Communities: Sources, Comparisons and Educational*

Challenges, edited by Günther Jikeli and Joëlle Allouche-Benayoun, 29–40. New York: Springer, 2013.

Widmann, Peter. "Der Feind Kommt Aus Dem Morgenland. Rechtspopulistische 'Islamkritiker' Um Den Publizisten Hans-Peter Raddatz Suchen Die Opfergemeinschaft Mit Juden." In *Jahrbuch Für Antisemitismusforschung* 17, 45–68. Berlin: Metropol, 2008.

Wiedeman, Johannes. "Angriff auf Tanzgruppe: Der alltägliche Antisemitismus in Hannover-Sahlkamp." *Die Welt,* June 26, 2010.

Wiedl, Nina. "Dawa and the Islamist Revival in the West." *Current Trends in Islamist Ideology* 9 (December 14, 2009). http://www.currenttrends.org/research/detail/dawa-and-the-islamist-revival-in-the-west.

Wieviorka, Michel. *The Lure of Anti-Semitism: Hatred of Jews in Present-Day France.* Translated by Kristin Couper Lobel and Anna Declerck. Leiden: Brill, 2007.

——. *La tentation antisémite: Haine des Juifs dans la France d'aujourd'hui.* Paris: Laffont, 2005.

Willsher, Kim. "Brutal Murder Was Anti-Semitic Crime, Says Sarkozy." *The Guardian,* February 22, 2006.

Wistrich, Robert. *European Anti-Semitism Reinvents Itself.* New York: American Jewish Committee, 2005.

——. *A Lethal Obsession: Anti-Semitism from Antiquity to the Global Jihad.* New York: Random House, 2010.

——. *Muslim Anti-Semitism – A Clear and Present Danger.* New York: American Jewish Committee, 2002. http://www.ajc.org/atf/cf/%7B42D75369-D582-4380-8395-D25925B85EAF%7D/WistrichAntisemitism.pdf.

Wolf, Eva, Jurriaan Berger, and Lennart de Ruig. *Antisemitisme in het voortgezet onderwijs.* Amsterdam: Anne Frank Stichting, 2013.

Yakira, Elhanan. *Post-Zionism, Post-Holocaust: Three Essays on Denial, Forgetting, and the Delegitimation of Israel.* Translated by Michael Swirsky. Cambridge: Cambridge University Press, 2009.

Young, Alford A. Jr. "Experiences in Ethnographic Interviewing about Race: The Inside and Outside of It." In *Researching Race and Racism,* edited by Martin Bulmer and John Solomos, 187–202. New York: Routledge, 2004.

Zick, Andreas, Andreas Hövermann, and Beate Küpper. *Intolerance, Prejudice and Discrimination: A European Report.* Berlin: Friedrich-Ebert-Stiftung, Forum Berlin, 2011. http://library.fes.de/pdf-files/do/07908-20110311.pdf.

Zick, Andreas, Beate Küpper, and Hinna Wolf. *European Conditions: Findings of a Study on Group-focused Enmity in Europe.* Institute for Interdisciplinary Research on Conflict and Violence, University of Bielefeld, 2009. http://www.amadeu-antonio-stiftung.de/w/files/pdfs/gfepressrelease_english.pdf.

Zuckermann, Moshe. *Antisemitismus Antizionismus Israelkritik.* Göttingen: Wallstein Verlag, 2005.

Zumbini, Massimo Ferrari. *Die Wurzeln des Bösen: Gründerjahre des Antisemitismus: von der Bismarckzeit zu Hitler.* Frankfurt a. M.: V. Klostermann, 2003.

Index

Italicized page numbers refer to illustrations.

DR. GÜNTHER JIKELI is a research fellow at the Moses Mendelssohn Center for European-Jewish Studies, Potsdam University, and at the Groupe Sociétés, Religions, Laïcités at the Centre National de la Recherche Scientifique (GSRL/CNRS), Paris. He earned his PhD at the Center for Research on Antisemitism in Berlin. He has taught at Indiana University, Potsdam University, and at the Technical University Berlin. From 2011 to 2012, he served as an advisor to the Organisation for Security and Cooperation in Europe on combating antisemitism. In 2013, he was awarded the Raoul Wallenberg Prize in Human Rights and Holocaust Studies by the International Raoul Wallenberg Foundation and Tel Aviv University.